# Political Tendencies in Louisiana

# Political Tendencies in Louisiana

REVISED AND EXPANDED EDITION

**Perry H. Howard**

LOUISIANA STATE UNIVERSITY PRESS

*Baton Rouge*

ISBN 0-8071-0944-4
Library of Congress Catalog Number 74-123205
Copyright © 1957, 1971 by Louisiana State University Press
Manufactured in the United States of America

Designed by J. Barney McKee

**To Vernon J. Parenton,**

who has, like a true citizen of his
native state, expressed through
all adversity—"la joie de vivre."

# Preface

This volume, based to some extent on my earlier work *Political Tendencies in Louisiana* 1812–1952, is an expanded and updated study of Louisiana voting patterns. It owes its origin, and whatever may be its merit, to the continued interest taken in political ecology by Rudolf Heberle. Dr. Heberle, now Louisiana State University Boyd Professor Emeritus, has offered me inspiration, guidance, and warm friendship since first taking me as a green graduate assistant who showed an interest in Louisiana politics and believing in my potential as a political sociologist. His own stature as a sociologist, already known to his students, was recognized by his peers when Professor Heberle in 1967 was elected vice-president of the American Sociological Association. It is a pleasure for me to be able to record my indebtedness to him and to add the hope that this revised edition may contribute to the field of political ecology which he so ably pioneered.

The chairman of my department, Walfrid J. Jokinen, and my colleagues provided the kind of atmosphere that makes scholarly pursuit a pleasure. I also wish to acknowledge the summer research grant given in 1964 by the Faculty Research Council of the Louisiana State University Graduate School as well as one of the first relief-time grants in the spring semester, 1967, established by Dean Irwin A. Berg for the College of Arts and Sciences.

A number of graduate students have assisted me. Maryland Anderson and Kay P. Whyburn assisted at various stages of statistical analysis and map making, and made frequent trips to the library. To Robert M. Kloss goes special gratitude. Throughout the period of research and writing, and regardless of his other duties, Bob gave unstintingly of his time and effort. His enthusiasm for the project remained a constant source of encouragement.

I want to thank Lynn Davidson, Sally Smith, and Ida Crockett who cheerfully provided careful typing whenever asked. My editor, Martha L. Hall, painstakingly considered every line of the manuscript, and much more clarity of expression resulted from her effort.

The present work is offered as a stimulant to further study of Louisiana politics. In the matter of basic data and analysis, much is owed to my colleague and friend George S. Tracy. Neither the fruitfulness of aggregate data analysis nor survey research has been adequately used in the study of this state's political behavior. We are looking for a new generation of more able methodologists and statistically inclined students who, without forgetting theory, will become motivated to carry on from here.

*Baton Rouge*
*July*, 1969

# Introduction

## 1. Political Tendencies and Political Ecology

The comparative method has been used to seek understanding of the nature of society.[1] Information derived from intranational contrasts must be considered useful in particular because data comparability both within and across time periods may be assumed to be enhanced. Furthermore, under such conditions, certain variables may be held constant while examining others.[2] Heinz Eulau in pleading the case for the comparative study of government has said: "There are enough units in the American political system to keep a whole generation of scholars busier than bees in perfecting comparative analysis."[3] The present work may be seen as an example of how potential, untapped resources on the state level may be released for the study of electoral continuity and change.[4]

The particular methodology which will be used here to study Louisiana politics is called "political ecology,"[5] and it may be said that in such an area, which touches upon historical sources, ecological data are indispensable. For it is possible to apply to ecological units both the logic of panel and multivariate analysis, to explore the impact of historical events upon communities, counties (or parishes), states, or other such units of different predispositions, and at the same time to take into account their social structure. The research on contem-

[1] Ralph H. Retzlaff, "The Use of Aggregate Data in Comparative Political Analysis," *Journal of Politics*, XXVII (1965), 797–817; Robert M. Marsh, *Comparative Sociology* (New York, 1967); Stanislav Andreski, *The Uses of Comparative Sociology* (Berkeley, 1965).

[2] Retzlaff, "Comparative Political Analysis," 813–14.

[3] Heinz Eulau, "Comparative Political Analysis: A Methodological Note," *Midwest Journal of Political Science*, VI (1962), 397.

[4] Seymour Martin Lipset, *Political Man* (Garden City, 1963), 384.

[5] Rudolf Heberle, *Social Movements* (New York, 1951); Rudolf Heberle, "On Political Ecology," *Social Forces*, XXXI (1952), 1–9.

porary behavior and social structure can ignore neither the weight of history nor ecological data.[6] In other words, to gain knowledge of continuity and change in politics requires long-term ecological research.

One of the main concerns of political sociology is the question of the interrelationships between political tendencies, parties, movements, and social classes.[7] It has been assumed that in Western political systems an analysis of the geographic distribution of support for a party or candidate points to what classes or categories of voters make up that support. Also, such an analysis leads to a more complete understanding of the fundamental processes of social integration and disintegration.[8] Seymour M. Lipset and Stein Rokkan, in tracing party systems and voter alignments in the West on a comparative basis, have stressed that four decisive contrasts have reflected differences in the national histories of conflict and compromise across the cleavage lines which have characterized the development of the modern nation state:[9] (1) the center-periphery (the central nation-building culture and resistance of distinct subject populations in provinces and outlying areas); (2) state-church (the newly established nation state and the historical corporate privileges of the Church); (3) land-industry (the landed interests and the rising class of industrial entrepreneurs); and (4) owner-worker (the conflict between owners and employers and between tenants, laborers, and workers). The manner in which the active nation-building elites historically dealt with these oppositions and the alternative alliances opted have decisively influenced the consequent class politics of Western societies. Finally, despite the cleavages, integration was nevertheless possible when consensus was generated, when avenues of expression were opened through which political choices were allowed to resolve conflict

[6] Juan J. Linz, "Ecological Analysis and Survey Research," in Mattei Dogan and Stein Rokkan (eds.), *Quantitative Ecological Analysis in the Social Sciences* (Cambridge, M.I.T. Press, 1969), 99.

[7] Heberle, *Social Movements.*

[8] Heberle, "On Political Ecology," 8–9.

[9] Seymour M. Lipset and Stein Rokkan (eds.), *Party Systems and Voter Alignments: Cross-National Perspectives* (New York, 1967), 14, 34.

and value differences, through what have been labeled "pluralistic" procedures.[10]

The methodology of political ecology has been developed to explain the political behavior of the people of a given area through inquiry into the factors which may influence voting. By correlating election returns with indicators of significant social characteristics, it is possible to ascertain the interests and predispositions which are present in an area as well as the social divisions which may be reflected in the voting. The continental scholar most influential in the development of the theory and techniques of political ecology, or what he called the *geographie de l'opinion politique*, was Andre Siegfried.[11] His interest in the subject came from his observations of the astounding consistencies in political opinion in areas of France despite the well-known instability of political parties. Siegfried was moved to seek the geographic factors which contributed to this apparently underlying stability. Mattei Dogan, an able successor in the tradition of Siegfried, has explained: "There is surely no direct causality, in the rigorous sense of the word, but there is some correspondence between nature of the soil, agrarian landscape, type of dwelling, distribution of land ownership, degree of stratification of society, the stronger persistence of traditions, and political orientation."[12]

Rudolf Heberle applied the techniques developed by Siegfried with the addition of more refined statistical methods in a comprehensive study of the Nazi vote in a region of Germany.[13] Later, after his migration to the United States, Heberle supervised a whole series of studies of Louisiana politics refining the methods of political ecology.[14]

[10] Robert M. MacIver, *The Web of Government* (New York, 1947); E. E. Schattschneider, *The Semisovereign People* (New York, 1960); Robert A. Dahl, *Pluralist Democracy in the United States* (Chicago, 1967); William Kornhauser, *The Politics of Mass Society* (Glencoe, Ill., 1959).

[11] Andre Siegfried, *Tableau de la France de l'Ouest sous la Troisième République* (Paris, 1913); Andre Siegfried, *Geographie Électorale de l'Ardeche sous la IIIᵉ République* (Paris, 1949).

[12] Mattei Dogan, "Political Cleavage and Social Stratification in France and Italy," in Lipset and Rokkan (eds.), *Party Systems*, 183.

[13] Rudolf Heberle, *From Democracy to Nazism: A Regional Case Study on Political Parties in Germany* (Baton Rouge, 1945).

[14] Rudolf Heberle and Alvin L. Bertrand, "Factors Motivating Voting Behavior in a One-Party State," *Social Forces*, XXVII (1949), 343–50; Perry H. Howard, "An

A veritable "school" of political ecology has been developed in France since the end of World War II, and most of its members have been students of, or have been influenced by, Andre Siegfried.[15] The term *sociologie electorale* has likewise been adopted by the Norwegian political scientist Sten S. Nilson, who published the first comprehensive treatise on the subject.[16] Another Scandanavian, Erik Allardt, at the University of Helsinki, has published a number of studies of Finnish politics, pioneering in the use of the statistical method of factor analysis of ecological data.[17] In the United States the foremost exponents of quantitative and regional studies of a more or less ecological nature have been Arthur N. Holcomb, Stuart Rice, George Lundberg, Harold F. Gosnell, V. O. Key, Jr., Samuel Lubell, and Walter Dean Burnham.[18] Political ecology, then, influenced by the kind of studies cited here, cannot be claimed to be the invention of any single nation.

Techniques of several of the social sciences are employed in ecological analysis, combining geographical, historical, sociological,

---

Analysis of Voting Behavior in Baton Rouge," *Proceedings of the Louisiana Academy of Science*, XV (1952), 84–100; Rudolf Heberle, George Hillery, Jr., and Frank Lovrich, "Continuity and Change in Voting Behavior in the 1952 Primaries in Louisiana," *Southwestern Social Science Quarterly*, XXXIII (1953), 328–42; Rudolf Heberle and Perry H. Howard, "An Ecological Analysis of Political Tendencies in Louisiana: The Presidential Election of 1952," *Social Forces*, XXXII (1954), 344–50; William C. Havard, Rudolf Heberle, and Perry H. Howard, *The Louisiana Elections of 1960* (Baton Rouge, 1963).

[15] François Goguel and Georges Dupeux, *Sociologie Electorale: Esquisse D'Un Bilan Guide De Recherches* (Paris, 1951).

[16] Sten S. Nilson, *Histoire et Sciences Politiques* (Bergen, 1950).

[17] Erik Allardt and Pertti Pesonen, "Cleavages in Finnish Politics," in Lipset and Rokkan (eds.), *Party Systems*, 325–66; Erik Allardt, "A Theory on Solidarity and Legitimacy Conflicts," in his *Cleavages, Ideologies, and Party Systems* (Helsinki, 1965); Erik Allardt, "Working Class Consciousness and Alienation: A Preliminary Ecological Analysis," *Sociologiske Meddelelser*, X (1965), 35–46; Erik Allardt, "Aggregate Analysis: The Problem of Its Informative Value," in Dogan and Rokkan, *Quantitative Ecological Analysis*, 41–51.

[18] Arthur N. Holcombe, *The Political Parties of Today* (New York, 1924); Stuart Rice, *Quantitative Methods in Politics* (New York, 1928); George Lundberg, "The Geographic and Economic Basis of Political Radicalism and Conservatism," *American Journal of Sociology*, XXXII (1927), 719–32; Harold F. Gosnell, *Grass Roots Politics* (Washington, D.C., 1942); V. O. Key, Jr., *Southern Politics* (New York, 1949); Samuel Lubell, *The Future of American Politics* (New York, 1951), and Samuel Lubell, *Revolt of the Moderates* (New York, 1956); and Walter Dean Burnham, *Presidential Ballots, 1836–1892* (Baltimore, 1955).

and statistical methods. The following assumptions can be said to guide such investigation: "The geographic characteristics of a region— topography, soil quality, resources, climate, physical accessibility, and nearness to markets by available routes—determine the development of the economy of that region—the kind and relative importance of agriculture, of manufacturing industries, commerce, transportation, and so forth. The economy determines the economic class structure— the planter and sharecroppers; family farmers, renters and hired help; factory owners and workers. The economic class structure determines the nature of local social and political issues as well as the local reaction to national issues."[19] It must be emphasized, however, that these assumptions must be subject to demonstration of their relevance to the political process in each case.

According to this scheme, geographical characteristics of an area are influential in the development of a particular economy, dependent, of course, upon the cultural values and the level of technology of the people involved. The economy, in turn, determines the objective class structure, and ultimately, political tendencies. Classes in this sense are seen as aggregates of individuals and families in similar economic positions, having the same or like goods and services to offer in the system of production and distribution. It follows that they will receive corresponding monetary rewards in the marketplace. It also means that people in the same economic position have similar "life chances," in Max Weber's sense; that is, they have like chances to obtain values and opportunities of primary importance for life and survival.[20] Thus the political ecologist must make a rather rigorous analysis of the social structure, and, in particular, he must identify the various social collectives and groups which result from the processes of social differentiation and stratification.

In the majoritarian system of political representation in most Western democracies, voting behavior has been viewed as a major aspect of political tendencies. Understanding "tendency" as an inherent disposition or inclination to move in a given direction,

[19] Heberle, *Social Movements*, 213–14.
[20] See Max Weber, "Classes, Status Groups, and Parties," *From Max Weber*, trans. and ed. by H. H. Gerth and C. Wright Mills (New York, 1946), 180 f.

and holding that the act of voting is influenced in some way by the underlying social structure, it is possible through the method of political ecology to make a judgment of what the vote means. It is possible to determine what political tendencies prevail and to demonstrate how these tendencies are related to social and economic factors of the social structure. Yet it is important to note that emphasis is placed upon collective rather than individual behavior. The sociological assumption is that the social behavior of people is determined by their participation in groups which are significant for them. The "factors" of analysis, then, are manageable. They are not random or unlimited because it is held that certain major influences (such as pecuniary evaluations) may be basic in a particular social system. Most of the political tendencies with which this study will be concerned have to do with the voting behavior of people who make up particular kinds of social collectives.

Samuel Lubell spoke of political tendencies as "voting streams." He found that Americans have always voted less as individuals than as part of a particular voting stream—flows of voter patterns which took original form from the economic contours of the country, as in the North or South, or from cultural outlook, as in religious preference or ethnic background. Lubell adds: "Since everything that happens to people affects their voting, each of these streams can serve as a river along which one can travel backward or forward, into American history."[21]

The basic sociological problem is to find out the extent to which the total vote for a party or a candidate is a group phenomenon, representing organization and consensus. In other words, the question is whether or not individual voters, when they cast their ballots, are aware of their identification with others as party or class members, regardless of their formal commitment to the purposes and interests of an organized group. Yet, at the same time, empirical observations have shown that not all social behavior is determined or conditioned by formal organization. To conceptualize this consideration the term "social collective" has been devised, by which is meant "groups of

[21] Lubell, *Revolt*, 261.

individuals or families, who are tied to one another by virtue of shared traditions or because of their common perspectives."[22] A social collective is unorganized, but large enough to continue its existence even though the membership should change. Consensus is said to remain "latent," held tacitly, and revealing itself under conditions or occasions when stimuli render it manifest. From this generic concept may be drawn the sociological meaning of "class" and "party," for collectives may contain subunits such as these and reflect, more or less, organized purpose. The "political tendencies" of parties and classes is another term for the characteristic voting behavior of such units.

Historically, parties have been the vehicles of class action. To be precise, it is necessary to recall that parties have likewise been utilized by other social divisions, such as the religious groups in England. A party is a social collective that is organized, a group with a rationally determined purpose to which the membership is committed. Once established, of course, a party may carry on a group existence of its own, recruiting support from the social categories and groupings which are in fact present in a society. The defining of "class" requires further comment, however. Is class referred to only if class consciousness is manifested? Is class a psychological concept? In the sociological tradition, as has been implied above, class has to be taken as an "objective" category. That is, social class, in this sense, is a social collective, an unorganized grouping or category held together by common interests or sharing similar functions in the economic system. A social class is said to be fully developed when the persons who make up the category recognize that they hold like class positions.

Students of the emergence of modern society, by using ecological data (the term "aggregate data" has been preferred by many social scientists), have accumulated evidence that one important correlate of class position is differential voting behavior. In recent years,

[22] Ferdinand Toennies, "Estates and Classes" (trans. Reinhard Bendix) from "Staende und Klassen" in Alfred Vierkandt (ed.), *Handwoerterbuch de Sociology* (1931), Ferdinand Enke Verlag, 617–28. Reprinted in Reinhard Bendix and Seymour M. Lipset (eds.), *Class Status and Power* (2nd ed.; New York, 1966).

however, there has been discussion of an "end of ideology" in the more Western affluent nations, such that a consensus takes the place of traditional cleavages. Yet the use of survey data has yielded findings which tend to confirm the historical continuity of political cleavage and ideological dissensus. David R. Segal has said that survey data argues "for the persistence of historical influences upon contemporary political alignments, and in fact, for the persisting import of economic relations as an important focus."[23] Much the same conclusion has been made by Lipset and Rokkan, who found that the relation between cleavage and party organization continues to hold. They said that the party systems of Western nations in the 1960's "reflect, with few but significant exceptions, the cleavage structures of the 1920's."[24] The alternatives open to parties as well as many party organizations, are older than the majorities of the national electorates. This important observation simplifies an historical examination of political tendencies, on the one hand, but requires a more thorough understanding of the class concept on the other.

The political ecologist must catalogue the "people," and identify and classify the social collectives and groups of a political unit that may be influential in the molding of political expression. In the analysis of an area traditionally devoted to agricultural enterprise, such as Louisiana, there arise further problems of definition. Historically, as was true for the South in general, planter-farmer class cleavage was manifested in political behavior. But it is essential to be able to determine who is a planter or farmer and what makes an agricultural enterprise a plantation rather than a farm. To provide answers for questions of this sort is to anticipate possible misunderstanding of concepts and interpretation of data which, in an ecological study of this kind, are of crucial importance. At the same time, it may be possible to clarify our general frame of reference by way of illustration.

It has been said that one searches in vain for a precise definition of the family farm. This is so because common usage, as well as

---

[23] David R. Segal, "Classes, Strata and Parties in West Germany and the United States," *Comparative Studies in Society and History*, X (1967), 81.
[24] Lipset and Rokkan, *Party Systems*, 50.

classifications of the United States Bureau of the Census, employs the term "farm" (and "farmer") as a vaguely inclusive category.[25] Of course, it is desirable to distinguish farm and plantation in terms of how the agricultural enterprise is organized, for the system of agriculture and also the size of holdings are basic to all rural social stratification.[26] It will be pointed out, as this study develops, that although data are often insufficient for making as adequate identification as desired, careful observations make it possible to characterize what is meant by these terms and where in the agricultural landscape the types so designated are located.

A clear-cut contrast exists between two systems of farming, two ways of utilizing the land potential: the so-called family farm and the plantation. As T. Lynn Smith put it, whatever else may be said of the family farm, "certainly it refers to the condition in which each farm family has sufficient land to occupy its members fully at agricultural pursuits, but not enough land to necessitate the steady employment of a great deal of supplementary labor."[27] To a considerable extent, operation of such a farm has been represented in the American agrarian myth as a "way of life." A community or an area based upon such a system of agriculture may be characterized by a maximum degree of social homogeneity, and this means that a minimum of social division occurs—the potentials for the development of social stratification and cleavage are limited.[28]

Large-scale agriculture is, in essentials, the factory system in farming. The plantation system technically refers to the latifundia of tropical countries, but in the United States, "plantation" has become the accepted term for the large-scale agricultural systems of the southern region. The elements necessary to the plantation system have been listed as four in number:[29] There must be an abundance of

[25] T. Lynn Smith, *The Sociology of Rural Life* (Rev. ed.; New York, 1947), 307. See Chap. 12, "Land Tenure," and Chap. 15, "Size of Holdings," for treatment of this problem.
[26] Lowry Nelson, *Rural Sociology* (New York, 1952), 261.
[27] Smith, *Sociology of Rural Life*, 307.
[28] Nelson, *Rural Sociology*, 265–67.
[29] Rupert Vance, *Human Factors in Cotton Culture* (Chapel Hill, 1929), 39.

fertile, cheap, level or rolling land; there must be a rather docile, cheap labor supply of low social status; management must provide not only an economic but a social supervision as well; and the products must be staples, easily cultivated cash crops for which no intricate marketing problem exists.

In such a system the owner may be a resident operator or an absentee manager with an overseer directing the activities of the laborers, who may be tenants, croppers, or wage hands. Of course, in antebellum days the labor force was Negro slaves, and the owners tended to live on location in the "big house" or mansion. Large scale agriculture consisted of the agricultural operations of merchants, bankers, and professional men who made up the "best families" of villages, towns, and small cities in the South.[30] The primary purpose of the plantation system was to make profits. Of course the family farm also seeks profit, but it is, in the first place, the home of the farmer. Where a plantation economy predominates an area, there is a greater degree of social stratification.

Historically, the small holding predominated the American rural scene, although an important exception was found in the South, where the fertile lands were preempted by the plantation system while the poorer lands became the seat of the family farm. The planter class was the ruling group, and many of its members developed a way of life congenial to a self-styled aristocracy. The social cleavage between farmer and planter classes revealed itself in political expression or tendencies.

The discovery of a political climate in a given area through an investigation of the human geography and social ecology will in fact show that experience is cumulative and that social factors influence the behavior of people. Purposes shift, however, and consensus may wax or wane; the economic base of the social structure may change. Moreover, collectives vary with the degree of social power at their disposal. These and other considerations must be reckoned with in the ecological analysis of voting behavior. But before turning to a description of the social ecology of Louisiana, it is desirable to comment

[30] Smith, *Sociology of Rural Life*, 313.

upon some methodological questions which have been raised concerning ecological analysis.

Aggregate data, which are used in ecological analysis, represent gross figures about certain categories of voters, but they do not reveal how individuals or subunits of those categories actually behave or what influences them. As long as the student recognizes this, he avoids the danger of attributing to an individual the behavioral characteristics of the groups to which he belongs. This is the "ecological fallacy," the fallacy of inference from ecological to individual correlation. Earlier attacks on the "ecological fallacy," however, have been replaced by considerable effort to spell out the assumptions and the limitations of inference from one level of description to another.[31]

A residue of unsupported assumptions is a disadvantage of ecological analysis when the researcher fails to label these assumptions as such.[32] While the survey researcher faces the contrary danger from the "ecological fallacy" in the "individualistic fallacy" of trying to generalize from individual behavior to collective relationships, the sample survey, nonetheless, has helped to verify hypotheses which ecologists have entertained and to improve the standard interpretation of events.[33] Increased experience has led students of voting behavior to recognize that the techniques used may be a function of the intentions of the researcher. Thus, Erwin K. Scheuch has pointed out that the preference for either individual or aggregate measurement is related to the differing strategies in theory construction. "Macro theories are easier to connect with aggregate data,

[31] Mattei Dogan and Stein Rokkan (eds.), *Quantitative Ecological Analysis*, "Introduction," 13. The initial statement of the problem comes from W. S. Robinson, "Ecological Correlations and the Behavior of Individuals," *American Sociological Review*, XV (1950), 351–57. It stimulated a considerable literature among which are Leo Goodman, "Some Alternatives to Ecological Correlations," *American Journal of Sociology*, LXIV (1959), 610–25; O. D. Duncan, Ray P. Cuzzort and Beverly Duncan, *Statistical Geography* (Glencoe, Ill., 1961); Hubert M. Blalock, Jr., *Causal Inferences in Non-Experimental Research* (Chapel Hill, 1963); Hayward Alker, *Mathematics and Politics* (New York, 1965).

[32] See John H. Fenton, *People and Parties in Politics* (Glenview, Ill., 1966), for a useful discussion of the use of aggregate and survey data.

[33] Heberle, *Social Movements*. The discussion of polls in Chap. 10 remains one of the best in the literature.

while micro theories and reductionistic explanations of systems are apparently more related to individual measurements."[34]

The method used depends upon the problem to be solved. Therefore, Robert R. Alford, in defense of the sample survey, has suggested that "particularly in the present period when class bases of politics may be dwindling, it is dangerous to infer on the social base of parties from ecological correlations."[35] On the other hand, the use of the growing number of datum archives to reclaim past political behavior inevitably must rest upon an ecological interpretation of aggregate data.[36]

In working with election returns as "scrolls of the past," as Samuel Lubell has called them,[37] the student is encouraged by the observation that aggregate data are the "hardest" data that can be obtained. The meaning and comparability of aggregate data vary less from area to area, from time to time, and from study to study than do most survey data.[38] Erik Allardt has tried to "get things straightened out" in the continued discussion of the use of aggregate data by suggesting that the main objective of ecological analysis is not to be found in the demonstration of correlations but in the area of causal explanation. Thus, the value of aggregate data lies in its informativeness because of the greater variety of events accounted for, in contrast to individual data that may have high probability but low informative content. Indeed, the deliberate and cold-blooded uses of the ecological fallacy make possible increased speculative and interpretive generalizations which avoid the pitfalls of research triviality.[39]

[34] Erwin K. Scheuch, "Cross-National Comparisons Using Aggregate Data: Some Substantive and Methodological Problems," in Richard L. Merritt and Stein Rokkan (eds.), Comparing Nations (New Haven, 1966), 133.

[35] Robert R. Alford, "Class Voting in the Anglo-American Political Systems," in Lipset and Rokkan, Party Systems, 70–71.

[36] Walter Dean Burnham, "The Changing Shape of the American Political Universe," American Political Science Review, LIX (1965), 8.

[37] Lubell, Revolt, 261.

[38] Austin Ranney, "The Utility and Limitations of Aggregate Data in the Study of Electoral Behavior," in Ranney (ed.), Essays on the Behavioral Study of Politics (Urbana, Ill., 1962), 96.

[39] Allardt, "Aggregate Analysis," 51.

In research strategy, ecological units may be classified in terms of presence and absence of social and economic variables, and the patterns of voting behavior of such units may be traced (or vice versa). In any case, the unit of analysis may be treated as a "voter type," and its tendencies may be compared with those of other such types within a particular political jurisdiction. This comes close to the election or voter "simulation," which, coupled with the increasing sophistication of electronic computer technology, promises to sharpen the conceptual and logical aspects of research design.[40]

By applying the techniques of factor analysis to a file of ecological variables for the 550 "communes" in Finland, the smallest administrative units in the country, Allardt derived analytical units (the five areas into which it was found the country could be divided) from the data units (the communes), so that ecological patterns instead of single variables could be compared for replication and specification in comparative research. It was possible to discover within-nation variations and regional imbalances. Regional imbalances were found to exist not only in the distribution of important variables (such as Communist strength) but also in ecological patterns or associations between variables (two patterns of radicalism, traditional and emerging). One important aspect of the research design, which facilitated causal interpretations of the ecological data, rested in the fact that the data units (communes) really corresponded to natural social areas that people were aware of and with which they identified themselves and others.[41] While "weaker" statistical tools will be used, Allardt's work has provided a rationale for the search for political tendencies in Louisiana. This study will trace within-state differences in terms of clusters of parishes (the county unit in all other American states) which are found to be similar in historical and socio-cultural background, and for which aggregative data are plentiful. These clusters of parishes will be labeled "voter type areas."

[40] Robert L. Chartrand, "Automatic Data Processing and the American Political Campaign," *The Library of Congress Legislative Reference Service*, TK 6565 C Sp 115 (1966). This is an exhaustive survey of the literature.
[41] Erik Allardt, "Implications of Within-Nation Variations and Regional Imbalances for Cross-National Research," in Merritt and Rokkan, *Comparing Nations*, 337–48.

The parish delineations used in this study do not presume to improve upon the generalized maps of Louisiana produced by Fred B. Kniffen (showing the natural regions of the state),[42] Roger W. Shugg (depicting a simplified regional division of Louisiana parishes),[43] or Alvin L. Bertrand (showing the location of ten rural social areas in the state).[44] The latter delineation was drawn from an analysis of aggregate data of the present number of sixty-four parishes taken mainly from the United States census (1950). The first two maps cited, however, were based upon the work of Samuel Henry Lockett and E. W. Hilgard. Lockett's map delineated natural boundaries from field notes taken in an extensive survey of the state around 1870 and was printed as "The Louisiana State University Topographic Map of 1873."[45] The Hilgard map was an agricultural one compiled from published reports on the cotton states for the tenth census of the United States (1880).[46]

Inspection of both of these early maps shows a striking degree of similarity as to location and details of the natural regions of the state. They closely represent the original natural conditions when upland and swamp, prairies and marsh, were little changed by human activities.[47] The establishment of voter type areas, which will be made in the pages to follow (see page 2), will draw upon the maps discussed above, modifying them, but only for the special purpose of facilitating the analysis of data drawn from political subdivisions.

[42] Fred B. Kniffen, *Louisiana: Its Land and People* (Baton Rouge, 1968).

[43] Roger W. Shugg, *Origins of Class Struggle in Louisiana* (Baton Rouge, 1939; paperback, 1968).

[44] Alvin L. Bertrand, *The Many Louisianas* (LSU, Agricultural Experiment Station Bulletin No. 496 [Baton Rouge; June, 1955]).

[45] Samuel Henry Lockett, "The LSU Topographic Map of Louisiana, 1873" (New York, 1873).

[46] E. W. Hilgard, *Cotton Production in the Mississippi Valley and Southwestern States*, V, Pt. 2 (U. S. Census Reports, 1880); see also Yvonne Phillips, "Land Use Patterns in Louisiana" (Master's thesis, Louisiana State University, 1950), where a number of state maps are presented, some based on aerial photographs.

[47] Kniffen, *Louisiana*, 10.

# Contents

CHAPTER XI                          *Page*
## The Future of Louisiana Politics                          **398**

# List of Tables

*Page*

CHAPTER VI

*Page*

CHAPTER VII

CHAPTER VIII                              *Page*

CHAPTER IX                                                    *Page*

CHAPTER X                              *Page*

*Page*

CHAPTER XI                                    *Page*

# List of Maps

Political Tendencies in Louisiana

# Louisiana Voter Type Areas

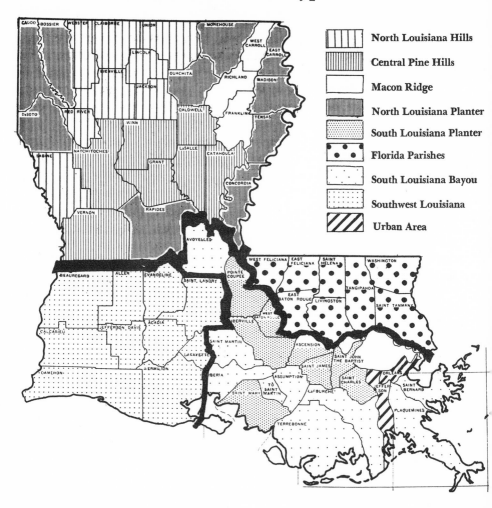

North Louisiana Hills

Central Pine Hills

Macon Ridge

North Louisiana Planter

South Louisiana Planter

Florida Parishes

South Louisiana Bayou

Southwest Louisiana

Urban Area

# CHAPTER I

# Foundations of Political Ecology in Louisiana

## 1. *Units of Ecological Analysis*

Louisiana is one of the Gulf Coast tier of states and shares general characteristics common to other states of the region, but there are striking differences in its geological foundation that set it apart. These differences are due to the Mississippi River, which flows through the state and extends its delta into the Gulf of Mexico.[1]

The alluvial valley of the Mississippi, shaped like a huge triangle with apex pointing north, begins at Cape Giradeau, Missouri, and fans out to the Gulf, covering most of South Louisiana. Today the dominant feature contributing to the Gulf Coast Geosyncline, the geologic process bringing a downwarping of the earth's crust under the Gulf shore, is the Mississippi River which on its changing courses through Louisiana dumped tons of sediment along the coast before settling in its present bed.

One of the distinguishing characteristics of the Louisiana section of the Gulf Coast is the fact there are relatively larger areas of marsh, swamp, and floodplain than are found in the rest of the region. The deposition contributed by the Mississippi system brought rich alluvial soils to Louisiana. The Mississippi Delta is said to begin at the northern borders of Pointe Coupee Parish across from the extreme southwest corner of the state of Mississippi, bounded on the west by Old River, the Atchafalaya, Bayou Teche, and Vermilion Bayou, and on the east by the bluffs above Baton Rouge, by Bayou Manchac, the Amite River, and the lakes above and to the west of New Orleans.[2]

---

[1] Richard J. Russell and H. V. Howe, "Cheniers of Southwestern Louisiana, *Geographical Review*, XXV (1935), 461.

[2] *Lower Mississippi River Delta*, Geological Bulletin No. 8 (New Orleans: Department of Conservation, Louisiana Geological Survey, 1936).

The present extensive delta and floodplain result from the action of epochs of geological time, during which the alluvial valley of the Mississippi has been filled and built up. Further geologic action has produced terraces preserved through regional tippings. These comprise the lower portions of the Florida Parishes and most of what is now called the southwest prairies of Louisiana.

If one studied a relief map of the state, he would find three major upland areas, surrounded by floodplains, terraces, and deltas produced by the Mississippi River and its tributary, the Red River. These uplands comprise what became known as the hill parishes of North Louisiana and the Florida Parishes to the east. Smaller but nonetheless important uplands are the Bastrop Hills north of Monroe, and Macon Ridge to the east, both within the Mississippi River floodplain in Northeast Louisiana. This geologic foundation provides a firm basis for subsequent topographic and soil type investigations.

The surrounding river systems take the shape of a large, roughly-described "Y." It is formed by the Mississippi, which flows south through the upper half of the state before turning southeastward to the Gulf, and by the Red River, which flows south and east from the northwest corner of the state, connecting with the Mississippi at Old River. An alternate route, taken when the Mississippi was in its flood stage, was down through the Atchafalaya basin, which was once a channel of the Mississippi and which would have tended to take the main channel of the river again, had not extensive engineering work been carried out at Old River.[3]

The left side of the Y cuts the geologically older uplands of North Louisiana into two parts. The section west of the Red River consists of hills in the north, giving way to the coastwise prairie as one proceeds south. Most of this area is highly eroded and gives the appearance of being more rugged than the hills really are. The middle upland section east of the Red River is a triangle pointing south, bordered on the east by the Ouachita River portion of the Mississippi system. This section consists of rolling hills (from two hundred to five hundred feet above sea level) extending over the Louisiana border into Arkansas. Within the Mississippi alluvial valley is found another older upland,

[3] Fred B. Kniffen, *Louisiana: Its Land and People* (Baton Rouge, 1968), 154.

Macon Ridge, which extends through the two parishes of West Carroll and Franklin and includes a portion of Richland.

North and east of the lower Mississippi, which forms the leg of the Y, there is another upland which becomes terrace on the entire southern edge, finally merging into the delta region. Here are included the bulk of the Florida Parishes, from the Felicianas to the Mississippi border marked by the Pearl River. The delta fans out at its base and actually embraces the entire area of swamp and marsh that makes up the Gulf Coast of the state. The alluvial valley, floodplain, and the upper delta of the Mississippi extend the width of two tiers of parishes in the north before spreading out to form the lower delta. Within this large area, and also up the Red River Valley, natural levees have been built up through deposition. Along the banks of river and bayou the land is thus generally above high water and is very fertile, making it the preferred location of plantation and farm. However, only short distances away the land becomes swampy and often inaccessible.

Although ecological characteristics will be described in conjunction with the analysis of voting tendencies as the study proceeds, it is desirable at this point to describe the basis for the delineation of voter type areas and at the same time it will be possible to present the most general aspects of the human ecology of each unit. The problem of boundaries is present in every geographic study, and the solution is always somewhat arbitrary, suiting the purpose at hand. At once, in an historical study of this sort, it is best to establish cartographic boundaries which show Louisiana as it was, as well as Louisiana as it is, but in any case to delineate areas within the state which consist of clusters of parishes—the political units of record. The voter type areas outlined in Map 1 represent a compromise, then, of the delineations made in the classic state maps described above. The attempt has been made to derive a cluster-of-parishes regional map, which does justice to the natural regions of the state, consisting of the three major features: lowlands (including coastal marshes, the Mississippi floodplain, and the Red River Valley), terraces (including blufflands, flatwoods, and prairies), and hills.[4]

[4] *Ibid.*, 8–9.

Nine voter type areas (Map 1) have been outlined, and at this point it will prove useful to list them, showing the appropriate parishes included in each:

*North Louisiana Planter Parishes* (10): Bossier, Caddo, Concordia, DeSoto, East Carroll, Madison, Morehouse, Ouachita, Rapides, Tensas.

*North Louisiana Hills* (8): Bienville, Claiborne, Jackson, Lincoln, Red River, Sabine, Union, Webster.

*Central Pine Hills* (7): Caldwell, Catahoula, Grant, LaSalle, Natchitoches, Vernon, Winn.

*Macon Ridge* (3): Franklin, Richland, West Carroll.

*South Louisiana Planter Parishes* (8): Ascension, Iberville, Pointe Coupee, St. Charles, St. James, St. John the Baptist, St. Mary, West Baton Rouge.

*South Louisiana Bayou Parishes* (8): Assumption, Avoyelles, Iberia, LaFourche, Plaquemines, St. Bernard, St. Martin, Terrebonne.

*Florida Parishes* (8): East Baton Rouge, East Feliciana, Livingston, St. Helena, St. Tammany, Tangipahoa, Washington, West Feliciana.

*Southwest Louisiana* (10): Acadia, Allen, Beauregard, Calcasieu, Cameron, Evangeline, Jefferson Davis, Lafayette, St. Landry, Vermilion.

*Urban Area* (2): Jefferson, Orleans.

The logical place to start a description of voter type areas is with the Urban Area, since New Orleans was the earliest major settlement of Europeans (1718), with the exception of Natchitoches (1714). In Orleans, and part of adjacent Jefferson Parish, is found an urban population which from the inception of statehood in 1812 has made up about 20 percent of the Louisiana population. From the Isle of Orleans, earliest settlement moved up the Mississippi River to the so-called German and Acadian Coasts (coasts referring to the natural levees of the river).

To move north and west from New Orleans is to come to the parishes beside and through which the Mississippi flows, from St. Charles to Pointe Coupee, and into which early settlers came, intent upon fashioning an agricultural enterprise resting upon this most fertile alluvial land. These are the South Louisiana Planter Parishes. Not all the Europeans who farmed along the river were wealthy plantation owners, although that was the rule, and the planters came to dominate the social and political life of the area. About 1720, German settlers had taken up residence along the German Coast above New Orleans in what are now St. Charles and St. John the Baptist parishes. Eventually, these people were to lose their language and their identity because of their absorption into the larger French population of the colony. Aside from the names, there is little that is German to be found along the German Coast today.[5]

Another group who were to make a lasting impression on the history of Louisiana were the Acadians, who first arrived and settled along the Acadian Coast which consisted of the two parishes of St. James and Ascension, directly upriver from the German Coast. From about 1760 on, Louisiana was to receive Acadian exiles from French Canada by the hundreds and thousands, seeking a place of refuge.[6] From the coast, they went west and down into the South Louisiana Bayou Parishes along the broad levees of Bayou LaFourche. They went to the Pointe Coupee settlement and thence westward up the Red River into what became Avoyelles Parish. By water they pushed across the Atchafalaya swamps to the levees of Bayou Teche all the way to the eastern borders of the prairies and Southwest Louisiana, where settlement beyond Opelousas and Lafayette was sparse until late in the nineteenth century. The Acadians proved to be hard workers like the German settlers before them and likewise became very good peasant farmers (*petits habitants* of river and bayous).

[5] *Ibid.*, 124.
[6] *Ibid.*, 127.

Vernon J. Parenton has made clear that the Acadian settlers were not destined to become absorbed and forgotten.[7] These poor farmers, strong in their Catholic faith, had large families, and held on to their ways, so much so that the entire section of the state eventually became dominated by a French culture, as the "Cajuns" absorbed nearly every alien group which came into contact with them. Parenton has found this a great contrast between the French in Canadian Quebec and the French of American Louisiana. On the latter scene, the process of acculturation and accommodation was such that the Acadians lost neither their French religion nor their characteristic culture. Five factors were found to be decisive in this process:[8] (1) intermarriage; (2) the dominance of the Acadian mother; (3) the influence of the French Catholic religion; (4) a strong solidarity or esprit de corps; and (5) the characteristic cultural outlook the Acadian called *la joie de vivre*.

Claude Jean Roumagnac found that by mid-twentieth century the bulk of the "Acadian" parishes, measured by means of a French-name inventory and records of Catholic religious affiliation, lay within the confines of the heavy lines in the base map for this study which locate the South Louisiana Planter and Bayou voter type clusters of parishes.[9] Only St. Landry, Lafayette, Evangeline, Acadia, Vermilion and Cameron are found outside, delineated in this study within the Southwest Louisiana area. Of Roumagnac's "core area," only St. Landry and Lafayette parishes fall outside what has been designated as the Bayou voter type area. It is important to recognize, however, that most of the parishes in the Southwest Louisiana voter type as well as the Florida Parishes area contain populations with a great many Roman Catholics. This is one reason for dividing North and South Louisiana at the line indicated on Map 1, at roughly the 31st parallel.

[7] Vernon J. Parenton, "The Rural French-Speaking People of Quebec and South Louisiana," (Ph.D. dissertation, Harvard University, 1948).

[8] T. Lynn Smith and Vernon J. Parenton, "Acculturation Among the Louisiana French,: *American Journal of Sociology*, XLIV (1938), 355–64.

[9] Claude Jean Roumagnac, "A Demographic Analysis of Selected Characteristics of the 'Acadian' Population of Louisiana, 1940" (Master's thesis, Louisiana State University, 1952).

Some hesitation accompanied the inclusion of Avoyelles Parish with the Bayou Parishes and St. Mary with the South Louisiana Planter Parishes, when in each case there was a break in the contiguity, and yet there was a logic for doing so. While Avoyelles, the parish which contains the confluence of the Red and Mississippi rivers, must be classified among the alluvial parishes of the floodplain, at the same time much of the area is given over to swamplands. Similarly the historical records indicate that this parish was less predominated by plantations than either set of planter parishes upriver or down. On the other hand, St. Mary Parish, while located within the floodplain, contains the natural levee of Bayou Teche which flows through it. But its alluvial portions became the seat of sugar plantations. Using the percentage of slaves in 1860 as a rough indicator of the relative domination of the plantation, it can be seen that Avoyelles, with 54.5 percent slaves, more nearly approximated the Bayou voter type (average 53.6 percent slaves), while St. Mary, with 77.6 percent slaves, was more nearly associated with the South Louisiana Planter voter type (average 71.0 percent slaves).

Sugar cane was the predominant staple grown along the lower Mississippi, as well as Bayou LaFourche and Bayou Teche. Due to the French influence, the field types here were generally the small arpent type (an arpent is about 192 feet) measured off a certain width along the high ground of the levee and extended back a greater length into the backland swamps.[10] However, plantation economy brought combinations of these narrow, ribbon-like fields under a single operation. Harold Hoffsommer has shown that the great bulk of acreage in the "sugar bowl" in 1940 was in the larger farms and that 7 percent of the cane operators had more than 70 percent of the total acreage.[11] Plantations have, historically, been operated in both the river as well as the bayou tier of parishes to the west of them, but they predominated in the river parishes. The picture is incomplete without consideration of the other side of agriculture in this sugar bowl area, for this was the heart of the area settled by

[10] Kniffen, *Louisiana*, 122.
[11] Harold Hoffsommer, *The Sugar Cane Farm* (LSU, Agricultural Experiment Station Bulletin No. 320 [Baton Rouge, 1940]).

the Acadian French. The *petits habitants* along bayou and streams of the backlands became peasant proprietors who grew cane as well as other crops used for home consumption on their small, lateral section farms. One must inspect with care the voting behavior of this complex area of Planter and Bayou parishes because of the extremes in ways of life and because sugar cane production was associated with the presence of expensive sugar mills which processed the cane crop on a commercial basis.[12]

The Florida Parishes are so-called because of the fact that the area was included as part of West Florida at one time, before it became part of Louisiana under the establishment of its statehood in 1812. The white settlers in this part of South Louisiana had been almost all Anglo-Saxon and Protestant and here, particularly in East Baton Rouge, East and West Feliciana, and St. Helena parishes a plantation system was developed, the staple being cotton rather than cane. There were historical circumstances that provided the homogeneity of this area as, in terms of relief, it is probably the most mixed of all the voter types. The strip of bluffland which extends southward from Vicksburg, Mississippi, covers most of East and West Feliciana and East Baton Rouge parishes, while Livingston, the southern half of Tangipahoa, and St. Tammany are classified as flatwoods terrace land. St. Helena, the northern half of Tangipahoa, and Washington parishes are a hill area with longleaf pine in predominance.

The voter type area cluster of parishes within South Louisiana, not yet fully described, has been labeled Southwest Louisiana. It now consists of ten parishes, all of which, as the state developed, were derived from the original parishes of Lafayette (which included the territory from which Vermilion Parish was derived in 1844) and St. Landry (which included all the rest of the area from the Atchafalaya River on the east, westward to the Sabine River). The cities of Lafayette and Opelousas were settled on the terrace blufflands which separated the Mississippi floodplain from the prairies on the southern half and the flatwoods on the northern half of the terrace land which

[12] J. Carlyle Sitterson, *Sugar Country: The Cane Industry in the South, 1753–1950* (Lexington, 1953).

stretched southwestward to the Texas border. While Calcasieu was derived as a parish from St. Landry in 1840 (including the area from which the parishes of Jefferson Davis, Allen, and Beauregard were established in 1912), the prairies remained relatively unsettled due to lack of adequate transportation until 1882 and the completion of the Southern Pacific Railroad.[13] Rapid settlement then began, and the prairies were used for the production of rice. It had been grown haphazardly by the Acadians, who had been the first stream of migrants to push into the area, but among the new settlers were many midwesterners who took up rice production in the place of other grain crops like wheat or oats by methods with which they were familiar. The large family-sized farm came to predominate, and the area resembles the Middle West in many ways.[14]

Within the northern reaches of Calcasieu, the terrace flatwoods sustained one of the finest stands of longleaf pine timber in the world.[15] This virgin stand was eyed by northern lumber syndicates soon after the railroad was completed, and by 1895 the mills in and around Lake Charles cut an annual production of 140 million board feet of lumber. Here, and farther north in the Central Hills, such heavy production continued until "by 1918 there were twelve million cutover acres and they were increasing by 250,000 to 300,000 annually. By 1920 operators saw the end and were looking westward to the virgin forests of the mountain and Pacific states.[16] The Southwest Louisiana Parishes of Beauregard and Allen, with the northern part of Evangeline, were joined with the parishes of the Central Pine Hills in the common designation of "the cutover parishes."

This large area in the central and west central section of the state was stripped of its virgin cover, and subsistence farming became the rule. When studied in the 1930's, it was found that the farm population

[13] Kniffen, *Louisiana*, Chap. 28; Donald J. Millet, Sr., "The Economic Development of Southwestern Louisiana, 1865–1900," (Ph.D. dissertation, Louisiana State University, 1964).

[14] T. Lynn Smith, Mary Byrd, and Karl Shafer, "Mobility of Population in Assumption and Jefferson Davis Parishes, Louisiana," *Southwestern Social Science Quarterly*, XVII (1936), 31–37.

[15] Donald J. Millet, "The Lumber Industry of 'Imperial' Calcasieu: 1865–1900," *Louisiana History*, VII (1966), 51.

[16] Kniffen, *Louisiana*, 165.

was generally composed of white farmers, with remaining lumber camps (tree farming was found to be effective in this region where rapid growth is sustained) showing a larger proportion of Negroes. Even so, a large portion of the farm population was engaged, at least part time, by the lumbering industry.[17] Often the departure of the lumber industry left the population with few resources and with farms whose utilization was poorly organized or whose fertility was low. Beauregard Parish, on the extreme southwestern edge of the cutover, typified this condition.[18] It will not be surprising to find signs of radical political tendencies within the cutover parishes.

The first major settlements of Louisiana took place in the South Louisiana Planter and Bayou areas and within the Florida Parishes. Early settlement by the French had also begun up the reaches of the Red River Valley, however, when Natchitoches was established to assert the French claim to lower Louisiana and as an outpost from which to develop trade with the Spaniards in Texas. It was not until after 1812 that sustained settlement was experienced in North Louisiana, and then it took place on the levees within the floodplain of both the Red River and the Mississippi. Here were established the parishes which became noted as the home of "King Cotton," plantations, and large numbers of Negro slaves. It becomes necessary, then, to delineate those parishes which will be classified as having been predominated by the cotton plantation, noting that while South Louisiana Planter Parishes were settled mostly by French, the settlers who came later to the northern alluvial parishes were American Anglo-Saxons.

The arbitrary nature of boundaries is revealed in the compromise involving ten parishes which form the North Louisiana Planter voter type area. Though it might be expected that all the alluvial lands of the Mississippi floodplain, which extend back the width of two parishes on the west side of the river, would be developed, away from

---

[17] T. Lynn Smith and Martha R. Fry, *The Population of a Selected Cut-Over Area of Louisiana* (LSU, Agricultural Experiment Station Bulletin No. 268 [Baton Rouge, 1955]).

[18] Bueford M. Gile, *Economic Utilization of Rural Land Resources in Beauregard Parish, Louisiana* (LSU, Agricultural Experiment Station Bulletin No. 322 [Baton Rouge, 1940]).

the natural levees, the entire area from Old River to the Arkansas line was subject to seasonal flooding. Thus settlement became concentrated along the front tier of parishes in the delta and along the levees of the Ouachita River in Morehouse and Ouachita parishes, and here the plantation system was established.

The problem of boundary is made more difficult in the parishes through which the Red River flows, because the alluvial valley is of relatively narrow width, and though the plantation predominated there, it soon gave way to the family farm in the hills beyond. One author, in tracing the geographic distribution of plantations in Red River Parish, as late as 1940, said: "Along the river [Red] the plantation system prevails, and the yield per acre is greater than in the hills. In the uplands the farms are usually small, and the yield per acre is not so great. In both sections there is a diversity of crops grown, but generally in the hills more crops are grown for home consumption than along the river."[19]

The question of boundary easily becomes one of compromise, where a judgment has to be made regarding the historical experience of a particular parish area, and a balance found between the number of plantations along the levees and the number of farms among the hills. It becomes a matter of relative dominance. For this reason, Caddo, Bossier, and DeSoto parishes have been added to the North Louisiana Planter Parishes, while Red River and Natchitoches, though early committed to the plantation, also saw the settlement of many farmers within the more extensive hill portions of these parishes. The judgment to classify these as Hill Parishes can be reenforced by again looking at comparative figures on percentage of slaves in 1860. Though the Natchitoches population (adjacent Red River Parish was not created until 1871) was 56.4 percent slave, up the Red River in DeSoto Parish the proportion was 65.0 percent slave, in Caddo 60.4 percent, and Bossier 70.4 percent, while the average for the North Louisiana Planter area was 72.9 percent slave, the highest proportion of all voter types areas in 1860. While Rapides was also given over to hills and swamp as well as alluvial lands, its population

[19] Marion T. Loftin, "Agricultural Extension and Cultural Change in Red River Parish," (Master's thesis, Louisiana State University, 1941), 14.

was 60.0 percent slave in 1860 and it was well known as a planter-dominated parish.

Though Macon Ridge is a bluffland terrace—an ancient upland within the surrounding Mississippi floodplain—in antebellum times it was given over to the plantation. There was also a sizable amount of family farming, and, particularly in the early decades of the twentieth century, a large number of farmers from the hill parishes took up residence in these parishes of Franklin, Richland, and West Carroll. Therefore, it was decided to treat these three as distinct from the adjoining Planter Parishes.

There remains the justification for delineation of the North Louisiana Hills and Central Pine Hills clusters of parishes. First glance at a natural regions or relief map shows that all fifteen parishes involved could easily be classified simply as Hill Parishes. But the basic index maps, referred to above, carefully distinguish two sets of hill areas, each traversed by the Red River. Both Lockett and Hilgard agreed that the soil in the parishes designated as the North Louisiana Hills was superior to that of the Central Pine Hills. Lockett labeled it "good soil" as compared to "thin soil," while Hilgard referred to the former as "oak uplands" and the latter as "pine hills" or, west of the Red River, as "oak, hickory, and pine hills" Kniffen has designated the difference as simply "shortleaf" and "longleaf" hills. It was Roger W. Shugg who claimed that the presence of the upland oak may be considered an indication of more fertile land than where the pine grew in abundance. Of course that oak was cut long ago, and most of the land is now in pine, but the original difference was important, as Shugg maintained that the yeoman slaveholders preferred boundaries of oak, leaving the pine forests to those without slaves. "The result was that by 1860 the area defined by oak trees merged into the black belt, produced almost all the cotton, and had the larger share of wealth in the uplands. The piney woods were sparsely inhabited by white people of little means."[20]

From the 1840's until the Civil War, the states of Alabama, Mississippi, Georgia, North and South Carolina, Virginia, Kentucky,

[20] Roger W. Shugg, *Origins of Class Struggle in Louisiana* (Baton Rouge, 1939; 2nd ed., 1968), 11.

and Tennessee sent their sons and daughters by the hundreds to Louisiana where they peopled the Hills Parishes.[21] This stock, yeoman farmers who established family farms from the forest wilderness, grew a cash crop of cotton as supplement in their subsistence economy. When possible, self-sufficiency was augmented through the purchase of a number of slaves. This practice was more prevalent in the North Louisiana Hills area and, as a consequence, portions of the parishes of Webster, Claiborne, Bienville, and Lincoln were known as a little plantation area, in contrast to the Hills home of the red-neck farmer. Moreover, after the Civil War, the total population of the North Louisiana Hills Parishes consisted of a greater proportion of Negroes than within the Central Pine Hills. Around 1900 the railroad came and along with it the sawmills and the systematic denuding of the pine hills. In recent years the North Louisiana Hills farmers have begun to supplement cotton production with beef cattle, dairying, and poultry farming enterprises. Peaches and watermelons are also specialties of the area. The level of living is relatively high in this cluster of parishes, and along with it, the educational level.[22]

In comparison, the Central Pine Hills area, with its vast acres of cutover, by the 1930's had become a depressed area economically. Alvin L. Bertrand found this area with the highest proportion of rural nonfarm inhabitants (indicative that many rural residents were not bona fide farmers), a low farm value index, and the lowest rank in value of farm products sold.[23] As is true of all cutover areas of the state, the proportion of Negroes is low. The Central Pine Hills area is one of small holdings scattered in the midst of large timber tracts where relatively little commercial agriculture is done, and where a majority of the rural residents work part time in lumber and pulpwood or allied industries.

In completing this brief general survey of the voter type areas,

[21] Robert O. Trout, "The People of the North Central Louisiana Hill Country" (Ph.D. dissertation, Louisiana State University, 1954).

[22] Alvin L. Bertrand, *The Many Louisianas* (LSU, Agricultural Experiment Station Bulletin No. 496 [Baton Rouge, 1955]), 14.

[23] *Ibid.* Areas 4 and 5 on Bertrand's delineation were found to be quite the same, except cut by the Red River.

the reader is reminded again of the arbitrary designation of parishes
to particular areas. Valid reasons can be found to place a number of
parishes in one rather than another set of parishes, but it should be
remembered that the primary objective is to generate summary data
for significant subunits of the state. For the earlier period, while
Louisiana was predominantly an agrarian state, the clusters of parishes
labeled voter types can be seen to distinguish planter and farmer areas,
between which political tendencies may be compared. Two Planter
units have been designated, one for North Louisiana and the other
for South Louisiana parishes. In contrast, there are three farmer
units, the two Hills areas and the South Louisiana Bayou Parishes.
Macon Ridge belonged originally to the Planter Parishes but in the
twentieth century this became farmer area. Finally, it is possible
to designate the Florida Parishes and Southwest Louisiana as intermediate in this scheme—mixed planter and farmer. As the discussion
above has tried to make clear, within each of these voter type areas,
such factors as soil conditions, history of settlement, ethnic origin of
population, and recent developments have created significant within-
state differences.

Changes in the economy of rural Louisiana have taken place since
the great depression and particularly since World War II. Formerly,
the three cash crops on which the rural people depended were cotton,
sugar cane, and rice, but now farming is more diversified with the
increasing spread of dairy and beef cattle operations. On sugar cane
plantations mechanization is virtually complete and this has led to
an increase in the size and decline in the number of operating units,
as well as to changes in labor relations from a paternalistic to a more
contractual pattern.[24] Large parts of the cutover areas are now under
reforestation, and revenue from oil production in nearly every part of
the state has lifted the level of living in most of the rural areas of
Louisiana.

At the same time, the increased importance of industrial development in the state has accelerated the growth of population in the
urban parishes of the state. The urban-industrial areas of Caddo-

[24] Roland J. Pellegrin and Vernon J. Parenton, "The Impact of Socio-Economic
Change on Racial Groups in a Rural Setting," *Phylon*, XXIII (1962), 55–60.

Bossier, Ouachita, Rapides, Calcasieu, Lafayette, East Baton Rouge, and Jefferson-Orleans now contribute half the state's population. In contrast to the increase of population in the urban parishes stands the decrease of population in most of the rural areas, more so in North Louisiana than in the south, however, where a number of rural parishes have shown moderate increases. About two-thirds of the state's people now reside in South Louisiana.

In areas where oil fields and large industrial plants provide the opportunity of employment outside agriculture, as in the river parishes between Baton Rouge and New Orleans, around the city of Lafayette, and in the coastal marshes in Plaquemines, St. Bernard, Jefferson, and LaFourche parishes, the beginnings of a rural industrial working class are noticable. In the cities, the past quarter-century not only has witnessed the formation of an industrial working class, but also a great increase in the proportion of white collar workers, of salaried employees in private enterprise and government service. Subject to verification, these classes appear to be recruited from rural areas and small towns, and this is not without consequence for their political attitudes and behavior. While political power in the past was nearly a monopoly of the coalition of businessmen and planters, reenforced by oil and other industrial interests, this situation was changed when Huey P. Long mobilized and activated the farmers and other "small people" and created a "countervailing" power combination. Today there is no doubt that labor is also an increasing factor, although the extent and nature of its influence remains a matter of investigation.

These cluster-of-parishes areas described above will be treated in this study as voter type units, as sets of data subject to all the limitations and strength of ecological analysis of voting behavior. The units have been constructed to facilitate the analysis of within-state differences in political tendencies on the part of elements of the electorate (planter-farmer, merchant-laborer, and so forth). It must be reiterated that the presumed relationships between the motivation of particular individuals and the collective responses of individuals recorded by voter types always are inferred.

# CHAPTER II

# Louisiana Experiences Representative Government

*1. Colonial Experience and the Framing of the Constitution of 1812*

The political history of Louisiana as a state must be viewed against a background of a century of colonial experience. When Louisiana entered the Union, the framers of its constitution met peculiar difficulties in establishing the instrument of a democratic government among a people devoid of such forms. Unlike other American states, Louisiana was never an English Colony.[1] Its political history before statehood in 1812 consisted of seventy years under France (1699–1769), thirty-two years under Spain (1769–1801), a short period (1801–1803) when Spain ceded Louisiana back to France, and finally the U.S. territorial years (1803–1812) after the Louisiana Purchase.

As a royal colony, Louisiana had been governed by laws emanating directly from France. During the short period when the colony was ceded to Spain, the Spanish had little influence on the French culture. The colonists resented the transfer, though admittedly the Spanish administration was the more efficient. The Civil Code of 1808, adopted under the territorial governorship of William C. C. Claiborne, was a combination of Spanish and French civil law plus certain elements of the Code Napoleon. Present-day civil law of the state in large part stems from the experiences under this arrangement. Under the French and Spanish, the Louisiana colonists were politically passive. They did not participate in civil administration to any extent, and apparently they were satisfied with the generally kind paternalism of their rulers.

Seven decades of French rule left a lasting mark, influencing the

---

[1] Melvin Evans, *A Study of the State Government of Louisiana* (Baton Rouge, 1931).

18

institutions and the attitudes of the people. Later Anglo-Saxon infusion never displaced, but only modified, the basic Latin institutions.[2] Under the Enabling Act of 1811, the United States Congress allowed the Territory of Orleans to call a convention and frame a constitution that it might become a state of the Union.

Ordinarily a constitution has a gradual development, being the product of the progression or retrogression of the community.[3] The majority of the original thirteen American colonies had been nurtured on Anglo-Saxon institutions. The colonists, after all, revolted against oppression under the prevalent political system, not against its common-law traditions. In the framing of the American Constitution there was little that was new, if there was much that was debatable.[4] In Louisiana the people had no such continuity of democratic experiences which might be articulated in an instrument of government. The differences in social structure and historical experience between Louisiana and the thirteen original states are obvious when their constitutions are compared. Not only was the political experience vastly different, but there was also a unity of interests in Louisianians which had been lacking in other colonies.

French colonists had pretensions of aristocracy and the main problem in Louisiana was to frame a constitution acceptable to the American Congress, one republican enough to satisfy the temper of the time. This becomes clear when the constitutional provisions for office of governor in the new state are examined. One student of Louisiana government has aptly summarized the differences mentioned above: "Louisiana too, had her symbol of external control, but in comparing the formation of her first Constitution to that of the revolutionary state constitutions, the differences remain more significant than the similarities. Of fundamental importance was the lack of a revolutionary struggle; no Louisianian's blood had been shed in their effort to rid themselves of external control. In addition, there was not the same internal conflict that had expressed itself

---

[2] *Ibid.*, 12.

[3] William Dart (ed.), *Constitutions of the State of Louisiana* (Indianapolis, 1932).

[4] Vernon L. Parrington, *Main Streams in American Thought* (New York, 1930), I, 279.

in the lively struggle between the yeoman class of farmers and the large planters and financial interests in the older states."[5] The first Louisiana constitution was dominated by the influence of an aristocratic society with strong French sympathies, just as the nine ensuing constitutions were to express the influence of some other dominant portion of the citizenry.

The prevailing attitude of this early elite was reflected in the pages of the *Louisiana Gazette* when it "urged the convention to adopt a short aristocratic constitution based upon a propertied electorate, and which provided for a governor not elected by suffrage."[6] The membership of the convention was composed of seventeen men of American descent and twenty-six of Creole, or French, ancestry. Among this elite-group were three future governors, five future United States senators, one future congressman, and a future minister to France.[7]

Casting about for models suitable to their needs, the framers decided upon the Kentucky Constitution of 1797. It had been written by a similarly conservative group, and in most cases the Louisiana convention used its exact language. The few original items in the Louisiana constitution included a section prohibiting the legislature from adopting any system or code. This indicates the dread which people of Louisiana held of the English common law, wholly mysterious to them. The Louisiana constitution emerged ultra-conservative and ultra-aristocratic.

The Constitution of 1812, far from being in accord with the spirit of the American Union, "had been so formulated as to satisfy the alien prejudices in favor of hereditary government existing in the state during its early years.[8] The preamble heralded the aristocratic attitude of the convention. It began: "We, the *representatives* of the people" and ended "do mutually agree *with each other* to form

[5] James W. Prothro, "A Study of Constitutional Development in the Office of the Governor in Louisiana" (Master's thesis, Louisiana State University, 1948), 30.

[6] Quoted in Phillip D. Uzee, "The First Louisiana State Constitution: A Study of Its Origins" (Master's thesis, Louisiana State University, 1938), 30.

[7] *Ibid.*, 15.

[8] Evans, *Study in State Government*, 33.

*ourselves* into a free and independent State."[9] This document contained no Bill or Rights; the first Louisiana constitution containing one was that of 1868.

The power vested in the executive branch likewise reflected past experience and the pervasive unity of the early plantation aristocracy. The action of the framers of the constitution was at variance with the practice of the earlier states, who had no reason to reject a strong governmental head. The broad appointive power of the governor shows the extent to which Louisianians wished to delegate authority to the executive.[10] This office of governor remains one of the most powerful in the nation, his appointive power being a major reason.[11] The governor was to be chosen by the assembly from the two highest on the list of candidates elected by qualified voters. He was required to be a citizen of the United States, a resident of Louisiana for six years, and the owner of taxable property valued at a minimum of $5,000. Emphasis must be placed upon these provisions empowered by the first Louisiana constitution, since the present study will in large part focus upon analysis of the electoral support of Louisiana governors, and because the problem of executive power remains an issue in Louisiana politics.

Two other problems of the initial state constitution—suffrage and representation—were to become major issues in Louisiana politics before 1860. "One but more often both were used in such a manner as to perpetuate the power of the large planters of the black belt and the commercial groups of New Orleans."[12] Article II, Section 8, stipulated that every free white male citizen of the United States who had resided one year in the county in which he offered to vote and who had purchased public lands or paid a state tax should enjoy the rights of an elector. Our analysis below will demonstrate how this property test limited suffrage in Louisiana.

[9] *Ibid.*, 28; italicized by Evans.

[10] Ben B. Taylor, Jr., "The Appointive and Removal Powers of the Governor of Louisiana" (Master's thesis, Louisiana State University, 1935), 151.

[11] Charles W. Tapp, "Development of the Constitutional Appointive Power of the Governor of Louisiana" (Master's thesis, 1964), 8.

[12] Emmett Asseff, *Legislative Apportionment in Louisiana* (LSU, Bureau of Government Research [Baton Rouge, 1950]), 10.

Finally, we must note the manner in which the framers of the 1812 constitution handled the matter of representation. This difficult question was reduced to four thorny issues: (1) the basis of representation; (2) the geographic unit for representation; (3) limitations upon the number of representatives per unit; and (4) the minimum and maximum number of members in each house. One student has concluded that these issues were vital because "they were the determining factors in whether New Orleans, the white belt counties, or black belt counties would control the legislature—New Orleans versus the rural parishes—small farmers in the white belt versus the large plantation owners in the black belt."[13] Representation, it turned out, was to be "equal and uniform" and, in the House, was to be based upon the number of qualified electors. The legislature was directed to take a census beginning in 1813 and every fourth year thereafter in order to determine from the tax lists which white males qualified to vote. Fourteen senatorial districts were to remain forever indivisible.

II. *The Genealogy of Political Parties in Louisiana*

A constitution outlines the profile of a political power structure. With limitations of suffrage and representation written into the document of 1812, access to power resulted in that "Government by Gentlemen" described with such clarity by Roger Shugg. In his incisive words, Louisiana was "ruled by a minority made up of planters, merchants, and lawyers" with the ballot "chiefly in the hands of landowners and shopkeepers."[14] It is in the interplay between such a political power structure and ecological features as described in Chapter 1 that political tendencies become manifest. This interplay between particular ecological balances and the political system of the state has produced several prolonged periods of politics in Louisiana that may be isolated in terms of certain dominating characteristics.[15]

---

[13] *Ibid.*, 10.

[14] Roger W. Shugg, *Origins of Class Struggle in Louisiana* (Baton Rouge, 1939; paperback, 1968), 121–22.

[15] William C. Havard, Rudolf Heberle, and Perry H. Howard, *The Louisiana Elections of 1960* (Baton Rouge, 1963), 17.

In the only early ecological study of Louisiana politics, James K. Greer asserted that the social and industrial activities of the state were influenced by two factors, topographical and geographical on the one hand, the nature and diversity of the population on the other.[16] If one can find interests requiring different policies, then he has found potent elements in the determination of political choices. Greer identified two such elements—*cotton*, a natural staple, and *sugar*, an artificial one. Here was an assertion of simple economic necessity leading to political organization: "Sugar could not be produced in Louisiana without the active protection of the central government, and the realization that this was an inexorable fact made the sugar growers, almost without exception, National Republicans, and later Whigs."[17]

Here was a conflict of interests—cotton and sugar country the attempted resolution of which led to support of political parties with differing views on the proper activity of government. Indeed, we can go further and extend Mr. Greer's list, trying to identify the oppositions which provide dynamic force in the social and political life of Louisiana society. Factors of both a power structure and ecological nature may be listed, without implying any particular sequence:

*Table 2–1*

ECOLOGICAL AND POWER STRUCTURES (OPPOSITIONS)

| Regional | planter parishes . . . . . | farmer parishes |
|---|---|---|
| | South Louisiana . . . . . | North Louisiana |
| | New Orleans. . . . . . . | country parishes |
| Demographic | French . . . . . . . . . | American |
| | black (Negro) . . . . . . | white |
| | native. . . . . . . . . | immigrant (Irish) |
| | youth. . . . . . . . . | aging |

[16] James K. Greer, "Louisiana Politics, 1845–1861" *Louisiana Historical Quarterly*, XII (1929), 381–425, 555–610; and XIII (1930), 67–116, 257–303, 444–83, 617, 54.

[17] Leslie M. Norton, "A History of the Whig Party in Louisiana" (Ph.D. dissertation, Louisiana State University, 1940).

| Religion | Roman Catholic . . . . . | Protestant |
|----------|--------------------------|------------|
| Classes | planter . . . . . . . . . | farmer |
| | merchant . . . . . . . . | laborer |
| | Bourbon . . . . . . . . | poor and white (red-neck) |
| | employer . . . . . . . | worker |
| Party | Whig . . . . . . . . . . | Jacksonian Democrat |
| | Republican . . . . . . . | Democrat |
| | Opposition . . . . . . . | Long candidate |
| Ideology | elitist . . . . . . . . . | populist |
| | white supremacy . . . . . | moderation |

Though quite obviously not all these sets operate at the same time in demanding resolution, many are related, as subsequent analyses are intended to show. There is a common theme, however, which has to do with the determination of suffrage and representation. A general conflict working in the American setting had to do with the question of the prerogatives of an elite in placing limitations on suffrage and the egalitarian tendency to demand its logical opposite—unlimited access to the suffrage. This can be illustrated with a simple cross tabulation as follows:

*Table 2–2*

A MODEL FOR TYPES OF SUFFRAGE

|  |  | Power Structure | |
|--|--|------------------|--|
|  |  | Elite (aristocratic) | Non-Elite (egalitarian) |
| Suffrage | Limited | NOT ALL can vote | |
|  | Unlimited |  | ALL can vote |

The framers of the first Louisiana constitution intended (with acceptance of the document) that "NOT ALL" might exercise the franchise. If the action of this elite was reminiscent of that of Tidewater Virginia, it likewise would be subject to the development of a similar opposition on the part of the yeoman farmer demanding political participation for "ALL."

Migration was to be a certain fact in the first half of the nineteenth-century South, and Louisiana was not immune to this process. Population increased dramatically between 1820 and 1840, more than doubling the number of potential voters, and these bringing with them the Jacksonian ideology of unlimited opportunity in a landed society.[18] Tension between planter and farmer would appear early in Louisiana, however, for while the plantation system provided access to the elite class in the South, generally, so long as fertile land was available, much of the alluvial lands were already preempted by the previously French colonists. The Americans who gained a foothold in the North Louisiana Mississippi Delta, Ouachita and Red River bottoms in the 1830's would tend to side with their planter compatriots in the southern parishes. Elitists were to engage in political contests with levelers infused with the rural populism of Jacksonian Democracy. But while the population of Louisiana increased ten-fold from statehood to 1860, the politically important category, white males twenty-one years of age and over, remained in the proportion of 29 percent of the total. Increased suffrage could only come from decreased limitations upon it.

The population increase through the 1830's, due primarily to the migration of natives from the states to the east and north of Louisiana, was steadily constant and created a population of extreme demographic youth. It may be instructive to compare Louisiana with Australian data for the 1870's, when the world's youngest frontier also experienced the full consequences of migration:[19]

---

[18] See a general interpretation for the South in Perry H. Howard and Joseph L. Brent III, "Social Change, Urbanization, and Types of Society," *Journal of Social Issues*, XXII (1966), 73–84.

[19] Edward Rosset, *Aging Process of Population* (New York, 1964). See charts and discussion of significance of age, therein.

*Table 2-3*

DEMOGRAPHIC YOUTH IN LOUISIANA
1830, AND AUSTRALIA IN 1871*

|  |  | Age Groups | | |
|  | Total | 0–14 years | 15–64 years | 65 and over |
| --- | --- | --- | --- | --- |
| Louisiana | 100% | 42.1 | 56.1 | 1.8 |
| Australia | 100% | 42.1 | 56.2 | 1.7 |

* Source: U.S. Census; Edward Rosset, *Aging Process in Population*, New York, 1964. Unless otherwise stated, the source of tables in this study has been the materials presented in Appendix A or B, or drawn from the context of the discussion.

Age, to be sure, carries with it important social and political consequences, but the age composition of the population in Louisiana increases the more in importance due to the significant internal differences to be found among the voter types based upon ecological regions.

According to Appendix A, Table 3, the frontier areas in 1830, especially the two Hill areas, the Bayou Parishes, and Southwest Louisiana, had young populations, but even the North and South Louisiana Planter types are shown to be proportionally younger than the statewide average. Migration to a developing area, together with rurality, may be said to account for these proportions, while, on the other hand, the relatively older populations of Jefferson and Orleans typify conditions of urbanism. Altogether, however, Louisiana in 1830, and indeed until the twentieth century, must be taken as a characteristically frontier society in the process of development.

III. *Nativism: 1812–1832*

Louisiana, like the rest of the South, manifested perennial devotion to the Democratic Party, although it supported the winning candidate in every presidential election from 1812 through 1856. In the first three presidential elections after statehood, the Louisiana Assembly supported the Jeffersonian and Madisonian Caucus in Congress.

The state supplied three electoral votes each for Madison (1812 and 1816) and Monroe (1820), but by 1824, tendencies were so balanced that the vote was split between Jackson and John Quincy Adams.

At the same time, the first few gubernatorial elections were in the nature of a skirmish between local factions, although cutting across this, the struggle for power between Frenchmen and Americans could be detected. The Florida Parishes, then four in number, were joined to Louisiana in the Act of statehood in April, 1812, although these parishes, settled by Anglo-Saxon Americans with Democratic leanings in politics, had not been represented at the constitutional convention. The outlook of the native Louisianian was exotic to the Americans, who migrated in ever increasing numbers to New Orleans, the Florida Parishes, and North Louisiana. It is understandable in terms of ethnocentrism why the issue in these early elections was carried by old Creole settlers against American newcomers. The Frenchman, in turn, was looked upon as a Frenchman by the English citizen or settler, though he might have been of the same political party.[20]

The cleavage was not so apparent, perhaps, in the first election for governor, when the former territorial governor, W. C. C. Claiborne, was chosen by the assembly over the Creole, Jacques Villeré. As Claiborne's term of office drew to a close it was clear he had welded the bonds of statehood. He had managed to win the admiration of her citizens and had headed Louisiana in the direction of successful representative government.[21] He went on to serve Louisiana in the Fifteenth Congress in 1817.

In 1816, despite attempts at keeping nativism out of politics, the French-speaking elite had again nominated illustrious son Villeré, while the Americans countered with Joshua Lewis. The Assembly chose Villeré, and his feared partisanship did not materialize. The Frenchman demonstrated his capacity to rule and his aristocratic sense of responsibility, as he made a sincere effort to close the breach between Creole and American.

[20] Greer, "Louisiana Politics," 388.
[21] Garnie W. McGinty, *A History of Louisiana* (New York, 1951), 126.

Thomas Robertson, candidate of the American faction, polled the highest vote in a field of four in 1820. The next highest vote was cast for the Creole Peter Derbigny. Louisiana had her first taste of representative government and had found no lack of able candidates. The elections of 1824 bring us to a point where a more exhaustive analysis can be made, since from this date there is a record of the vote by parishes as well as statewide.

With the maps to be used to support analysis of Louisiana politics, the decision was made to plot the distribution of voter support on the basis of four sets of percentages. The intervals used will make it possible to trace the extremes of support and opposition as well as the "swing" vote either side of 50 percent. That is, where a parish vote (or voter type average) consists of a very high or very low percentage for candidate or party, it is reasoned that a corresponding community of interests exists within the unit. Contrawise, where a parish contains a number of competing interests, the variance will be greater (the vote will approximate more nearly 50 percent). Maps outlining the vote by parish will be used in conjunction with tabular presentation of voting behavior by voter types, in order to catch subtleties of local variation. Illustrated here is a general scheme to determine whether or not there exists a community of interests:

*Table 2–4*

VARIANCE IN THE VOTE: CONSENSUS AND CONFLICT

| | | Variance | |
| --- | --- | --- | --- |
| | | Small (00–39% 60–100%) | Great (40–49 50–59%) |
| Community | Much | CONSENSUS | |
| of | | | |
| Interests | Little | | CONFLICT |

There may be, of course, *geographic* cleavage such as an extreme difference in the vote of planter or farmer parishes as well as *social* cleavage within areal units such as exists between workers and merchants. While a high or low percentage vote for a candidate or party may be an indicator of agreement or consensus, the question remains of *what a vote means.* The reader may discover the incredibly high vote in some parishes, a phenomenon which was not unusual in this period. When a candidate wins by an extremely high margin, it might reflect solidarity and a real political consensus, or it may be the voice of a vocal few. Such a possibility is great in view of the small population of certain parishes. On the other hand, the strong support registered for a winning candidate might reflect abstention from voting on the part of the opposition. Likewise, one might interpret this phenomenon as the result of indifference of all but the "following" of the local boss.

The gubernatorial elections of 1824, 1828, and 1831 intensified the opposition between French and American. "Until the election of 1834 the most important issue in state elections for Governor was whether the candidate was 'Creole' or 'American,' ... After 1834, party politics became more important."[22] While in the earliest elections the Americans took credit for Claiborne and Robertson, the French claimed Jacques Villeré. Now, after the election of the American Henry Johnson in 1824, the French dominance was reached as, successively, Pierre Derbigny and A. B. Roman assumed the governor's chair. Indeed, the Americans had nominated two candidates in 1824, as had the French. In fact, the combined vote for the two French candidates would have produced a majority in this election as well, 52 percent of the total vote cast.

In checking the distribution of the gubernatorial average percent "French" vote in the period 1824–31, it was expected that the areas which contained the longer-established parish populations would provide the highest vote in support of French interests. Thus South Louisiana Planter as well as Bayou voter types both fall in the top interval of voter support. There was here, as in the more urban Jefferson and Orleans parishes, a homogeneous population sharing a consensus of opinion. On the other hand, the Florida Parishes and North Louisiana Planter voter types both indicated a more decided

---

[22] Edwin A. Davis, *Louisiana: The Pelican State* (Rev. ed.; Baton Rouge, 1969), 154.

preference for the American candidates at this time. Here was the frontier, yet to be developed, populated already, however, by migrants from the older American states. Finally, it can be seen that at this period the Southwest Louisiana voter type registered a French preference in line with the fact that the French towns of Opelousas and Lafayette constituted most of this area's population.

A glance at Map 2–1 indicates that without exception the French support fell in the parishes of old Louisiana. The third interval support found in Natchitoches is not an exception, for it will be remembered that this parish was settled by the French. The Florida Parishes and North Louisiana were even now filling up with migrants with a more decided democratic leaning than preferred by the French. A cleavage is revealed in the overwhelming nine out of twelve parishes with percentages below 50 percent falling into the first interval of support for the French (00–39.9 percent) in comparison with the sixteen out of eighteen parishes above 50 percent falling in the fourth interval of support (60–100 percent). All but one of the nine were to be found in North Louisiana, while none of the sixteen were.

In this period, neither emerging party nor the issue of nativity had obstructed impartiality. Evidence of this is to be found in the affiliations given by the first incumbents sent from Louisiana to the United States Congress. The House was closer to the people, who voted for candidates, and its composition revealed the nascent French-Whig ascendancy of the period from 1813 to 1836. On the other hand, 43.7 percent of the senators elected by the upper house of the Louisiana Assembly gave no party affiliation. Continuance of the French-American opposition would remain an influence on Louisiana politics, but there were other interests emergent in the 1820's which refocused the political struggle.

Louisiana was to become a meeting ground of national tendencies in the 1820's. A clarity of interests and party support resulted from that emerging structure, the plantation economy in agriculture. In the end, sugar and cotton planter might share an identity of interests, but since the cotton planter settling the Florida Parishes and North Louisiana was the more recent arrival on the Louisiana scene, he had brought with him a political preference for the Virginia

# "French Ascendancy," 1824, 1828, 1831

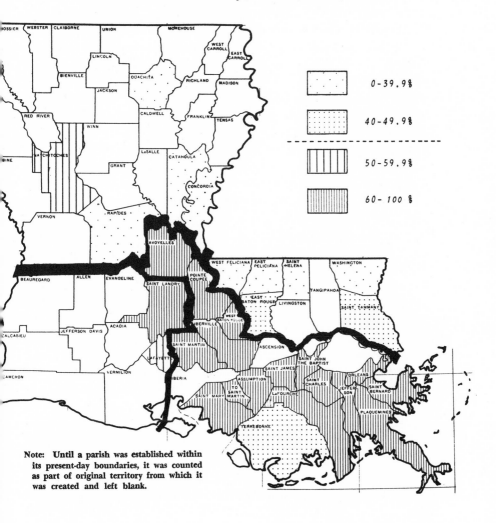

Note: Until a parish was established within its present-day boundaries, it was counted as part of original territory from which it was created and left blank.

Caucus and later, Jacksonian Democracy. The program of the National Federalists had found sympathy from the native Louisianians, the sugar planters and the attendant commercial interests in the city of New Orleans. At the same time, backwoods Democrats were arriving in Louisiana in increasing numbers from the same stream as the cotton planters, but they came too late to strike it rich.

Though in the 1830's the labels changed as organized political parties became established throughout the country, the two basically different views of the ends of government remained. The Whigs of John Quincy Adams and Henry Clay lined up against the Jacksonian Democrats. The Whig program envisaged the state as the originator of ambitious programs of internal improvements whereas the Jacksonians wanted the state kept simple and frugal. The middle-class Whiggery of Clay represented the influence of the maturing settlement, as in South Louisiana, while Jacksonianism was nothing less than frontier coonskin populism with its simple agrarian *laissez-faire*.[23] The emerging alignments were obscured in the presidential elections of 1828 and 1832, however.

The average percentage statewide vote in favor of the candidacy of Andrew Jackson for President in 1828–32 in Louisiana was 60.5 percent, suggesting that perhaps the state would become a bastion for the Democrats. Louisiana voters of all persuasions responded to the popularity of the hero of New Orleans. Still, the conservatism of Louisiana showed itself in the closeness of the vote in 1828, the first year presidential electors were chosen by popular vote.[24] John Quincy Adams received 4,095 votes to Jackson's 4,604. A student of the period explained Andrew Jackson's support: "Jackson's endorsement came from the city of New Orleans, and from the 'interior.' His personal popularity will largely explain his victory in the city. The 'interior' cotton farmer had no need or desire for the application of the protective principle. No West Indian latifundia challenged their staple."[25]

---

[23] Parrington, *Main Streams*, II, 138–39; Howard and Brent, "Social Change."
[24] Mary L. McLure, "The Election of 1860 in Louisiana," *Louisiana Historical Quarterly*, IX (1926), 606.
[25] Norton, "A History of the Whig Party," 63.

# Average Jackson Vote, 1828 and 1832

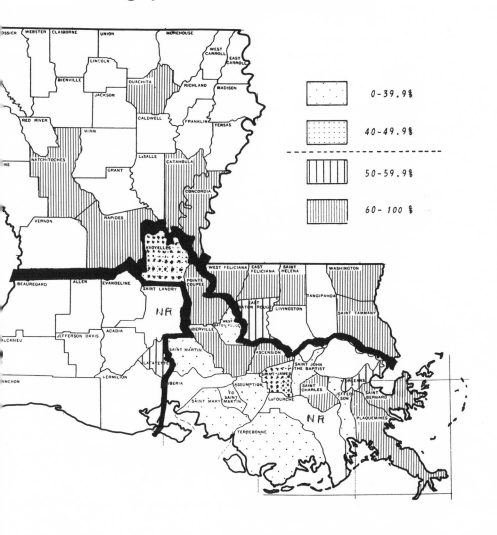

Map 2–2 is designed to show the degree of support for Jackson so that comparisons may be made with the degree of French support in the gubernatorial elections of this period. The popularity of Jackson in the interior is clearly seen, as the Florida Parishes and North Louisiana emerge as the seat of Democratic strength. Conservative forces with anti-Jackson sentiment were found in the parishes predominantly sugar producing. In the first of these elections, the year 1828, New Orleans voted for Jackson by only 52.9 percent. This shows the cleavage of the electorate between American and European migrant labor on the one side, the great commercial interests and native French on the other side. Again, the north-south difference is seen in the fact that apart from East Baton Rouge all the Florida Parishes and North Louisiana fell within the highest interval of Jackson.

The pulling power of the hero is to be found, however, if the vote of parishes in the gubernatorial elections analyzed above is compared with that of the presidential election. Then, a decided French shift toward Jackson can be seen as percentage intervals are compared:

*Table 2–5*

FRENCH PARISHES SHIFT TO JACKSON, 1828

| 60–100% French to 60–100% Jackson | 60–100% French to 60–100% Jackson | 60–100% French to 60–100% Jackson |
|---|---|---|
| Pointe Coupee | Orleans | St. James |
| Iberville | | Avoyelles |
| St. Charles | | |
| St. Bernard | | |
| Plaquemines | | |

| 50–59% French to 60–100% Jackson | 40–49% French to 60–100% Jackson |
|---|---|
| Natchitoches | St. Tammany |

Nonetheless, in general profile, the pro-French and anti-Jackson tendency was present on the map as expected.

If enthusiasm for Andrew Jackson ran so high in Louisiana, then voter turnout should have been greater in the presidential elections than in the elections for governor. Using the meager data available, it is possible to compare both in the elections of 1828. It was discovered that voter turnout was greater for the presidential than for the gubernatorial election, the prevailing condition up to 1860, in fact:

*Table 2–6*

VOTER TURNOUT, PRESIDENTIAL AND
GUBERNATORIAL ELECTIONS, 1828

|  | White Males | Presidential 1828 | | Gubernatorial 1828 | |
| --- | --- | --- | --- | --- | --- |
|  | 21 years +<br>1830 Census | Votes | Percent<br>Turnout | Votes | Percent<br>Turnout |
| Total. . . . . . . | 24,914 | 8,600 | 35% | 7,367 | 30% |
| Orleans. . . . . . | 8,011 | 1.412 | 17% | 1,135 | 13% |
| Rest of Parishes . . | 16,903 | 7,188 | 42% | 6,232 | 36% |

From these figures the difference in turnout is unmistakable in all three categories. In the analysis of subsequent periods, voter turnout in the rural parishes of the interior will be found to be even greater. The significance of the extremely low turnout in Orleans Parish cannot be stressed enough, although such a condition was to be expected within this rapidly growing city. Here, the most important consideration is that, apparently, earlier students of suffrage in Louisiana persisted in using the total counts, rather than differentiating parish units, and hence exaggerated on the low side.[26]

[26] Shugg, *Origins of Class Struggle,* and Asseff, *Legislative Apportionment.*

# CHAPTER III

# Two-Party Politics, Louisiana Style
# 1834-1852

## I. *The Whig Ascendancy*

Diverse opinions on many issues had brought a political squaring off among Louisianians, so they were ready to align themselves with one or the other—Whigs or Democrats—when national party organizations came into the state. This shift from nativism to party opposition is simple to trace by observing the events which led the Whigs to organize against the forces of Jackson. The Jacksonian Democrats developed strength rapidly after the first national nominating convention in 1831 and the successful reelection of President Jackson. The party support became nationally established as Jackson forces effectively destroyed the dominance of "King Caucus" which had allowed Congress to effect the ascendancy of New England and Virginia in the Presidency. Now a presidential party held the reins of government, and with the acknowledged wizardry of Martin Van Buren at the disposal of the Democratic Party, the continued removal of restrictive suffrage requirements, particularly along the nation's frontiers, seemed to hold great promise for the Democrats.[1]

Democratic success was to be checked, however, for "the meeting in the Spring of 1834 which produced the Whig Party had more material from which to construct an opposition to the Democrats than had been available for years."[2] The *Whig Almanac* of 1838 summarized the factions which combined to give substance to the new party as follows: (1) most of the former National Republicans (Federalists), supporters of Adams and Clay, advocates of the

---

[1] Ralph M. Goldman, *The Democratic Party in American Politics* (New York, 1966), 128, 42, 43 ff.

[2] Walter Dean Burnham, *Presidential Ballots, 1836–1892* (Baltimore, 1955), 1–2.

American system; (2) nullifiers and states' rights men; (3) many of those known as anti-mason; (4) "stay at home" voters drawn from their apathy by the alledged usurpation of executive power; and (5) disaffected Jackson men appalled by the high-handed conduct of the President. The Jacksonians were probably the most significant element in the combination, for, without them, the Whig Party would have lacked national scope. With them the Whigs became cross-sectional.[3]

In Louisiana the Whigs found support from planters on both sides of the nativity (French-American) cleavage, although it was the conservatism of South Louisiana which prompted the greater support. While the great popular hero Jackson won elections with ease in Louisiana, his party was not able to effect this national success in local elections. For the Democrats did not succeed in winning the governorship until 1842. In the elections of 1834 the Whigs successfully elected Louisiana's entire delegation to Congress and from two-thirds to three-fourths of the state legislature.[4] A severe rebuke to the Jackson forces was given when native son Edward Douglass White was elected governor over the Democratic candidate John B. Dawson.

The Whigs adherence to the nationalistic program of the old Federalists and their organized opposition to the leveling tendencies of the Jacksonians drew 60 percent of the gubernatorial vote to White. The election was said to have been conducted in a way to arouse class consciousness,[5] each party seeking the French vote and the increasingly important New Orleans Irish vote. A summary of the qualifications of the two candidates is revealing:

Edward D. White was proclaimed as an uncompromising Whig, a fast friend of protective tariff, a jealous advocate of internal improvements, a warm and substantial friend of the United States Bank, and a firm and consistent exponent of the American System.

---

[3] *Ibid.*, 3.

[4] Mary L. McLure, "The Election of 1860 in Louisiana," *Louisiana Historical Quarterly*, IX (1926), 606.

[5] Leslie M. Norton, *Readings in Social Science: Louisiana 1699–1876* (Baton Rouge, 1936), 109; Garnie M. McGinty, *A History of Louisiana* (New York, 1951), 137.

John B. Dawson was zealously supported by the Democrats, who represented him as a firm and pure public man, a friend of the people, a supporter of the Union of the states, and an advocate of low tariff, and an unflinching enemy of the United States Bank.[6]

The Whigs' success in their campaign was remarkable; even the hero of the Battle of New Orleans had not been able to command the support given to White in that city, and it was obvious from the beginning that Dawson's appeal could never match Jackson's. Within the parishes, the new Whig support suggested the pattern of a French-American split. Dawson gained pluralities in the Florida Parishes and in North Louisiana. Evidence of the economic interests involved is found in the more than 80 percent vote registered in White's favor in several sugar producing parishes where the principle of protective tariff was to become paramount. All South Louisiana gave majorities for White, who, after all, was the Whig representative of the old aristocracy. The contrast in the support given the Whig in Concordia and in newly created Catahoula Parish is likewise indicative of the economic dimensions of Whiggery. The vote in Concordia was 54.6 percent for White, whereas Catahoula, in the bordering Central Pine Hills, with more farmers whose subsistence agriculture did not require any shift from the Democracy, registered 29.3 percent for the Whig.

While the electoral vote of Louisiana returned to the Democrats in 1836, the popular vote was extremely close—3,842 votes for Van Buren to Harrison's 3,383, or 51.7 percent Democratic. One writer has found that the continued Democratic advantage had been due to the patronage built up in the state,[7] and this may be the reason, within French Louisiana, that of the seven parishes which had supported Jackson before, all but New Orleans remained Democratic in 1836. After this election, South Louisiana was found to be predominantly Whig. Indeed, the control of local affairs in the state, secured in 1834, remained with the Whigs until the early 1840's when it passed into the hands of the Democrats, where it remained, exclusive of New Orleans, until the war.

[6] Norton, *Readings*, 109.
[7] McLure, "Election of 1860," 606–607.

An overall glimpse of the profile of Louisiana's response to presidential politics in this period may be gained by making comparisons of the voting tendencies of the nation, the South, and the state (Appendix A, Table 2). In these calculations we follow the lead of W. Dean Burnham in his most useful compilation of presidential ballots utilizing the geographic sections currently established by the Bureau of the Census. As Burnham put it, "While they are admittedly inferior politically to such designations as 'South,' 'Border,' 'Midwest,' and others, it had to be recalled again that the Far West of 1836 lay in Illinois and Missouri rather than on the Pacific coast."[8] Better to choose a uniform standard even if it is not a politically optimum one.

The uniformity in the variation, election to election, in Democratic support among the three units, is striking. Remarkable, as well, is the closeness to 50 percent in each case. As was hypothesized above, the higher the percentage support, the higher the consensus within the unit, and the closer to 50 percent, the greater the cleavage. This was a period of national stability in voting behavior, when "neither political party at its maximum was able to gain more than approximately 53 percent of the national vote."[9] Areas of lasting support were extensive during this period, lined up on either side for Democratic or Whig counties. The location and composition of these bedrocks of party loyalty have been summarized:[10]

*Table 3–1*

DEMOCRATIC AND WHIG COUNTY PROFILES IN THE NATION

| Democratic Counties | Whig Counties |
| --- | --- |
| low-income | high-income |
| mountainous, upland, and frontier regions | flat or gently rolling |
| settled by Scotch-Irish and other latecomers | populated by society with greater wealth, prosperity, fewer latecomers |
| underpopulated | more densely settled |

[8] Burnham, *Presidential Ballots*, xv.
[9] *Ibid.*, 55.
[10] *Ibid.*, 56–57.

These generalizations obviously fit the South, with the opposition between farmer and planter, and, of course, Louisiana may be seen as the epitome of a cleavage pattern.

The average range of difference among the Democratic percentages in nation, South, and state in the period between 1836 and 1852 can be calculated as 1.13 percent. While the nation and South differed by only one-half of one percent, the greatest difference, between Louisiana and the national percentage, was only 1.7 percent. A closer parallel may have existed had it not been for the ups and downs somewhat more prevalent in Louisiana than for either of the other two units. In fact, internal reactions to economic crisis in the late thirties, which helped give the Presidency to the Whigs in 1840, led to the Democratic reversal which accounted for nearly half the difference between Louisiana's Democratic support and the national percentages. Here is an example of how closely, sometimes, the election returns follow economic well-being, and it may be instructive to pause long enough to trace something of the socio-economic aspects of the developing Louisiana society in this period.

## II. *Boom Times in Louisiana*

The decade of the 1830's saw boom times in Louisiana.[11] The state developed in the early nineteenth century like a frontier success story moving from territorial status in 1803 and to statehood in 1812 to become the commercial center of the South in the 1820's. In this decade the advocates of cotton began moving into the regions north of the 31st Parallel, which, with the exception of French influence in Avoyelles Parish, very nearly divided the state, north and south. Below the parallel, the advocates of sugar expanded the growth and the processing of that staple so much that it was in this region that population growth was most noticeable (Appendix A, Tables 4, 5, 6). In 1820, 40 percent of the state's total white population was found in South Louisiana (South Louisiana Planter and Bayou parishes, Jefferson Parish, and Southwest Louisiana, but excluding New

[11] Merl Reed, "Boom or Bust—Louisiana's Economy During the 1830's," *Louisiana History*, IV (1963). The following is taken from Reed unless otherwise cited.

Orleans). Ten years later this figure had risen to 45 percent. During this same decade the slave population in South Louisiana rose from 48 to 54 percent of the state's total.

The white population within South Louisiana rose 23 percent, 1820–30, but they bought many slaves to produce their sugar crops, causing a dramatic increase of 103 percent in the slave population within this area. Population increased in South Louisiana in the decades to come, but the rate of change and proportionate number of whites and slaves within "old" Louisiana had peaked in 1830. The boom of the 1830's brought rapid growth and development along the Red as well as the Ouachita and Tensas rivers. In Southwest Louisiana the line of settlement skipped the prairies west of Lafayette and Opelousas and picked up in the Calcasieu River area.[12]

The state's white population increased by 77 percent between the censuses of 1830 and 1840, largely in North Louisiana and New Orleans and at the expense of rural South Louisiana. The parishes which make up North Louisiana almost doubled in the number of whites (91 percent increase) while Orleans parish whites increased at the rate of 118 percent. It was in this decade that the Irish began to migrate to New Orleans,[13] but while up to the war the city's white population would approximate nearly 40 percent of the state's, 1840 marked the census year in which the rate of increase peaked.

In North Louisiana, however, the population, both white and slave, continued to grow; and the rate of increase for both was 111 percent in the decade ending in 1850. While the number of whites residing in Orleans Parish continued to approximate some 40 percent of the state's total, the number of slaves declined precipitously so that by 1860 only 4 percent of the state's slave population were found in Orleans. The slave contagion had spread into rural South Louisiana and the Florida Parishes, but the number of both whites and slaves declined in proportion to the state's total. It was in North Louisiana, where cotton became king, that the proportional numbers

---

[12] *Ibid.*, 36.
[13] Ruby Nell Gordy, "The Irish in New Orleans, 1845–1855" (Master's thesis, Louisiana State University, 1960); Earl F. Niehaus, *The Irish in New Orleans, 1800–1860*, Baton Rouge, 1965).

of both whites and slaves continued to increase up to the census of 1860.

The percent increase in the white population in the North Louisiana Planter voter type in the decade of the 1830's was 90 percent and in the next decade rose to 110 percent. Also, whereas the rate of increase in slaves was 177 percent in the former decade, it fell to 92 percent in the latter. It was in the 1830's that the extensive peopling of the Tensas Basin began, and the distinctive features of plantation landscape appeared. Many of the plantation cores in what became Tensas, Madison, and Carroll parishes as they were carved out of Concordia became well-known as rural centers and the focus of many social functions. In this period settlers rapidly transformed the wilderness into an agricultural bonanza. A way of life and pattern of settlement was established that continues today.

But as this pattern of settlement followed the river bottoms into Ouachita and Morehouse Parishes, and, until 1861, along the levees of Bayou Macon, the Macon Ridge unit in between remained more like the two Hills units. Here again the difference between voter type areas are obviously delineated by natural and cultural conditions.[14]

Not all Louisiana was devoted to the plantation economy and Roger Shugg has demonstrated that the state, commonly thought of as the land of the planters, actually contained a greater number of farmers than planters.[15] This measure is stated in terms of operators, however; in terms of size and crop production, the plantation predominated. Even though the majority of slaveholders held fewer than ten slaves each, it was the concentration that counted, and where the plantation was prevalent the number of slaves was great.[16] This means that for lack of a better index, a parish may be depicted as being planter or farmer, depending upon the proportion of slaves to the white population.

While a look at the figures will show that in the two Hills voter

[14] Yvonne Phillips, "Settlement Succession in the Tensas Basin" (Ph.D. dissertation, Louisiana State University, 1953), 5.

[15] Roger W. Shugg, *Origins of Class Struggle in Louisiana* (Baton Rouge, 1939; paperback, 1968), Chap. 8, "Survival of the Plantation System."

[16] James K. Greer, "Louisiana Politics, 1845–1861," *Louisiana Historical Quarterly*, XII (1929), 389.

type areas the number of slaves increased in the 1830's and 1840's at a greater rate than the number of whites, proportionately there were fewer slaves in these parishes than among any other voter types. But there was apparent, even then, a distinct difference in the rates of increase between what Shugg called the Oak Hills and the Central Pine Hills. He pointed out that the uplands which sustained the growth of oak rather than pine were the more fertile,[17] and this fact may explain why the somewhat greater white and, at the same time, large slave rates of increase took place as the lands in the planter areas became preempted. The Central Pine Hills area remained relatively unpeopled up to the Civil War.

Nevertheless, the clear contrast between farmer and planter units may be seen by comparing the relative proportion of slaves within the populations. While in the North Louisiana Planter voter type area the proportion of slaves to whites averaged around 70 percent in the three decades from 1830 to 1850, in the two Hills voter type areas the proportion of slaves actually declined from 38 to 24 percent in this period. One can readily detect the difference indicated by the proportion of slaves when he observes the state average hovering close to 50 percent in the six pre-war decades.

Another way of observing the one sided slave-farmer ratio in the Hills Parishes is to check individual parishes. Hilly Caldwell, a parish newly created in 1839, had a population of 1,354 whites but only 649 slaves in the census of the next year. The presence of slaves, and therefore of slaveholders, in the hills may explain why the voter support here was, in this period, nearer 60 percent than 100 percent. There was not complete solidarity, even in the hills.

Whereas in North Louisiana the contrast between farmers and planters consisted of a differential among parishes, in South Louisiana these same classes resided within the *same* parishes. While this is so, there were proportionately fewer from the planter class within the Bayou Parishes in the heart of Acadian country than elsewhere. (In 1840 the Bayou voter type population was 54 percent slave while the proportion of slaves to whites in the South Louisiana Planter

---

[17] Shugg, *Origins of Class Struggle*, 11.

area was 70 percent.) J. C. Sitterson has shown in his study *Sugar Country*[18] that in the South Louisiana Planter Parishes even before the American period, French and Spanish planters had acquired large holdings. At the same time a layer of Acadian and Spanish peasants (*petits habitants*) had established their smaller holdings in the "back" away from river and bayou. In the years after the acquisition of Louisiana by the United States, however, many planters began to enlarge their holdings and to dominate the rural economic life.[19] Shugg believed that in many of the sugar parishes the farmer vote was influenced by the position of the planter elite.[20] For the most part it could be said that Acadians kept to themselves—the rural French lived in something like ancestral fashion—honest, steady, plodding;[21] but, as Vernon J. Parenton has shown with such clarity, all the while luring those with whom they came into contact to *their* way of life.[22]

A number of factors, in summary, contributed to the "boom or bust" economic situation in the 1830's: population growth, both white and slave; frontier development, mostly in North Louisiana; internal improvements; manufacturing; trade, commerce; wholesaling.[23] Development of the economy was closely dependent upon banking and finance, and a system of private as well as state supported banks was maintained, with the State Bank getting its start as a land bank capitalized at four million dollars in 1824. But what the banks did with the money has been called "a travesty upon economic growth."[24] By too often following the profit motive rather than more secure investment outlets, the bankers created a forerunner of that monstrosity of Reconstruction, the Louisiana Lottery.

The nationwide panic of 1837 and the depression which followed placed a stigma on the Democratic administration. In Louisiana,

[18] J. Carlyle Sitterson, *Sugar Country: The Cane Industry in the South, 1753–1950* (Lexington, 1953).
[19] Vernon J. Parenton, "The Rural French-Speaking People of Quebec and South Louisiana" (Ph.D. dissertation, Harvard University, 1948), 341.
[20] Shugg, *Origins of Class Struggle*, 148–49.
[21] Greer, "Louisiana Politics," 387.
[22] Parenton, "Rural French-Speaking People."
[23] Reed, "Boom or Bust," 46.
[24] *Ibid.*, 48.

the effect of the crisis was immediately felt in a decline in the price of native products.[25] The panic caused fifteen New Orleans banks to suspend payment, paralyzing business and spreading consternation among planters and commercial people alike. Such a consequence might not have guaranteed a Whig victory in the gubernatorial election of 1838, but it helped, and in 1840, Louisiana continued the Whig tendency in the presidential election; for the first time, Louisiana's electoral votes were given to other than the Democratic Party.

In the gubernatorial race between Whig candidate former Governor André Roman, and the Democrat Denis Prieur, voters gave support where, during the economic crisis, their interest should best be served. Roman won with 52.8 percent of the vote. Both candidates cut into the sugar country and the Florida Parishes but the balance of power lay in the cotton country where Roman held a distinct advantage. Concordia Parish gave near unanimous support to the Whig, for example, while newly established Caddo Parish in the Red River plantation area went 69.5 percent for Roman.

In the 1840 presidential election, the Whig candidate General Harrison swept the state, scoring heavily in both North and South Louisiana Planter voter type areas. Out of the nine parishes established in North Louisiana at this time, the Democrat candidate carried but two—Carroll and Union. Below the 31st Parallel, the Democrats won four of the six Florida Parishes, but otherwise only Plaquemines and Assumption, the vote in Ascension Parish having been a tie.

This was the high-water mark of Whiggery in the office of governor, however. In the 1838 election, the margin of victory was narrow, and with the population outside South Louisiana steadily increasing, as has been shown above, the success of the Whig Party became doubtful. In 1842, the Democratic Party captured the governorship with Alexandre Mouton, a state legislator from Lafayette Parish, who received 60 percent of the popular vote and became Louisiana's first Democratic governor. The Louisiana Whigs now suffered from the same malady which had given them victory in 1838—unsound

[25] *Ibid.*, 51.

banking policies, enacted by the legislature over Roman's protests. This time, the Whigs held firm in the Planter areas from Madison Parish down the Mississippi to St. Charles Parish. The Democratic candidate swept the Florida Parishes, Southwest Louisiana, and the Hill areas.

In view of the general excellence of the qualifications of Louisiana's Whig governors, it might have been regretted that they could win no more. Of course they did not become voiceless; Whigs were in strong representation in the Louisiana Assembly throughout the 1840's and most of the 1850's, some of the reasons for which will be presented below. The two strongest economic elements of the state continued to show Whig tendencies. "These, the merchants and the sugar planters, were the aristocrats of Louisiana. They had a community of interest which was satisfied by the Whig platform; and as elections approached, they expressed themselves as preferring a party nominee who was a 'gentleman.' This usually meant that they preferred the nomination of a wealthy sugar planter."[26] Little wonder the Whigs could get nowhere with the rural Democrats and their strongly developed sense of equality!

Two-time Governor Roman had represented this elite. He was a sugar planter from St. James Parish, on the west side. About his qualifications there is no argument. He was a wise and progressive leader. He worked for the improvement of public education; he established a model penal system; he formed a well organized militia; he worked for the extension of communications and the encouragement of science and agriculture. Crossing party lines, Roman endorsed Jackson's stand against the Nullification Ordinance of South Carolina.[27] He tempered conservatism with political responsibility.

III. *The Move to Constitutional Change, 1845*

Influenced by the continuous arrival of the small-farmer class of settlers from neighboring and Atlantic seaboard states, with their Jacksonian doctrines that all political offices should be elective by

[26] Norton, *Readings*, 113.
[27] McGinty, *History of Louisiana*, 135.

the people and that every man should possess the franchise, the people of Louisiana, as early as 1842 and 1843, evinced strong approval to holding a constitutional convention. The desire to drive aristocracy and privilege from government was the animus of the entire Jacksonian movement so that no wonder Whig politicians called themselves conservative and the Democrats destructive.[28] By 1845 the Democrats were numerous enough to prevail, and Solomon Downs led representatives from his "Red River Democracy" to the Baton Rouge convention. The actual enabling act passed the assembly on March 18, 1844, and the convention was held the next year.

It may seem strange in retrospect, after Louisiana almost doubled the mortality rate which Jefferson had prescribed for constitutions—10 in 110 years—that the first constitution lasted for 30 years. However, the social classes whose delegates had written Louisiana's first organic law were satisfied with the results. A consensus existed in the aristocratic period of rule from 1812 through 1824 as to those constitutional powers properly delegated to the governor.[29] By the early 1840's the balance of power had shifted enough for Jacksonian principles to prevail. The mounting strength of the Democrats who felt that they were living in the nineteenth century under a seventeenth century government upset the old order at the polls.[30] The main "aristocratic" provisions which were objectionable were the property qualifications for holding office, the great appointive power of the governor, and the inequality of senatorial representation.

In this period of two-party politics in Louisiana loyalties were more nearly divided between two groups of equal strength than they were ever to be again.[31] Regarding the concept of good government and the position of the governor, a great cleavage existed between the two parties. The fact that the Democrat Party was a rising party with leveling tendencies made it certain that meaningful

[28] Greer, "Louisiana Politics," 388.
[29] Charles W. Tapp, "Development of the Constitutional Appointive Power of the Governor of Louisiana: 1812–1921" (Master's thesis, Louisiana State University, 1964), 66.
[30] James W. Prothro, "A Study of Constitutional Developments in the Office of the Governor of Louisiana" (Master's thesis, Louisiana State University, 1948), 9.
[31] Ibid., 102.

debate would take place. The great issues may be reduced to these
two simple questions: (1) Should the government represent the
simple public needs and desires of the entire population? (2) Should
the government establish a restrictive order under the auspices of
those gentlemen of principle and property who best know the needs
of the unthinking masses?[32] The Constitution of 1812 had answered
these questions in terms far different from what was desired in 1845,
even though in the end result the new document might not seem
such a radical improvement.

Both sides were guaranteed representation when the results of
the election of delegates were made known. The convention was
composed of thirty-nine Whigs and thirty-eight Democrats. One
Whig editor exulted: "Thank providence our Constitution will be
safe from the agrarian and leveling view of the radicals; of the numbers
elected to the Convention 48 are conservatives, enough to satisfy
us that none but changes absolutely necessary will be made in the
Constitution—that the Judiciary will not be elective by the people—
thus securing to us one of the greatest boons we were struggling
for."[33] Despite such forthright admissions to privilege, the constitution
written in 1845 was a liberal document compared with that of 1812.
It was prefaced by words far different from those embodied in the
preamble of the first constitution. Gentleman rule was still maintained,
but a concession had been made by the elite. Now the people could
act for themselves, for the Constitution of 1845 began: "We the people
of Louisiana, do ordain and establish."

No one went away from the convention completely satisfied—an
inevitable situation with party cleavage so great. Compromise had
been achieved over opposition. Some Whigs were dissatisfied because
the new instrument was too democratic. The convention president,
Joseph Walker, and the Democratic radicals signed, but purely as
compromise; the constitution was not democratic enough for them.

The Whigs strove to avoid letting down the restrictive bars
completely. The governor was no longer required to meet a property
qualification, but he must be thirty-five years of age and a resident

[32] *Ibid.*, 32.
[33] Norton, *Readings*, 122.

of Louisiana for at least fifteen years. (The 1812 constitution had required the governor to be a resident for six years.) The office of lieutenant governor was established, legislators were no longer held to a property qualification, and some offices formerly appointive were made elective. The conservatives successfully maintained the judicial bulwark, for judges were still to be appointed by the governor, with the consent of the Senate.

One of the hot issues to be resolved had been the problem of representation, for both House and Senate were grossly unrepresentative of the people. The delegates spent a great deal of their time debating this issue. Actually, the legislature had acted to meet the demand for periodic reapportionment four times through 1826 but not again until 1841. And though the legislature then obeyed the constitutional charge to reapportion, it failed to obey another constitutional provision which required that representation be equal and uniform. This was a serious matter in a state with its population increasing so rapidly through in-migration.

The situation had been quite good at the time of the reapportionment in 1826, variation being not as great as it would later develope. A brief table provides data for a look at comparative representation in the Louisiana House in 1826.

*Table 3–2*
REPRESENTATION IN THE LOUISIANA HOUSE, 1826*

|  | Percent of Representatives | Percent of White Males 21 Years + |
|---|---|---|
| North Louisiana | 16% | 16% |
| Florida Parishes | 20% | 18% |
| South Louisiana | 50% | 41% |
| Orleans Parish | 14% | 25% |
|  | 100% | 100% |

* Source: Asseff.

The principal cause of the inequities which continued to increase during the 1830's and early 1840's was simply the sheer number of people populating the developing frontier, whites unable to vote, and hence failing to count as electors, because they remained disfranchised and might not meet the property restriction. The population within the black belt planter areas was more settled and more affluent as well, and therefore had a larger number of qualified electors. But while many would have agreed that a qualified elector system was to be preferred to total population as a basis for representation, it was, for the reason outlined, inequitable. The black belt gained proportionally in representation at the expense of the white belt and New Orleans because a much higher percentage of the whites was able to vote in the black belt. In summary, Emmett Asseff has listed, besides long residence and other qualifications set up for voting, three other reasons for the increasing malapportionment; (1) intimidation; (2) ignorance and indifference; and (3) poor transportation to the polls which were usually some distance away.[34]

The constitutional convention in 1845 considered six plans upon which to base representation. The planter parishes would have preferred total population (slaves counted as three-fifths) while the farmer parishes would have preferred to establish representation on the basis of white population. New Orleans would have preferred taxable property as a basis, since it paid about two-thirds of the state's taxes. The convention had agreed, already, to limit Orleans to one-fifth of the representatives so that its leaders were more interested that no limitations be placed upon the number at some future date. Overrepresented on the basis of qualified electors, the large planters sought even greater control by changing the basis of representation to total population while the white belt opposed any change to total population. Here was a test of strength for the opposition known as farmer-planter, or Democrat-Whig.

In the compromise that was achieved, New Orleans held the balance of power in the House; the convention resolved the issue by reapportioning the Senate on the basis of total population and the House on the basis of qualified electors.[35] It was said that Orleans

<hr />

[34] Emmett Asseff, *Legislative Apportionment in Louisiana* (LSU, Bureau of Government Research, [Baton Rouge, 1950]), 14–15.

[35] *Ibid.,* 16.

joined the black belt in striking this compromise. The number of members of the House was to be established between seventy and one hundred, while the number of senators was to be fixed at thirty-two, but no parish might have more than four senators. It is easy to imagine that access to the power structure was not to be materially aided by these rulings. Less than a decade was to pass before the planters in alliance with urban merchants were to undo these arrangements.

If the conservatives held the line against the encroachments of democracy on the apportionment issue, it may have appeared that greater gains were obtained regarding the suffrage limitations. Indeed, as finally written, the Constitution of 1845 granted suffrage to all white males twenty-one years of age or over who had been citizens of the United States for two years and residents in the state two consecutive years next preceding the election, and the last year in the parish in which he offered to vote.

*Table 3-3*

COMPARISON OF THE CONSTITUTIONS OF 1812 AND 1845

|  | Constitution of 1812 | Constitution of 1845 |
|---|---|---|
| Race . . . . | White | White |
| Sex . . . . . | Male | Male |
| Age . . . . . | 21 years + | 21 years + |
| Citizenship . . | United States | United States |
| Property . . . Requirement . | Paid state tax or purchased public land | ——— |
| Residence . . in State | ——— | 2 consecutive years, while absence from state more than 90 consecutive days disrupts aquisition of residence |
| Residence . . in Parish | 1 year | 1 year |
| Place of . . . Voting | ——— | Parish of residence or in cities, election precinct in which one resides |

These requirements were aimed at thwarting the influence of immigration. While no mention has been found of outright dissatisfaction with these provisions, it does seem that comparison with the earlier limitations, which were superseded, suggests there might have been.

One cannot be sure about the resulting consequences of these changes in the suffrage requirements, in particular the additions concerning residence. At the time, the removal of the property test was considered a major step in the extension of democracy. Perhaps the surest way to tell is to determine the extent to which, following the constitutional change in the suffrage, an upsurge in voting took place. The following will provide the data to compare rates of increase in the number of votes cast in presidential elections with those for governor in the years before and after 1845:

*Table 3–4*

NUMBER OF VOTES CAST IN PRESIDENTIAL
AND GUBERNATORIAL ELECTIONS, 1836–60

| | Presidential Elections | | Gubernatorial Elections | |
|---|---|---|---|---|
| | Number of Votes | Percent Change | Number of Votes | Percent Change |
| 1836 | 7,425 | – – – – | – – – – | |
| 1838 | – – – – | | 13,748 | – – – – |
| 1840 | 18,912 | 115% | – – – – | |
| 1842 | – – – – | | 14,307 | 41% |
| 1844 | 26,865 | 42% | – – – – | |
| Constitutional Change | | | | |
| 1846 | – – – – | | 23,354 | 63% |
| 1848 | 33,866 | 26% | – – – – | |
| 1850 | – – – – | | 36,115 | 55% |
| 1852 | 35,902 | 6% | 33,061 | – 8% |
| Constitutional Change | | | | |
| 1856 | 42,873 | 19% | 42,707 | 29% |
| 1860 | 50,500 | 18% | 41,041 | – 5% |

If now, after the work of the constitutional convention of 1845, the principle that "ALL" (see Table 2–2) could vote had been established, the record of votes cast reveals no great rush to exercise suffrage rights. The removal of suffrage limitations may, indeed, have stimulated greater participation in gubernatorial elections, but the increased number of votes cast simply brought the total closer to the number who had been voting in greater volume in presidential elections. Using the number voting for President, it is clear that the increase in voting had resulted from the rising number of males of voting age rather than the removal of limitations. In view of the great upsurge in the rate of population increase in the 1830's due to migration to the frontiers of Louisiana, this is not surprising.

The figures showing the rate of increase in voting provide evidence that in such a dynamic, developing society the previous limitations had not been too formidable to be overcome. At the same time, the question remains regarding the manner in which the addition of residence requirements may have inhibited the exercise of suffrage. The changes in the constitution ratified in 1852, which reduced the length of residence to one year within the state and six months in the parish, did not lead to any dramatic increase in the number of votes cast in Louisiana elections.

The year 1844 proved to be pivotal in the history of political parties in Louisiana,[36] for it was in this year that the Democrat Party had wrested political power from the Whigs in a close and heated presidential election. The Democrats had already gained the governorship for the first time in 1842, and now they were consolidating their gains. The Whigs henceforth would remain a strong minority party, for as has been shown above, the conservative forces in Louisiana demonstrated plenty of vitality in the constitutional convention. The Whigs would, however, proceed to transform themselves into the Know-Nothings or Americans and ultimately try—but fail—to become good Democrats. John Slidell assumed the leadership of the Democratic Party in the state in 1844 and attained both local and national fame by swinging the presidential election to Polk through his local control.

[36] McLure, "The Election of 1860," 607.

John Slidell adroitly took advantage of a weakness in the voting regulations, a constitutional directive which indicated that each voter must poll his vote within his county of residence. At that time, Orleans "county" consisted of the parishes of Orleans, St. Bernard, and Plaquemines. Calling on Irish and other citizens available, Slidell simply floated two steamboat loads of Democrats down the Mississippi to Plaquemines, creating a majority of what had been a minority.[37] Machine politics had been introduced into Louisiana, the "fraud" gave the state, and thereby the Presidency, to Polk, and Slidell became a kingpin in the party. The evidence is to be found in straightforward arithmetic. Whereas the Whigs had carried Louisiana in the previous election, it seemed certain that they would have repeated in 1844, but for the edge gained by the maneuvering of Slidell. The Democratic vote carried the state with an edge of 699 votes. It appears certain that these votes had been furnished by Slidell's itinerant voters. The parish of Plaquemines had a total vote of but 53 in the 1836 presidential election and only 290 in 1840. In 1844, however, the total vote had risen to 1,044, only to fall again in 1848 to 537 votes. It was in reaction to the Plaquemines fraud that the delegates to the constitutional convention the following year placed in the 1845 instrument the regulation that one must vote in the parish of residence.

IV. *The Louisiana "Democracy" and Whig Competition*

In the first election after the adoption of the new constitution, the Democratic Party in 1846 successfully supported the gubernatorial candidacy of Isaac Johnson, who received 54 percent of 23,354 votes. The Democrats also gained a majority of two in the Senate, whereas the Whigs held a majority of three in the House. There seemed to be little difference in the alternative bases of representation in this election at least. Johnson was a member of the predominantly Anglo-American West Feliciana aristocracy, and his administration left little to choose from, so far as accomplishments were concerned, between

[37] Greer, "Louisiana Politics," 12.

the new Democrats and the old Whigs. Johnson was not a strict party man, either, and he appointed some Whigs to office and tried to steer a middle course on the slavery question, now becoming a national issue.

The Democratic vote had given Johnson pluralities over the two Whig candidates in thirty of the forty-three parishes, indicating his wide-spread appeal. The heaviest Democratic voting was to be found in North and Southwest Louisiana, and of course in the Florida Parishes, where Johnson was the native son. This was the first election in which nearly all the parishes of the hills and prairies registered support in the highest interval of Democratic support, and this may have been a result of the lowered suffrage qualifications. The sugar parishes remained the seat of Whig support. However, parishes from cotton country likewise emerged in this election with Whig leanings. Wherever there was a sizable layer of planter classes within the northern parishes, a fairly even split of the vote occurred. A very definite tendency toward Whiggery had emerged. The significance in the distribution of the Democratic vote in the election of 1846 was twofold; it marked the strong Democratic tendency in the hills and the emergence of a Whig leaning among portions of the planter groups in the river-cotton country.

Two years later, in 1848, the Whigs became enthusiastic concerning their chances in the next gubernatorial race, but they were falsely inspired. After the Democratic defeat in 1846 the Baton Rouge *Gazette* had in fact lamented: "We have lost all hopes of seeing the Whigs in the ascendency for years to come. They have committed political suicide and exist no more as a party."[38] In the short run, at least, it was not to be as bad as anticipated, because the Mexican War served to revive the fortunes of the Whig Party. At the same time, however, Louisiana Whigs were to become somewhat ambivalent, since they had fears about the potential competition of Texas in sugar production. The Democrats, many with friends and relatives in Texas, and caught up in the fever of expansionism, were enthusiastic.

[38] Williams Adams, "Louisiana and the Presidential Election of 1848," *Louisiana History*, IV (1963), 131.

The Wilmot Proviso was advanced nationally, in meeting the problem of the annexation of Texas, to effect the exclusion of slavery from any new acquisitions. The storm of protest raised by southern politicians showed the determination of the dominant elements of the Democratic Party to struggle for their views on slavery. In the face of this sectionalism, it remained to be seen whether the traditional cleavages could remain in Louisiana politics. As a spokesman of Louisiana Democrats, Governor Johnson had answered in these words:

> Noninterference of congress with the slavery question is the surest means of preserving the Union, and that doctrine should be insisted on with an unflinching resolution never to surrender it. To any proposition, therefore, to compromise that doctrine, the South, with bitter and humiliating experience before her, will turn a deaf ear. Submission to incipient oppression prepares men for the yoke, and compromises on this question are nothing else than anti-slavery victories. The oft repeated, galling, and unprovoked aggressions of anti-slavery leave no room to anticipate a cessation of hostilities, and the South had been sufficiently warned that, if it is wise to hope for the best, it is equally prudent to prepare for the worst. It is far better to be lawless than to live under lawless rule.[39]

The Democrats had handicapped themselves, however, for President Polk had been allowed to categorically state he would serve only one term, and as with Governor Johnson, the Democrats faced the issue of slavery by "still trying to solve that problem by an exercise in Language."[40]

Whig hopes had risen with the discovery of a public hero in the tradition of Jackson, General Zachary Taylor, who could employ his military fame to obtain the Presidency. Even Henry Clay had been led to remark, "I wish I could kill a Mexican." Taylor's victory was assured when the Democrats split in New York State, and Van Buren led "Free Soilers" in opposition to the Democratic nominee, Lewis Cass, also a general in the Mexican War. The results

[39] Quoted in John C. Merrill, "Louisiana Public Opinion on Secession" (Master's thesis, Louisiana State University, 1950), 91–92.
[40] Goldman, *The Democratic Party*, 52.

were extremely close, the Whigs winning nationally with 48 percent of the vote cast. General Taylor was a native son, and the Louisiana Whig carried the state with 54.6 percent of the vote. The parishes he carried outlined the planter areas of both cotton and sugar country. The Whigs must have known from past experience how strong Louisiana was in support of military heroes at the polls. Then, as now, "old soldiers never die."

The presidential election of 1848 presaged at least three definite trends which were borne out in future Louisiana politics. They have been identified by Fife as: (1) Slavery as the dominant feature of political debate; (2) The basic weakness of the Whig Party; (3) The collapse of the Whig Party on the state level, ending, to this day, a two-party system in Louisiana.[41]

On the eve of Taylor's campaign, Louisiana had a Democratic governor and a Whig legislature that had elected a Democrat to the United States Senate. Just as the Whigs had held the office of governor despite the election of Jackson, so now the Democrats in 1850 proceeded to win the election for governor despite the Taylor popularity. But the results were close; Joseph Walker, native of New Orleans and president of the constitutional convention of 1845, won with 51.4 percent of the vote, a slim majority of little more than a thousand votes over the Whig John B. Plauche. The campaign followed national issues, among which was the Wilmot Proviso; the Democrats opposed, and the Whigs favored it. The geographic distribution of the highest support for Walker indicates that the backing of the farmer was indeed apparent. The bulk of the Democratic support came from the interior parishes which had voted that way before. The increased solidarity of the cotton and sugar plantation parishes in support of Whiggery was such, however, that the total vote was nearly evened between the parties.

Under stipulations of the new constitution, the citizens of Louisiana would vote for governor in 1852. The Democrats chose as their candidate Paul O. Hebert, resident of Iberville Parish and of Acadian

---

[41] Thomas W. Fife, "The Presidential Election of 1848 in Louisiana" (Master's thesis, Louisiana State University, 1959).

lineage. Again, as in the last election, the Democratic margin was very slim, this time a majority of less than 2,000 votes. Hebert's main support came from the hill farmers of the interior parishes, and from the Floridas. Once more cotton and sugar planters showed their like-mindedness in joint support of the Whig candidate, Louis Bordelon. Over half of Hebert's slight lead might have been secured in New Orleans, where he obtained 56.4 percent, a majority of some 1,200 votes.

In the presidential election, Louisiana supported the Democrat, Franklin Pierce, but the Louisiana Democrats had not put up a united front and he won by only 51.9 percent of the total vote cast. It was almost a carbon copy of the preceding gubernatorial election, for Pierce, with a majority of 1,392 votes, barely topped the 1,200 edge of Hebert. In fact, on the Whig side the consistency was remarkable. Of the sixteen parishes carried by the Whigs in the election for President, all but one, St. Bernard, had also given majorities for Bordelon in the governor's race. These parishes outlined the borders of conservatism in Louisiana, bridging from North Louisiana Planter Parishes to those of South Louisiana Planter and Bayou voter type areas.

Still, within a state which had been recipient to thousands of Jacksonian migrants, the Democrats became divided. The impending dissolution of the National Whig Party and the consequent weakening of Louisiana Whigs presented the Democrats with a secure situation in which to conduct a factional quarrel. Events would prove the folly, however, of meeting the issues of the slavery crisis in a one-party situation. The Democrats divided into factions under the leadership of two dominant personalities. John Slidell had demonstrated his finesse, becoming boss of Louisiana politics through building combined support from the New Orleans Irish and the Jacksonian farmers of the interior. United States Senator Pierre Soulé provided leadership for the opposing faction and a block of support from the sugar parishes. The personal ambitions of these two men for political power forced them to choose between the opposing viewpoints on slavery held within the Democratic Party.

## v. *An Analysis of Political Tendencies, 1834–1852*

It is time to attempt to summarize the voting tendencies which appeared in the period of two-party politics from the 1830's through the early fifties. The most pertinent fact was the almost even split in the support of the two national political parties, Whig and Democrat. The average support for the Democrats, statewide, had been 50.3 percent in the five presidential elections and 48.1 percent in the six gubernatorial elections. Analysis must proceed, then, to find and account for any within-state variation from these averages. The accompanying maps and tables will make the task more simple. First, one can make note of the parish rank-order coefficient of correlation of plus .69 computed between the two arrays of voting returns. On the extremes, the relationship between the average Democrat vote for president and governor is clear in a comparison of the voting behavior of parishes:

*Table 3–5*

AVERAGE NUMBER OF PARISHES BELOW AND ABOVE
50 PERCENT: PRESIDENTIAL DEMOCRATIC, 1836–52,
AND GUBERNATORIAL DEMOCRATIC, 1834–52

| Presidential 1836–52 | Gubernatorial 1834–52 | | |
|---|---|---|---|
| | Parishes Above 50% | Parishes Below 50% | |
| Parishes Above 50% | 24 | 2 | (26) |
| Parishes Below 50% | 5 | 17 | (22) |

The Maps (3–1, 3–2) provide confirmation that the parish distribution of these intervals of voting percentages clearly divides on regional lines. Parishes above 50 percent Democratic support are to be found mostly in the Hills voter units, the "American" Florida Parishes, and Southwest Louisiana. The other side of the cleavage is made up

# Average Presidential Democratic Vote
## 1836-1852

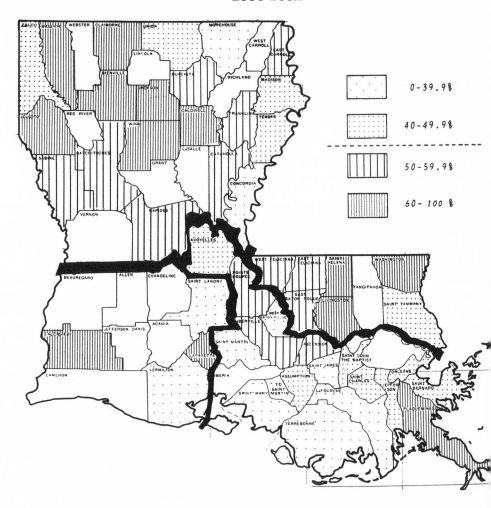

# Average Gubernatorial Democratic Vote
# 1834-1852

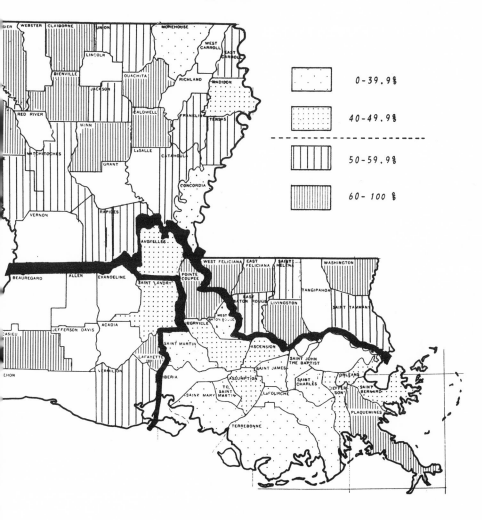

of parishes located in South Louisiana, in both the Planter and Bayou voter type units as well as in urban Jefferson and Orleans parishes. Added to these must be planter parishes along the "front" in the Mississippi Delta and region of the Ouachita River. Whiggish principles brought cotton and sugar interests together, although some ambivalence remained in view.

Of the five parishes with percentage votes below fifty in the presidential election but above for the gubernatorial, all except Vermilion wavered close on either side of the dividing line, with the aforementioned parish moving from the first interval, below 50 percent, to the 50–59 percent interval. On the other hand, Iberville and Ascension each moved from just above to just below the 50 percent line. The majority of these were planter parishes where the degree of Democratic support was most likely to vary.

The parish distribution of Democratic support, measured by the four sets of percentage intervals, shifts from a rather uniform dispersion for presidential voting into the direction of greater Democratic leaning in voting for governor. This tendency may be traced listing the number of parishes by intervals for the two kinds of elections:

*Table 3–6*

AVERAGE NUMBER OF PARISHES IN PRESIDENTIAL DEMOCRATIC PERCENTAGE
INTERVALS, 1836–52 AND GUBERNATORIAL, 1834–52

| Interval | Presidential Democratic | Gubernatorial Democratic |
|---|---|---|
|  | Number of Parishes | Number of Parishes |
| 00–39% . . . . . . . . . . | 10 | 10 |
| 40–49% . . . . . . . . . . | 12 | 9 |
| 50–59% . . . . . . . . . . | 13 | 14 |
| 60–100% . . . . . . . . . | 13 | 15 |

Overall, however, the most important observation that can be made is on the consistency in parish voting behavior in the period under discussion. Next to the stability of the voting behavior in the elections of 1834–52, greatest significance would lie in the discovery of any within-state difference between the behavior of the voter type units which have been delineated. While the state averages hovered at 50 percent in this period of two-party politics, Table 3–7 presents data which reveal that the degree of Democratic support varied widely among the voter types. This means that the general tendency—cleavage between Democrat and Whig—was a function of further sets of opposition: North and South Louisiana; planter and farmer classes; urban and rural residence.

In the decades under discussion, the population of New Orleans made up 32 percent of the state's total white population, but the city contained only 13 percent of the slaves. When it came to voting, however, the proportion of the total number of votes cast by New Orleans was sizable, averaging 25 percent for both presidential and gubernatorial elections. The pertinent data can be summarized in tabular form:

*Table 3–7*

NUMBER AND PERCENT OF VOTES CAST IN PRESIDENTIAL
AND GUBERNATORIAL ELECTIONS, 1834–52,
NEW ORLEANS AND STATE

| Pres. Election | Gubn. Year | State Vote | New Orleans Vote | Percent of State | Percent Democrat | State Percent Democrat |
|---|---|---|---|---|---|---|
| . . . . | 1834 | 10,211 | 1,500 | 15% | 36.2% | 40.7% |
| 1836. . . . . . | | 7,425 | 1,341 | 14% | 49.6% | 51.7% |
| . . . . | 1838 | 13,748 | 3,092 | 23% | 50.1% | 47.2% |
| 1840. . . . . . | | 18,912 | 4,429 | 23% | 39.5% | 40.2% |
| . . . . | 1842 | 14,307 | 2,205 | 15% | 44.3% | 55.4% |
| 1844. . . . . . | | 26,865 | 5,638 | 21% | 46.3% | 51.3% |
| . . . . | 1846 | 23,354 | 5,905 | 39% | 50.1% | 54.0% |
| 1848. . . . . . | | 33,866 | 10,130 | 30% | 45.2% | 45.4% |
| . . . . | 1850 | 36,115 | 10,387 | 28% | 51.1% | 51.4% |
| 1852. . . . . . | | 35,902 | 9,573 | 27% | 50.6% | 51.9% |
| . . . . | 1852 | 33,061 | 9,751 | 29% | 56.4% | 53.0% |

A number of interesting facts emerge from inspecting these figures. In the first place, whereas voting behavior in the state had been characterized by the closeness of the election returns, New Orleans remained consistently Whig in presidential preference but just barely Democratic in most of the elections for governor. This appears all the more surprising in the face of the determined effort on the part of the Democrats to organize the immigrant vote. This had been possible because the city had been divided into municipal districts, the First, predominantly Creole in population, the Second, American, while the Third was made up of immigrant population.[42] The "fighting, drinking, politicking" Irish element was organized, and it made the difference in local elections when a small bloc vote could swing a close contest.[43] Later on in the 1850's, the fear of the manipulation of this immigrant vote encouraged a nativist movement in Louisiana politics.[44]

The immigrant vote was not only Democratic, but it was also somewhat limited by the suffrage restrictions on length of residence. Still, it is instructive to note that although the New Orleans total vote had nearly doubled after the 1845 constitution was ratified, the Whiggish support had remained in about the same proportion as before. The Whig Party had found support from bankers, merchants, and the professional classes because of their economic interests, which, according to Greer, "needed a high tariff, or banks, or internal improvements at Federal expense. The same classes among the Democrats were more conservative on the issue of change because of their material interests than the average Democrat."[45] One could add that these material interests crosscut the differences in nativity between the older French and newer American settlers.

The variance in votes was greatest, then, in the Urban Area where differences in class and background led to a quite even split of the electorate between Whig and Democrat. No such cleavage of interests could be found to approximate so closely the 50 percent in the rural parishes of the interior. Here there were differences, but the variation in percentage support for Whig or Democrat was found to exist

[42] Gordy, "The Irish in New Orleans," 51.
[43] Niehaus, The Irish in New Orleans, 71.
[44] Fife, "Presidential Election of 1848; " W. Darrell Overdyke, "History of the American Party in Louisiana," Louisiana Historical Quarterly, XVI (1933), 84–91, 256–77, 406–26, 608–27.
[45] Greer, "Louisiana Politics," 393.

between voter type units. This was a function of the difference, in turn, between the two diverse types of agriculture—the plantation system and the small-scale family farm. The distribution of planters and farmers in pursuit of these ways of life within the state has been delineated already. It is possible, therefore, to take the voter types made up of groups of parishes showing degrees of planter and farmer dominance and observe their voting behavior. The most obvious indicator is the proportion of the state's slave population found in each of the voter type units. Each one may be placed in rank and compared with its rank order support of the Democratic Party.

*Table 3–8*

AVERAGE PRESIDENTIAL AND GUBERNATORIAL DEMOCRATIC
PERCENTAGES 1834–52 AND PROPORTION OF STATE SLAVE POPULATION
BY VOTER TYPE AREAS

|  |  | Average Democratic Percent 1834–52 | | Rank Order | |
| Unit | Proportion of State's Slaves | Pres. | Gubn. | Slave | Vote |
| --- | --- | --- | --- | --- | --- |
| South Planter. . . . . . | 22% | 43% | 42% | 1 | 7 |
| North Planter. . . . . . | 21% | 48% | 53% | 2 | 5 |
| Florida Parishes. . . . . | 14% | 58% | 63% | 3 | 2 |
| South Bayou . . . . . . | 13% | 45% | 42% | 4 | 6 |
| Southwest . . . . . . . | 6% | 55% | 58% | 5 | 4 |
| Central Pine Hills. . . . | 4% | 61% | 60% | 6.5 | 1 |
| North Hills . . . . . . | 4% | 59% | 59% | 6.5 | 3 |

The historical increase of population in Louisiana, together with the history of voting, which have been traced in detail above, support the hypothesis that: The greater the number of slaves within a voter type unit, the less the degree of support for the Democratic Party. The units which rank first in the state's slave population should rank last in percentage of Democratic vote. The tendency points in that direction, the hypothesis being confirmed by a minus .6 rank-order coefficient of correlation. The extremes make it clear: the two Planter units, with 43 percent of the state's total slaves, voted an average 46 percent Democratic, while the two Hills voter types, with 14 percent of the slaves, provided an average 60 percent Democratic vote.

Even the South Louisiana Planter voter type is not found to fall in the lowest (00–39%) interval of Democratic support. While from all accounts the sugar producing parishes leaned in the direction of the Whigs because of the perennial concern over a protective tariff for the tropical staple, there existed, at the same time, factors which inhibited total Whig solidarity in this voter type area; and the same thing could be said for the Bayou voter type unit in this period as well. Throughout the decades preceding Secession, numbers of American planters from the other states made their way into South Louisiana sugar parishes, often, as in the case of Assumption, preempting and consolidating holdings along river and bayou. This provided one potential source of Democratic support, the other coming from descendants of the Acadians, scattered throughout the "sugar bowl," *les petits habitants de bayou.* Voter turnout data show that, although inarticulate, the "Cajuns" must have been active at the polls.

Planter and farmer, alike, had embraced the Democratic Party throughout the South, but in Louisiana, as elsewhere, black-belt planters could be characterized by the tendency to support the national Whigs in presidential politics. This same sympathy for the Whigs was extended to statewide elections as well. This Whig tendency on the part of the cotton planter is explained in terms of vested interests and elements of a states' rights position.[46] Whereas the Southern Whigs of the 1830's had found a common cause in the opposition to the leveling influences of Jacksonian Democracy, by 1844 the Whigs had established a unity and consensus behind the program of "internal improvements" developed by Henry Clay.

The Florida Parishes at first glance seem to provide an exception to the expected inverse relation between number of slaves and Democratic votes. This voter type may be considered less homogeneous, in this period, than the others. East Baton Rouge and the two Feliciana parishes contained slightly more than 80 percent of

[46] Arthur C. Cole, *The Whig Party in the South* (Washington, D. C., 1913), vii–viii, 341–43.

the slaves held in the seven parish area, or 26,531 of the total of 32,969 slaves. Nevertheless, an explanation must be made for the fact that, at the same time, these three planter parishes provided an average 58 percent Democratic vote in this period while the farmer from pine flats and hills in the remaining four parishes of the Floridas swelled the average voter support to 62 percent Democratic. The planter class had settled earlier in the western part of this area around Baton Rouge, St. Francisville, and Clinton, then farther north along the Mississippi Delta. Moreover, migrants had brought with them the Jacksonian prejudice, and in both the periods of nativism and two-party politics, the settlers managed to elect several native sons to high positions in the Louisiana power structure, all as Democrats.

The period of two-party politics was one in which the Whigs and Democrats stood each other off at the polls. The balance was secured by the nearly 60 percent Whig preference of the planters, countered by the 60 percent Democratic preference of the farmers from hill and bayou. All the while, the vote in New Orleans broke even between the parties. These votes can be considered a genuine exercise of suffrage, for while key positions within the power structure were filled by the conservative elements, the leadership of "The Louisiana Democracy" by such politicians as Solomon Downs and John Slidell guaranteed that the electorate had meaningful choices at the election box. At any rate, though malapportionment continued to be an issue in antebellum Louisiana, voter turnout at the polls increased in these decades, stimulated, no doubt, by the two-party competition.

While the state total turnout figures had led investigators to conclude that voter apathy as well as elite domination prevailed in Louisiana, it can be shown in fact that, outside urban New Orleans, a voter turnout in proportions considered praiseworthy even today, prevailed. The proportion ranged from the 20 percent in Orleans to close to 70 percent in the voter types made up of interior parishes.

Two-party competition characterized Louisiana politics through the elections of 1852. A decade earlier, however, the Democrats had captured the governorship they were to hold until Secession. The party composition of the Louisiana delegation in Washington

(Appendix A, Table 12) likewise showed the beginnings of the tendency toward Democratic support, which, in the 1850's reached high proportions. The Democratic Party was counted as party preference for 81 percent of incumbents in the Senate, while in the House, party preference shifted from 35 percent Democratic to 58 percent in the period 1837 through 1852. The law profession continued to be the main vehicle for this kind of political mobility, even though it may be important to note the increased proportions of planters, who served in both Senate and House.

# CHAPTER IV

# The Downfall of the Whigs
# and Impending Secession
# 1852-1860

## 1. *The Constitution of 1852 and Continued Malapportionment*

The Jacksonians in Louisiana continued to be dissatisfied with the constitution.[1] The governor's appointive power still was too great and his term of office too long, and suffrage requirements engineered by the elite continued to rankle them. Roger Shugg's authoritative work puts it this way: "Suffrage and representation determine what republican government can do: in Louisiana it could do nothing against the will of the slaveholding minority of the population."[2] The Constitution of 1845 was so much more liberal by contrast to the one of 1812, however, that the electorate had endorsed it by a vote of 12,277 to 1,395.

Mercantile interests in New Orleans likewise remained dissatisfied with the instrument of 1845. They sought further constitutional change because of restrictions on the right of the legislature to borrow money, its ban on charter banks, its prohibition of loans to internal improvement companies such as those constructing levees, and its restrictions on the life of corporations.[3] With two sorts of reforms being sought, the one to liberalize suffrage and representation and the other to extend commercial privilege, it is not surprising to find the Democrats proposing the former and the Whigs the latter.

Democratic Governor Joseph Walker opposed calling another

---

[1] Charles W. Tapp, "Development of the Constitutional Appointive Power of the Governor of Louisiana" (Master's thesis, Louisiana State University, 1964), 8.

[2] Roger W. Shugg, *Origins of Class Struggle in Louisiana* (Baton Rouge, 1939; paperback, 1968), 134.

[3] Emmett Asseff, *Legislative Apportionment in Louisiana* (LSU, Bureau of Government Research, [Baton Rouge, 1950]), 19; Shugg, *Origins of Class Struggle*, 134–35.

convention, but public support for the move was widespread. The Whigs, with increased strength gained by the alliance of cotton and sugar planters, were quick to see their opportunity and campaigned vigorously and successfully in the election of delegates. But because Jacksonianism had so popularized the word "democracy," they realized that they could not be so openly and vindictively anti-democratic as they had been in earlier campaigns.[4] Instead of proclaiming democracy the mother of all mischiefs, the later Whigs welcomed it as an effective aid in vote getting. The Baton Rouge *Gazette* hid its enthusiasm by saying, when the Whigs filled two-thirds of the seats of the convention with eighty-five delegates to the Democrats' forty-five: "The Whigs have an awful responsibility resting upon them, and it behooves every Whig to work with diligence and to present to the people a constitution wise in its construction, liberal in its provisions and worthy of the great state of Louisiana and of the Whig Party. We now have it in our power to place Louisiana beyond the reach of Locofocoism and to retain its government in our hands for years to come."[5]

The constitution adopted in 1852 was thus an ironic document, sponsored in the name of democracy but conceived in terms of economic considerations.[6] If the Whigs had seemed to be generous to the farmer, they had exacted a price. Diverse elements had pushed the 1852 convention, and its work reflected them. It met the demands of the people for a more democratic structure; every political office became elective, including the judiciary, and the terms of office were shortened. At the same time, the economic reforms desired by the merchant classes were also made. The Whigs worked hard and, in the changes made concerning representation, saw the perpetuation of their control of government, for total population was made the basis of representation in the lower chamber, matching the gains of 1845, when the Senate was based upon total population. This meant that planter interests would control the legislature, because their

---

[4] James W. Prothro, "A Study of Constitutional Developments in Louisiana" (Master's thesis, Louisiana State University, 1948), 62.

[5] *Ibid.*, 62.

[6] Tapp, "Development of Constitutional Appointive Power," 32.

slaves would count in their favor. The Democrats had argued with some justification that "one Whig master and his 1,000 slaves possessed representation in the General Assembly equal to 1,001 free, white Democrats."[7]

The poor parishes, short of slave property, protested, in vain, the 1852 constitution, feeling that slave representation destroyed the "essence of republicanism," placed the African and the white man on the same level and thereby stamped "upon this Government the odious principles and character of an aristocratic Government."[8] A popular but ineffective denunciation of "nigger rule" was raised, and for the first time in Louisiana the economic issue was beclouded by race prejudice. The efficient leadership of Judah P. Benjamin was underscored, however, when the state ratified the document by a small majority, 19,383 to 14,989.[9]

Population and voting data show how the Whig triumph at the convention succeeded at the ballot box. An analysis of the vote cast for governor in 1850 shows that the farmer held his own in voting

*Table 4-1*

ELECTORAL PARITY INDEX, 1850, BY VOTER TYPE AREAS

| | Proportion of State Total | | Electoral parity index |
|---|---|---|---|
| Unit | Votes | Population voting age | |
| North Louisiana Hills | 7 | 6 | + 1 |
| Central Pine Hills | 5 | 3 | + 2 |
| No. La. Planter Parishes | 14 | 10 | + 4 |
| So. La. Planter Parishes | 12 | 7 | + 5 |
| Florida Parishes | 10 | 7 | + 3 |
| So. La. Bayou Parishes | 13 | 8 | + 5 |
| Southwest Louisiana | 7 | 5 | + 2 |
| Jefferson | 2 | 8 | − 6 |
| Orleans | 30 | 46 | − 16 |
| | 100% | 100% | 0 |

[7] Leslie M. Norton, *Readings in Social Science: Louisiana 1699–1876* (Baton Rouge, 1936), 161.
[8] Shugg, *Origins of Class Struggle*, 142.
[9] *Ibid.*, 136, 142–43.

(on a one-man, one-vote basis) but that in elections of representatives, the farmer found the voting deck stacked against him. If voter type units are matched according to the proportion that each contributed to the state totals of the voting age population and to the votes cast, a simple index of electoral parity may be computed, expressing the difference between the two.

All the "interior" parishes actually contained more of the total vote cast than their corresponding share of white males of voting age, but the difference was greater in the planter areas. The farmer areas simply did not have as many potential voters. In the urban area, immigrants to the city were disfranchised by residence requirements, and Orleans Parish, which contained 46 percent of the state voting age population, accounted for only 30 percent of the votes cast.

When the proportion of representatives elected to the legislature from the voter type areas is considered, however, a quite different pattern is discovered. For, after 1852, what counted was the total population, which included slave holdings, and this worked easily to the advantage of the planter elite wherever they dominated a parish. In fact, if the proportions of the total number of slaves are ranked alongside the proportions of total representation held by each voter unit, a near perfect rank-order coefficient of correlation can be computed: plus point nine. The arrays, omitting New Orleans, are distributed as follows:

*Table 4–2*

PROPORTION OF STATE SLAVE POPULATION, 1840–50,
AND REPRESENTATION, 1854, BY VOTER TYPE AREAS

| | Slaves, 1840–50 | | Representatives, 1854 | |
|---|---|---|---|---|
| Voter Type Unit | Proportion of total | Rank | Proportion of total | Rank |
| So. La. Planter Parishes . . . . . | 22 | 1 | 15 | 2 |
| No. La. Planter Parishes. . . . . | 21 | 2 | 18 | 1 |
| Florida Parishes . . . . . . . | 14 | 3 | 11 | 3 |
| So. La. Bayou Parishes . . . . . | 13 | 4 | 11 | 3 |
| Southwest Louisiana . . . . . . | 6 | 5 | 7 | 5 |
| Central Pine Hills . . . . . . . | 4 | 6.5 | 3 | 7 |
| No. La. Hills . . . . . . . . . | 4 | 6.5 | 7 | 5 |

The effect which follows from using the aggregate population as a basis of representation is clear. The figures show a regular gradient from planter to farmer areas, from alluvial to hill parishes. Following Asseff,[10] the number of representatives which black and white belt parishes and Orleans Parish would have elected under the three different bases of representation are:

*Table 4-3*

NUMBER OF REPRESENTATIVES IN BLACK AND WHITE
BELT PARISHES UNDER DIFFERING BASES OF SUFFRAGE

|  | Total population | Electors | White population |
|---|---|---|---|
| Black Belt . . . . | 46 | 38 | 34 |
| White Belt . . . . | 19 | 20 | 19 |
| Orleans . . . . . | 23 | 30 | 35 |
|  | 88 | 88 | 88 |

Looked at in this way, an explanation is found for the constitutional limitation on the number of representatives allowed from Orleans Parish. It had been provoked by a fear that the rapidly growing urban area would dominate the legislature. However, Orleans representation came more into line with the other voter type areas as the state grew and population distributed more widely. This approach obscures the geographic distribution of representation, and therefore the same data should be studied according to voter type area unit.

Representation based upon the elector plan (where the number was determined by voter turnout in previous elections), or the total number of whites, gave the farmers a chance, but, on the basis of total population there was no way for farmers of the hill and frontier parishes to gain parity with the planters. They were simply outnumbered. The combined representation of the farmers in the House, based on population in Southwest Louisiana and the Hills was

[10] Asseff, *Legislative Apportionment.*

*Table 4–4*

NUMBER OF REPRESENTATIVES UNDER DIFFERING
BASES OF SUFFRAGE BY VOTER TYPE AREAS

| Voter Type Unit | Total population | Electors | White population |
|---|---|---|---|
| No. La. Planter Parishes. . . . 15 | 15 | 11 | 9 |
| So. La. Planter Parishes . . . 13 | 13 | 8 | 7 |
| Florida Parishes . . . . . . . 10 | 10 | 8 | 7 |
| So. La. Bayou Parishes . . . . 10 | 10 | 10 | 9 |
| Southwest Louisiana . . . . . 6 | 6 | 6 | 5 |
| North Louisiana Hills . . . . 6 | 6 | 9 | 7 |
| Central Pine Hills . . . . . . 3 | 3 | 4 | 4 |
| (N) | 88 | 88 | 88 |

fifteen; for the two planter areas, twenty-eight. Based on the electors
or white population plans, the farmers would have drawn evenly,
for representation was nineteen to nineteen and sixteen to sixteen,
respectively.

Other states of the Old South were governed by slaveholders;
but only in Louisiana before the Civil War, were slaveholders able
to shape legislation through the representation of their slaves.[11]
For the majority of the people, it made little difference, then, whether
power was held by Slidell or Benjamin, Democrats or Whigs, the
country or the city. Together, planter and merchant, black belt
and city ruled the state. With such opposites vying for advantage,
Louisiana politics would continue to be lively.

II. *The American Party in Louisiana*

Success of the Whig elements in perpetuating their place in the power
structure did not guarantee continuance as a political party. Although
Louisiana was to remain a bastion of conservatism, the Whig Party,
as a vehicle of that sentiment, was to fail. A constant conservatism
led the Whigs to compromise in regard to the slavery issue, but the

[11] Shugg, *Origins of Class Struggle,* 140.

northern wing of the party had become radically antislavery by the 1850's and the southern organization of Whigs, unsuited to act as champions of the slave power, declined and disappeared. Attempts to revive the party continued until the outbreak of war.

While the Whig Party from its beginning, in the 1830's, had advocated the protection of vested interests, during the 1840's the Democrat Party had found states' rights a congenial justification for slavocracy, expansionism, and the demand for cheap land. The Democrats' concern for vested interests undermined the position of the Whigs. From this time on, Arthur C. Cole has pointed out, the Whigs of the South were Unionists.[12] In South Louisiana the sugar industry required a high capital expenditure because its production required machine manufacture as well as slave agriculture.[13] This was one reason a large majority of Louisiana sugar planters expressed opposition to Secession.[14] With less in the way of capital investment, the cotton planters, who in the thirties and forties had aligned themselves with the Whiggery of South Louisiana, now tended toward the Democrats and their States' Rights defense of slavery and Secession.

In the gubernatorial election of 1856, the American Party (Know-Nothing) became a serious factor in Louisiana.[15] Know-Nothing as a vehicle of political expression had been introduced in Louisiana in February 1854, encouraged by the demise of the Whig Party. The state was second only to Virginia in establishing Know-Nothing councils. Know-Nothingism (members were told to say "I don't know" to questions about the party) may be seen as unique here, for nationally it had repudiated the Catholics. Even so, the bulk of the membership of the old-line Whig Party found haven in the ranks of the American Party. They, after all, had believed that Democratic success had come from voting the New Orleans Irish and other foreign elements against them. The anti-Democratic tendency of

[12] Arthur C. Cole, *The Whig Party in the South* (Washington, D.C., 1913), 342.

[13] Shugg, *Origins of Class Struggle*, 98.

[14] J. Carlyle Sitterson, *Sugar Country: The Cane Industry in the South, 1753–1950* (Lexington, 1953), 205.

[15] Vance Lynn S. Jeanfreau, "Louisiana Know Nothings and the Elections of 1855–1856," *Louisiana Studies*, IV (1965), 222–64.

the old Whig combined with the anti-foreign sentiment, overruling the solidarity of Catholicism.

The religious question vexed would-be supporters of the American Party, and the immigrant tide also complicated matters by threatening to weaken southern sectionalism, thereby creating a second problem for the party in Louisiana.[16] Many natives within the state feared the foreigners but, at the same time, desired to preserve both slavery and the Union. Still a third difference encountered by Know-Nothingism in Louisiana was in the rivalry of the Democrats, who wanted to maintain their own dominance even though they were divided among themselves.

The wellsprings of the American Party lay in the corruption within the old parties, but while Know-Nothingism rapidly reached its zenith in 1856, it just as rapidly dwindled to an ineffective opposition, statewise. It was the existence in New Orleans of a large foreign element and the irritating memories of past Democratic machine politics that kept the Know-Nothings vigorous there until the Civil War.[17] In New Orleans politics, disorder had become commonplace by 1854 as streets became battlegrounds of the Irish and the Know-Nothings. The new group was similar to the Native American Party of the 1840's which had been formed by such men as Judah P. Benjamin in order to reform the ballot and the naturalization laws. But the Know-Nothings were more ambitious than this, and were counting upon the well-known fact that the Whigs were smarting over defeats and ready to jump aboard the bandwagon.

It was "The Democracy" under John Slidell which had undermined the Whig ascendancy. It had liberalized the government in the 1840's, had established white manhood suffrage, and in mobilizing the Irish immigrant in New Orleans and the Jacksonian farmer in the interior parishes, had driven the Whigs "into the futile chauvinism of the Know-Nothing movement."[18] In John Slidell, Louisiana had found one of the many of her citizens destined to rise to national prominence.

[16] *Ibid.*, 227, 228.
[17] James K, Greer, "Louisiana Politics, 1845–1861," *Louisiana Historical Quarterly*, XIII (1930), 272.
[18] Shugg, *Origins of Class Struggle*, 153.

Slidell had been elected to Congress in 1844, and as his popularity grew he effected a strongly unified party organization back home that was new to Louisiana. He and Solomon Downs, whose seat in the U.S. Senate Slidell won in 1853, controlled the Democrat Party in the state.

Slidell was not without opposition within the Democratic Party; former Senator Pierre Soulé competed for the reins of the party up to the Secession. His support rested upon a more conservative foundation, however, and he was never able, in the 1850's, to mount a successful attack upon the position of Slidell. It was said that Soulé lost all possibility of leadership in the Democracy when he was outmaneuvered by John Slidell in 1853. At that time Soulé men enjoyed the rumor that "King John" would be made a minister to Central America. But Slidell, who did not intend to be trapped out of his position of power in Louisiana, declined, and when Soulé vacated his seat in the Senate to accept a mission to Spain, Slidell was in a strategic position.[19]

The Democrats became divided nationally when, after 1854, Stephen Douglas reopened the whole slavery issue in Congress by introducing the Kansas-Nebraska Bill.[20] This act would repeal the Missouri Compromise and, by implications, the Compromise of 1850 through the device of "squatter sovereignty." Thus settlers, or "squatters," who went into these territories, were to decide for themselves by popular vote whether they would have slavery or not. Northern Democrats, northern Whigs, northern Know-Nothings, and the Free Soil Party were all outraged. Douglas' action served not only to split the Democrats; it had the effect of destroying the Northern Whigs, aiding the development of the newly formed Republican Party and opening the door to Know-Nothings. The American Party provided a voice of protest against immigration, and now, also provided an opposition to the Democrats in the South. In Louisiana, John Slidell continued steadfast within the presidential

---

[19] Greer, "Louisiana Politics," 70.
[20] Walter Dean Burnham, *Presidential Ballots, 1836–1892* (Baltimore, 1955), 61–2; Ralph M. Goldman, *The Democratic Party in American Politics* (New York, 1966), 54.

branch of the Democratic Party while Pierre Soulé became the local leader of the Douglas faction of the Democrats.

By 1855, almost the whole state had been swept by a wave of enthusiasm for the Know-Nothings. The American Party's candidate for governor was the former Whig, Charles Derbigny, while the Democrats, appearing to divorce themselves from the national administration, whose attitudes on Cuba had alienated many in Louisiana, nominated Robert C. Wickliffe. He was another of the Feliciana elite, who had conducted himself with such distinction in the state legislature that he was boomed as a gubernatorial possibility. Wickliffe was a Douglas supporter and influenced the state nominating convention to endorse the Kansas-Nebraska Act as just legislation. The Louisiana Democrats then pledged co-operation with the northern Democrats so long as this branch accepted the rulings of Congress on slavery as set forth in the Act.[21]

Although backed by sugar parish Whigs, the Know-Nothing candidate found some strong support in cotton country as well as in South Louisiana Planter and Bayou Parishes. Paradoxically, perhaps, Derbigny lost several of the sugar planter parishes, but Wickliffe carried the parishes in the Soulé stronghold because he supported Douglas. The Democrats lost some ground in the Florida Parishes, but in the heartland of the Louisiana Democracy, the Hills, the farmers stood solid. Some Planter areas, both North and South, continued to demonstrate their anti-Democratic tendency, and as expected, the New Orleans vote went Know-Nothing, but only by 50.9 percent.

Remnants of the American Party remained visible in the 1860 election for governor. The national Know-Nothings ceased to function in 1857, but the New Orleans organization still controlled the city politics. The large foreign population and the constant immigration of still more remained factors working for them. In this way the Americans could say they were the bulwark against Democratic

[21] Thomas B. Landry, "The Political Career of Robert Charles Wickliffe "(Master's thesis, Louisiana State University, 1939), 21; Norton, *Readings*, 158; W. Darrell Overdyke, "History of the American Party in Louisiana," *Louisiana Historical Quarterly*, XVI (1933), 84–91, 256–77, 406–29, 608–27.

manipulation of these groups. The climax of their organized activity reached its peak in 1858. Speaking in 1859, Pierre Soulé summed up the political situation in these prophetic words: "Partyisms are entombed in the past. The American Party, the Whig Party, exist no more as national or even state parties, though we may at times still see their shadows flit around our municipal halls and elective precincts. Their scattered fragments are in *process of assimilation with the two factions into which the Democratic Party is divided.*"[22]

The gubernatorial election of 1860 became a struggle for control of the Democratic Party, and Soulé faced Slidell for the showdown. The firmly entrenched support of Slidell prevailed in the nomination of Thomas O. Moore. In final desperation, Soulé organized an opposition party—a coalition of "purifiers," or anti-Slidell Democrats, and the remnants of the American, or Know-Nothing, parties—which nominated Thomas J. Wells. The campaign boiled down to "for or against Slidell." Slidell's victory was predictable from the beginning. The important thing was that the electoral balance of two decades had been destroyed, with Moore receiving 62 percent of the votes cast. Soulé's candidate obtained majorities in only two parishes, Orleans and Terrebonne, although the Jefferson vote had been a toss-up.

With the statewide support for Thomas Moore so strong, an interpretation of the voting percentages favoring the Slidell faction may be carried out best through analysis of the combined votes of the gubernatorial elections of 1856 and 1860. The former year had seen a contest between the established and transitional parties while the latter election had been a battle of factions. Slidell sentiment in 1860, although widespread, had been most generally found concentrated in Hill Parishes or prairie, where his machine strength was organized. This vote was a vote for the Democracy. In 1856, for example, the four Hill Parishes of Bienville, Jackson, Caldwell, and Winn had registered votes averaging 68 percent support for the Democratic candidate Wickliffe, who had been a Douglas man. In 1860 the same four parishes recorded votes of over 70 percent for Moore, who,

[22] Norton, *Readings*, 163, italics added; see also Mary L. McLure, "The Elections of 1860 in Louisiana," *Louisiana Historical Quarterly*, IX (1926).

with Slidell's backing, was in the other camp. The hill farmer voted Democratic out of tradition and did not look behind the party label. The same could not be said for those parishes where planter groups were dominant; opinions appeared to be divided. Sugar parishes along the river marked the continuation of a trend toward the Democratic Party. Parishes of the upper Mississippi appeared on the list of Slidell supporters, although Madison and Concordia, Know-Nothing in 1856, were weaker in support of Moore's candidacy. Factional support was divided, but the only clear pattern which can be discovered was what may be identified as a compulsive drive to Democratic solidarity.

If the election of 1852 marked the denouement of two-party politics in antebellum Louisiana, those of 1856–60 were a fitting Democratic finale. A cross-tabulation of parish percentages above and below the 50 percent mark in these elections indicates the drive to Democracy:

*Table 4–5*

AVERAGE NUMBER OF PARISHES BELOW AND ABOVE 50 PERCENT,
GUBERNATORIAL DEMOCRATIC 1850–52 AND 1856–60

|  | 1850–52 Average Dem. | 1856–60 Average Dem. | | |
|---|---|---|---|---|
|  |  | Parishes Above 50% | Parishes Below 50% | (N) |
| Parishes Above 50% |  | 96% (28) | 4% (1) | (29) |
| Parishes Below 50% |  | 62% (10) | 38% (6) | (16) |

Even among those parishes which fell below 50 percent Democrat in the elections of 1850 and 1852, the drift toward the Democratic column in the period 1856–60 is clearly discernable (Map 4–1), as former Whig parishes became Democratic. Only the Urban Area and North and South Louisiana Planter voter type areas with 45.0, 57.5, and 56.6 percent, respectively, fall below the 1856–60 state Democratic average of 57.8 percent.

# Average Gubernatorial Democratic Vote
# 1856-1860

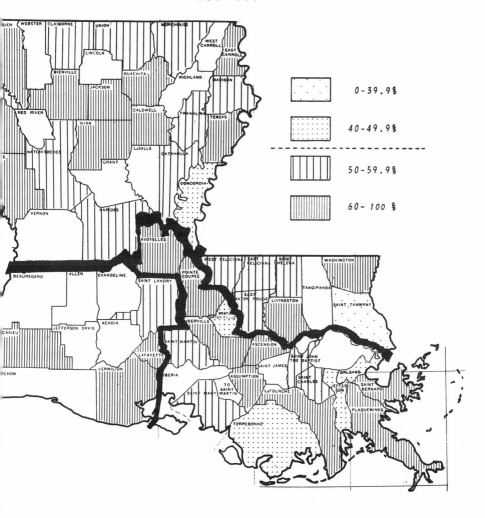

In the 1856 party convention in Baton Rouge, a sharp conflict arose between the Slidell and Soulé factions regarding which candidate, Douglas or Buchanan, possessed the greater pretensions to the presidency.[23] Local debate became academic at the 1856 national convention where "King John" Slidell led the Buchanan forces in the three-way battle with the Pierce and Douglas factions. On the sixteenth ballot Buchanan led Douglas 168 to 122 votes, the latter withdrew his name, and the former was nominated for President. Slidell's victory was capped by the addition of a rising young southerner, John C. Breckinridge, as Buchanan's running mate.[24]

Back home in Louisiana, old Whigs in the state thought that in Buchanan the Democrats had made a good choice.[25] He was the third "doughface" put up by the Democrat Party in three elections, which indicates the deadlock that the Democrats experienced and their desire to compromise North and South for harmony. As events turned out, Buchanan stood "as the last of an old political tradition, just as the Democratic Party of 1856 stood as the last ante-bellum party which completely transcended the Mason-Dixon lines."[26]

In the hope of attracting dissident Democrats as well as Whigs, the American Party, in 1856, nominated former President Millard Fillmore, who had succeeded after the death of the Whig President Taylor. As a sponsor of the Compromise of 1850, he was representative of the last of another old political tradition—solution by compromise.[27]

The results of the 1856 presidential election in Louisiana showed that it was still strongly Unionist in feeling and that it was groping after reforms in the political machinery that would bring compromise and avoid conflict. Fillmore received 20,709 votes to 22,164 for the Democrat Buchanan. The American Party had missed carrying the state by less than 2 percent of the total vote cast (Map 4–2). There

---

[23] Greer, "Louisiana Politics," 103.
[24] Goldman, *The Democratic Party*, 54.
[25] Greer, "Louisiana Politics," 105.
[26] Burnham, *Presidential Ballots*, 64.
[27] *Ibid.*, 64.

# Presidential Democratic Vote, 1856

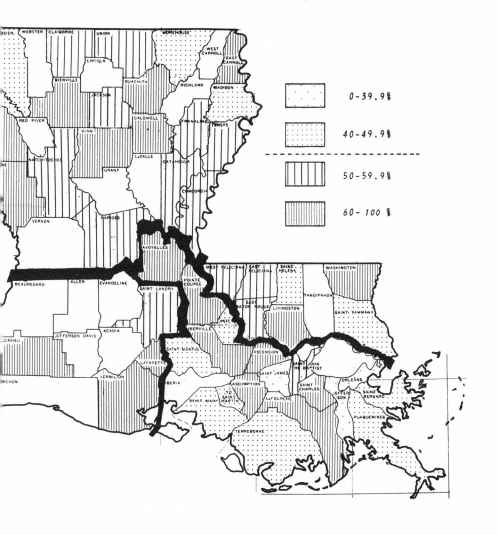

remained decidedly more cleavage here than in the South as a whole, where the American candidate obtained only 43.6 percent of the votes cast. Indeed, across the South there was an increase of Democratic support, as even such bastions of Whiggery as Tennessee voted for the Democrat Buchanan.

In Louisiana, Buchanan carried thirty-four parishes to Fillmore's fifteen. Some of these last had been Whig through every presidential election since and including that of 1840: Morehouse, St. James, St. Mary, St. Martin, Terrebonne, and West Baton Rouge. Thirteen of the parishes Buchanan carried likewise had always voted Democratic: Bienville, Calcasieu, Caldwell, Claiborne, DeSoto, East Feliciana, Franklin, Jefferson, Lafayette, Livingston, Plaquemines, Sabine, St. Bernard, West Feliciana, and Winn.[28]

There was a decline, overall, in the number of parishes showing continued opposition to the Louisiana Democracy. This was hidden by the 54 percent vote in favor of the American Party cast in New Orleans, enough to balance interior losses and keep the state total close to 50 percent. The Democratic percentage found in the Planter voter type areas shows that many former Whigs chose to take their chances with the Democrats, rather than support this hybrid party of expediency, the Americans.

A recent analysis of Know-Nothing strength in the South makes it possible to compare the 1856 vote in Louisiana and determine in more detail the factors involved in the election. James Broussard has used to advantage the county election returns which in recent years have been made more readily available to the scholar. From an examination of these votes he concludes that four major factors seem to have affected the strength of the American Party in the slave states: (1) the presence of a Whig majority in the period from 1836 to 1852; (2) the prevalence of Union feeling as measured by the 1860 presidential vote; (3) the proximity of a large foreign-born population; and (4) the presence of a large number of slaves.[29]

The first three factors worked to the advantage of the Americans,

[28] Greer, "Louisiana Politics," 113.
[29] James H. Broussard, "Some Determinents of the Know-Nothing Electoral Strength in the South, 1856," *Louisiana History*, VII (1966), 18.

while in general, slaveholding interests, desiring to keep party solidarity and, distrusting the abolitionist tendency of the Americans, worked against them.

It is possible to array the southern states by American percentage of the vote in 1856 and divide it into top, middle, and bottom thirds. These sets of intervals may be cross-tabulated with an arrayed index divided into thirds and based upon a combination of Whig strength, Unionism, foreign-born population, and slave population (inverted). This allows Broussard to confirm the following hypothesis: States possessing high degrees of Whig strength, Union sentiment, and foreign-born population, and having few slaves, gave the highest vote to the American Party in 1856. Louisiana emerges as something of an exception to this. It falls into the top third of American vote, but into the middle third of the index of American advantage. An analysis which retraces the presentation made by Broussard, comparing Louisiana with data on the South as a whole, will reveal the reasons why.

One would expect presence of the foreign-born population to be the factor most likely to influence the American vote in Louisiana. Urban New Orleans, including Jefferson Parish, made up over 40 percent of the total number of whites in the state, and, in turn, the proportion of foreign-born among the urban population in 1860 had been slightly more than 40 percent. Therefore, when Broussard found that the American showing in the South was directly related to the presence or absence of a large foreign-born population, it is not surprising that the American showing in Louisiana was related even more so. In the South as a whole, the American gain or loss over the percentage of Whig showing in 1852 was found to be a plus 13.3 percent in counties with over 25 percent foreign-born, plus 2.9 percent in counties with 10 to 25 percent foreign-born, and minus 3.4 percent in counties with less than 10 percent foreign-born. In Louisiana the spread was greater. The vote in urban Orleans and Jefferson increased from 49.5 percent Whig in 1852 to 72.0 percent American four years later, or a gain of 22.5 percent. On the other hand, off in the interior parishes, which made up the other two categories of foreign-born, losses of minus 0.6 percent and minus 6.9 percent occurred, and this was a greater falling away from the traditional Whig support than in the South.

This was not the only, or even the most important factor. Confirmation is found for what was intimated above, that the Whigs from both cotton and cane production areas held firm. While Broussard seems correct in assuming that Whig counties in any given category would show more inclination to support Fillmore than would Democratic counties of the same category,[30] county (parish) data for Louisiana show a tendency toward greater Whig support. Whig counties (1836–52) in the South, 50 percent or more Negro and therefore containing many slaveholders—made up 52.4 percent of the American support; in Louisiana this support amounted to 75 percent—a 23 percent increase over the South.

Further, by using the county votes in 1860 as evidence for Unionist or States' Rights inclinations, it was found that old party loyalties determined how the American Party was viewed. In both the South and Louisiana, three-quarters of the Unionist Whig (1836–52) counties appear in the American column in 1856. But whereas only one-quarter of the southern States' Rights Whig (1836–52) counties voted American, 15 percent more of the Whig parishes in Louisiana that had voted for Breckinridge in 1860 did so. Whig counties of States' Rights persuasion switched strongly to the Democratic ticket in 1856, while Whig counties sympathetic to the Union went just as overwhelmingly American.[31] "Swing" counties in the South which oscillated between Whig and Democratic candidates, before, now turned Democratic in 1856, but again, while Louisiana followed in the direction of the South in this, the degree of such a swing was some 20 percent less.

Finally, where Broussard found that by 1856 the slave counties in the South were in the midst of a massive swing to the Democracy, in Louisiana no such movement was apparent.[32] Where the Whig advantage in slave counties (counties over 50 percent slave compared to all other counties) in the South dropped from an average 15 percent

---

[30] *Ibid.*, 8.
[31] *Ibid.*, 12.
[32] *Ibid.*, 14.

in the four presidential elections before 1852 to less than 1 percent in 1852, and increased to an American advantage of 4.6 percent, the Whig advantage in Louisiana averaged 17 percent and actually increased to 18 percent in 1852, while the American advantage held at a level almost twice as high as that for the South—8.7 percent in 1856.

Thus, Louisiana stands as an exception to the rule among the Deep South states, ranking much higher in Whig strength, Union sentiment, and foreign-born population, and drawing close to Mississippi, Alabama, and South Carolina only on the rank of slave population. Moreover, within-state differences among Louisiana parishes, discovered by comparing the parishes ranked by American strength with an index of American advantage, shows a gradient on which planter voter types stand at the top and farmer voter types toward the bottom. While a shift in the direction of Democratic solidarity in the face of threat to the institution of slavery can be found in Louisiana, in 1856, reaction was not as vehement in Louisiana as elsewhere. This conclusion is borne out by observing what happens when the vote of the parishes with Democratic majorities in 1856 is projected to 1860:

*Table 4-6*

NUMBER OF PARISHES BELOW AND ABOVE 50 PERCENT
PRESIDENTIAL DEMOCRATIC 1856 AND 1860

| Parishes Democratic, 1856 | Parishes Southern Democratic, 1860 | | |
|---|---|---|---|
| | Above 50% | Below 50% | (N) |
| Above 50% | 73% (24) | 27% (9) | (33) |
| Below 50% | 33% (5) | 67% (10) d | (15) |

Thus while twenty-four out of the thirty-three parishes (73 percent) in the Democratic column in 1856 contributed majorities in 1860, ten out of fifteen parishes (67 percent), which held American majorities in 1856, refused to go Southern Democrat in 1860.

III. *The Louisiana Election of 1860 and the Secession of 1861*

In the words of W. Dean Burnham, "the election of 1856 had resulted in a postponement of the evil day of wrath which was to come."[33] By the spring of 1860 the event predicted by the election of 1856 had occurred—the North moved toward the Republican Party while the Democratic Party was at last split into sectional factions. The map of the election of 1860 is a picture of a nation breaking in two. In the North, the Republicans and northern Democrats contested for the vote; in the South, Democrats, with their candidate, Vice-President Breckinridge, opposed the Constitutional Union Party and its candidate, John Bell of Tennessee. The election results showed Abraham Lincoln victorious with 160 electoral votes, nearly 20 more than the needed majority, while Breckinridge followed with 72 electoral votes, ahead of Bell's 39 and Douglas' 12. The Republicans had gained the electoral votes of all 16 states north of the Mason and Dixon line, as well as those of California and Oregon. Bell's 39 electoral votes from Kentucky, Virginia, and Tennessee, provided the dividing line between the Republicans and the rest of the southern states, all of which gave their electoral votes to Breckinridge.

A further clarification of the internal divisions is shown in the following table:

*Table 4–7*
PARTY VOTES, PRESIDENTIAL ELECTION,
1860, IN NATION, REGION, AND STATE

|  | Republican (Lincoln) | Northern Democrat (Douglas) | Southern Democrat (Breckinridge) | Constitutional Union (Bell) |
|---|---|---|---|---|
| United States . . | 38.9% | 29.5% | 18.0% | 12.6% |
| "South" . . . . | 1.0% | 9.4% | 48.5% | 41.1% |
| Louisiana . . . . | – – – | 15.0% | 45.0% | 40.0% |

While Douglas' electoral vote had placed him last in the presidential race, his percentage of the popular vote had placed him second.

[33] Burnham, *Presidential Ballots*, 71.

His stand for compromise on the slavery issue was such that his support spanned the sectional cleavage, while Breckinridge and Bell received most of their support from the South. In terms of popular vote cast in the South, however, the Southern Democrats did not secure a clear majority. Rather, at the juncture of November, 1860, the South stood with a slight majority of its voters indicating a desire for compromise. Likewise, in Louisiana, the forces of moderation, split in their vote between Douglas and Bell, prevailed against the southern candidate of the Democracy.

The factional battle staged by the Democratic Party during the gubernatorial election of 1860 in Louisiana was carried over to the presidential campaign. John Slidell led his faction out of the national Democratic Party and followed other southern states in backing the candidacy of John D. Breckinridge for President. The Soulé faction was seated at the Democratic convention at Baltimore, and when Stephen A. Douglas won the nomination, the Soulé forces gave enthusiastic support. The newly formed Constitutional Union Party with many former Whigs as members nominated John Bell for the Presidency, hoping to forestall disunion. Many conservative planters and merchants backed the Union Party in Louisiana.[34]

In lining up the candidates, the New Orleans *Crescent* wrote the following:

Hon. John Bell, of Tenn., representing the Constitutional Union Party, composed of Whigs, Democrats, American and Union men generally, who wish to preserve the Constitution and Union against all assaults upon either . . . The Hon. Abraham Lincoln, of Illinois, representing the Black Republicans, sectional, "irrepressible conflict" party, who believe that this country was made for "niggers" instead of white men, and whose ultimate objectives embrace not only the political subjugation but the social ruin and destruction of the people of the Southern States . . . The Hon. S. A. Douglas, representing those who claim to be the regular, simon-pure, "original Jacobs" Democracy, and who have a special weakness for what they themselves call "popular" and their opponents "squatter" sovereignty in the Territories. . . . The Hon. John C. Breckinridge, the representative of the

[34] Norton, *Readings*, 169–70.

remainder of that Party in the Southern States, with a sprinkling here and there, in the States of the North.[35]

The rival Baton Rouge *Daily Gazette and Comet* summed up the party platforms:

1. Bell and Everett stood for "Constitution and Union."

2. Douglas and Johnson stood for the rights of the people of the territories to regulate their own domestic institutions.

3. Breckinridge and Lane stood for slavery in the territories with congressional legislation to establish it; progressive free trade; against the general system of internal improvements; free seas; filibustering; and annexation of Cuba.

4. Lincoln and Hamlin stood for Tariff and incidental protection, against African slave trade, and for the Homestead Bill.[36]

With such a wide spectrum of political principle from which to choose, Louisiana voters had no difficulties in finding a stance in keeping with the state's traditional tendencies. In Louisiana, at least, the real contest lay between Breckinridge and Bell, for even though the Soulé faction opted for Douglas, influential members of the power structure in South Louisiana and New Orleans pushed the candidacy of John Bell. As one student of the election has put it: "The results show most convincingly that the majority of the people were still conservative and union-loving. A combination of Bell and Douglas factions could have changed the electoral vote. Old Whigs and New Liner Democrats had voted the ticket they believed would save the Union."[37]

During the campaign, the Bell forces had seemed confident of victory, having made a vigorous appeal throughout the state. In New Orleans they had formed political clubs and were quickly followed in this by the other parties. The Bell-Everett clubs were most in

---

[35] Quoted in John C. Merrill, "Louisiana Public Opinion on Secession" (Master's thesis, Louisiana State University, 1950), 91–92.
[36] McLure, "Election of 1860," 665–66.
[37] *Ibid.*, 667.

evidence, and a rough correlation could be found between club activity and the vote received by the party.[38] New Orleans went Unionist with Bell receiving 5,215, Douglas 2,998, and Breckinridge 2,645 votes. The elated Bell forces were now sure they would gain a sweeping statewide majority. The city vote proved no indication of the trend, however. Breckinridge carried the state by less than 2,500 votes. Such a close contest, in which the southern Democrats received 22,681, the northern Democrats 7,625, and the Constitutional Union Party 20,194 votes—in all, 50,500 votes were cast, some 8,000 more than had ever been cast in an election in Louisiana before—indicates the importance of the issue. The parties seemed to have split the state's opinion.

In making within-state comparisons to determine where support for these divergent positions was based, one set of votes can be disposed of easily. A full 45 percent of the Douglas vote in Louisiana had been cast in urban New Orleans and Jefferson Parish. The bulk of the support for the other two contenders, Breckinridge and Bell, lay elsewhere, as the urban proportions of the state vote cast for each was 12 percent and 31 percent, respectively. After eliminating the Douglas urban support, 32 percent of the remaining vote was found to come from the Soulé stronghold of Ascension, Assumption, and Lafourche parishes, the only three in the state to provide pluralities for Douglas. The rest, 2,878 Douglas votes, were distributed among the other 43 parishes.

The neat pattern of cleavage found in the distribution of the average percentage Democratic support, 1836 to 1852, becomes obscured in the delineation of the 1860 vote (Map 4–3). It is no longer so clearly a matter of North and South Louisiana, or farmer and planter. Still, a comparison of the number of parishes found within each set of percentage intervals, using the elections 1836–52, 1856, and 1860, finds a great deal of consistency (Table 4–8). The most striking fact about the earlier period of two-party politics had been the nearly even proportion of parishes in each interval set. On a majority basis, the split in vote for this period had been 46 percent of the parishes

[38] Jerry L. Tarver, "Political Clubs in New Orleans in the Presidential Election of 1860," *Louisiana History*, IV (1963), 119–29.

## Presidential Southern Democratic Vote, 1860

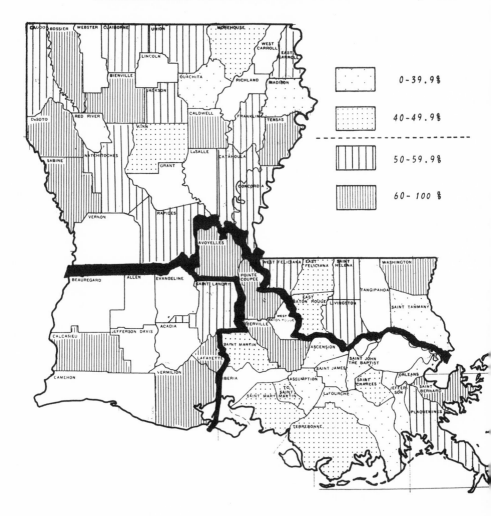

0 - 39.9%

40 - 49.9%

50 - 59.9%

60 - 100%

Table 4–8

NUMBER OF PARISHES, PRESIDENTIAL DEMOCRATIC,
1836–52, 1856, AND 1860, BY PERCENTAGE INTERVALS

| Percentage Interval | Number of Parishes Democratic | | |
|---|---|---|---|
| | 1836–52 | 1856 | 1860 (So. Dem.) |
| 00–39% . . . . . . . . . . . . . | 10 | 3 | 11 |
| 40–49% . . . . . . . . . . . . | 12 | 12 | 8 |
| 50–59% . . . . . . . . . . . | 13 | 14 | 15 |
| 60–100% . . . . . . . . . . | 13 | 19 | 14 |
| | (48) | (48) | (48) |

Whig and 54 percent of them Democratic. As had been determined above, the 1856 election served to draw Democratic votes from the more conservative side of the cleavage, so that the proportion of Democratic parishes increased by 15 percent. In the election of 1860, however, it is apparent that another shift in parish support took place so that instead of a 69–32 percent Democratic advantage in 1856, it was reduced to 60–40 percent Democratic. Still, a falling away from the Whig, or conservative side is seen, statewide, when Orleans Parish support is discounted.

Perhaps the most important thing to note is the regularity with which parishes remained within the same interval of support. Thus, of the nineteen Union parishes in 1860, all but five, or 74 percent, had been Whig in the period 1836–52. Four of these shifters to the Union side were planter parishes—Ouachita, Ascension, East Baton Rouge, and East Feliciana—while the fifth, Winn, was a farmer parish. On the other side, of the twenty-nine parishes which gave majorities to the southern Democrats, all but eight of them, or 72 percent, had been Democratic in the period of two-party competition. Three of these shifters to States' Rights were Planter Parishes, Caddo, Concordia, and Tensas. Two each were Bayou and Southwest Louisiana Parishes, Avoyelles and St. Bernard, St. Landry, and Vermilion parishes, while the eighth, Union, was North Louisiana Hills.

This pattern of stability, together with shifting support, is representative of the enigma surrounding the results of the 1860 presidential election and subsequent move to Secession. It is difficult to find definitive tendencies with which to make a judgment. One thing sure is the shift in support on the part of thirteen parishes, half of which were dominated by planter interests. But of these seven parishes, four shifted from Democrat to Union (two cotton and two sugar) while three shifted from Whig to States' Rights (three cotton). There is no explanation here, on the ecological level. The same holds true for the six parishes with more of a farmer orientation.

Within-state differences by voter types provide little more by way of explanation, although the decision between Breckinridge and Bell may be seen to rest in Red River country, which could not be captured at this late hour from John Slidell's machine. The four voter types which ranked highest in support of Breckinridge are found in North Louisiana among both Hill and Planter units, and in Southwest Louisiana. But all voter types, save the last named, could be labeled as "swing" parishes, with high variance in the voting percentages. While it is true that many small farmers voted their traditional Democratic prejudice, and that large slaveholders tended to switch from Whiggery to States' Rights in this tense election, still, someone in the parishes making up all the voter types had voted for Union. In fact the regularity in support for Bell at close to one-third of the total vote cast in all units is striking.

The expectation that cotton planters would give unified support to the southern Democracy, since cotton was king, was not borne out in Louisiana. For this reason it is not possible to find a clear-cut relationship between slaveholding and the support for Democratic States' Rights in 1860. It has already been shown how the cotton parishes maintained a Whig tendency, even where slaves outnumbered whites by ten to one. Cotton was king and dependent upon slave labor, but the prosperity shared with sugar planters in the fifties was perhaps too great to risk losing without first exploring all roads to moderation. These were conservatives, and the Whig Party had been the home of conservatism, as well as aristocracy, in Louisiana. Up to Secession, these vested interests found sympathy with the Whig brand of States' Rights.

On the extremes of the political tendency the differential is clear; where the Democratic support was lowest the voter types ranked highest in proportion of slaves, and where the Democratic tendency was greatest the proportion of slaves was least. In the middle range, however, the relationship breaks down, for here the support of Slidell and Soulé factions obscures the pattern. Parishes with a high proportion of slaves, such as Rapides, Avoyelles, Assumption, and Ascension, as well as the Democratic Felicianas, were counted in the ranks of this faction. Table 10 in Appendix A shows the relationship to political tendencies in that slaves were a wealth-producing property.

If the cleavage between conservative planter and Democratic farmer was the predominant political tendency in the three decades before the war, then the breakdown of the Whig Party organization and the division of the Democratic Party into Slidell and Soulé factions left large groups of Louisiana voters politically voiceless when the issue of Secession became crucial. In this situation the forces of Slidell captured the state for the Democracy. A chance was lost to register a stand for moderation. Contemporary accounts tell of how the election of Lincoln frightened the slaveholders and led them to "desperate actions born of fear. . . . They were not angry at what happened in the long sectional controversy of the past, but intensely apprehensive of what the North might do in the future."[39]

The leadership in Louisiana did not wait long after the November election to find out what the Republicans might do. John Slidell had thought the South might rule within the Union, but now he found no alternative to Secession. Governor Thomas O. Moore had been hand-picked by the Slidell machine, and in December of 1860 he had called a special session of the Assembly and asked for an immediate election of delegates for a convention to be held on January 23, 1861, to consider the Secession. Action now rapidly followed action in the drama which soon became a tragedy.

The election for delegates was conducted on January 7, 1861, with all the form of a regular political campaign, and resulted in the

[39] Shugg, *Origins of Class Struggle*, 161.

triumph of the "state-action" or "immediate secession" factions.
A great many unanswered questions surround the action. Why was
so little time taken to call the legislature into session, to agree upon
holding a convention, to elect delegates, and why were the official
election returns suppressed until three months after the convention
had finished its business when a tabulation of parish votes was
released through a party organ, the *Delta*? So much remains obscure
that the suspicion of conspiracy has been raised. Yet, while it is true
that slaveholders were in the majority among the delegates, this
circumstance resulted from constitutional action taken back in 1852
when aggregate population was made the basis of representation.
The Secession convention could be called revolutionary in the sense
that the Assembly did not submit the question to popular referendum
as required by the constitution. In summing up the evidence
concerning these acts by the Louisiana "government of gentlemen,"
Roger Shugg states that "coercion and precipitate action all indicated
successful minority pressure rather than a conspiracy," and that
"the undemocratic procedure by which secession was accomplished
'was in pursuance of class and oligarchical political methods to which
the slave section of the country had been well accustomed.' "[40]

The fact that the Secession movement took place so soon after the
presidential election of 1860 makes it possible to investigate the
voting results of both by looking at the votes of parishes in the same
way that panel studies of voting trace changes of decisions on the
part of individuals who are reinterviewed over a period of time.[41]
This will be done below by using the unofficial parish tabulations
of the popular vote on Secession delegates, even though there is
some question regarding their veracity. While the rounding off of
votes and an occasional padding may have taken place, the tabulation
of total vote favorable to the Secessionists of 20,448 to 17,296 required
no great distortion. Students have, at any rate, accepted the number
of delegates to have been 83 Secessionists and 47 Cooperationists.[42]
When a computation using the questionable parish returns to recon-

[40] *Ibid.*, 169.
[41] Seymour Martin Lipset, *Political Man* (Garden City, 1960), 378.
[42] Shugg, *Origin of Class Struggle*, 164.

struct the support of delegates along the required lines of representative and senatorial districts is made, the results match. The location of the Cooperationist delegates can be determined by use of the parish tabulations of popular votes. Therefore it is possible to present data comparing Secession parish votes with the presidential vote of two months prior.

A coefficient of correlation between the rank order of parish support of Breckinridge and Secession of plus point 580 has been made. The 25 percent of variance thus accounted for is located at the extremes of the arrays, among the parishes which were discovered to be consistently Whig or Democrat in the previous decades. This is not as strong a regularity as might be expected, however, and therefore further analysis is called for in explanation.

The delineation of the Secession vote by parish (Map 4–4) makes it clear that the split in the vote was at least two-pronged. On the one hand stands the cleavage of hill-farmer and planter, especially in North Louisiana. On the other hand, the Secession vote can be seen to divide the state between North and South as well. Compared to the presidential vote two months before, more parishes fall at the extremes of percentage support for or against Secession. On the level of parish voter types, the units holding for moderation on the issue of Secession can be identified as Hill, South Louisiana Planter, and the Florida Parishes (Appendix A, Table 9). All the parishes in Southwest Louisiana opted for Secession, with the North Louisiana Planter unit nor far behind, nine parishes to one in favor of Secession. Sugar parishes in the South Planter area were split on the issue, as was the Bayou voter type area. Evidence of the ultimate effect of the malapportionment built into the Constitution of 1852 is found in the more than 40 percent of the total Secession vote contributed by the two Planter units and the Bayou Parishes. Still, it is also possible to note that the proportions of both Secession and Cooperation totals were quite evenly divided between the two interior sections, north and south.

More telling of the effect of using aggregate population as the basis of representation is the computed figure of the proportion of delegate strength which the forty-seven Cooperationist members

# The Vote for Secession, 1861

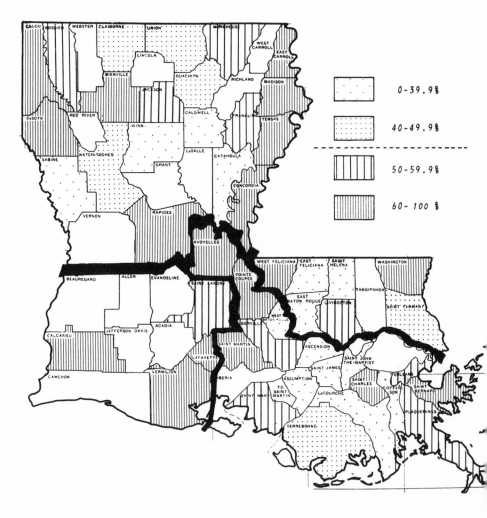

contributed to the total. It was found that 48.5 percent of the white males of voting age in the state had elected 32 percent of the delegates, and that the parishes involved held but one-third of all the slaves in Louisiana.

It is possible to extend the above analysis of the parish votes in 1860 as compared to the long-time tendencies measured by average percent Democrat in the presidential elections from 1836 to 1852. Whatever shifting occurred in 1860 can be traced further to the parish votes for delegates to the Secession convention. For the purpose of analysis—the Whig or Democratic average percentage of 1836–52, Union or Southern Democrat, 1860, Cooperation or Secession, 1861, and percent slaves, 1860—all can be tabulated by sets of parishes.

When the possible combinations are broken out, it is discovered that a heterogeneous set of the five Democratic parishes which had swung moderate in 1860 by voting Union (Set 3) continued this trend in supporting Cooperation in 1861. On the other hand, all but one of the eight Whig parishes which swung to Southern Democrat in 1860 (Sets 7, 8) remained radical in 1861 in support of Secession. At the same time, of the fourteen parishes which held to the moderate position through the presidential election (Sets 1, 2), these split almost 50–50 as eight stayed moderate and six swung radical to Secession. Finally, of the twenty-one parishes consistently Democratic through 1860 (Sets 5, 6), three-quarters of them supported Secession in 1861. The six parishes (Set 5) which swung from consistently Democratic to the moderate position can all be identified as hill-farmer parishes which refused to follow the Democratic compulsion to the ultimate of disunion.

Once more the question of the relationship between slaveholding and Secession can be considered and this time an association may be seen to exist. That is, the number of slaves proportionate to total population is highest in all parishes which voted for Secession. Still, in only the Hill Parishes, which had made the moderate swing to Cooperation in 1861, was the proportion slaves below 50 percent. Planter Parishes were distributed across the spectrum of opinion on the Secession issue, but it must be noted that in the two sets of

*Table 4-9*

COOPERATION AND SECESSION PARISHES, 1861,
BY PRESIDENTIAL VOTE, 1860; BY WHIG, OR DEMOCRATIC, 1836–52,
WITH PERCENT SLAVE, 1860

| | Whig 1836–52 Union 1860 | | Dem. 1836–52 Union 1860 | | Dem. 1836–52 So. Dem. 1860 | | Whig 1836–52 So. Dem. 1860 | |
|---|---|---|---|---|---|---|---|---|
| | (1) Coop. | (2) Sec. | (3) Coop. | (4) Sec. | (5) Coop. | (6) Sec. | (7) Coop. | (8) Sec. |
| (N) | 8 | 6 | 5 | — | 6 | 15 | 1 | 7 |
| Percent Slave | 52% | 74% | 58% | — | 48% | 62% | 36% | 65% |
| | Assumption | Madison | Ascension | | Caldwell | Bienville | Union | Avoyelles |
| | Lafourche | Morehouse | East B.R. | | Catahoula | Bossier | | Caddo |
| | Jefferson | St. Charles | E. Feliciana | | Claiborne | Calcasieu | | Concordia |
| | St. James | St. Martin | Ouachita | | Natchitoches | Carroll | | St. Bernard |
| | St. John | St. Mary | Winn | | Sabine | DeSoto | | St. Landry |
| | St. Tammany | (Orleans– | | | St. Helena | Franklin | | Tensas |
| | Terrebonne | proportion | | | | Iberville | | Vermilion |
| | West B.R. | slaves not | | | | Jackson | | |
| | | figured in | | | | Lafayette | | |
| | | total for | | | | Livingston | | |
| | | this set) | | | | Plaquemines | | |
| | | | | | | Pt. Coupee | | |
| | | | | | | Rapides | | |
| | | | | | | Washington | | |
| | | | | | | W. Feliciana | | |

parishes most heavily slaveholding, the swing to the radical position occurred at different times. Both had shown Whig tendencies in the period of two-party competition, but the set consisting of Madison, Morehouse, St. Charles, St. Martin, and St. Mary remained Union in 1860, becoming radical only when the issue of Secession reached a showdown.

One further refinement will be made by following through the analysis made by Seymour Martin Lipset in explanation of the emergence of the one-party South.[43] Lipset finds in seven southern states (Virginia, Alabama, Georgia, Mississippi, North Carolina, Tennessee, and Louisiana) a similar voting pattern to that discovered for Louisiana. That is, the strength of the Secessionist candidate Breckinridge lay with the whites living in those areas in which the slave population was least. Again, this would lead one to expect that the Whig slaveholders who backed Bell in the presidential election would continue as the principal source of Unionist sentiment, while the counties with few slaves would back Secession, in continuance of the tendency for Breckinridge. Such an expectation was fulfilled in neither Louisiana nor in the South. In Lipset's analysis the expected relationship between slaveownership and voting Unionist shown in the presidential election was completely reversed in the referenda. The counties with many slaves supported Secession, and those with few slaves backed the Union. The following is an adaptation of Lipset's data, comparing his South with Louisiana voting behavior:

*Table 4–10*
LOUISIANA AND SEVEN SOUTHERN STATES'
RELATIVE POSITIONS OF COUNTY (PARISH)
IN PROPORTION TO SLAVES AND PRESIDENTIAL VOTE, 1860,
AND SECESSION VOTE, 1861

| Relative Position of County (Parish) in Proportion of Slaves | (N) | Counties (Parishes) | | |
|---|---|---|---|---|
| | | Number for Breckinridge | Number for Secession | Number for Union |
| HIGH    7 So. States | (181) | 94 | 130 | 51 |
| Louisiana | (16) | 8 | 12 | 4 |

[43] Lipset, *Political Man*, 378 ff.

| MEDIUM | 7 So. States | (153) | 87 | 92 | 61 |
|--------|--------------|-------|-----|-----|-----|
|        | Louisiana    | (16)  | 10  | 8   | 8   |
| LOW    | 7 So. States | (203) | 130 | 75  | 128 |
|        | Louisiana    | (15)* | 12  | 7   | 8   |

* Excluding New Orleans.

Presented in this way, the shift in identification with the issue of Secession is easily located in the areas with both high and low proportion of slaves. It can be calculated that 20 percent more of the high-slave counties in the South supported Secession than voted for Breckinridge. The shift in Louisiana is found to be relatively similar, with 25 percent more for Secession. On the other extreme an opposite shift took place as 27 percent fewer low-slave counties in the South supported Secession than voted for Breckinridge; in Louisiana the figure is 33 percent less.

Lipset wanted to make one more cross-tabulation through which he hoped to make clear what happened in 1860–61. His figures are presented (Appendix A, Table 11) alongside comparable ones for Louisiana, including data on voter types. He states his case this way: "In the presidential election, men continued to vote along traditional party lines. When, however, party labels vanished and the issue became one of secession versus Union, the class of economic factors previously inhibited by party loyalties broke through. The slaveholders voted for secession in the referenda, while those living in areas with few slaves voted for the Union."[44] While admitting this generalization, Lipset went on to admit that party loyalties continued to have some effect on voting behavior. Thus, in the southern counties under consideration, nearly two-thirds of the high-slave counties which had been predominantly Whig in presidential voting continued this conservative tendency by voting to remain with the Union. On the other hand, one-half the low-slave counties which had supported Breckinridge shifted to a Union vote, while 86 percent of the low-slave counties which had opposed Breckinridge continued their Union support in 1861.

[44] *Ibid.*, 380.

Turning to the comparable data on Louisiana it can be seen that it follows the general pattern characteristic of Lipset's South and reiterates conclusions made above. The contribution to Secession and Union support on the part of each voter type is clearly visible. Lipset's writes:

> The old well-to-do Whig slaveowners and their followers continued in 1860 to oppose the southern demagogues from the lower nonslaveowning strata of the white population, and the latter remained loyal to the party of Jackson even after it became the party of slavery and secession. But once the die was cast and the vote represented an issue rather than a party, enough of the Breckinridge supporters opposed secession and enough backers of Bell, the Constitutional Unionist, supported it to make it accurate to say that, in proportionate terms, the slave-owners voted for secession and the non-slaveowning whites opposed it.[45]

In Louisiana it was farmer and sugar planter who joined forces, for neither desired to resort to bloodshed in the protection of vested interests. But there were not enough hill Democrats or sugar-bowl Whigs to halt the now inevitable move for disunion.

Inexorable circumstance had done its work. Party strife and failure, unequal representation, and cumulative political experience brought the tragedy of Secession. And in Louisiana, the tragic was touched with the ironic—for how curious that it had been Josiah Quincy of Massachusetts, who had protested Louisiana's admission to the Union in 1811, and the abolitionists of Massachusetts who vehemently protested her secession half a century later.

[45] *Ibid.*, 381.

# CHAPTER V

# Another Look at Reconstruction

## 1. The Electoral Foundation of Post-Bellum Politics: An Ecological Panel

The curves derived from plotted changes in total and voting populations decade by decade in Appendix A, Table 1 and Table 2 for nation, section, and state provide dramatic evidence of the hiatus created by the actions culminating in the Secession of 1861. It is as if a great tear had split the political fabric of society. Although the Civil War did not destroy the Democratic Party as a national organization, the party captured the presidency but two times before 1912, and its proportion of the popular vote emerged above 50 percent only in the disputed defeat of its candidate in 1876. In the defeated section, a struggle for power is revealed in the narrow percentage advantage the Democrats held over the Republicans. In Louisiana, however, said to be the state that bore the most severe Reconstruction experience,[1] close contest with the Republicans was, up to 1876, followed by a surge of extreme Democratic solidarity.

The gap between total population and voting age population narrowed in Louisiana after the war, for now, the Negro was reckoned to be a human being and a citizen whose vote made him an important pawn in the struggle for political power. The closeness to which the curve of voter registration approached that of voting age population is evidence of that. The Negro moved to center stage in the political drama of Reconstruction and its aftermath in Louisiana.

The Democratic Party remained strong in the old centers of Jacksonianism in the South, but also gained the support of and was even captured by the old Whig-supporting plantation owners and

---

[1] Willie Malvin Caskey, *Secession and Restoration of Louisiana* (Baton Rouge, 1938), vii.

their merchant cohorts in the cities. At the same time, the Republicans were able to gain the support of the poor whites from the mountain South who had backed the Whigs in the thirties and forties. This group had voted Consitutional-Union in 1860 and against Secession in 1861, fought for the Union, and remained loyal to the Republican Party through Reconstruction, the period of white supremacy, and the age of Roosevelt and Truman.[2]

Seymour Martin Lipset suggests that an "ecologial panel analysis" which investigated shifting county votes over a long period of time "would probably show that the two groups which were unstable in 1860–61 have been a potential source of change in the one-party South ever since Reconstruction."[3] The expectation would be for the old Whig classes to become Democratic, but miscast outside the Republican Party which became the inheritor of the Whig tradition. Well-to-do strata and areas which had remained Unionist in 1860 and Cooperationist in 1861 would be expected to have a propensity to shift to the Republicans today. On the other side, the Democratic farmer counties which shifted to the moderate side in 1861 "appear to be the same counties which, after the Civil War, backed agrarian third parties or 'populist' factions within the Democratic party, and which remain in the party now while the old Whig strata bolt to the Republicans as a reaction to the restored liberalism of the national Democratic party."[4]

While the profile of county support of Secession or Union is expected to remain in evidence as the voting behavior in subsequent electoral contests is traced, it cannot be expected that the pattern will be confirmed in detail in individual southern states. Thus, with the data used to show the voting behavior of Louisiana parishes in response to the issue of Secession or Union held constant in a panel, projected future tendencies based upon these propensities can be studied. Such an ecological panel analysis does reveal regularities in postwar politics but with only some similarity to the general expectation. (See Appendix A, Table 13)

[2] Seymour Martin Lipset, *Political Man* (Garden City, 1960), 383.
[3] *Ibid.*, 383.
[4] *Ibid.*, 383–84.

In the panel analysis, a difference is expected to be found in the subsequent votes of parishes which had favored Secession or Cooperation in 1861. The panel of Secession parishes, it is hypothesized, should number more in support of the Democratic Party than is true for Cooperation parishes, and the Secession panel should be on the Democratic side in the contest with the Populist-Republican fusion in 1896, and become anti-Long after 1928. There is a general confirmation of these expectations. Though both Secession and Cooperation parishes succumbed to the Democratic persuasion after Redemption in 1876, a hint of moderation is found on the Cooperationist side in 1896, before this tendency was obscured by the Bourbon ascendancy after the great disfranchisement of 1898, and the Louisiana version of the one-party South was perfected. Difference on the Cooperation side appears again in parish support of Longism, but in contemporary Louisiana it seems that some other variables must act to cancel out the Secession-Cooperation cleavage.

In the period of Reconstruction when the triumphant Republicans drew newly enfranchised Negro support at the polls, there was already a difference in the degree of support for the Democratic Party in both presidential and gubernatorial elections. More Cooperation parishes lined up on the Republican side, as is shown by the proportion of parishes within each panel found in the below 50 percent Democrat interval. Even after 1876, when the Democrats learned to use the Negro vote to advantage in overcoming the Republicans, relatively more Cooperation than Secession parishes continued to record a Republican sentiment. It is found that, consistently, the group of parishes in South Louisiana which had always been on the moderate side held out against the Democratic compulsion. Thus, for example, during the presidential elections in the period from 1880 to 1892 while of the total panel of Cooperation parishes only 15 percent could be placed in the below 50 percent Democrat interval, these South Louisiana parishes held out with 37 percent of them in the anti-Democratic interval.

The anti-Democratic Party sentiment in the Cooperationist parishes is clearly visible again in 1896 when the Democrats forced a showdown with the Republicans and their Populist friends. At this time, while the proportion of Fusionist parishes among the South Louisiana set was 40 percent, the proportion reached 100 percent among the North Louisiana Hills set of parishes which had optioned for Union in 1861. With the rise of Longism in 1928, still another clear distinction is found between Secession and Cooperation parishes. While North Louisiana Hills, frustrated in their Populist hopes a generation before, led the way, it is important to note that the parishes which sustained Longism along with the Hills units were the Whig-Union-Republican-Moderate set from South Louisiana. Finally, as a radical response to the contemporary civil rights issue seemed to obscure the differences between the panels, the moderation of South Louisiana could still be found intact, with most of the parishes involved in support of deLesseps Morrison and the Democratic Party. Now the set of parishes which included Secessionist Orleans, St. Charles, St. Martin, and St. Mary joined. The Secession-Cooperation cleavage had been superseded by a North-South Louisiana cleavage. Succeeding chapters must be devoted to an attempt to show how this happened.

Part of the answer to the question of what happened to the Secession-Cooperation cleavage can be found by observing that while the general expectations are confirmed, in making an ecological panel analysis two crucial considerations were omitted: (1) sixteen new parishes created after the war, many of them in Southwest Louisiana and populated by settlers with a background of different political experience; (2) most important, perhaps, differential location of the Negro population among the parishes after the war which might lead to a consequent acceptance of the "mind of the South" in differing degrees.

The Secession-Cooperation, or radical-moderate issue is entangled, then, with the Negro question. The presence of the Negro as a voter and competition for his political support which continued until 1898 could be expected to influence voting behavior within the parishes where his number was proportionally greater. When this period of mass politics was ended in the Bourbon white supremacy which built the "solid South," it could be said that the Negro question was resolved, not to be raised again until the second half of the twentieth century, after Longism has broken the ascendancy of the Bourbons. This section cannot be concluded, then, without an investigation of the Negro's presence after the war, within the population, and on the voter rolls before taking up once more the historical narrative.

The search for the Negro presence after his emancipation from slavery can begin looking again at the ecological panel which measures the proportion of Secession or Cooperation parishes with few or many slaves. As was shown in Chapter 4, the proportion of Secession parishes with a ratio of slaves to whites above 50 percent was greater than for the Cooperation parishes. To put it another way, 40 percent of the Cooperation parishes had a slave ratio below 50 percent compared to the 29 percent in the case of Secession parishes. The important consideration, however, is to find whether this difference in the degree of Negro presence continued after the war. It did, although the Secession panel showed more consistency, 29 percent of the parishes therein remaining in the below 50 percent interval in all three cases: (1) the slave ratio in 1860; (2) Negroes in the population up to 1900; and (3) the percentage Negro voter registration. The only shifts are to be found in the distribution of parishes in the two above 50 percent intervals. On the Cooperation side, while the proportion of parishes with few Negroes seemed to decline after the war, the proportion of parishes with few Negro voters registered had increased. A further explanation through a more detailed investigation seems in order.

The computation of rank order coefficients of correlation between parish arrays of percentage slaves, percentage Negroes after the War, and the percent of Negroes registered to vote, should make it possible to determine the constancy of the Negro presence.

*Table 5–1*

PARISH RANK ORDER COEFFICIENTS OF CORRELATION
BETWEEN ARRAYS OF "NEGRO PRESENCE," 1860–1900

| | Parishes | | |
| --- | --- | --- | --- |
| NEGRO | Percent Slaves 1860 | Percent Negroes 1870–1900 | Percent Negroes Registered 1880–88 |
| Slaves 1860 | – – – – – | + .866 | + .876 |
| Negroes 1870–1900 | – – – – – | – – – – – | + .821 |
| Registered 1880–1888 | – – – – – | | |

There is clearly an areal continuity here, indicating that, while the newly freed slave did engage in some geographic mobility, to a very large extent the freeman remained a resident in the general location of his previous servitude. The rank-order coefficient for the relation between slave and Negro location, before and after the war, accounts for 75 percent of the variance in the parish arrays. Even more, 77 percent of the variance, is accounted for in the computation of the relationship between parish slave location and that of percent Negro of the total parish voter registrations. Here is further evidence in confirmation of the tendency for parishes which had high ratios of slaves to arrange, through registration, for high ratios of Negro voters. In other words, it appears that three-fourths of the parishes tended to register Negroes, after the war, up to their proportionate number in the population.

The fact that the degree of regularity drops when the rank order arrays of Negro residence and Negro registration after the war are compared, from three-fourths to two-thirds of the variance, can best be explained through reference to the accompanying maps (Maps 5-1 and 5-2). It can be seen that the slave population had followed the river systems so that the delineation of high slave ratio suggests a letter "Y". The delineation of the average ratio of Negroes from 1870 through the census of 1900 shows that the Negro continued to reside in the plantation parishes along the alluvial bottoms, but with some differences. That is, the Negro presence tended to be relatively greater after the war, in the Ouachita River area, along Bayou Macon, up the Red River bottoms, and into the Hill Parishes along the Arkansas border. While the eye may find little difference between the delineation of Negro residence and Negro registration, yet an inspection of the array of parish percentages indicated an important regularity. When an increase in the proportion of a parish population that was Negro took place, the relative number of Negro voters registered was less.

When the same data is assembled by voter types (Appendix A, Tables 15 and 16), this tendency for an increase in Negro population to be followed by a lesser proportion of Negro registration is located in North Louisiana voter type areas. On the other hand, when a unit

# Percent Slaves in Population, 1860

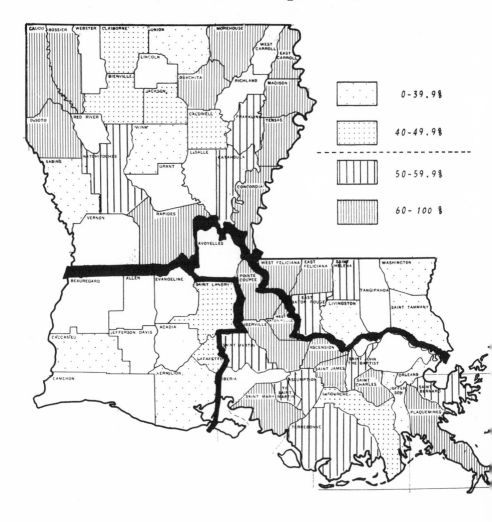

0 - 39.9%

40 - 49.9%

50 - 59.9%

60 - 100 %

experienced a decrease in its Negro population, the proportion of Negro voters registered tended to approximate the population ratio. The central Pine Hills followed this pattern, which had characterized the South Louisiana voter type areas. The North Louisiana Hills, Macon Ridge, and even the North Louisiana Planter unit, all had proportionally fewer Negroes registered as voters.

To locate the Negro presence is extremely important, for any analysis of post-bellum politics in Louisiana must take into consideration the mass conditions that prevailed. That is, the general tendency from 1867 to 1898 was for nearly all to become registered to vote, who were voting age and male, white or black. But while a vigorous competition prevailed in the electoral contests, one important element of that competition was a struggle to control or to make use of the Negro vote, first by the Republicans and later by the Democrats. Negro ratios in the voter types are found to be greatest in the antebellum plantation units. Checking the percentage of the state registration of 1888 which each voter type contributed, it can be seen that a potential advantage existed in the very units which had ruled Louisiana before the war as a consequence of the determination of representation.

Thus, it can be calculated that the North and South Louisiana Planter units, together, contained 31.2 percent of the total voter registration in 1888. At the same time, however, this nearly one-third of the registration of voters was made up of but 18.5 percent of the state's white registrants, while 46.1 percent of the Negro voters resided in the Planter units. Two other units are found which contained proportionally more of the state's Negro voters than of the white voters. These are the Florida Parishes and the Bayou Parishes where planters were also present in relatively large numbers. The freemen of these parishes remained economically dependent upon their former masters who had controlled them as slaves. Within such a framework post-bellum politics would be played.

# Average Percent Negro in the Population
## 1870-1900

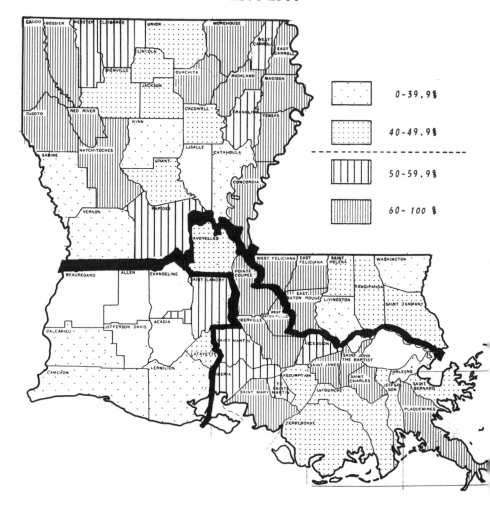

II. *Picking up the Pieces: 1862–1867*

If it is true, as Frank L. Owsley put it, that Louisiana was to become *"the* horrible example of Reconstruction,"[5] certainly the circumstances surrounding Secession and the eventual occupation of New Orleans and adjacent parishes in the spring of 1862 by federal troops gave no indication to forecast such an outcome. The parties' failures led to Secession, but if it were correct that the war had been fought for a slaveholding minority, a great many Louisiana voters had seemingly voted for moderation. Her Unionist supporters intended that compromise on the slavery issue be explored thoroughly. While many of these voters ultimately became Secessionists, they were moderate, and sought a method of deliberation and cooperation. Moreover, the presidential vote of 50,500, over half of which could be labeled as moderate, became important because it would form the basis for Lincoln's "10 per cent plan," in the restoration of rebel states to the Union. The 1860 election map indicates that South Louisiana, where the majority of voters was to be found, had been overwhelmingly Unionist. Because of this Lincoln chose Louisiana for his plan to restore a Confederate state when, in a state election, the number of votes counted amounted to 10 percent of 1860 vote. The people were to be allowed to pick up the pieces of statehood and begin afresh the struggle for political power.[6]

General Benjamin F. Butler entered the city of New Orleans on May 1, 1862, but sixteen months after Louisiana had seceded. It is thus reasonable to believe that remnants of Union sympathy remained intact, especially in New Orleans, where the laboring classes had never found favor with slavocracy. The Confederates, from whose ranks the former power structure had been manned, were discredited. Now, the once out-voted lower classes found the political balance had tipped to their side, and that an outside force in the form of federal troops had a hand on the scales. Federal occupation did not preclude the

---

[5] Caskey, *Secession and Restoration*, xii.

[6] Ultimately there were three plans for re-entry; (1) Lincoln's reorganization; (2) Johnson's restoration; and (3) the Radical's reconstruction; Gerald M. Capers, *Occupied City* (Lexington, 1965) gives a fresh account.

possibility of the formation of an acceptable civil government even though positions were reversed and the Unionists now held control. It was politically logical for the Lincoln administration to desire successful restoration of the most deeply southern state. This led W. M. Caskey to argue that this period of Louisiana history best be designated as reorganization rather than reconstruction.[7] He differed with Roger Shugg, who a year later wrote that the occupation precipitated within the state first a social revolution and then a counter-revolution.[8] In Shugg's view, the revolution began with the establishment of a government under Northern auspices. But this interpretation tends to read the events of 1862 through glasses colored by subsequent events. Maybe Reconstruction could not have been otherwise, yet, objectivity requires the assumption that the motives of Louisiana Unionists and Federals alike were above suspicion, and that the evidence suggests the verdict.[9]

A harsh Reconstruction did occur in Louisiana, but the question is: Was it inevitable? After the war, Louisiana faced many problems, four major ones having been listed by Professor Edwin Davis: (1) the restoration of state and local self-government; (2) the rebuilding of agriculture; (3) the development of industry to supply basic home needs; and (4) the definition of the place in society of the newly freed Negro. Davis adds, "Louisianians would have liked to be left alone to solve their own problem in their own way, but this, of course, was not to be."[10]

Whether or not they acted from motives of expediency, citizens of Louisiana who found themselves now within the lines of the federal troops had no choice but to work with the military and civil representatives of President Lincoln. A Union Association had sprung up in New Orleans by late May. With encouragement from Washington, it was organized by Michael Hahn, a former Douglas supporter who had migrated before the war from Bavaria.[11] There was no shortage of

[7] Caskey, *Secession and Restoration.*
[8] Roger W. Shugg, *The Origins of Class Struggle in Louisiana* (Baton Rouge, 1939; paperback, 1968), 196.
[9] *Ibid.*, Shugg devoted but two pages on the years 1862–63.
[10] Edwin A. Davis, *Louisiana: The Pelican State* (Baton Rouge, 1959), 220.
[11] Caskey, *Secession and Restoration,* 57, 108.

potential members ready to espouse the movement. So-called "Great Union Demonstrations" were held throughout the summer preparing the population, so that in September, 1862, a total of 67,920 Louisianians had taken the "oath" of allegiance to the Union and to the Constitution.

The Unionists agreed in the main with President Lincoln that a state could not legally leave the Union. They were quite ready when General Shepley, Lincoln's Military Governor, in June, 1862, prepared to restore partial civil government within the state by calling a congressional election in the first and second districts which constituted the occupied territory.

In December, 1862, Benjamin F. Flanders and Michael Hahn were elected congressmen from these districts. In the first district the total vote cast was 2,543, more than half the total vote of 4,011 in the congressional election in 1859. In fact, Flanders received 366 more than a majority of the 1859 vote. The total vote in the second district was likewise more than half that of 1859, 4,874 compared to 8,944, and here, Hahn's 2,581 votes constituted a majority of 54 over his three opponents.

Caskey explains why a vote of 7,417 was a signal triumph and boded well for future Reconstruction. Although 15,000 voters were registered in 1862, registration was not a voting requirement during the occupation, and several thousand potential voters were away in the armies. Further, in the last five elections before the war, the average vote in New Orleans had been only 7,310.[12]

But the reestablishment of a civil government rested upon the decision of the House of Representatives to accept the credentials of Flanders and Hahn. On February 17, 1863, after weeks of debate, Hahn delivered a convincing speech in which he contended that New Orleans was a Union city, and not a hotbed of Secession.[13] The final vote for seating the two members was 92 to 44.

Many were heartened by this beginning, and anticipation ran high after Congressman Hahn revealed that Lincoln promised him hopes of a speedy organization of state government. However, the Louisiana

[12] Ibid., 65.
[13] Ibid., 73.

phase of the war was not to be completed so easily. General N. P. Banks, who replaced Butler, began his campaign to bring the entire state into federal control in 1863. But it was more than two years later that General Kirby Smith laid down his sword in June of 1865. Another delaying factor was lack of agreement among the Unionists as just *how* to effect restoration.

At frequent Union meetings all agreed on the wish to eliminate maritial law, but the Unionists were divided on the main issues of the day. One group, who called themselves the Conservatives, consisted largely of Union-minded slaveholders, who, with much at stake, had been ready to repudiate Secession and to preserve the Union, but earnestly hoped to preserve slavery. The Conservatives wanted to stand upon the Constitution of 1852 and the fundamental issue was whether Louisiana should be restored to the control of their kind under the old constitution, or put in the hands of a majority of loyal white people under a new organic law.[14]

The other faction of Unionists, the Free State Party, became dominant in the Union Association, and, with not so much at stake as the planters among the Conservatives, grew more radical and "it seems to have recognized that a social revolution was in the making, . . . contended that slavery was dead, and that a convention should frame a constitution that would meet the needs of the new conditions, . . . a constitution by which both the rights of 'white men' and a 'free soil state government' would be secured."[15] This group would triumph, in the end, not only through currying the favor of General Banks and the federals, but also by virtue of its appeal to New Orleans labor, which, always inclined to economic radicalism, had by 1863 organized the Working Men's Union League. Its platform called for objects cherished by immigrant laborers before Secession: (1) the abolition of slavery; (2) the removal of every Negro from Louisiana by colonization; and (3) the admission of all white men to suffrage with no restrictions to residence.

In January of 1864, General Banks ordered that an election be held for state offices, and further, that in April, delegates should be elected

[14] Shugg, *Origins of Class Struggle*, 198; Caskey, *Secession and Restoration*, 75.
[15] *Ibid.*, 77.

for a constitutional convention. Why this order of sequence was given has not been examined. The Free Staters nominated Michael Hahn for governor and Madison Wells for lieutenant governor, while the Conservatives gave opposition with the nomination of J. G. A. Fellows. A radical faction of the Free State Party backed B. F. Flanders, who was advocating swift moves to enfranchise the Negro. "Hahn's speeches articulated the class interest of labor in New Orleans and exposed the reactionary danger of pleas by the conservatives for political laissez faire and restoration of the old order. . . . Numerous if not preponderant among their supporters at the polls was labor."[16] For this reason the election of Hahn cannot therefore be considered surprising, and the results must have been gratifying to the military authorities who were ever so anxious that the total vote cast meet the 10-percent-of-1860 quota, and at this juncture had tried to discourage support of Flanders.

The administration ticket won with huge majorities, Hahn supporters piling up 6,171 votes out of the total of 11,355 votes cast. Fellows was second with 2,959 votes, and Flanders a poor third with only 2,225. Indeed, the total vote that General Banks reported was twice as much as Lincoln's requirement; the vote of 5,771 polled in New Orleans alone would have sufficed. The new state government quickly received the blessings of President Lincoln, who recognized Hahn as civil governor under the old constitution and also invested him with the powers then being exercised by General Shepley, the military governor. Almost as quickly, however, numbers of Unionists had begun to question the legality of the whole proceedings. Although they did not prevail, these Unionists argued that Banks had violated the consitution by arbitrarily deciding upon an election date, and by his manner of defining qualifications of voters. The Free State government was established, however, and Louisianians turned to the task of formulating the organic law of the first free state.[17]

The constitutional convention of 1864 was attended by white delegates from the federally occupied part of the state only, but was construed to represent the entire loyalty of the state. Although the

[16] Shugg, *Origins of Class Struggle*, 199.
[17] Caskey, *Secession and Restoration*, 107, 110, 115.

delegates understood the problems of the state, Shugg labeled the resulting document as revolutionary, and his judgement seems accurate when the background of these delegates is considered. According to Shugg, labor was even more prominent in the constitutional convention of 1864 than in the election of governor earlier that year.[18] Mindful of the issues of the 1850's these *nouveau arrivé* undoubtedly intended to redress their old grievances concerning the machinations whereby in 1852 the planters had built their power by gaining control of the General Assembly.[19] This was one reason, perhaps, why no Negro suffrage was put forth at this time. It was said that "any granting of the suffrage itself to the Negro might well serve to re-establish the control of those on whom the Negro must depend for his livelihood."[20]

A more compelling factor working against Negro suffrage was the position of the federal authorities. General Banks had assumed that to extend the franchise to the Negro at this time would fly in the face of the wishes of Congress and northern citizens. It would not be acceptable to establish a government dominated by Negroes, who were a majority of the population.[21] New Orleans "free colored" had earlier gone to Washington to speak directly to President Lincoln in favor of at least the partial recognition of their political rights. Lincoln had then written Governor Hahn asking him to consider "whether some of the colored people may not be let in."[22]

The convention delegates had early demonstrated strong sentiment against Negro suffrage, and, while later in the session a resolution was passed authorizing the legislature "to pass laws extending suffrage to such other persons, citizens of the United States, as by military service, by taxation to support the Government, or by intellectual fitness, may be deemed entitled thereto," the word "Negro" did not appear

[18] Shugg, *Origins of Class Struggle,* 200.
[19] Charles W. Tapp. "Development of the Constitutional Appointive Power of the Governor of Louisiana" (Master's thesis, Louisiana State University, 1964), 28.
[20] James W. Prothro, "A Study of Constitutional Developments in the Office of the Governor of Louisiana" (Master's thesis, Louisiana State University, 1948), 73.
[21] Tapp, "Development of Constitutional Appointive Power," 35.
[22] Caskey, *Secession and Restoration,* 130.

in the document adopted.[23] At this time, before ratification of the Civil War amendments, it was generally thought that Negroes were not citizens.

The suffrage was extended, in 1864, to all white males of twenty-one years age or over who could meet the one-year residence requirement. The constitution established representation on the basis of qualified voters, with no restrictions to be placed upon New Orleans. It revived the 1845 restriction on banks and corporations. A progressive income tax was inaugurated. Minimum wage and maximum hours for laborers in public work were established. There should be public schools for black as well as white. Finally, slavery was abolished, this being the first Louisiana constitution to mention the term. As one student of Louisiana constitutional development has said, it seemed for a brief moment that the political outsiders, the poorer whites, had been victorious.[24]

With this new dispensation of power placed in the hands of loyal white citizens, who found they could hope to work under the moderate stance of the Lincoln administration, Louisiana, it appeared, was off to a good start in re-establishing her statehood. The constitution was ratified on July 23, by a large majority of those who voted, but with less than the 10 percent of the vote desired by the Federals. Little enthusiasm was found for elections believed to be under partisan control. While it might be expected that eventually returning Confederates would repudiate such a constitutional document, there might be something to gain by going along with it; besides, there was hardly any other choice. Confederates might find themselves able to work with Lincoln and Johnson, as had the natives of Unionist sentiments. The political actions of the returned Secessionists, however, would be bound to lead to conflict with the Radical wing of the Republican Party if and when it gained the upper hand in Washington.

The first legislature to meet under the new constitution assembled in New Orleans on October 3, 1864. In adressing the body, Governor

[23] *Civil Action No. 2458* (U.S. District Court, Eastern District of Louisiana, Baton Rouge Division), *U.S.* vs. *State of Louisiana*, John Minor Wisdom for the majority, 13.
[24] Tapp, "Development of Constitutional Appointive Power," 40.

Hahn displayed his Unionist convictions as he decleared: "While this state was thus momentarily placed by the bad men who had conspired against the national authority in armed hostility to the Union, no patriot ever conceded or with truth and propriety admitted, that its people had ever sanctioned the atrocious doctrine of secession; and although for a time, under rebel control as under Federal military occupation the inalienable rights of the state were in abeyance, they were never lost or surrendered."[25]

In this vein, then, Hahn concurred in the legislature's resolution of proscription against Confederates. This resolution favored prosecution on charges of perjury and treason of the Confederate leaders of the state, including such antebellum notables as John Slidell and Judah P. Benjamin. At the same time punishment should be imposed upon all the legislators who had gone along with the Secession convention, all those who had signed the Ordinance of Secession, or who had failed to renounce their treason and swear loyalty to the United States. All persons who found themselves included in this proscription were, in addition, barred from legal citizenship. As Leslie M. Norton has put it: "Such a measure was a prophetic indication as to the nature of the Reconstruction of the State of Louisiana according to vindictive policies of the Northern extremists and radicals."[26]

Shortly after this, however, Hahn resigned the governorship in order to serve as United States Senator. He was succeeded by Lieutenant Governor James Madison Wells, who promptly indicated a more conciliatory attitude towards the Confederate veterans returning in numbers by the spring of 1865. Although many felt that the recently adopted constitution was invalid, Governor Wells proceeded to call an election for state officers that year in accordance with the new instrument of government. Wells was nominated by the Democrats, and another group, appreciative of the merits of Louisiana's wartime governor, Henry W. Allen, nominated him for the post. This was little more than gesture, and Wells was elected by a large majority of 80.2 percent.

[25] Leslie M. Norton, *Readings in Social Science: Louisiana 1699–1876* (Baton Rouge, 1936), 185.
[26] *Ibid.*, 185.

Wells had by proclamation given full legal status to the Confederate parishes which had held out until the end of the war. His attitude was constructive: "Whatever may have been the cause of the outbreak and however bitter may have been the feelings engendered in the hearts of some, it is better that all such matters be buried out of sight forever. It is not the past, but the present and future, we have to deal with. You must go to work to organize civil government in your respective parishes."[27] They did, and in the statewide elections defeated the Free Staters and gained control of the legislature.

A contemporary summed up the feeling toward Wells in a letter written to former Governor Moore, exiled in Cuba: "Governor Wells bears . . . the same happy relation to Louisiana that President Johnson bears to the whole South. Their instincts, if not of the States' Rights school are yet for *justice to the South* and they are and will show themselves to be true to their instincts. . . . Governor Wells from a combination of circumstances . . . [is] the most fortunate selection which could be made to carry out the true policy—the President's policy— the patriot's policy—a reconstruction of the Union on the basis of the perfect equality of the states."[28]

A look at the distribution of the election returns in favor of Governor Wells shows the appeal, so far, of his actions. In fourteen parishes out of the forty-eight voting, Wells received 95 percent or more, and there was a pattern in the distribution. It might be supposed that this electorate was anxious to put the affairs of government in order once more. Along the Mississippi, the parishes voted overwhelmingly for Wells. These were planter areas; the cotton parishes, which had moved for Secession, and also the sugar parishes, which had been in the ranks of the Cooperationists in 1861. Now they were in accord once more. The bulk of the voter types had followed suit, leaving only five parishes that had not given a majority vote for Wells. This was still, however, a minority electorate, as the total vote was only 27,809, the lowest since the election of 1846.

[27] *Ibid.*, 186.
[28] Quoted in Walter M. Lowry, "The Political Career of James Madison Wells" (Master's thesis, Louisiana State University, 1947), 84.

The nature of the support given Wells in the election of 1865, in which representatives of all antebellum groups were to be found, seemed another assurance that Louisiana would be able to achieve successful restoration. There were, however, other politicians to contend with. Henry Clay Warmoth, for instance, considered in Louisiana histories to have been a carpetbagger, was claimed by the Radical Republicans in Louisiana to be the delegate to Congress from the "territory" of Louisiana; they felt the existing Democratic government based upon the 1864 constitution was fraudulent. Washington recognized neither Warmouth nor the two elected senators.

During the first two years of Wells's administration circumstances arose which brought on Reconstruction and forced Louisiana government into the hands of "avaricious adventurers and ignorant Negroes."[29] First was the Black Codes, enacted by the Democratic-controlled legislature to aid local police juries in bringing order to the wandering, disorganized, and unemployed Negroes, cut adrift by emancipation. This action, taken by their former masters, reduced the Negro to a "condition which lay between peonage and serfdom."[30] Although the Black Codes made the Negroes work and prevented their idle wanderings, the angered Republicans and northern Radicals could claim that the Negro was returned to the status of slavery.

Such legislation under the plans of restoration endorsed by the Johnson administration gave northern Radicals a golden opportunity to mobilize public opinion in favor of a mandate for the Congress to "reconstruct" the Confederate states. It was not the Black Codes themselves, but the Radicals' use of them, which brought them into disrespect. There was little chance for a happy solution. Since the southerners pragmatically assumed the necessity to effect social control of Negroes whether by a general, the Bureau (Freedman), or the state legislature, they were vulnerable to attack when judged before the absolute doctrines of liberty and equality for all. Their methods were

---

[29] Norton, *Readings*, 186.
[30] Shugg, *Origin of Class Struggle*, 213.

more especially subject to attack when they were misrepresented to the conscience of the nation.[31]

Things went from bad to worse as the Democratic-controlled Louisiana Legislature split with Governor Wells. Wells had apparently been a man of moderation and sympathy for the problems of his state; he was also the only governor to serve during restoration and Reconstruction who was a native Louisianian. After his election in 1865, however, he experienced trouble with the legislature, for while he had shrewdly enlisted the support of the numerically strong and influential ex-Confederates in furtherance of his own political fortunes, these previously dominant groups had ambitions of their own.[32] Wells had pressed for the ratification of the Fourteenth Amendment in the General Assembly session beginning in December of 1866. His support of the amendment displeased the conservative Democrats, but, this was no time for the ex-Confederates to assert themselves and expect the social and political orders to fall back into the old slots. While the Negro problem had to be solved, no new Black Code, no matter how mild, could stand for long in Louisiana. Meanwhile, Radical Republicans were organizing in New Orleans, with ambitious plans for how best to gain political control of the state.

The coup de grâce occurred as an unanticipated result of reconvening the constitutional convention of 1864 on July 30, 1866. The bill for a new constitutional convention had been passed by the General Assembly, whose Democratic members wanted to write a document reclaiming their former ascendancy; it was vetoed by Governor Wells, reintroduced, and passed the second time by the requisite two-thirds majority. Only the intercession of President Johnson, who, fearing this would open the door to Radical control, halted the move.[33] On the other hand, Radical Republicans in Louisiana likewise wanted a new constitution—for entirely opposite reasons. The Radical leaders sought to keep the way to their own political future open through the enfranchisement of the Negro and

---

[31] Roland Paul Constantin, "The Louisiana 'Black Code' Legislation of 1865" (Master's thesis, Louisiana State University, 1956), v.

[32] John R. Ficklin, *History of Reconstruction in Louisiana* (Baltimore, 1910), 104.

[33] Norton, *Readings*, 189.

by denying the vote to ex-Confederates. But any new convention generally representative would be overwhelmingly Democratic. The Radicals found what seemed an ingenious solution to their quandary in an unusual resolution passed by the convention of 1864: "Be it resolved that when this convention adjourns it shall be at the call of the president, whose duty it shall be to reconvoke the convention for any cause."[34]

The New Orleans Riot of 1866 was the primary reason the Radical Republicans were able to wrest control of Reconstruction from President Johnson, and it had been precipitated by the resistance to efforts to reconvene the convention of 1864. With the convention in session at Mechanic's Institute Hall, armed white men lay in wait nearby as a group of Negroes marched down the street to the hall. One shot triggered a desperate fight, resulting, according to official reports, in 38 deaths and the wounding of 146.[35] Shugg has called it a "massacre" provoked by white radicals "to transfer the franchise from Confederate veterans to freed men."[36] If the white Democrats regretted the incident, they nevertheless blamed it upon the Radicals and Negroes, and if "behind the July 30 explosion of blind rage lay a fundamental inability of the whites to accept the emancipation of slaves and its revolutionary implications," now it appeared that "the wind had been sown and the whirlwind reaped."[37]

Congress passed the Reconstruction Act in March of 1867 which divided the recalcitrant southern states into districts. General Philip H. Sheridan was appointed commander of the Fifth Military District, including Texas and Louisiana. He ordered Governor Wells to vacate his office and in his place appointed Benjamin F. Flanders. When, further, Sheridan ordered a new registration of voters, the results of which showed two-third of the total to be Negro, hope faded for the perpetuation of Democratic control of state affairs.

Although this registration was made under the supervision of

[34] Donald E. Reynolds, "The New Orleans Riots of 1866, Reconsidered," *Louisiana History*, V (1964). 7.
[35] *Ibid.*, 5–6, 13.
[36] Shugg, *Origins of Class Struggle*, 216.
[37] Reynolds, "Louisiana Riots," 14, 27.

federal officers, its significance cannot be overemphasized. Not only was this the first recorded registration of voters statewide, but also this list of franchised voters would become the electorate which would choose delegates to the constitutional convention of 1868, as well as substantially that which would cast ballots for gubernatorial and presidential candidates that year. Furthermore, now the federal authorities were determined to extend the franchise to include the Negro. It becomes important, therefore, in the analysis of the votes in subsequent elections, to be able to locate his presence among the parishes.

The Louisiana Legislative Documents of 1869 show that 129,716 citizens were enfranchised to vote in the registration of 1867. Of this total, 45,189 were whites but almost twice as many, 84,527, were Negroes. The white registration count was 82 percent of the total number of whites who had voted in the presidential election of 1860 and is evidence of the disruptions which war and Reconstruction created (Appendix A, Table 14). The radical proportions within the electorate would be close to 50–50 in the decades to come, but at this time, with North Louisiana but recently reconciled to the war's end and to federal control, the Negro clearly represented the balance of power. For, while in the election of 1860 the North Louisiana parishes had contributed 38 percent of the total vote cast, this area made up but 32 percent of the statewide 1867 registration, and now 76 percent of the North Louisiana electorate was Negro. It was little better in the South Louisiana parishes where there was a gain of 4 percent in the state totals (from 37 percent of the vote cast in 1860 to 41 percent of the registration in 1867), but where 67 percent of the electorate was now Negro. Meanwhile, in the urban New Orleans area, where 27 percent of the total state registration was but 2 percent more than its contribution to the 1860 vote, white registrants made up 36 percent of the state total; more white voters were registered in 1867 than had voted in 1860. At the same time, here as well, the Negro voters outnumbered the whites, with 54 percent of the area total.

Since 65 percent of the state's registered voters were Negro, white supremacy would be difficult to maintain.

III. *Politicians of Fortune: Carpetbag Government, 1868–1876*

The coalition of ex-Confederates and Unionists sharing common views with Governor Wells might have indicated that in a few years members of the old power structure would dominate once more. But, in 1866, Wells joined forces with the Democratic radicals and his remarks at that time anticipate a struggle between radical and conservative. Wells said that only by giving all Negroes the right to vote could the large Democratic or conservative majority possessed by the ex-Confederates in Louisiana be overcome.[38] Actually, it made little difference in the outcome that the Democrats had become divided, for, in 1867, General Sheridan called for a constitutional convention to be held the next year in order that Louisiana meet the conditions that Congress imposed upon the former Confederate states. They must ratify the Fourteenth Amendment which extended the legal protection of the federal government to include the Negro, and they must grant him the suffrage.

The nearly equal number of Negro and white delegates among the ninety-eight admitted to the convention clearly showed how the new electorate, registered to vote in 1867, would behave. The convention of 1868, one of the first constitutional assemblies ever convened in the United States without distinction of race or color,[39] proceeded to fashion a political instrument which, in comparison with that under which members of the antebellum power structure operated, was extremely radical. It was the first constitution in Louisiana containing a bill of rights, using a phrase from the Declaration of Independence. Schools were desegregated and discrimination in public conveyances prohibited. A literacy test was rejected, and the Negro was granted the suffrage while at the same time restrictions were placed upon unrepentant ex-Confederates. Residence requirements were established in such a way that the political fortune hunters swelling the population of New Orleans could begin to act with the full privilege of citizenship. This meant that with the aid of native scalawags Republican domination would be guaranteed, providing the Negro vote could be

[38] Lowry, "James Madison Wells," 119.
[39] Norton, *Readings*, 190.

influenced. It would be possible to outmaneuver, if not to outnumber, the Democrats.

The thesis of Roger Shugg that the Constitution of 1868, following closely that of 1864 extending the rights of white labor in Louisiana, was a second social revolution, has been contested. Charles Tapp points out that the events of 1868 cannot be seen as part of the historic pattern of constitutional development in Louisiana, but as outside the mainstream—a detour as it were. While it is true that both the movements of 1864 and 1868 shared the similar element of discontent, the Constitution of 1864 had been approached with delegates who understood the problems of the state. There was no such common bond in 1868 among a congery that included Negroes, emigrant Yankees, demobilized federal soldiers, and whites who disliked planter domination. Tapp draws the telling conclusion that the Constitution of 1868 was written not because the delegates were effecting a genuine social revolution but because of events that had been set in motion outside the state.[40]

What the Constitution of 1868 really did was to change the substance of Louisiana politics: what had been a contest among whites with opposing interests became a contest among whites for Negro support. In this contest it is supposed that the Republicans, who had posed as benefactors of the Negro race, held the natural advantage. The parade of corruption and governmental abuses ushered in by the newly elected carpetbag administration, consisting of Republicans and their Negro front men, served to widen a breach between many Louisiana whites and the blacks. The white response to these circumstances forged an alliance between the poor white and the remnants of the planter-merchant oligarchy of former times.[41]

The constitution had been adopted by the eligible voters, and in the subsequent election for state offices, Henry Clay Warmoth was elected governor. His lieutenant governor was Oscar J. Dunn, a Negro. The relationship between Negro registration and support for the carpetbagger is suggested in the closeness of the state-wide

[40] Tapp, "Development of Constitutional Appointive Power," 45, 47.
[41] Ibid., 47–47.

averages, 65 and 63 percent respectively. A more detailed confirmation is found in the distribution of percentages by voter type areas:

Table 5-2
PERCENT NEGRO VOTER REGISTRATION, 1867,
AND PERCENT VOTE FOR HENRY C. WARMOTH, 1868,
BY VOTER TYPE AREAS

| Unit | Percent Negro Registration | Percent Warmoth Vote |
|---|---|---|
| North Louisiana Hill | 50% | 50.1% |
| Central Pine Hill | 61 | 62 |
| North Louisiana Planter | 88 | 72 |
| Florida Parishes | 67 | 49.9 |
| South Louisiana Planter | 72 | 82 |
| South Louisiana Bayou | 64 | 67 |
| South West Louisiana | 53 | 75 |
| Urban Area | 65 | 52 |

The two Planter areas with the highest proportion of Negroes registered showed the greatest Warmoth support, while the inverse generally was true for farmer areas. The central Pine Hills Negro registration was inflated by Natchitoches Parish (80 percent) while in Southwest Louisiana, St. Landry had a Negro registration of 60 percent as opposed to the area average of 53 percent. Reconstruction began in earnest under a Republican coalition made up of Negroes, scalawags, and carpetbaggers. Louisiana was to witness an unprecedented struggle for political advantage where, it has been said, "Republican politicians organized the Negro vote, massed it, and carried it to the polls."[42]

The question of the Negro's fitness for self-government is pertinent, for without education and with no previous political experience, the undignified and inappropriately frivolous behavior of Negro represen-

[42] Norton, *Readings*, 192–93.

tatives in the General Assembly was predictable.[43] The issue of Negro participation in Louisiana politics was a serious one, because his presence tipped the balance of power to the Republicans. It was to combat this advantage that Democrats organized secret societies such as the Knights of the White Camellia in order to terrorize and intimidate the Negro and secure white supremacy.

The first official record of intimidation and violence came with the contest for President in the fall of 1868. The Republicans won nationwide with General U. S. Grant, but in Louisiana the Democrats managed to influence the Negro vote and the state's electoral vote went to the Democratic candidate, Governor Horatio Seymour of New York. The Republican spokesman, Governor Warmoth, claimed that Democratic success in Louisiana was obtained through the most disgraceful acts of intimidation. A record of both the presidential vote and acts of intimidation are available, statewide, and at this point an analysis of their distribution will be made.

In 1868, the Democrats were able to carry but 47.3 percent of the presidential vote, nationally, and their success was not much better across the South, where 55.5 percent of the total vote was Democrat. In Louisiana, however, where the electorate was voting for President for the first time since the war, an overwhelming 70.7 percent of the votes favored the Democratic candidate. This surge of voting solidarity was not sustained throughout Reconstruction, for in the election of 1872 and 1876, Louisiana, with Democratic support of less than 50 percent, trailed the South and the nation. Of course, the critical question is which tendency was the exceptional one. On the one hand, there exists the evidence of the close antebellum contest between Democrat and Whig. On the other hand, a look forward reveals the Democratic solidarity manifested after the end of Reconstruction (Appendix A, Table 2).

The more extreme degree of solidarity manifest in 1868 is apparent when the relative proportion of parishes with Democratic votes above and below 50 percent is compared:

---

[43] *Ibid.* An example of the moral tone of the legislature is seen in the words of one member who called upon the Speaker to recognize him: "I rise to a point of order—this bill is a swindle." 193.

*Table 5-3*
NUMBER OF PARISHES BELOW AND ABOVE 5o PERCENT,
PRESIDENTIAL DEMOCRATIC, 1868, AND AVERAGE, 1868–76

Number of Parishes
Democratic Percentages

| Election | Below 50% | Above 50% | |
|---|---|---|---|
| 1868 | (19) | (37) | Democratic Violence |
| 1868–76 | (26) | (56) | Republican Control of Election Machinery |

Although it is clear that in 1868 the parish voting tendency was for Democratic majorities, what is even more important is that, of the parishes which had voter support above 60 percent, exactly half of them were over 99 percent Democratic, and over three-quarters of them were more than 80 percent Democratic. This high degree of solidarity of the 1868 parish distribution might indicate a determination to oppose Radical Republican interference in Louisiana politics, the same solidarity that condoned Democratic violence. On the other hand, the conflict manifest in the relatively high degree of variance found in the Reconstruction set of elections suggests that Republicans were having some success with the electoral machinery in Louisiana. These generalizations are supported by further statistical analysis and by historical record.

It is within-state differences in the voting behavior of parishes that explain the 1868 Democratic surge of solidarity. A surprising regularity is found by comparing the percentage votes of the clusters of parishes called voter types in this study. A close relationship exists between voter type Democratic percentages in the 1868 presidential election and the average for those of the 1868–76 period. A rank order coefficient of correlation of +.995 can be computed, for in only two voter types was there a shift in the relative ranking of Democratic percentages. Where a voter type area like the North Louisiana Hills remained high in Democratic support throughout the Reconstruction elections, in 1868 it was at its highest.

Since the question of how the new electorate would vote is crucial, a further step is to compare it with Negro registration. With the suffrage of the Negro an established fact, the expected outcome in 1868 should be a Republican victory at the polls. Logically, if voter turnout was uniformly high and if all Negroes voted Republican, defeat of the Democrats was assured. But in 1868 this did not happen as the following tabulation shows:

*Table 5-4*

PERCENT NEGRO REGISTRATION AND PERCENT
PRESIDENTIAL DEMOCRATIC, 1868, BY NORTH AND
SOUTH LOUISIANA VOTER TYPE AREAS

| Voter Type | Percent Total Voter Turnout | Percent Negro Registration | Percent Democratic Vote |
|---|---|---|---|
| No. La. Hills | 92% | 50% | 99.8% |
| Southwest La. | 91 | 53 | 99 |
| Pine Hills | 83 | 61 | 83 |
| Bayou | 78 | 64 | 60 |
| Floridas | 91 | 67 | 65 |
| So. La. Planter | 87 | 72 | 38 |
| No. La. Planter | 83 | 88 | 55 |

To control Negro voter registration by frequency distribution among voter types is to determine whether the Democratic support was more or less than that expected if all Negroes voted Republican.

*Table 5-5*

FARMER-PLANTER GRADIENT IN PERCENT NEGRO
REGISTRATION COMPARED TO PERCENT PRESIDENTIAL
DEMOCRATIC VOTE BY VOTER TYPE AREAS

| Parish Voter Types | Percent Negro Registration | Percent Democratic Vote |
|---|---|---|
| North Louisiana | 72% | 73% |
| South Louisiana | 68% | 50% |

After noting that the percentage turnout of voters in the non-urban areas of Louisiana was uniformly high in 1868, a number of generalizations may be drawn. While there was no one-to-one correspondence between percent Negro registration and percent Democratic vote, a regularity can be observed. The greater the proportion of Negroes registered within a voter type area, the lower the percentage of Democratic support. The relationship moves in the expected direction but more than that, a distinctive division within the gradient is to be found. There is a farmer-planter cleavage but more than that, the Democratic percentage is much greater than expected even if all Negroes within the farmer areas voted Republican.

An explanation of the general correspondence between the degree of Negro registration and support of the Republicans in 1868 can be found among the following: (1) Negroes were persuaded to vote Democrat; (2) contrary to expectation, Negroes were committed Democrats; (3) the Democratic votes had been stuffed into the ballot boxes; or (4) Negroes had been intimidated by terror and violence. All of these are possibilities. Certainly more violence occurred in those parish areas that were highest in support of the Democrats.

A joint committee on the conduct of the presidential election of 1868 reported to the General Assembly. In the tabular summary presented here, the ratio of the number of acts of violence for every one hundred ballots cast is compared to the percentage Democratic vote by voter types. The farmer unit consists of the two North Louisiana Hills voter type units together with Southwest Louisiana; the mixed unit contains the South Louisiana Bayou and Florida Parishes; as indicated the two planter units are left separated.

*Table 5–6*
RATIO OF NUMBER OF ACTS OF VIOLENCE, PRESIDENTIAL ELECTION, 1868,
AND PERCENT DEMOCRATIC VOTE BY VOTER TYPE AREAS

| Units | Percent Democratic vote | Ratio acts of violence per 100 voters |
|---|---|---|
| Farmer . . . . . . . | 90 | 54 |
| North La. Planter . . . | 68 | 34 |
| Mixed. . . . . . . . | 60 | 27 |
| South La. Planter . . . | 38 | 9 |

In 1868 the Democratic consensus was localized, and the state's electorate had divided, with North joining Southwest Louisiana in contributing the largest proportion of the Democratic vote. In these areas nearly three-fourths of the violence occurred, as well. In Reconstruction presidential elections, the contours of Democratic support rose highest in the Hills Parishes, across Southwest Louisiana and the Florida Parishes. The behavior of the North Louisiana Planter unit is not so easily explained, however. Within-unit difference is found both for the degree of Democratic support and for the proportional contribution to the statewide violence of 1868.

While the northern Planter Parishes had contributed 26 percent of the total violence, fully two-thirds of it occurred in the parish of Franklin, intermediate in location between planter and farmer areas. Likewise, while nearly 90 percent of the registered voters here were Negro, in 1868 the unit had averaged 68 percent in Democratic support. A distinct difference in support is discovered, however, when parishes are aggregated into Mississippi Delta and Red River categories, with Rapides serving as a geographic link between the two:

*Table 5-7*

NORTH LOUISIANA PLANTER VOTER TYPE AREA PERCENT
PRESIDENTIAL DEMOCRATIC, 1868, AND AVERAGE, 1868-76

| | Percent Democratic 1868 | Percent Democratic 1868-76 |
|---|---|---|
| MISSISSIPPI DELTA | 22% | 23% |
| Carroll | | |
| Madison | | |
| Tensas | | |
| Concordia | | |
| RAPIDES | 42% | 32% |
| RED RIVER | 100% | 60% |
| Bossier | | |
| Caddo | | |
| DeSoto | | |

The cluster of parishes far up the Red River showed the same complete
Democratic solidarity as had the neighboring Hill Parishes, and while
the average Democratic support here during the Reconstruction period
receded to 60 percent, it was dissimilar to the other Planter categories,
which were solidly Republican in support. At least one factor
contributing to the higher Democratic percentages up the Red River
is the greater proportion of whites among the voters there, 22 percent
compared to 9 percent in the Delta.

At this time, Rapides and the four Planter Parishes fronting on the
Mississippi River can be seen, together with the South Louisiana
Planter Parishes, to profile on the map what may be called the
"fracture line" of subsequent Louisiana politics, held together by the
Negro presence. Why did South Louisiana as a whole and the Planter
units in particular provide such comfort to the Republicans? Ante-
bellum Union sentiment, the acquisition of many plantations by
Yankee arrivals, the registration of the Negro population, and the
sugar bowl's concern with Republican tariff policy—all led South
Louisiana to Republican ascendancy.

If a resort to violence in the conflict of Reconstruction could help
account for the Democratic surge in the presidential election of 1868,
the tactics of Republicans to count themselves in helped produce the
Republican majorities of 1872 and 1876. In the struggle for power,
violence and disorder prevailed, despite the presence of federal troops,
and gubernatorial elections became one important battleground. In
this conflict "no race, class, or party could lay virtuous claim to clean
hands."[44] The violence attendant upon and resulting from the 1868
presidential election had prompted the Republican-dominated
General Assembly to change the registration and election laws. An
"election," or "returning board" was established, empowered to
examine, pass on, and throw out all votes considered fraudulent.
"This law placed dictatorial powers in the hands of the Governor,
and that Governor was Warmoth."[45]

While Governor Warmoth quickly acquired almost unlimited
power for his administration of state affairs, and even managed to win

[44] Shugg, *Origins of Class Struggle*, 226.
[45] Norton, *Readings*, 194.

the adoption of a constitutional amendment in 1870, which would have made him eligible for re-election, by the end of 1872, this first Reconstruction regime in Louisiana collapsed with the attempted impeachment for wrong-doing of the governor. Not that Warmoth's quest for power or his misuse of authority was involved in this defeat. It was "both the opposition's jealousy of Warmoth's leadership and its own desire to control the state, rather than any wish for reform, which caused the collapse of the Warmoth regime."[46] Nor did Warmoth's fall bring relief from Louisiana's Reconstruction; the practice of politics in the grand style pioneered by Warmoth became Republican standard procedure. Furthermore, the Democrats, noting the methods and successes of the Republicans adopted and applied them in the new era after 1877.

Reconstruction was in full swing, and with elections coming up in 1872 a whole series of caucuses and nominating conventions was held as numerous interests maneuvered for advantage in the power struggle. Coalitions became transitory. The local Republicans had begun to quarrel among themselves as early as 1870, and at least two factions emerged. Each determined to grasp control of state affairs through electoral success, for, by now, the fruits of victory were exceedingly precious in terms of personal status, political power, and economic gain.

One Republican faction drew its power from federal patronage, and the members of this "customhouse crowd" desired to give nothing less than full support to the Grant administration to guarantee its continued advantages. The Republicans wanted control of the General Assembly in 1872 so that they could engineer means of reducing the power of Governor Warmoth, who had fallen out with the Grant forces.

The other Republican faction gravitated to the administration of Warmoth, and they hoped to hold their advantage through the powers of his office. In the face of widespread corruption, which in this period was not confined to one state or section, Carl Schurz and other leaders of note created a new organization, the

[46] Althea D. Pitre, "The Collapse of the Warmoth Regime, 1870–72," *Louisiana History*, VI (1965), 187.

Liberal Republican Party. When, in 1872, both Liberal Republicans and Democrats supported the nomination of Horace Greeley of New York for the presidency in opposition to Grant, Governor Warmoth had found a base from which to operate in the attempt to keep his control of Louisiana affairs.

Events began to move more swiftly when, in late 1871, the first of three successive Negroes to hold office, died—Lieutenant Governor Oscar J. Dunn. In the struggle to replace him, Warmoth succeeded in having his ally, State Senator P. B. S. Pinchback take the position. Strengthened by this move, the so-called Pinchback faction caucused in May and nominated Warmoth for governor and Pinchback as his running mate. Warmoth declined on the grounds that many delegates had wanted to make an alliance with the customhouse faction, and Pinchback was given first place on the ticket.

A faction of Liberal Republicans was organized within the state, and it too put a slate of candidates into the field. The Democrats were busy with their own plans to regain control, and to further complicate matters a new group, the Reform Party had nominated candidates. This party, which had been organized in December of 1871, was composed for the most part, of former Whigs and prominent citizens who had been opposed to the Slidell Democracy and who now were willing to forget party names and party considerations in order to reform allegedly existing abuses in the state government.[47]

By mid-August fully five state tickets had been announced. They included the following:

Table 5-8
STATE TICKETS IN 1872 PRESIDENTIAL AND GUBERNATORIAL ELECTIONS

| Party | | Governor | Lt. Governor |
| --- | --- | --- | --- |
| Republican | Customhouse | William Pitt Kellogg | C. C. Antoine |
| | Pinchback | P. B. S. Pinchback | A. B. Harris |
| | Liberal | D. B. Penn | John S. Young |
| Democratic | | John McEnery | B. F. Jonas |
| Reform | | George Williams | B. F. Jonas |

[47] John Edmond Gonzales, "William Pitt Kellogg: Reconstruction Governor of Louisiana" (Master's thesis, Louisiana State University, 1945), 10.

This imposing array was reduced to two tickets, however, in a series of maneuvers for fusion. The Louisiana Liberal Republicans wanted to fuse with the Democratic-Reform-Pinchback groups, but the first two named refused coalition with the Pinchback group. Then Pinchback joined forces with the Customhouse faction and was persuaded by them to accept the office of Congressman-at-large. The Liberal Republicans, Democrats, and Reformers at last agreed to a fusion that resulted in a two-ticket contest on November 4, 1872:

*Table 5–9*
FINAL STATE TICKETS, 1872 ELECTIONS

|            | Governor       | President      |
|------------|----------------|----------------|
| Republican | W. P. Kellogg  | U. S. Grant    |
| Fusion     | John McEnery   | Horace Greeley |

The Louisiana Democrats thought that fusion with the Liberal Republicans and the Warmoth adminstration held a great chance for victory, and so it seemed, for the Governor used his returning board to advantage. When the returns came in, victory was claimed by McEnery, but the rival returning board of the Kellogg faction spelled doom for the Democrats. Two rival governments actually were established after this, but this was Reconstruction, and because the federal government officially recognized the customhouse factions, the count of their returning board was accepted, and their candidate for governor placed in office through force of arms.

It was political irony worth noting[48] that the Democrats, who had heaped so much scorn upon Warmoth earlier, should now go down in defeat with him. For, with the support they had been able to muster, the Democratic Party's move for fusion had seemed a wise one. The returns, which had been made official, gave Kellogg a majority of over seventeen thousand votes; the New Orleans compilation was allowed to stand with a six-thousand majority for McEnery. It was in the country parishes that the Republicans allegedly piled up

---

[48] Norton, *Readings*, 196.

their count. All accounts agreed that fraud was prevalent, and since the administration in Washington desired a Republican outcome in any case, even if McEnery really had carried the state by a majority, it is doubtful if he would have been permitted to take office.[49]

Even President Grant himself was not sure who had won, for in summing up the problem in 1875, he said: "It has been bitterly and persistently alleged that Kellogg was not elected. Whether he was or not is not altogether certain, nor is it any more certain that his competitor, McEnery, was chosen. The election was a gigantic fraud, and there are no reliable returns of its results. Kellogg obtained possession of the office, and *in my opinion has more right to it than his competitor.*"[50]

Charge and countercharge echoed all the way to the halls of Congress where, if no definite conclusion could be reached, at least, a thorough canvass of the counts of the two returning boards was made. As General Grant had easily won, the Republicans felt no need to question Louisiana's presidential vote. The rival counts are tabulated here, however, with the contested gubernatorial counts, in order to demonstrate the astonishing regularity with which the electorate allegedly voted:

*Table 5–10*

1872 ELECTION RESULTS PROMULGATED
BY RIVAL RETURNING BOARDS

|  | Democratic Count | Republican Count |
|---|---|---|
| Greeley | 66,467 (53%) | 57,029 (44%) |
| Grant | 59,975 (47%) | 71,663 (56%) |
| TOTAL | 126,442 | 128,692 |
| McEnery | 64,467 (54%) | 55,249 (43%) |
| Kellogg | 56,373 (46%) | 72,890 (57%) |
| TOTAL | 120,840 | 128,139 |

[49] Gonzales, "William Pitt Kellogg," 28.
[50] *Ibid.*, 26, italics added.

While the Republican returning board's count of total votes cast for both governor and President was more consistent than the Democratic count, it is the extremely close similarities in the proportions of votes for the candidates of the two parties which warrants attention. In the results of the gubernatorial election, there was no simple difference that a reversal of numbers could change. These differences resulted from a cumulation of consistent variations in reporting election results on the parish level. In the Republican count, which was allowed to stand as official, Kellogg's margin over McEnery was almost twice as great as that of McEnery over Kellogg in the count of the Democratic returning board.

Further analysis showed that in as many as twenty-four parishes the returning board counts were in substantial agreement:

Table 5–11
COUNT IN 24 PARISHES ON WHOSE VOTES
RETURNING BOARDS AGREED IN 1872

|  | Democratic Count | Republican Count | Registration White | Registration Negro | Margin of Majority |
|---|---|---|---|---|---|
| Democrat. . . . | 36,679 | 33,817 | 52,979 |  | 476 |
| Republican . . . | 36,203 | 35,590 |  | 51,469 | 1,673 |

In this set of parishes the average between the two majorities gave Kellogg a margin of a thousand votes. Moreover, the Democratic vote and white registration and the Republican vote and the Negro registration correspond. Not so, however, in the remaining thirty-four parishes, regarding whose vote the controversy raged. It was here that the glaring discrepancy in the number of Republican votes showed up:

Table 5–12
COUNT IN 34 PARISHES ON WHOSE VOTES
RETURNING BOARDS DISAGREED IN 1872

|  | Democratic Count | Republican Count | Registration White | Registration Negro | Margin of Majority |
|---|---|---|---|---|---|
| Democrat. . . | 27,788 | 22,432 | 34,786 |  | 7,618 |
| Republican . . | 20,170 | 37,300 |  | 42,879 | 14,668 |

Assume there was the same regularity between registration and vote in the second set as in the first, and it is clear that the Democratic returning board did not give enough votes to the Republican candidate. "If the same ratio of republican votes was given for the 42,000 colored registered voters as of democratic votes given by 34,000 white registered voters, which was 27,788, the republican vote would be 35,000 instead of 20,170."[51] On this basis alone, the combination of Kellogg's majorities in the two sets of parishes would have guaranteed victory.

Checking the number of parishes with major discrepancies between the counts of the rival returning boards, within the Louisiana voter types, it was found that the distribution divided the state quite evenly. Few units were not suspected of suffrage fraud, 45 percent of the parishes with discrepancies being found in North Louisiana. In all, some 68 percent of the parishes with suspect returns belonged in the two Planter units and the South Louisiana Bayou voter type.

Assuming that most Louisiana voters in the election of 1872 were motivated by the belief that their vote would count, the distribution of support shown by either set of election returns was in a predictable direction. That is, *Hills* units and those of the southwest prairies, where in general the white registration outnumbered the colored, gave highest Democratic support, regardless of whose count was used. In striking contrast to the political tendencies of these farmer parishes was the solid pattern of Republican support within the parishes traversed by the Louisiana river systems. Of the twenty-three such parishes which in profile fill up the "Y" outlined by the courses of the Red and Mississippi rivers, only urban Orleans gave a majority to the Democratic candidate in the election of 1872. Here was the fracture line of Louisiana politics in clear display, for the most part Planter Parishes with a unity of Republican support held together, of course, by the presence of the Negro. The pattern to be typical in the future appeared—but in reverse, so to speak.

This was a struggle to the political death. Governor Kellogg, with federal troops at his elbow, showed no disposition toward moderation;

[51] *The Louisiana Adjustment: Governor Kellogg's Election in 1872 and the Fraud of the Fusionists* (New Orleans, 1875), 11.

his rule was absolute, and the steady erosion of Louisiana's economy continued. One historian has declared that government under the carpetbaggers could only be labeled, in modern parlance, "a racket."[52] Because of two inescapable dilemmas, one of a racial and social character and the other racial and economic, the Radical Republicans found themselves in a situation where a failure to find resolutions could lead only to violence.

The Republicans' first dilemma was that their electoral majority consisted of Negro votes. A cumulative tension developed; reliance upon the ballots of one race, the weaker one at that, led to a counter tendency toward a united hostility on the part of the other race. In this circumstance the Negro was unreliable, for whatever his political allegiance, he was bound to white planters out of economic necessity.

The second dilemma was more subtle, but just as thoroughly alienating to the white electorate. Since the Republican radicals lacked the confidence of white business interests and relied upon the federal army for their power, they were unable to draw upon the customary supports found in the economic development of the state. The carpetbaggers turned to political exploitation and fed at the trough of public revenues. As a result taxes went ever higher, without increased benefits and with the effect of further depressing trade and agriculture.

It was in response to the financial ruin fostered by war and increased by Reconstruction that led to the action which has been called the Louisiana "unification movement" of 1873.[53] The terrible burden of taxes and public debt imposed by the Republicans prompted businessmen and planters from New Orleans and South Louisiana to attempt to solve their problems rationally through a political unification of the races. These reformers seemed confident that the Negro could be controlled, if his allegiance to the Republicans could be broken. A primary source of conflict would be eliminated, and Louisianians would be free to follow their eonomic interests in a more congenial atmosphere. T. Harry Williams found these reformers to be motivated

---

[52] Shugg, *Origins of Class Struggle*, 231.
[53] Vincent J. C. Marsala, "The Louisiana Unification Movement of 1873" (Master's thesis, Louisiana State University, 1962).

by economics and not the desire to raise the status of the Negro to first class citizenship.[54] The pragmatic realism of these citizens notwithstanding, economic reform was not achieved now by the union of the races. Little support was in evidence from either the whites or the blacks, and professional leadership was lacking.

Racial strife continued, meanwhile, and Louisiana became an armed camp in 1873 as a result of the "Colfax riots" in Grant parish which caused the death of a number of Negroes. Once more federal authorities found further necessity for keeping troops in the state. The Negro had found a place in Louisiana politics, but his position was not a comfortable one. Salvation for the Democrats lay in the overthrow of Negro rule and the Republican Party. Negro suffrage was a stern fact, and the block of Negro votes was an important stake in the political struggle. There were a number of ways to deal with the reality, the most extreme of which was terror.

The first inclination was to discredit the Negro at the polls. The planter would ensure that his former slave looked ridiculous as a citizen. The events which actually followed lend credence to the remarks of P. B. S. Pinchback, Louisiana's only Negro governor who had served briefly at the time of the attempted impeachment of Warmoth: "Democrats in many portions of the State instigated and thrust the most ignorant colored men that could be found for election to the Consitutional Convention with the view of making that Constitution of 1868 a farce; and in order to make success certain they put no competing candidate in the field. . . . The illiterate men returned home successful statesmen and from that day to this nearly every man in Louisiana has felt himself every inch a statesman and from this policy has arisen in a great degree the ignorance that has found its way into the public offices of our state."[55]

There were other ways to meet the problem of the Negro vote. After the defeat of 1872, in the local elections which preceded the

[54] T. Harry Williams, *Romance and Realism in Southern Politics* (Baton Rouge, 1966), Lecture 2.
[55] Pinchback before the House of Representatives, June 8, 1874; quoted in Agnes Smith Grosz, "The Political Career of P.B.S. Pinchback" (Master's thesis, Louisiana State University, 1943).

next gubernatorial election, the Democrats prepared for drastic action. In 1874 the secrecy of the Knights of the White Camellia and the Ku Klux Klan was abandoned, and on April 27th, in Opelousas, the first White League was organized. It openly vowed to overthrow Kellogg and the Republicans and re-establish the white man's party. The Shreveport *Times* put it this way: "The carpetbaggers' careers are ended; we are determined to tolerate them no longer; and if they care for their infamous necks, they had better stop their work right now and look out for a safer field for rascality. If a single hostile gun is fired between the whites and blacks, every carpetbagger and scalawag that can be caught will in twelve hours be hanging from a limb."[56] Federal control made it impossible to overthrow Negro rule in a legal manner, so it was decided to circumvent the Negro domination by subterfuge or extralegal action.

The White League began to demand the resignation of Republicans in local as well as state offices, and the demands led the Kellogg administration's organized forces to counteract the League's armed militia. When on September 14, 1874, the Crescent City White League successfully fought a pitched battle with Kellogg's forces, took control of the city, and established the Democrats in the State-house, President Grant was called upon to send sufficient troops to put down the White Leaguers, and the tide turned against the Radicals in Louisiana, forecasting the success of the Redeemers in 1876.[57]

In 1876 the Democrats overcame the carpetbag government, and since the total votes increased by between 17,000 to 40,000 over that of the previous election, it is not feasible to believe that redemption was gained merely by suppressing the Negro vote. The Democrats may have stuffed ballot boxes, but, in fact, the Redeemers went all out to woo and win the Negro. Their task was made easier, perhaps, because the cumultative results of carpetbag misrule weighed heavily against the Republicans. The exploitation of the state coffers by these political adventurers, and the fact that the Negro had gained little in the process, weakened Republican chances.

[56] Norton, *Readings*, 196.
[57] Wisdom, *U.S.* vs. *State of Louisiana*, 17.

It became evident early in the campaign that the Negro vote would again play the deciding factor, and the *Picayune* keynoted the policy of the Democrats: "We must convince the Blacks that we are in earnest in our expression of good will, and they, for their part, must evince a disposition to meet us half-way. As ours is the superior race, at least by culture and experience, it becomes us to take the initiative. Let us endeavor to persuade the colored people that an alliance of the two races is necessary to the preservation of their common safety."[58]

Francis T. Nicholls, the Democratic nominee for governor, promised not to let the carpetbag returning board count him out should he win the election, and he kept his word by beating the Republicans at their own game; he made a deal. The Republicans needed every vote they could get for their presidential candidate Rutherford B. Hayes to defeat the Democrat Samuel J. Tilden. It was the closeness of that race that enabled Nicholls to keep his chair.

After the November 7th election Tilden could count on 184 electoral votes, only one vote short of winning. But those votes included victories in the carpetbag states of South Carolina, Florida, and Louisiana where there would be Republican-controlled returning boards to recount. These "visiting statesmen" from the North arrived in Louisiana where the Democrats had won by a majority of eight thousand votes, a margin not easily brushed aside. Easy or not, the returning board gave the election to Hayes.[59] Then they swapped the Republican presidential count for the Democratic gubernatorial count.

After Hayes was made president with the help of this Louisiana deal, he removed the returning board appointee for governor— S. B. Packard—and recognized the Nicholls government. Federal troops were withdrawn from Louisiana, and Packard surrendered the Statehouse to the White League which had been protecting Nicholls. Reconstruction was over.

Again, as in the elections of 1872, the regularity with which the electorate allegedly voted is discerned, and now, the stability of Reconstruction voting behavior can be noted:

[58] Quoted in Hilda Mulvey McDaniel, "Francis Tillou Nicholls and the End of Reconstruction" (Master's thesis, Louisiana State University, 1946), 29.

[59] John D. Hicks, *The American Nation* (Boston, 1945), 142.

*Table 5–13*

1876 ELECTION RESULTS PROMULGATED
BY RIVAL RETURNING BOARDS

|  | Democratic Counts | Republican Counts |
|---|---|---|
| Tilden | 83,723 (52%) | 70,508 (48%) |
| Hayes | 77,174 (48%) | 75,315 (52%) |
| TOTAL | 160,897 | 145,823 |
| Nicholls | 84,487 (52%) | 71,198 (48%) |
| Packard | 76,477 (48%) | 74,624 (52%) |
| TOTAL | 160,964 | 145,822 |

The Nicholls vote, distributed among the parishes, showed that, if the Negro voted Democratic in some numbers, he had little influence on the results. The parishes which contained predominantly Negro registered voters were carried by the Republicans. Although the planter elite retained control of the Democratic Party, as always, they owed victory to the weight of the farmer vote. Most of the parishes in the highest quartile of the arrayed Nicholls vote were located in the hills and prairies. The ancient Democratic prejudice remained a factor to be reckoned with.

And what of the traditional Whig tendencies? All of the parishes of the sugar country were high in the number of Negro voters and, together with New Orleans, they were the sources of Republican strength. Joined with the Negro predominance in the Red River and Mississippi Delta parishes, these Republicans were still a formidable force, and would remain the chief opponents of the Democrats in electoral contests up to 1896. The official count had showed Nicholls the victor, but with only 52 percent of the 160,964 votes cast. This was the largest number of votes ever tallied in a Louisiana election.

It is possible now, to show the general distribution of Democratic and Republican tendencies in the Reconstruction period (Maps 5–3 and 5–4). This can be done by presenting a tabular summary of parish voter type behavior which combines both gubernatorial and presidential elections. The parish average voting percentages distributed in a scatter-diagram are collapsed into four sets of frequency intervals:

Table 5–14
PRESIDENTIAL DEMOCRATIC, 1868–76, AND
GUBERNATORIAL DEMOCRATIC, 1872–76, BY
PERCENTAGE INTERVALS BY VOTER TYPE AREAS

Number of Parishes

| Unit | LOW-LOW Gub. 0–49% Pres. 0–49% | LOW-HIGH Gub. 0–49% Pres. 50–100% | HIGH-LOW Gub. 50–100% Pres. 0–49% | HIGH-HIGH Gub. 50–100% Pres. 50–100% |
|---|---|---|---|---|
| So. La. Planter Parishes . . | 7 | – – – | 1 | – – – |
| So. La. Bayou Parishes. . . | 4 | 3 | 1 | – – – |
| No. La. Planter Parishes . . | 6 | 3 | – – – | 3 |
| Central Pine Hills . . . . . | 1 | 2 | – – – | 3 |
| No. Louisiana Hills . . . . | 2 | 1 | – – – | 4 |
| Florida Parishes . . . . . | 2 | – – – | 1 | 5 |
| Southwest Louisiana . . | – – – | – – – | – – – | 5 |
| Urban Area . . . . . . . | 1 | – – – | – – – | 1 |
| STATE TOTAL . . . . . . . | 23 | 9 | 3 | 21 |

Cross-tabulated as a scatter-diagram, it would appear that the few parishes falling into the middle ranges, together with those from the voter type units generally high in Democratic support, but with some parish exceptions in the low percentage intervals, prevent the generation of a high correlation. Yet, a cleavage is apparent and in the expected directions. Planter units gave little Democratic support in either gubernatorial or presidential elections, while farmer units registered high support. It is important to note now, however, since an analysis of tendencies in subsequent elections will show a dramatic shift, that planter parishes from both North and South Lousiana had been placed in the low-low percentage interval of Democratic support.

Finally, it is informative to examine the congressional delegation during the years of the Republican domination (Appendix A, Table

# Average Presidential Democratic Vote
# 1868-1876

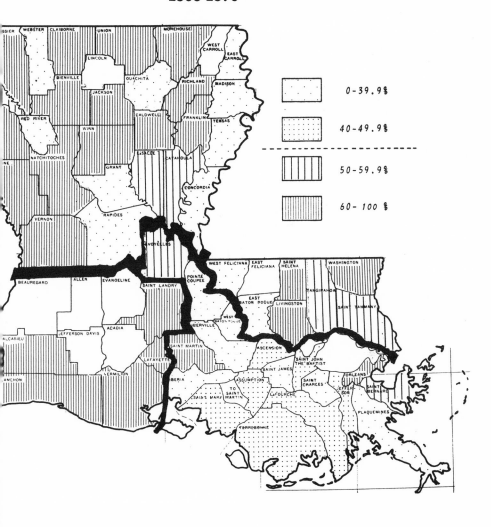

# Average Gubernatorial Democratic Vote
## 1872-1876

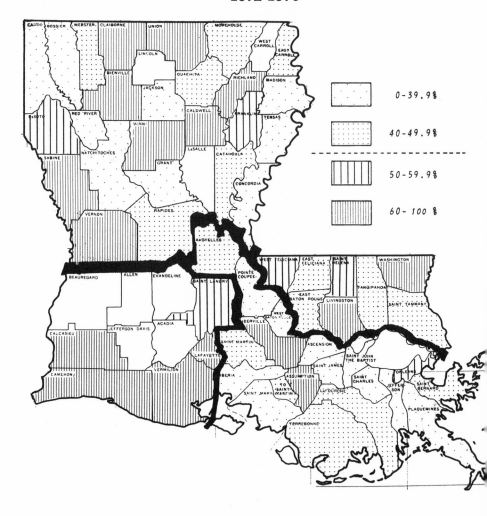

0 - 39.9%

40 - 49.9%

50 - 59.9%

60 - 100 %

12). The background of the delegates is about what one would expect it to be in this period of unrest and uncertain social mobility in Louisiana. Republicans predominated, of course, but where antebellum delegates had been drawn mostly from among lawyers, now there was not only an increase in the number of military officers and just plain adventurous politicians, but, also, proportionally many more delegates from the planter class.

## iv. *Louisiana Redeemed*

Although the withdrawal of troops in 1877 did open politics to the Democratic Party of the Redeemers and ended the federal attempt to enforce an egalitarian Louisiana, it did not immediately establish white supremacy. There were still many parishes where Negroes were entrenched in local office, and that institution of Reconstruction, the Louisiana Lottery Company, remained a force of political influence. It had donated funds to the administration of the Redeemers in 1877 and, with great strength in the legislature, was seeking to perpetuate its influence by an extension of its charter.

Governor Nicholls, however, now began his opposition to the lottery; he vetoed the legislative enactment, but the lottery company with help from the federal courts was not defeated until 1892. In 1879 the company joined the legislature in calling for a constitutional convention, a counter move to the revolutionary instruments fashioned in 1864 and 1868. It is not surprising to find that the Constitution of 1879, in reaction to Reconstruction, imposed strong restrictions upon the legislature and granted executive powers rivaling those of 1812.

This constitution was written by white men whose primary objective was to reaffirm white supremacy. Yet, there was no overt move to disfranchise the Negro at this time. In the first place, any move in this direction would bring intervention by the federal government. More important was the belief of the Democratic elite that the black man's vote could be controlled and that it would prove to be politically useful against either Republicans or poor whites. The Negro was bound to the white planters by economic necessity and thus, economic proscription—one of the most common and mild of the Democratic

threats because it carried no physical terrors—was also one of the
most effective.[60] The attitudes of the new ruling group were
reactionary, as the events of subsequent decades proved.
The emergent Bourbon elite demonstrated the goal of their
redemption in the elections of 1878. In that year white supremacy
was established through Democratic fraud, violence, and intimidation
against the Negro. A contemporary wrote in 1903: "The election of
1878 marked a final overthrow of the Republican party in Louisiana.
In 1876 we had elected Nicholls governor on a state ticket, but it
took 1878 to finish the work. So complete was the overthrow of the
Radical-Republican-Negro party . . . at that election, that from that
time to this, it has never been able to elect a constable, even in the
parish."[61]
The Democrats, taking no chances, had fanned the flames of white
solidarity and reigns of terror had been established in several parishes
in an attempt to intimidate the Negro voter. These disclosures reveal
the extent to which Reconstruction became a rationalization, justifying
actions as severe as allegedly had been practiced earlier by the former
rulers. Otis A Singletary has discovered the duplicity of the Democrats' actions. At first they had refused to recognize the reign of terror
in 1878, but the Democratic Redeemers were actually too proud of
their achievements to remain discreetly quiet. They claimed that the
Negroes had voluntarily voted the Democratic ticket, but the records
of actual violence belie this. A favorite Democratic rationalization was
that the actions were not the result of prejudice against the Negro
as Negro, but against the Negro as political leader. "From a moral
point of view, the Negro was, on the average a good citizen; the Negro
politician vile. From a political viewpoint, both were bad."[62] Therefore, whether accidently or incidently, the Negro was an object of
white terror in 1868, and as W. J. Cash put it, the Democratic Party

[60]Allie Bayne (Windham) Webb, "Methods and Mechanisms Used to Restore
White Supremacy in Louisiana, 1872–76" (Master's thesis, Louisiana State University,
1948), xiv.
[61] Quoted from a letter of Newton C. Blanchard to John R. Ficklin, Feb. 9, 1903,
in Otis A. Singletary, "The Reassertion of White Supremacy in Louisiana" (Master's
thesis, Louisiana State University, 1949).
[62] Singletary, "Reassertion of White Supremacy," 68.

became the "institutionalized incarnation of the will to White Supremacy."[63]

In the emerging reality of white supremacy the important question is, who gave electoral support to the standard bearers of this movement. A planter-merchant elite re-established itself in the political sun, but it could stay there only through gaining support of the farmer groups and a portion of the Negro vote, or through intimidation of either or both. The Jacksonians of the 1840's could effectively escape the fear of the Negro as slave, but could the farmer-Democrat of the seventies and eighties afford to ignore him? 

While the after-effects of Reconstruction and redemption were said to have elevated the poor and white in the ranks of southern society, such was far from true.[64] The plantation system survived and began to assume many colonial characteristics; and this was also the tendency in the new southern industry. After the war, as planters failed and plantations went on the block, rising urban groups stepped into the class of the landed gentry. Merchants, lawyers, and doctors bought plantations as speculative investments, and this tended to push the price of land beyond reach of the small cotton grower.[65]

Two attendant developments worked against the lower classes in the South—the crop lien system and share cropping. While the Negro became a share cropper and supported the continued dominance of the plantation, the white farmer became caught in the crop lien system. The Jacksonian hill farmer in Louisiana had been concerned about the race question only when his way of life was threatened in 1860; there were few Negroes in his area, and he naturally protested the necessity of fighting someone else's war. Moreover, as Cash has pointed out, the farmer of the South had not been directly exploited by the plantation system as such, either; the farmer could act as a relatively free agent with society.[66]

Events in the 1880's, however, would deem to give substance to the

[63] Wilbur J. Cash, *The Mind of the South* (New York, 1941), 107.
[64] Shugg, *Origins of Class Struggle*; C. Vann Woodward, *Origins of the New South* (Baton Rouge, 1966).
[65] Rupert Vance, *Human Factors in Cotton Culture* (Chapel Hill, 1929), 65.
[66] Cash, *Mind of the South*, 39.

thesis of Roger Shugg concerning incipient class struggle as well as Bourbon fanning of the flames of racial prejudice. With the development of the crop lien system, the white family farmer became dependent upon the cotton merchant through indebtedness, and the merchants and planters controlled the (new) Democratic Party. Dissenters had to face the established hierarchy of the one political party to achieve redress of a grievance.

Here lay the foundations for group struggle culminating in the political explosion of the 1890's. Fear of economic insecurity caused the farmer to use the Negro as the political whipping boy, just as in another age, the fear of the Communist threat was to lead goodhearted men to condone the slander of the liberal.

# CHAPTER VI

# The Bourbon Ascendancy

## 1. Solidarity in the Hills, 1879–1892

The Constitution of 1879 became the heavy anchor of the new order, a governing circle which proved to be a closed corporation under the leadership of men like Louis A. Wiltz, John McEnery, and their business and planter associates. Governor Nicholls had been the Bourbon in 1876, representing the historical stereotype, but in Louisiana politics the name soon became associated with the anti-Nicholls faction of the state's Democratic Party as, in a sense, politics became a war between professionals and amateurs.[1] Economic advantage was furthered on the Cotton Exchange, in railroading, and through the lottery. The historian Gayarré had written that Louisiana suffered so much in Reconstruction it would "gladly embrace any change in government, submit to any other species of despotism."[2]

The ascendancy of the Bourbon Redeemers can be said to have marked the conservative reaction to Reconstruction. Politicians allied themselves to a merchant-banker-planter combination, wherein the men of money usually dominated, hoping to establish a stable economy by working with the politicians. It has been suggested that a strong entrepreneurial spirit operated within the Bourbon man, carried forward from urban-commercial development in the prewar society. From this category, and not from a particular class, came representatives imbued with that spirit of enterprise characteristic of a "New South." "Malevolence toward the political carpetbagger ambivalently switched to a hearty welcome for the economic carpetbagger."[3]

[1] Clarence H. Nichols, "Francis Tillou Nicholls, Bourbon Democrat" (Master's thesis, Louisiana State University, 1959), 168.
[2] Quoted in William Ivy Hair, "The Agrarian Protest in Louisiana, 1877–1900" (Ph.D. dissertation, Louisiana State University, 1962), 157.
[3] Nichols, "Francis Tillou Nicholls," 15.

Occasioned by the depression of 1873 and the extravagances of the carpetbag legislatures, the best known policy of the Bourbons had become financial retrenchment. The Redeemers' response had been to tighten the fiscal belt, and in consequence there ensued a decline in public schools, and charitable institutions barely managed to survive. More importantly, when prosperity did return, the principle of governmental parsimony had already been established.[4]

It was in the political sphere, however, that the Bourbon ascendancy was most acutely felt. If, after 1876, Bourbon misrule replaced radical misrule, the succession of Democratic governors was unable or unwilling to curb it, and the majority of the people, white or black, became exploited economically and politically. "Survival of the fittest" for the Bourbons came to mean that all whites, regardless of their walk of life, must cooperate in the repression of the Negro voting majority. In the decade of the 1880's, as the registration of Negro voters went up, Republican voting strength went down.[5]

The Bourbon appeared to accept the Negro's place in politics more readily than did the poorer whites, but if they saw the Negro vote as merely an unfortunate legacy from Reconstruction, they did object strenuously to the Negro as political leader. The Negro vote had been used to advantage in wresting Louisiana from the Republicans, and now the principle of white supremacy would be used to offset the agrarian threat to cut across color line and gain political control.[6]

If the dominating elements of the Democratic Party now intended to make the state safe for white democracy, they must turn to the Hills for support. The farmer parishes had never voted anything but Democratic. The Hills were Jacksonian and at the Secession crisis, Unionist. In the past, before the presence of the Negro voter had become a reality, the natural majority of the Democratic Party in the state had been demonstrated. The quest for political certainty now required the dogma of solidarity. An investigation of the distribution of Democratic support in the period 1879–92 reveals the pattern of Bourbon success.

[4] *Ibid.*, 17.
[5] Hair, "Agrarian Protest," 164.
[6] Nichols, "Francis Tillou Nicholls," 15–16; see Paul Lewinson, *Race, Class, and Party* (New York, 1932).

While the Democrats managed to elect Grover Cleveland President twice in this period, the national Democratic vote held to less than 50 percent (Appendix B, Table 2). At the same time, however, the Democratic presidential vote in Louisiana increased to safe proportions with the Bourbon ascendancy. In the following tabular summary can be found a forecast of the "solid South' in future presidential politics:

*Table 6–1*
VOTING BEHAVIOR IN THE PERIOD, 1879–92

| Election | Democratic Support | | Voter Turnout | |
|----------|------|------|------|------|
| Year | Gub. | Pres. | Gub. | Pres. |
| 1879 . . . . . . . . . . . . | 63% | — | 74% | — |
| 1880 . . . . . . . . . . . . | — | 62% | — | 60% |
| 1884 . . . . . . . . . . . . | 67 | 57 | 60 | 50 |
| 1888 . . . . . . . . . . . . | 72 | 73 | 73 | 45 |
| 1892 . . . . . . . . . . . . | 44 | 77 | 67 | 43 |

The percentages of support and turnout show how, as Democratic solidarity became an established reality, the proportional Democratic support increased while the turnout of voters in presidential elections decreased. Competition for leadership within the Bourbon democracy, however, led to increased variance in the vote and, at the same time, turnout remained high in gubernatorial elections. While, it will be recalled, the number of parishes which supported the Democratic

*Table 6–2*
NUMBER OF PARISHES BELOW AND ABOVE 50 PERCENT,
PRESIDENTIAL AND GUBERNATORIAL DEMOCRATIC,
1868–76 AND 1879–92

| | | Below 50% Democratic | Above 50% Democratic |
|---|---|------|------|
| 1868–76 | Gubernatorial . . . | 31 | 25 |
| | Presidential . . . . | 26 | 30 |
| 1879–92 | Gubernatorial . . . | 15 | 44 |
| | Presidential . . . . | 6 | 53 |

Party in above and below 50 percent intervals remained quite balanced in the Reconstruction period, a dramatic shift is discovered after Redemption.

In the elections during the period 1879–92 a sizable shift in the number of parishes whose electorate voted in the Democratic majority took place. As has been anticipated above, the greatest increase occurred in presidential support, so much that the proportion of parishes above 50 percent in Democratic support was 36 percent more in the latter period.

Not only was there a shift in parish support toward the Democratic Party after redemption but also apparent (Maps 6–1 and 6–2) is the sharp cleavage that increased between the parishes of North and South Louisiana. Low variance together with geographic contiguity were such that a small number of parishes clustered in South Louisiana remained strongly Republican, while nearly all the rest of the parishes became Democratic in the top interval of percentage support.

The Republican Party did survive in the state until 1900 through federal patronage and through the formidable candidates it continued to field against the Democrats. However, these factors alone cannot explain the large Negro vote in the sugar country which brought to the Republicans the label of the "black" party.

Of course predominant Negro registration would guarantee a Republican majority in most sugar parishes, but why did the Negro vote here while his participation in elections was discouraged and his vote intimidated in cotton country? For one thing, the sugar plantation, although devastated by the events of the war years, continued to remain the stable economic unit of the area, despite changes of hands. Large landholdings were kept intact, sharecropping was far less prevalent, and the Negro was a wage hand. It is tempting to hypothesize that the lack of widespread Negro intimidation in South Louisiana is attributable to the French cultural background and the presence of the Catholic church. This view will be tested later, in the 1950's, when necessary data are more readily available. It may also be stated that the more "tolerant" mood in regard to Negro voting in the sugar country happened to coincide with the planters' Republican leanings, which were of an economic basis. The sugar planters were

# Average Presidential Democratic Vote
## 1880-1892

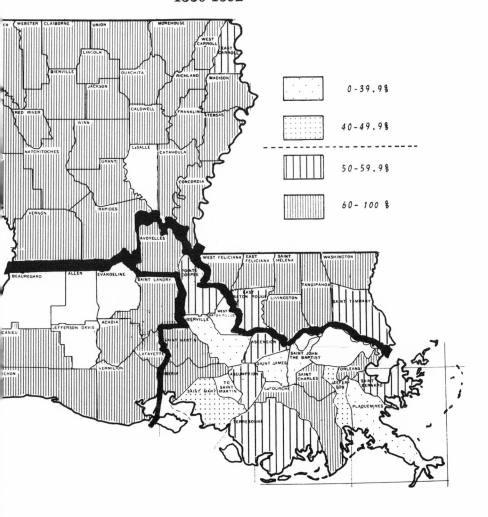

# Average Gubernatorial Democratic Vote
# 1879-1892

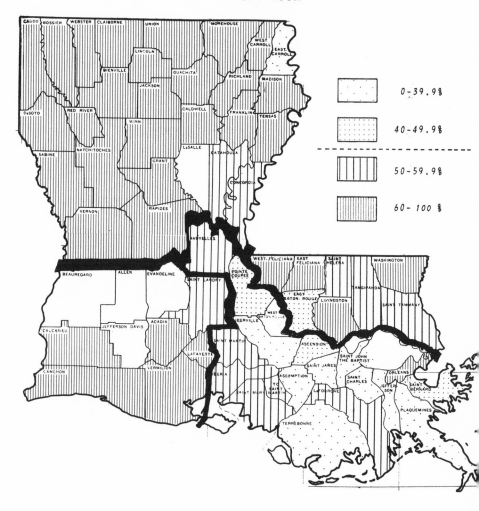

in sympathy with Republican notions of tariff which served to protect the artificial staple.[7]

In 1879, following the ratification of the new constitution, the Democrats had elected Louis A. Wiltz governor of Louisiana. The term of Governor Nicholls had been shortened by one year in retaliation to his opposition to the lottery. Of the total vote cast, 63 percent had favored Wiltz. His majority of over 31,000 was a large increase over the rather close majority—some 8,000 votes— which Nicholls had received in 1876. However, nearly 30,000 fewer votes were cast in this election than in 1876, and, assuming the Negro vote to be a Republican one, there was a decrease of some 15,000 Negro votes. Suggestion of intimidation and influence appeared once more.

Although support of the Republicans remained high in the sugar country of the southern delta, in the election under discussion, the political fracture line up the Red River and along the upper Mississippi Delta appeared disrupted. Parishes like Madison and Tensas, and Natchitoches and Rapides, all of which were weak in support of the Redeemer Nicholls in 1876, now returned a majority for the Demotic candidate. These parishes contained populations in which Negroes outnumbered whites, and in which the voter registration figures favored the Negroes (Appendix B, Table 15).

Ten parishes returned a Democratic vote of more than 98 percent. This was solidarity; or it might just as realistically have been the effect of intimidation, machine pressure, or ballot box stuffing. Most of these parishes had consistently given Democratic majorities, but never in such proportions as these. Moreover, the predominant group in each was the farmer. These were the Hill Parishes where the Negro had never resided in great numbers. At least, this was the situation in most of the parishes under consideration. It will be recalled (Chapter 5) that in the two decades since 1860 many Negroes had actually migrated into the parishes bordering Arkansas. Such parishes as Winn and Sabine had, on the other hand, shown decreases in Negro population.

The incidence of this high voting percentage would not assume such

[7] J. Carlyle Sitterson, *Sugar Country: The Cane Industry in the South, 1753–1950* (Lexington, 1953).

significance were it not for two things: (1) it occurred in a clustering of parishes and; (2) the same tendency continued to appear in the next two gubernatorial elections as well. Stretching from Franklin and Richland on Macon Ridge, through Ouachita, Lincoln, Jackson, Bienville, Winn, and across the Red River into DeSoto, Sabine and Vernon parishes in the Hills, this core of Democratic solidarity was fringed by parishes which had also produced relatively high votes for the same party.

This pattern of voter solidarity again appeared in the next gubernatorial election of 1884. Once more the seat of Republican opposition was found in the sugar country, with some vestiges of Republican tendency shown in Grant, East Carroll, and Webster. This time, however, there were twelve parishes with a vote favoring the Democratic candidate, John McEnery, by more than 98 percent. West Carroll and Tensas joined the block of solid Democratic parishes, and these had compiled votes of over 80 percent for the Democratic candidate in the previous election. West Carroll, another Macon Ridge parish, contained a Negro population that slightly outnumbered the whites in the count of this decade. But in Tensas, the Negroes outnumbered the whites by ten to one. Tensas was a parish of planters, of course, which had registered high Republican votes in the years of Negro support of the carpetbaggers.

The results of the gubernatorial election of 1888, when Governor Nicholls had been elected for a second time, showed a slightly different distribution of voting support. There was not only the appearance of Democratic support in sugar planter parishes like Ascension and St. Mary, there also appeared to be a shift in the distribution of parishes with strong Democratic leanings in the Hills. Seven of the parishes which had given over 98 percent support to the Democrats continued to do so. However, West Carroll and Richland counted less support in this election, as did Winn Parish in the heart of the Hills. Rather, Cameron and East Feliciana rounded out the group of parishes which approached consensus.

With the discovery of this core of Democratic solidarity, it is possible to use the Hills Parishes as a baseline, from which to determine the source of the agrarian protest, which was to reach its peak in

Louisiana in the nineties. Voting data for the eighties shows that the Democratic solidarity in support of the Bourbon ascendancy had come from the farmer parishes, and yet, the history of populism in Louisiana, as in the nation, records the protest and political actions of the dissident farmer, aiming to overcome the failure of the two major parties to help him. The question for Louisiana, is what explains the dramatic and radical shift of the Hill farmer away from Democratic fortunes? There are indications that farmer solidarity was less real than it appeared.

The protest movement fashioned by Louisiana farmers should be taken, of course, as part of the general reaction to national trends in post–Civil War America. The most important consideration can be stated simply:[8] "The history of American agriculture between 1850 and 1900 was marked by two great occurrences. One was the trans-formation. The other was the arising of a vast mass movement of protest." The transformation was the shift of agriculture from a self-sufficient base to commercialization, a trend which developed rapidly after 1850. The farmer, tied to the market by his cash crop, had become a direct participant in modern industrialism, and fully subject to the uncertainty of commercial fortune. But while the American farmer had thus entered the modern world, he continued to be identified by the old agrarian myth which had celebrated the virtue of the yeoman farmer. It was the agrarian myth which led the farmers' movement into the pursuit of broad political goals and ideological mass polices to reduce his discontent, even though, all the while, his problems remained basically economic in character.

In addition to the problems that came with commercialism of agriculture, here, as in other southern states, there were the added burdens of occupation and Reconstruction after the war. In the period from 1860 to 1900 the value of farm land in Louisiana had decreased by some $137 millions of dollars. The plight of the state can be appreciated by observing the contrast with the nation:

---

[8] Virgil Williams, "The Economic Philosophy of the Farmers' Movement, 1850–1900" (Master's thesis, University of Texas, 1956), 55.

*Table 6–3*

VALUATION OF PROPERTY, NATION, AND STATE, 1850–90

| Year | United States Millions of dollars | Louisiana Millions of dollars | Louisiana as a percentage of United States |
|------|-----------------------------------|-------------------------------|--------------------------------------------|
| 1850 | $3,967 | $98.5 | 2.6% |
| 1860 | 7,980 | 247.9 | 3.1 |
| 1870 | 9,412 | 91.3 | 0.9 |
| 1880 | 12,404 | 76.7 | 0.6 |
| 1890 | 16,439 | 110.4 | 0.7 |

Before the Civil War the agricultural richness of Louisiana was proverbial, but, afterwards, the state was doomed to decades of relative impoverishment.[9]

The difficulties of Louisiana's agricultural economy are further manifest in the comparative figures tracing production of what became the major cash crop—cotton:

*Table 6–4*

COTTON PRODUCTION, NATION AND STATE, 1850–90

| Year | United States Thousands of bales | Louisiana Thousands of bales | Louisiana as a percentage of United States |
|------|----------------------------------|------------------------------|--------------------------------------------|
| 1850 . . . . . . | 2,136 | 179 | 8.6% |
| 1860 . . . . . . | 3,841 | 778 | 20.0 |
| 1870 . . . . . . | 4,352 | 350 | 8.1 |
| 1880 . . . . . . | 6,606 | 508 | 7.8 |
| 1890 . . . . . . | 8,653 | 659 | 7.7 |

Despite the fact that increasing acreage was devoted to cotton, in the last half of the century. Louisiana's contribution to the nation's cotton production totals failed to reach the 1850 percentage figure. This difficulty of recovery from war and Reconstruction is the more telling

[9] Garnie W. McGinty, "Changes in Louisiana Agriculture, 1860–1880," *Louisiana Historical Quarterly*, XVIII (1935), 407–29.

inasmuch as cotton production was a southern specialty, and obviously Louisiana had suffered a greater setback than other southern states. The rosy contention that the New South in emergence was marked by the successful establishment of the yeoman farmer through the breakup of the plantation, may have served the public relations of the Bourbon oligarchy, but it turned out to be contrary to fact.[10] The spokesmen of the New South had founded their assertion upon the census and quoted figures to prove it. In the period from 1860 to 1880 it would appear that the number of southern farms had been doubled, while, at the same time, the average farm had been cut to less than half its previous size.[11] Actually, the picture, based upon such figures, "represented everything the Southern farmer *was not* and *had not.*" The new myth, however, "fulfilled the old Jeffersonian dream of an independent yeomanry, self-sufficient lords of a few acres."[12] Certain it was that this independence did not extend to political affairs. The inadequacies in census reporting hid the real situation, as Shugg ably demonstrated by using Louisiana data.[13] The census marshals had failed to distinguish between tenants and proprietors—the several tracts held by a planter were not registered as a unit, but as the farms of tenants who had taken the place of the former slaves.

In the struggle for economic reconstruction, the plantation *system* survived, even though drastic changes in landownership often took place. Moreover, as the South committed itself ever more completely to the perilous profits of a one-crop agriculture, there followed the steady drift from the cotton plantation to cotton tenancy.[14] As the whole South went to work after the war, the greatest shortage was not labor, but a supply of ready cash. The southern farmer could not get the "advances" that were available to his counterpart in the West, because the banking system of the region was inadequate. Two

[10] C. Vann Woodward, *Origins of the New South* (Baton Rouge, 1966), Chap. 7.
[11] Roger W. Shugg, *The Origins of Class Struggle in Louisiana* (Baton Rouge, 1939; paperback, 1968), 235.
[12] Woodward, *Origins of New South*, 175.
[13] Shugg, *Origins of Class Struggle*, 235–36; but compare with Fred A. Shannon, *The Farmer's Last Frontier; Agriculture 1860–1897* (New York, 1945), 81–83.
[14] Rupert Vance, *Human Factors in Cotton Culture* (Chapel Hill, 1929), 53.

practices were innovated which served to sustain economic enterprise as a whole but which, in the long run, worked against any general "rise of the poor whites" or the former slaves.[15]

The sharecropping system put the Negro to work, as well as an increasing number of hard-pressed white farmers. An even more widespread practice prohibited any significant establishment of the farmer on the land as "lord of his acres." This was the innovation of the crop lien credit system whereby the farmer pledged his crop to be handled by the merchant when it was harvested.[16] In theory, these practices might have reconstructed southern agriculture, save for a factor inherent within the system itself—the precariousness of the one-crop (cotton) economy.[17]

The trend towards concentration on the cotton industry accelerated after the war as an avenue to a ready source of cash. In commercializing cotton, however, the southern farmer and planter became dependent upon the world market. The South, producing on the average more than half the world supply, became the bellwether of cotton prices. With more and more cotton being grown, the prices dropped steadily in the period from 1870 until the late nineties. Whereas cotton prices averaged 13.8 cents per pound in the 1870's, in the next decade the average was 9 cents per pound, and in 1894 it reached the rock-bottom level of 4.6 cents per pound. One careful student of Southern cotton culture notes that with every bad year there came social unrest and innumerable panaceas.[18]

As a result of these practices the lower classes, white farmers and Negroes alike, became dependent upon the very class (planters and merchants) which was to emerge dominant in political affairs. Farming had become a financial instead of an agricultural interest. Cotton was the money crop exacted by landlords, living in towns, and the tenant's interest in diversification and food supplies was disregarded.[19] As it often did, political power rested upon property.

---

[15] Shugg, *Origins of Class Struggle*, Chaps. 8 and 9.
[16] Shannon. *Farmer's Last Frontier*, 90.
[17] Vance, *Human Factors*, Chap. 5.
[18] *Ibid.*, 113.
[19] *Ibid.*, 65.

The Redeemers became the ones to benefit, for as Woodward has put it, in speaking of the situation in Georgia, "once Redemption was effected, the upland plebeians found they had redeemed the state from the carpetbagger only to lose it to the lowland bosses."[20]

No figures on tenancy are compiled for the United States before 1880, but since that time the percentage steadily increased for the cotton states:

*Table 6–5*

TENANT FARMERS AS PERCENT OF ALL FARMERS, NATION, REGION, AND STATE, 1880–1920

|            | 1880 | 1890 | 1900 | 1910 | 1920 |
|------------|------|------|------|------|------|
| U. S.      | 26%  | 28%  | 35%  | 37%  | 38%  |
| South      | 36   | 38   | 45   | 45   | 44   |
| Louisiana  | 35   | 44   | 58   | 53   | 57   |

Again, it is evident, from comparing the tenancy figures, that Louisiana was harder hit than most. While, for the nation and the region, there was 9 percent more tenancy in 1900 than 1880, in Louisiana, 23 percent more had gone down into tenancy than had been the case two decades before.

Figures such as these belie the rise of the yeoman farmer. Farmers may have survived the ordeal of reconstruction better than the planters had, and had tended to increase in number after 1873, but tenancy spread faster than proprietorship. Shugg found that in the years from 1873 until 1880 the ratio of proprietors to croppers and tenants in Louisiana changed from 60:40 to 55:45. The conclusion was reached that "the increase of great estates throughout the century had such a cumulative effect that although Louisiana had contained more farms than plantations in 1860, it was dominated by agrarian monopoly in 1900, when its proportion of absentee ownership and overseer management was the largest in the South, and highest, except for Wyoming, in the entire United States."[21] The plantation system remained in Louisiana and, with it, a steady rise in tenancy. Negro and poor white

[20] Woodward, *Origins of New South*, 80.
[21] Shugg, *Origins of Class Struggle*, 241.

had found a place on the land, a position bringing with it an increasing sense of insecurity and despair. And, as A. L. Stinchcombe has reported is generally the case, tenancy relations lead to political instability.[22]

If the direction of analysis now turns to focus upon voter type differences in the incidence of economic well-being, it is possible to move closer to an explanation of the shift in Democratic solidarity in North Louisiana after the 1880's. Two indices will be used, the first a comparison of percentages of farms owned and the second having to do with percentage increases in the amount of acreage devoted to cotton production. The former index provides a measure of the opposite situation from agricultural tenancy, farm ownership, and this provides a means of determining within which clusters of parishes the farmer class remained relatively secure in the eighties:

*Table 6–6*

DIFFERENCE IN PERCENTAGE FARM OWNERSHIP,
1880 AND 1890, BY VOTER TYPE AREAS

| Voter Type | 1880 | 1890 | Difference |
|---|---|---|---|
| North Louisiana Hills . . . . . . . . . . | 86% | 54% | − 32 |
| South Louisiana Planter. . . . . . . . . . | 80 | 54 | − 26 |
| Macon Ridge . . . . . . . . . . . . . . | 54 | 28 | − 26 |
| North Louisiana Planter . . . . . . . . . | 45 | 20 | − 25 |
| Central Pine Hills . . . . . . . . . . . . | 75 | 62 | − 13 |
| South Louisiana Bayou . . . . . . . . . . | 72 | 60 | − 12 |
| Florida Parishes . . . . . . . . . . . . . | 64 | 52 | − 12 |
| Southwest Louisiana . . . . . . . . . . . | 72 | 72 | 0 |

There are few surprises in the parish distribution of lowered average percentages of farms owned. In general the planter-farmer cleavage is seen clearly although the North Louisiana Hills and Southwest Louisiana areas are exceptions demanding explanation. The more simply explained exception to the pattern is the latter area where, beginning in the 1880's, railroad lines were extended, stimu-

[22] Arthur L. Stinchcombe, "Agricultural Enterprise and Rural Class Relations," *American Journal of Sociology*, LXVII (1962), 165–76.

lating sawmill industry in what was almost virgin territory. At the same time, migrants from the Midwest began settlement on the prairies, thought to be undesirable for agriculture, and with mechanized devices, began the cultivation of rice.[23]

Not so easily explained is the contrast in decreasing farm ownership between the two Hills sections of North Louisiana, and yet, it is precisely here that it would be useful to learn why the Democratic solidarity in the Hills had split. The Hills Parishes stretching to the Arkansas border contained proportionally more farm owners than any other voter type unit in 1880, but these North Louisiana Hills recorded the greatest relative loss in farm ownership in the decade of the eighties. At the same time, the adjacent Central Pine Hills, while also high in farmer predominance, experienced but a third the loss of the former set of parishes.

One circumstance which led to more economic insecurity of the people residing in these parishes was the degree of increased commitment to the production of cotton at a time when the market price had begun a drastic decline. When the voter types of North Louisiana are controlled on this measure (three-fourths of the state's cotton production occurred here), a number of other variables can be compared:

*Table 6-7*
NORTH LOUISIANA VOTER TYPE AREAS, COTTON PRODUCTION,
PERCENT NEGRO, AND GUBERNATORIAL DEMOCRATIC VOTE IN SELECTED YEARS

| Voter Type | Change in Percent Cotton Acreage 1880–90 | Percent Slave 1860 | Average Prop. Negro 1870–1900 | Gubn. Dem. Ave. 1879–92 | Percent of State Total | | | |
|---|---|---|---|---|---|---|---|---|
| | | | | | 1888 White Regist. | 1888 Dem. Vote | 1892 Dem. Vote | 1896 Dem. Vote |
| No. La. Planter | + 30% | 73% | 77% | 75% | 10% | 26% | 24% | 22% |
| Macon Ridge | + 27 | 56 | 60 | 89 | 1 | 2 | 1 | 4 |

[23] Donald J. Millet, "The Lumber Industry of 'Imperial' Calcasieu: 1865–1900," *Louisiana History*, VII (1966).

No. La.

| Hills | + 66 | 42 | 45 | 80 | 10 | 10 | 13 | 8 |
|---|---|---|---|---|---|---|---|---|
| Cent. Pine |
| Hills | + 30 | 52 | 36 | 66 | 6 | 6 | 3 | 3 |
| STATE | + 47 | 48 | 49 | 62 | — | — | — | — |

Now, it becomes clear, the North Louisiana Hills not only became heavily committed to cotton production in the eighties but also, in these parishes there was an increasing proportion of Negro residents. This is in sharp contrast to the Central Hills, where proportionally less acreage was devoted to cotton and where the proportion of Negroes within the population actually decreased. On the basis of this cumulative evidence and with what will be said below regarding subsequent voting behavior, one can believe the hypothesis of H. M. Blalock, Jr., when he describes a "threat curve": "If whites are to maintain a constant power advantage over Negroes their degree of mobilization relative to that of Negroes must . . . increase with percentage Negro."[24] More generally, this author goes on to predict that, as a power threat increases, it is likely that greater emphasis upon the use of organizational and ideological techniques will be found.[25] This happened in both of the North Louisiana Hills voter type units, for different reasons and with different results.

While, as Map 6-2 shows, North Louisiana was solid in its support of the Democratic gubernatorial candidates in the elections from 1879 through 1892, it has been revealed above, that solidarity was most extreme in a set of parishes stretching across the northern hills. Democratic solidarity was broken, however, in the 1892 gubernatorial election. In the split that occurred, one set of parishes went "radical" while the other set remained "conservative." A comparison of the two Hills voter type areas in Table 6-7, above, shows that while the contribution of the parishes of the Central Hills to the state Democratic vote was reduced by half in 1892 over that of 1888, in the North

[24] Hubert M. Blalock, Jr., "A Power Analysis of Racial Discrimination," *Social Forces*, XXXIX (1960), 56. See also his *Toward a Theory of Minority-Group Relation* (New York, 1967).
[25] Blalock, "A Power Analysis," 58.

Louisiana Hills, its proportional share of the Democratic vote had increased in the 1892 election.

What is even more important to note, is that in the election of 1888 the Planter area was contributing decidedly more to the sum of the Democratic vote than was the North Louisiana Hills unit, each with 10 percent of the white voter registration. As if learning to follow suit, the Hills showed this tendency in the 1892 elections. What does this mean?

The imbalance between proportional shares of white voter registration and Democratic vote means that the redeeming Bourbons had lifted a page from the manual of practice followed in the heated and protested Reconstruction elections. It was for this reason that Woodward had said that "political democracy for the white man and racial discrimination for the black were twinborn."[26] Records of the time plainly show that Louisiana white men, especially in the northern part of the state, voted the straight Democratic ticket. Consider the following contrasting figures for the year 1888:

*Table 6–8*

NEGRO AND WHITE VOTER REGISTRATION AND
GUBERNATORIAL DEMOCRATIC VOTE, 1888

|  | The State | No. La. Planters | Ten Parishes with Democratic Solidarity |
|---|---|---|---|
| Democratic Vote | 136,746 | 35,192 | 15,076 |
| White Registration | 126,884 | 10,403 | 10,184 |
| Negro Registration | 127,923 | 33,294 | 9,603 |
| Percent More Democratic Votes Than White Voters | 8% | 67% | 50% |

Obviously, it took a lot of solidarity on the part of both white planters and farmers to keep the state safe for Democracy, or else the Negro, seeing the folly of his ways, had renounced the Republicans and joined the Democrats in the assertion of white supremacy.

In reality, the Democrats had taken up the "Ouachita plan,"

[26] Woodward, *Origins of New South*, 211.

attributed to John McEnery, who had declared in its favor that "it is time that the law shall be silent and [we shall] uphold our liberty at all hazards."[27] Negro voters were told that if they did not vote right that they would be counted right, at any rate. The Negro was prevented from voting but he was always counted.[28] The huge majorities for the Democratic candidates had been equated with the chastity of white womanhood, the memory of the Confederate dead, and the Divine Wisdom of Heaven—a difficult combination to beat. It was said that "colored cemeteries were bastions of strength for the party of white supremacy" and that a "dead darkey always makes a good Democrat." William Ivy Hair thus draws the irony of the age by commenting that in 1890, whites of voting age had outnumbered Negroes in the census count.[29]

Louisiana farmers, as a general rule, could not have been expected to prefer the Republican-Negro rule any more than had the planters. In fact, when the ancient Jacksonian Democratic heritage of hill farmers is studied, the Democratic prejudice of the farmer appears to have been a force to be reckoned with by the more conservative Democrats and Whigs. Now the redeeming Bourbons had no difficulty in drawing upon Democratic support from the hills beyond the bottom lands. The farmer would go along with Redemption in the hope that at long last his vote might further political freedom for his kind.

The end result of the farmers' Democratic solidarity was something else, however. Drawing upon information obtained from a leading Populist in Louisiana, Melvin J. White was able to discover one of the basic issues of the day.[30] The Bourbons had fashioned a device which gave the planter the same kind of advantage he had prior to the war, when legislative apportionment had been based upon total population. Now, delegates to the Democratic state convention which nominated candidates for state offices were apportioned among the parishes

[27] Hair, "Agrarian Protest," 166.
[28] Allie Bayne (Windham) Webb, "Methods and Mechanisms Used to Restore White Supremacy in Louisiana, 1872–1876" (Master's thesis, Louisiana State University, 1948).
[29] Hair, "Agrarian Protest," 168.
[30] Melvin J. White, "Populism in Louisiana During the Nineties," *The Mississippi Valley Historical Review*, V (1918), 6–7.

according to the number of Democratic votes cast in previous elections. This Bourbon device left the farmer out in the cold. It worked with great success in the Fifth District which included most of the delta and farm parishes of Northeast Louisiana. In the four river parishes, 11.3 percent of the adult white males had seventy-five delegates, while, in the other eleven parishes of the district, 88.7 percent of the whites of voting age were represented by seventy-nine delegates. Thus the Bourbon planters retained control of the state, relying upon the alleged *Negro* Democratic vote. The same Bourbon hands held both economic and political power. If this is what Redemption meant, then there was nothing offered in the white supremacy of the planters to the farmers to stop them from risking all to gain economic and political reform.

It is now possible to present, in summary, a comparison of some of the elements which help to explain the break in the near 100 percent Democratic solidarity in the Hills. Set one (I) which consists of the four parishes of Jackson, Sabine, Vernon, and Winn is readily distinguished from set two (II) which consists of the six parishes of Bienville, DeSoto, Franklin, Lincoln, Ouachita, and Richland in terms of the following:

*Table 6–9*

VOTING BEHAVIOR OF TWO SETS OF PARISHES
WITH DEMOCRATIC SOLIDARITY, 1868–92

1. The Southern Democratic Vote in 1860 . . . . . . I  (51%)
                                                  II  (53%)

2. The Vote for Secession, 1861 . . . . . . . . . . . I  (34%)
                                                  II  (67%)

3. The Foster Democratic Vote, 1892 . . . . . . . . I  (35%)
                                                  II  (62%)

4. The Populist Vote, 1892 . . . . . . . . . . . . . I  (51%)
                                                  II  (12%)

5. Percent Increase Cotton Acreage, 1880 to 1890 . . . I  (+ 74%)
                                                  II  (+ 31%)

6. Change in Percent Farms Owned, 1880 to 1890 . . .   I   (11% less)
                                                       II   (33% less)

7. Change in Percent Negro Population, 1880 to 1890 .  I   (8% less)
                                                      II   (14% less)

8. Percent Democratic Vote More Than White Voters, 1888  I   (2%)
                                                        II   (32%)

The discipline needed by the Bourbons to build the wall of white supremacy against the still opposing Republicans, if carried to extreme, would have made North Louisiana a closed society. In contrast, South Louisiana, with a greater degree of competition for the vote, remained more open. Yet, it was precisely in the northern parishes that voter elements had shown a tradition of protest of and independence from the ruling class.

II. *The Populist-Republican Fusion: 1896*

The agrarian movement was nothing new. Its offensive against the Bourbon oligarchy of the nineties began as far back as the early seventies.[31] And though the coming together of the Populist and Republican forces in the 1890's may seem, in retrospect, a desperate move, it is also probable that the happy prospect of almost certain victory four years hence was a factor. Also, protest was in the air throughout the nation in the latter part of the century, and as it became obvious that organization might accomplish much toward solving the economic problems of agriculture, Louisiana farmers seized their chance.

Although Southerners joined Westerners in protesting discriminatory freight rates and the rights of merchants to fix prices on what the farmer bought and sold, as well as against tariff-protected trusts, there was an important difference in their complaints. The bulk of the population of the South consisted of farmers, whose grievances help to explain the political struggles of the nineties. There,

[31] Arthur S. Link, "The Progressive Movement in the South, 1870–1914," *The North Carolina Historical Review*, XXIII (1946), 172–95.

a planter-merchant domination of politics was a constant source of resentment among the humbler whites of the uplands. In many southern states (although not yet, in Louisiana) the Negro was disfranchised and lacked leaders and political knowledge within their own class.

Only owners of large farms and plantations were in a position to lead a revolt against the Bourbons and their city allies, presiding over the development of Henry Grady's "New South."[32] In some states the need was met by a Ben Tillman or a Tom Watson, who urged voters to reverse the position of the Bourbons by espousing the dogma of agrarianism for the South and a glorification of the farmer and his way of life, while waging war upon the industrial East.[33] As Woodward put it in his study of the New South: "The political strategy of Southern Populists was based on combinations and alliances along regional, class, and racial lines." The first of these was an alliance between the South and the West. The second combination was a joining of farmers and city and factory workers in common cause, while thirdly, a political union of the Populists with Negro farmers and laborers was attempted. Every phase of this strategy was a challenge to the power structure, which had sought to divide all the elements Populists were trying to unite.[34]

In their pursuit of economic self-interest, the movement of the southern Populists promised to introduce once more a pluralism in political life. It inevitably must "collide full tilt with the whole edifice of Southern politics," which has been described by Professor T. Harry Williams as including the following: (1) An attachment to images of the past; (2) A separation of economics and politics; (3) An entombing one-party system; and (4) A folk unity forged by Reconstruction.[35] Although the agrarian reformers mounted a vigorous effort (and actually claimed to have won the gubernatorial election in 1896), there

[32] Francis B. Simkins, *The Tillman Movement in South Carolina* (Durham, 1926); C. Vann Woodward, *Tom Watson, Agrarian Rebel* (New York, 1938).
[33] Woodward, *Tom Watson*, 166.
[34] Woodward, *Origins of New South*, 252.
[35] T. Harry Williams, *Romance and Realism in Southern Politics* (Baton Rouge, 1966), 52.

was no Tom Watson to mobilize the masses, and in no other state was the Populist cause so hopeless.[36]

The economic concerns of the agrarian radicals led them to what should be called an "interest politics."[37] They wanted elements of debtor and commodity reform, both of which indicate the "built in" inconsistency of the farmer's class position. The farmer, staunch representative of the "old" middle class, makes his living by selling, but he also does capital buying from powerful sellers, and the farmer's income is often affected as much by buying as by selling; in addition, the farmer is often heavily in debt.[38] If, in reaction to such cross-pressures, the farmer entered politics, and if, as in Louisiana, his revolt was crushed, the resulting frustration would be all the more humiliating and distressing.

There now has been provided substance to verify Lucia Daniel's account of conditions in Louisiana which led to the Populist revolt. The wrath of the farmer had been aimed at: (1) The middleman (whose debtor he was); (2) The manufacturer (whose prosperity he envied); (3) The government (which he had too little voice in); and (4) The political party (which placed the interests of others before his).[39] Here, as elsewhere, the agrarian movement served as a safety valve for farmer discontent, as it tried to take over the Democratic Party. Should the Bourbons refuse to make room for the farmers, then the movement provided the framework to launch a third political party.[40]

At this point, a summary outline of the history of the Farmers' Alliance and Populism in Louisiana will be presented, and then an analysis of the tendencies revealed in the gubernatorial election of 1892 will be made. The sequence of events characterizing the agrarian movement in Louisiana follows:

[36] Hair, "Agrarian Protest," v.

[37] C. Vann Woodward, *The Burden of Southern History* (Baton Rouge, 1960), 153.

[38] Norbert Wiley, "America's Unique Class Politics: The Interplay of the Labor, Credit, and Commodity Markets," *American Sociological Review*, XXXII (1967), 533, 536.

[39] Lucia E. Daniel, "The Louisiana People's Party," *Louisiana Historical Quarterly*, XXVI (1943), 1062.

[40] Hair, "Agrarian Protest," 290.

1. The Farmers' Alliance was established about 1876 in Texas and spread from there into Louisiana.

2. A state agency of agriculture set up the Louisiana Agricultural Society in 1886 to encourage reforms of agriculture.

3. A Farmers' Alliance and/or Farmers' Union appeared in North Louisiana in 1888.

4. In 1890 the beginnings of a People's Party was made when a candidate was run in the congressional campaign from the Fourth District in Northwest Louisiana. The Winnfield *Comrade* was established October 3, 1890.

5. The People's Party was fully established October 2, 1891, and fielded candidates for state offices in the election of 1892.[41]

A wind of reform swept through Louisiana farmer parishes during the eighties, but it should be remembered that, at the same time, local politics had reflected the undemocratic character of the congressional and statewide politics. Hence a desire for political reform was added to the agenda of economic reforms. Indeed, William Hair has found the proximate causes of the rise of the Populist Party (or People's Party as it was officially chartered in Louisiana) in these circumstances.[42] In the 1890–91 session of the United States Congress, the Louisiana delegation had refused to endorse the Populists' sub-treasury plan, which would have eased the credit of American farmers. Alliance men of the Fourth Congressional District had backed a candidate with majority support of the delegates to the nominating convention, but he was deprived of the nomination by trickery. In anger the Winn Parish delegation bolted, went home, organized a new convention, and nominated T. J. Guice to oppose the nominee of the district convention. It was during this campaign that Farmer's Alliance men bought out the only newspaper in Winn and started to publish the

[41] The main points are taken from Hair, "Agrarian Protest"; Daniel, "Louisiana People's Party"; White, "Populism in Louisiana"; Henry C. Dethloff, "The Alliance and the Lottery: Farmers Try for the Sweepstakes," *Louisiana History*, VI (1965), 141–59.
[42] Hair, "Agrarian Protest,"

*Comrade at* Winnfield.[43] Somewhat earlier a roving reporter acting as subscription agent for the *American Non-Conformist*, published in Winfield, Kansas, had spoken at Baton Rouge, and had instructed hill farmers in the ways of revolt. Hardy L. Brian, so inspired, was named editor of the *Comrade*. He was a man of energy and ability who served the People's Party as its first secretary and as chairman of its state central committee.

Turning, thus, to politics, the farmers of the hill parishes sought reform of the state convention system which allowed the black parishes to control the hill or white parishes. The Populists also sought to reduce the appointive power of the governor, which was also detrimental to the hill farmers. As the election of 1892 approached, however, the greatest issue facing the Louisiana voter was the question of the charter renewal of the Louisiana State Lottery Company.

The election of 1892 threatened Bourbon solidarity, as five candidates entered the race for governor, when the Lottery issue split the parties in Louisiana.[44] Urban reformers from the New Orleans Lottery League had persuaded Alliance men to join in nominating a gubernatorial candidate who would oppose the Lottery. The rural reformers had expected to be able to name the Democratic candidate, but they were put off by urban leaders who argued that the Alliance candidate, Thomas Scott Adams, would not run well in the city. Thus, in the end, anti-Lottery Democrats nominated four-term state senator Murphy J. Foster, who had the blessings of Governor Francis T. Nicholls.

In opposition to the anti-Lottery move, Old Regular Democrats supported the nomination of a former Bourbon governor, Samuel D. McEnery. This mean that he had the support of the New Orleans Ring Democrats, the black belt parishes, and the Lottery company. Fearing that solidarity would indeed be breached, the Democrats conducted a statewide vote to solve the issue of candidacy in March. This move was the forerunner of the party primary in Louisiana. When a returning board found that Foster had become the choice of the Democrats, McEnery decided to run anyway.

[43] White, "Populism in Louisiana," 5–6.
[44] Dethloff, "The Alliance and the Lottery,"

Murphy J. Foster had fought the Lottery in the legislature. He was a planter from St. Mary, and in the fight against the Lottery, he had gained many friends. It was said that he had "led the forces of morality to victory over the graft and corruption that permeated the state government." If it were true that the Democrats' dogma required absolutes, then they had found the man for the job, a man versed in the imagery of persuasion. Concerning the Lottery, Foster had asked that "the mothers of this land when they kneel with their little ones at prayer to teach them to pray: Lead us not into this temptation, deliver us from this evil and save us from this polluting monster."[45]

The Democratic split invigorated both Republicans and Populists. The Republicans conducted one of their perennial factional quarrels as Henry C. Warmoth and William P. Kellogg differed over the lottery question. Neither would be denied, so the Republicans ended up with two factions in the race for governor. Warmoth supported the anti-Lottery Republican candidate, John E. Breaux, and charged that the Democrats had betrayed the interests of both sugar planters and Negroes. The Radicals behind Kellogg supported a lottery Republican, A. H. Leonard, and this faction backed the cause of the Negro.[46] The People's Party nominated the sheriff of Winn Parish, Richard L. Tannehill, as their candidate for governor, many Alliance men having turned to this party when they failed to dominate the Democratic Party. But now that the race was on, the Lottery issue lost significance because the United States Supreme Court upheld the constitutionality of the anti-lottery postal law.[47]

A political struggle of gigantic proportions is revealed in the distribution of the vote for the five gubernatorial candidates of 1892. Something went wrong with the old Democratic unity, and the "real" candidate of the party, Foster, received but 44 percent of the total vote cast. Even without the defection of McEnery, the Democratic

---

[45] Quoted from New Orleans *New Delta*, Aug. 8–9, 1890 in Sidney J. Romero, Jr., "The Political Career of Murphy J. Foster" (Master's thesis, Louisiana State University, 1942), 19.

[46] Dethloff, "The Alliance and the Lottery," 152.

[47] Philip D. Uzee, "Republican Politics in Louisiana, 1877–1900" (Ph.D. dissertation, Louisiana State University, 1950).

Party would have polled some 12 percent fewer votes than in the previous election.

Though the Lottery question had lost force, the candidates had lined up more or less on that basis, even the Populists, who associated the Lottery with the Bourbon domination. Hence even though the Democratic-Republican cleavage must be assumed to crosscut, it is noteworthy to find the sharp split in the vote between North and South Louisiana. While the ratio of lottery to anti-Lottery vote statewide was in the proportion of 43 percent to 57 percent, in North Louisiana the proportion was 21 percent to 79 percent. Moreover, of the twelve parishes which Foster took by more than 70 percent, eight of them were in North Louisiana, while of the parishes in which the Lottery candidates carried pluralities, only one of the fourteen was in North Louisiana. Perhaps the issue of the Lottery had a regligious or cultural connotation. At any rate, the distribution of highest support for the candidacy of Foster clustered along the Arkansas border, although his home was in South Louisiana. There, the only overwhelming Foster support was found in his home parish of St. Mary, and neighboring St. Martin and Acadia.

A number of tendencies appear in a summary distribution of the votes in the election of 1892, as presented on page 179.

Most notable in this election was that the solidarity of a decade had been broken. It was broken in the North and Central Pine Hills, where the People's Party candidate made heavy inroads, and it was broken in South Louisiana where, in sugar country, the Republicans slipped badly. For the first time since restoration, the Republican Party failed to gain a majority here, taking the support for both Republican factions.

In spite of Populist inroads, North Louisiana Democrats managed to hold their own in the 1892 gubernatorial race, even though considerably more Republican votes appeared here than in the decade past. Likewise, the traditional Democratic leaning of Southwest Louisiana remained evident, as well as a trend toward the newly formed People's Party. The same was true of the Florida Parishes, where, in fact, the distribution of support for the five candidates most typified the statewide totals. Within this unit resided an accurate

*Table 6-10*

GUBERNATORIAL ELECTION, 1892, VOTE FOR CANDIDATES BY VOTER TYPE AREAS

| Unit | | Anti-Lottery Democrat Foster | | Lottery Democrat McEnery | | Lottery Republican Leonard | | Anti-Lottery Republican Breaux | | People's Party (Populist) Tannehill | |
|---|---|---|---|---|---|---|---|---|---|---|---|
| | | Percent of State | Percent of Unit | Percent of State | Percent of Unit | Percent of State | Percent of Unit | Percent of State | Percent of Unit | Percent of State | Percent of Unit |
| North La. Planter | (16%) 100% | (24%) | 65% | (9%) | 14% | (10%) | 10% | (8%) | 8% | (3%) | 3% |
| Macon Ridge | (3%) 100% | (2%) | 42 | (3%) | 24 | (1%) | 6 | (7%) | 25 | (1%) | 1 |
| North La. Hills | (9%) 100% | (13%) | 62 | (4%) | 10 | (5%) | 9 | (1%) | 4 | (25%) | 15 |
| Central Pine Hills | (5%) 100% | (3%) | 26 | (4%) | 20 | (2%) | 6 | (4%) | 5 | (42%) | 43 |
| South La. Planter | (13%) 100% | (11%) | 37 | (10%) | 19 | (30%) | 38 | (10%) | 5 | (1%) | 1 |
| South La. Bayou | (12%) 100% | (10%) | 38 | (15%) | 34 | (15%) | 20 | (13%) | 7 | (2%) | 1 |
| Florida Parishes | (9%) 100% | (10%) | 47 | (18%) | 24 | (10%) | 18 | (7%) | 7 | (7%) | 4 |
| So. West Louisiana | (10%) 100% | (11%) | 50 | (6%) | 16 | (7%) | 11 | (23%) | 17 | (10%) | 6 |
| Urban Area | (23%) 100% | (16%) | 31 | (41%) | 48 | (20%) | 15 | (17%) | 5 | (1%) | 1 |
| STATE | (100%) 100% | (100%) | 44% | (100%) | 26% | (100%) | 17% | (100%) | 7% | (100%) | 6% |

179

cross-section of the electorate, Negro and white planters in St. Helena and the Felicianas, farmers in the piney hill parishes to the east of them, and an urban element in Baton Rouge.

In urban New Orleans, the Ring managed to hold tight with the Lottery issue by supporting McEnery. Still, urban reformers could be heartened by the 31 percent of the city vote which went for Foster, especially when anti-Lottery sentiment was not widespread in New Orleans.

The second largest share of support of any candidate was provided for the People's Party by the Central Pine Hills. There and in the North Hills, 67 percent of the Tannehill vote was cast. Indeed, a highly significant result of this election was the emergence of support for the People's Party, not only because of the strength of this support, which reaches as high as 75 percent Populist in some parishes, but also, because of its location. The break in the near-perfect Democratic solidarity of the Hill units in the eighties was more striking in its suddenness. Vernon, Winn, Grant, and Catahoula formed a tier of adjacent parishes, broken only by a thin stretch through which the Red River flowed, in which pluralities were won by the People's Party. Moreover, there were seven other parishes with sizable Populist votes clustered about the core group.

At the same time, the Florida Parishes and Southwest Louisiana had provided 17 percent of the total Populist vote. Here was a tendency that could bridge the cleavage of North and South Louisiana. From the Hills of North Louisiana, then, to the piney woods of the Florida Parishes in the southeast and beyond the prairies in the southwest, the farmer had sought a voice to protest the condition of things. His economic ailments had transcended his quest for white supremacy.

In the gubernatorial election of 1892, the color line was not apparent in the political support within the voter units. The Democrats had done well, on the whole, but a Republican-Populist fusion could portend victory over a divided Democratic front. In such a situation, the Negro vote might again provide the balance of power.

The gubernatorial election had been held on April 19, 1892,[48] and

[48] Dethloff, "The Alliance and the Lottery," 156.

in the presidential election of the following November, a fusion of Populists and Republicans and Negroes took place for the first time.[49] The Democrats carried the state by 77 percent of the vote, yet a precedent had been made, and the possibilities marked. For the Republican-Populist fusion had led to majority votes in four parishes. One was Plaquemines at the mouth of the Mississippi, while in North Louisiana the Populist fervor continued in Winn, Grant, and Lincoln parishes. Governor Foster was not unmindful of these events, and by 1894 was ready to face the agrarian menace and launch the Bourbon offensive, as the congressional elections of that year revealed the instability of the parties and the growing Populist unrest.[50]

A glance at Appendix A, Table 1, charting the curves of populations and voter participation shows a healthy recovery from the hiatus produced by the Civil War. It shows voter registration reaching, and actually surpassing, the census count of males twenty-one years of age and over. While interest in presidential elections appeared to decline, the upward trend in the gubernatorial voting curve is indicative of the intense political contest which must have taken place. This is all the more dramatic, inasmuch as the struggle is shown to have peaked in 1896. The precipitous drop after the elections of that year makes it a kind of watershed in Louisiana politics.

In the decade of the nineties, then, the chances looked as good for the Republicans as for the Democrats, with political competition enlivened by the entrance of dissident farmers. Carpetbagger-scalawag influence had been lessened, and opportunity for fusion with the farmers of the white race had been discovered. Both sides recognized the potency of fusion, which ultimately rested with the Negro. Thus returned the voting element which had been suppressed since the end of Reconstruction, through fraud, violence and intimidation. Once again the rival parties courted the Negroes for their votes.[51]

Expecting a close race in 1896, the Bourbons aimed first for a big

---

[49] Allie Bayne (Windham) Webb, "A History of Negro Voting in Louisiana, 1877–1906" (Ph.D. dissertation, Louisiana State University, 1962), 193.

[50] Hair, "Agrarian Protest," 301; Daniel, "Louisiana People's Party," 1098.

[51] Edwin Aurbera Ford, "Louisiana Politics and the Constitutional Convention of 1898" (Master's thesis, Louisiana State University, 1955), 46–47.

turnout at the polls, and then proceeded to the suffrage reforms which would establish the Bourbon ascendancy. Their four solutions to the "Negro question" had found support as early as 1894: (1) Recommendation of a constitutional committee for a poll tax; (2) An understanding clause; (3) Educational qualifications, favored by the governor and the Democratic caucus; and, (4) In the event of a defeat, powers granted to the legislature to restrict changes to the first session of 1896, and removal of all requisites for the Confederate veterans.[52] However, neither the Democratic Party nor Governor Foster had the courage to insist on finding a solution. One student of the period has suggested that after the bitter struggle of 1896, the Democrats' victory made the farmers willing to demand the legal disfranchisement of the Negro, a demand to which the Bourbons acquiesced.[53]

The political scene became even more open, when the sugar interests were hurt by the tariff of 1894. Louisiana planters, many of them ex-Democrats like E. N. Pugh of Ascension Parish, joined forces with the opposition.[54] They set up the National Republican Party of Louisiana in September, and vowed to be national on national issues but "lilywhite" at home. The Democrat press promptly ridiculed this group and demanded to know how any lilywhite party in Louisiana could bear the name of Republican.[55] With this turn of events, the fortunes of the Democrats were surely imperiled, considering the cluster of anti-Foster support which had been given in sugar country in the previous election. Rumor spread among the sugar planters that the Republicans and the "pops" would unite and nominate a complete state ticket.[56]

For the first time in many years the Democrats, in 1896, faced major opposition outside the regular Republican Party. The main issue in the Democratic campaign was Negro suffrage and white supremacy, and in retrospect the 1896 gubernatorial election was important for several reasons (1) It was the last time the fusionists would play a

[52] Ford, "Constitutional Convention," 43.
[53] Webb, "History of Negro Voting," v.
[54] Sitterson, *Sugar Country*, Chap. 16.
[55] Philip D. Uzee, "The Republican Party in the Louisiana Election of 1896," *Louisiana History*, II (1961), 335.
[56] Ford, "Constitutional Convention," 54.

major role in Louisiana politics. (2) It showed how close the Democrats could come to losing their control, as Foster was to lose a majority of the white parishes. (3) It turned out to be the last time a Louisiana governor would be allowed to succeed himself in office for many decades.[57]

The Populists and National Republicans proceeded to negotiate a fusion ticket consisting of three Nationals and four Populists, with J. N. Pharr, a National Republican, as the candidate for governor. The Democrats charged that Pharr, a prohibitionist, was also the candidate of the Negro, and many conservative Democrats in sugar country gave substantial sums to prevent what they feared would be a return of Negro rule.[58] Pharr's words regarding the Negro were indeed different from the views of the Democrats when he said: "I was reared with the Negro and worked side by side with him for twenty odd years. I may say for all my life, I never have found him other than a good laborer and as honest as most other men. If he has cut a bad figure in politics, we are to blame for it."[59]

The Democrats' opposition gained strength when the regular Republicans endorsed the fusion.[60] Their convention was a replica of every Republican convention for the past twenty years, as Warmoth and Kellogg battled it out. Kellogg wanted a separate ticket, while Warmoth wanted to endorse the fusion. This time the Warmoth faction was able to prevail.

Of such a tripartite fusion of diverse elements, whose only unifying force was the desire to beat the Democrats, the Thibodaux *Sentinal*, on February 8, 1896, made the following summary evaluation: (1) The Populist favored a paternalism of the most pronounced type and favored communism and free silver. (2) The National Republicans were white supremacists who had no use for the "niggers" except to vote them. (3) The regular Republicans wanted to repeal the separate car and anti-miscegenation laws.[61]

[57] *Ibid.*, 68.
[58] Sitterson, *Sugar Country*, 340.
[59] Romero, "Murphy J. Foster," 76.
[60] Uzee, "Election of 1896," 336–37.
[61] Quoted in Uzee, "Election of 1896," 337.

For good or bad, the Negro still had a vote in 1896, and this worried the Democrats. Foster, who had fought for party unity throughout his political career, now faced his most severe test. Governor Foster believed that only with the Democrats in power could the commonwealth prosper and, of course, this meant the Negro vote must somehow be managed. This meant white supremacy.

The intrusion of the problem of Negro suffrage irked the fusionists, as they stood to gain by the Negro vote. The Populist branch was also antagonistic to Foster as a result of the Governor's action in his first term. *The Louisiana Populist* had claimed that the "first thing Foster did after he was counted into office was to take the farmers by the nape of their necks and the slack of their trousers and dump them outside the party lines."[62] If the farmer wanted to try his luck with the People's Party, then the Democrats concluded they could do without him. The election results in 1896 proved the Democrats to be correct.

When the votes were counted, it was revealed that the Democrats had won with 56 percent of the total vote cast. Foster claimed 116,216 votes to Pharr's 90,138. Fraud was claimed, and with justification, since Foster's largest majorities had come from parishes where the Negro registration was heaviest.[63] The fusionists were sure the Democrats had stuffed the ballot boxes to ensure victory. Populists and National Republicans, as well as former Democrats, fearing such an outcome, had tried to make sure every election commissioner and poll official in the parishes with a Negro majority was a trusted Democrat because "the Negro vote would have to replace the white ones."[64] The election results showed the Democrats had been able to meet the challenge.

The distribution of the parish support of Foster showed the classic fracture line in Louisiana politics, along the river Y. (See Map 6–3). Only Natchitoches Parish, of all those through which flow the Red and the Mississippi rivers, failed to provide a majority for the Democrats. The Bourbons dominated the parishes touched by

[62] Romero, "Murphy J. Foster," 64.
[63] Daniel, "The Louisiana People's Party."
[64] Uzee, "Election of 1896," 339.

# Murphy J. Foster Vote, 1896

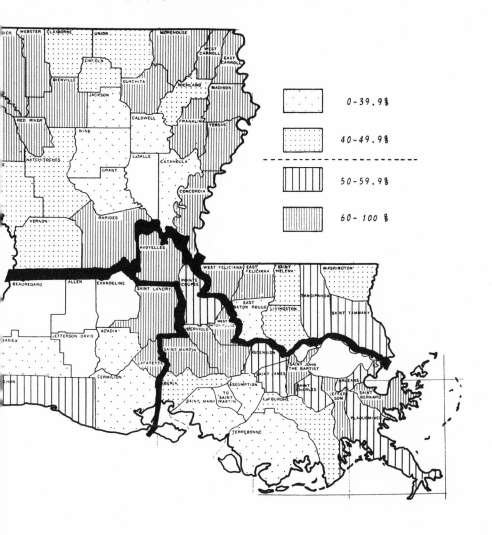

alluvial soil, where to this day, a large proportion of Louisiana's Negro population resides, a mark of the plantation system. Farmer and planter parishes stand out in sharp relief.

More refined analysis is shown in the distribution of the 1896 Democratic vote through within-state differences by voter types:

*Table 6–11*

MURPHY J. FOSTER VOTE, 1896, BY VOTER TYPE AREAS

| Unit | Number of Parishes | | | |
| --- | --- | --- | --- | --- |
| | 0–39% | 40–49% | 50–59% | 60–100% |
| No. La. Planter Parishes | — | — | — | 10 |
| Macon Ridge | — | 1 | — | 2 |
| No. Louisiana Hills | 1 | 4 | — | 3 |
| Central Pine Hills | 4 | 2 | — | — |
| So. La. Planter Parishes | 1 | — | 4 | 3 |
| So. La. Bayou Parishes | 2 | 2 | 1 | 3 |
| Florida Parishes | 1 | 3 | 2 | 2 |
| Southwest Louisiana | 3 | — | 1 | 2 |
| Urban Area | — | — | 1 | 1 |
| STATEWIDE | (12) | (12) | (9) | (26) |

The strong voice of the farmer is manifest in the "People's" vote in the Hills. In fact, wherever the farmer predominated in a parish in 1896 the Democratic candidate was defeated. While 60 percent of the parishes voted a majority for the Democrats in 1896, they were concentrated in their distribution. Almost three-fourths of the parishes supporting Foster were located in North Louisiana, within or adjacent to the Planter cluster, or within the South Louisiana Planter area and the Florida Parishes.

Fusion was best supported in those parishes where the Negro was not predominant. Almost the only exception is found in South Louisiana, where the cane planter had supported the anti-Bourbon Democratic cause. The parishes in the Hills areas, which had shown Populist tendencies in 1892, were the ones where the fusion of 1896 was successful, although half of the fusion parishes were to be found elsewhere. The vote for fusion had fashioned a bridge between North and South Louisiana.

Concerning the defeat by the Bourbons, the editor of the Winnfield *Comrade*, Hardy Brian, concluded: "We refused to take up the gun [and] so we lost. The fight will be won some day, but by. . . [unchristian] methods."[65] The farmers from rural uplands and bayous had found their voice, but in so doing they had uncovered their common enemy, the Democrats. The farmer would not be heard from again until the advent of Huey P. Long.

Despite defeat at the polls, the influence of the Alliance and Populist movements in Louisiana, as in the South, was profound. It shook to the foundations the supremacy of the Bourbon oligarchy. It effected, for the first time since the Civil War, a genuine cleavage within the Democratic Party, and what is most important, it forced the Democratic Party to look forward, and to become for a time almost as progressive as the Populist party.[66]

Francis B. Simkins showed how the Populism struggle was the last of three periods of southern politics following the Civil War. The first of these, Reconstruction, failed in its objective to give the Negro political rights, even though the principle of equality may have survived as a promise. The second period saw the Bourbon rule re-establish the cult of the southern gentleman and the practicality of seeking political power in alliance with business interests. Populism, finally, helped win rights for the agricultural majority and for the whites in general. Simkins cited the notable results accomplished in this last period, of how "the common whites were taught to exercise effectively their political power through the Democratic primaries; discriminatory legislation against the political and social rights of the Negro created the sort of equilibrium the South had long desired."[67] Whatever the course of events in other parts of the South, however, the political struggles in Louisiana in no way produced such notable results, perhaps because here the social and political discipline exacted by the Bourbons was more severe.[68]

[65] Hair, "Agrarian Protest," 292–93.
[66] Link, "The Progressive Movement," 177.
[67] Francis B. Simkins, *The South, Old and New* (New York, 1948), 269.
[68] V. O. Key, Jr., *Southern Politics* (New York, 1949), 550 ff.

III. *The Great Disfranchisement of 1898*

The Bourbons' "reconstruction," which was to shape the course of
Louisiana politics in the twentieth century, was completed in 1898.
The Democrats had managed to meet the challenge of the Populist-
Republican fusion. The destiny of Louisiana was in safe hands,
although there remained difficulties in the fact that Negro registration
was highest in the very parishes Governor Foster had won to preserve
white supremacy.[69] Some further safeguard was needed to prevent
the rebel farmer class or Negro voters from again threatening the
status quo. For the eighth time in the state's history a constitutional
convention was called.

Although it was generally felt that much of the 1879 constitution
was obsolete, the deeper reason for calling the convention was to create
a document that would limit Negro suffrage. Members of the white
power structure who had acquiesced to the Negro equality forced
by Radical Republicans, now had their chance to reestablish racial
segregation in Louisiana. And now it was the once adamant nation
who acquiesced—possibly because the myth of the Old South had
become more believable, and possibly because it was occupied with
its own ethnic and industrial problems.[70]

The members of the convention who wrote the Constitution of 1898
interpreted their mandate from the "people" to be to disfranchise
as many Negroes and as few whites as possible without violating the
Fifteenth Amendment to the federal Constitution. The intention was
stated plainly by the president of the convention, Ernest B.
Kruttschnitt, who had also chaired the convention of 1879: "We have
here no political antagonism and I am called upon to preside over
what is little more than a family meeting of the Democratic Party
of the State of Louisiana. . . . We are all aware that this convention
has been called . . . principally to deal with one question . . . to
eliminate from the electorate the mass of corrupt and illiterate voters

[69] Ford, "Constitutional Convention," 145–56.
[70] Perry H. Howard and Joseph L. Brent III, "Social Change, Urbanization, and
Types of Society," *Journal of Social Issues*, XXII (1966), 73–84.

who have during the last quarter century degraded our politics."[71] Of the 120 members convened in New Orleans, in February of 1898, to fashion a new power structure for Louisiana, 86 were natives of the state, and 110 of them were college graduates. Generally, they were conservative but, on the suffrage issue, reactionary.[72]

Several of the new constitutional provisions reflected the temper of the age. Legislative provisions, for example, increased the power to control corporations, a Populist idea. The legislature could no longer enact either local or special legislation. The governor was made ineligible to succeed himself. Yet, detailed restrictions on legislation were continued despite the fact that Negro dominance was no longer a threat. The shadow of Reconstruction hung over the convention of 1898.

A suffrage that could withstand scrutiny of the United States Supreme Court was the Democrats' chief aim. Their scheme was to provide several alternative suffrage requirements. If the Negro could not be refused the vote under one provision, then he could be banned under another. Certain educational and property qualifications were required by all voters, except any whose fathers or grandfathers had been legal voters in 1867. This meant that four classes of men would be allowed to vote: (1) literates; (2) tax-paying property owners; (3) sons of property owners; and (4) men who had voted in 1867, or their descendants.[73] It was this action which assured the successful completion of the struggle for reconstruction.

Governor Foster had been influential in leading the move to change the constitution. His message concerning the 1898 constitutional action reveals, perhaps, the dominant attitude which prevailed within the membership of his party: "The white supremacy for which we have so long struggled at the cost of so much precious blood and treasure, is now crystallized into the Constitution as a fundamental part and parcel of that organic instrument, and that, too, by no subterfuge or other evasions. With this great principle thus firmly imbedded in the Constitution, and honestly enforced, there need

[71] *Journal of the Constitutional Convention of 1898* (Baton Rouge, 1898), 9.
[72] Ford, "Constitutional Convention," 125.
[73] Constitution of 1898, Article 197.

be no longer any fear as to the honesty and purity of future elections."[74]

The ultimate consequences of this principle will become apparent in the analysis of twentieth-century politics. The immediate results were to reduce the registration by more than the estimated twenty to thirty thousand whites which the "grandfather-clause" provison had proposed to cover. A distinguished lawyer delegate to the convention, conscious of the moral dilemma and the paradox in the actions of 1898, remarked "By the irony of fate, as it were, this ultra-conservative convention was called upon as its chief duty to do the most radical thing known to legislation; to falsify the accepted teachings of history and roll back the wheels of political revolution without bloodshed; to take away the ballot from almost, if not quite, a majority of the voters of the state."[75]

The registration statistics, before and after 1898, and the gubernatorial vote in the election of 1900, provide an eloquent finale to the struggle for supremacy:[76]

*Table 6–12*
REGISTRATION BEFORE AND AFTER 1898,
AND GUBERNATORIAL VOTE, 1900

|  | White Registration | Negro Registration | Total Registration |
|---|---|---|---|
| January 1, 1897 | 164,888 (56%) | 130,444 (44%) | 294,432 (100%) |
| March 17, 1900 | 125,437 (96%) | 5,320 (4%) | 130,757 (100%) |
| Decrease in Registration | 38,551 | 125,124 | 163,675 |

|  | Total Gubernatorial Vote | Total Democratic Vote | Percent Turnout |
|---|---|---|---|
| 1896 | 206,324 | 116,216 | 74% |
| 1900 | 76,870 | 60,206 | 56% |
| Decrease in Vote | 129,484 | 56,010 | |

[74] *Louisiana Senate Journal*, 1898, 33–35.
[75] T. J. Kernan, "The Constitutional Convention of 1898 and Its Works," *Transactions*, Louisiana Bar Association (1899), 56–57.
[76] See Riley E. Baker, "Negro Voter Registration in Louisiana, 1879–1964," *Louisiana Studies*, IV (1965), 332–49.

The number of voters in 1896 had been the greatest in history, an indication of the issue at stake. Seventy-four percent of the registered voters had gone to the polls. In the gubernatorial election of 1900, there was a double-edged difference. Only 76 percent of the number of whites who had registered in 1897 did so in 1900, and of these, only 61 percent bothered to vote. The Democrats had not only succeeded in their disfranchisement, they had discouraged the very use of suffrage by the constitutionally elegible voters.

The registration of voters had reached its peak in 1897, the year following the attempt at fusion, when there was still hope that the votes of the farmer and the Negro spelled victory. This strong numerical position was to be of no avail, for, in the registration which preceded the gubernatorial primary election of 1900, the total count was only 45 percent of what it had been. The decrease in Negro registration was over 95 percent, as the proportion of Negroes in the electorate fell from 44 percent to a mere 4 percent. The suffrage clauses had done their expected work. What remains to be explained, however, is the decrease in the number of white registered voters. Almost 40,000 fewer white people registered in 1900 than in 1897.

It must be made clear at the outset, as Professor Henry C. Dethloff has shown, that "it cannot be substantiated that twenty-five per cent of the white voters were *disfranchised* by the convention of 1898. . . . The grandfather-clause and another part of section 5 allowed every previous white voter to register *if he so desired.*"[77] The contention *can* be made, however, that the impact of the actions of 1898 produced a widespread apathy among white voters, many of whom found it fruitless to concern themselves with politics. Evidence of this can be drawn from a number of indicators, including the parish distribution of gain or loss in registration, differences in the total vote between 1896 and 1900, and the proportional distribution of the white registration in 1908 (Appendix A, Table 16).

In twelve parishes, the white registration actually increased in 1900 over that of 1897. At least half of these twelve were planter parishes, in both North and South Louisiana. In certain parishes an

---

[77] Dethloff, "The Alliance and the Lottery," 158, n 72, italics added.

increase in white population had occurred, blunting the general decrease in voter registration. The move of whites into West Carroll, for example, was the forerunner of a large migration into the Macon Ridge parishes which would occur after 1910. An overall gain was likewise registered in Vernon and Washington Parishes, where increased lumber operations had already brought an influx of white population. The statewide distributions of losses in white registration, particularly evident in hill and bayou parishes, was a mark of the indignity which had been imposed upon farmer groups.

The number of whites registered to vote before the 1900 gubernatorial election was nearly as high as in 1888, and by 1908, the number of whites registered came within 130 of equaling the 153,174 registered white voters in 1896. No definite advantage accrued to any particular voter type. In fact, as the figures in Appendix A, Table 16 show, the relative advantage of farmer over planter parishes in North Louisiana, for example, remained nearly the same between 1888 and 1908: 3.6 percent more of the total white registration as compared to 3.0 percent. Further analysis below will show that, in fact, the number of whites registered was not a fair indication of the propensity to vote in the one-party primaries of the Democrats.

In the frame of reference used to analyze voting behavior in this study, it could be said of political life in Louisiana after the troublesome presence of the Negro was eliminated that ALL, EXCEPT OTHER were to be admitted (See Table 2–3). If, a half century later, the Negro was to be brought back in, as America sought to "socialize conflict,"[78] just the opposite was intended by the Bourbons, in the South and in Louisiana, at the turn of the twentieth century. The potentials of 1896 had been drastically blunted by the power structure fashioned by the framers of the Constitution of 1898. Segregation was sanctioned as a way of life.[79]

The crucial significance of 1898 lay in what V. O. Key called "developments beyond the constitution and laws." While a lively

[78] E. E. Schattschneider, *The Semi-Sovereign People* (New York, 1960); Harry A. Bailey, Jr. (ed.), *Negro Politics in America* (Columbus, 1967).

[79] C. Vann Woodward, *The Strange Career of Jim Crow* (2nd rev. ed., New York, 1966).

two-party competition prevailed before the war, save for the imported conflict between Radical Republican and Democrat, the previous bipartisanship failed to re-establish itself after the war. If, during this era, occasional cleavage between planter and farmer emerged, it was finally defeated by the combined forces of *discipline* and *repression*. Suffrage restrictions and the one-party system were the consequence. Social discipline tended "to bind a large proportion of the whites, especially the whites of substance and property to the Democratic party," and "measures and actions calculated to repress those opposed to the dominant, 'respectable' coalition"[80] were taken.

In general outline, the pattern of support for the People's Party and its Republican allies remained a significant one in subsequent Louisiana politics. Meanwhile, this pattern was frustrated, when the lower classes failed to gain the political upper hand in the struggles of the half century just completed. White farmers tried to beat the Bourbons in fusion with the Negro, and failed. It has been claimed that many disillusioned Populists found solace in white supremacy. But even this brought no respite, since the deeper question was *which whites* should be supreme?[81] In Louisiana a planter-merchant elite had captured the Democratic Party and treated the Louisiana version of the "solid South" as if it were a closed corporation. The endemic patterns of elitism and ascription continued to prevail.[82] The aspirations of the common man were thwarted, and Louisiana might well be said to have commenced a long convalescence of a seriously arrested socioeconomic development.

IV. *Machine Politics and "Good Government" Opposition: 1900–1916.*

With opposition effectively eliminated, the Democratic Party had a clear field in Louisiana politics. The sole problem became one of keeping control of the party machinery. The Bourbons were not at a loss in knowing what to do. There were allies to be had in the city. New Orleans had regularly polled about 20 percent of the total

[80] Key, *Southern Politics*, 551.
[81] Woodward, *New South*, 328.
[82] Seymour Martin Lipset, *The First New Nation* (Garden City, 1967), 246.

statewide vote. For purposes of representation in the state legislature, the city of New Orleans, even in antebellum days, had been divided into districts (wards), each of which sent a representative to the legislature. With the ward utilized as a unit, city voters could be organized into an effective political machine. The selection of a gubernatorial candidate with a reasonable degree of strength outside the city, granted he had the ability to deliver the city vote, would be tantamount to victory. Organized in 1897, the New Orleans Choctaw Club, the Ring, or the Old Regulars, as they became known to their friends, developed a machine along these lines and began to play an influential part in the politics of the state.[83]

Experience was to show that intraparty factional struggles could be just as bitter as the previous struggles between parties. But factional politics are not the same as two-party politics, if for no other reason than that issues become blurred. Nor is the problem of patronage the same. In spite of this, the factions tend to follow socioeconomic divisions within the population. And in Louisiana, a champion of the have-nots would be long in coming.

Before the white primary of the Democratic Party replaced the general election in importance, however, the Bourbons found it necessary to defeat the dying efforts of the opposition. That there was little difficulty in this can be seen by reviewing the distribution of the statewide vote in the general elections of 1900 and 1904. The statewide average support for the Democratic winner in 1904 was 84 percent, and only South Louisiana Planter and Bayou voter types recorded support below this average.

The state Democratic convention nominated the incumbent state auditor, William W. Heard, for governor in 1900. He was the preference of Governor Foster. In opposition, the regular Republicans nominated Eugene S. Reems, while the lilywhite Republicans and Populists joined to support the candidacy of Donelson Caffery. Although the campaign was spirited, the result was never in doubt. Heard became governor with 78 percent of the vote of 76,870 being cast in his favor. The parish distribution of the 1900 and 1904 vote

[83] George M. Reynolds, *Machine Politics in New Orleans, 1897–1926* (New York, 1936).

revealed in classic profile the final domination of the Bourbons (Map 6–4). In 18 of the then 62 parishes within the state, the total vote for Heard had been over 90 percent. Solidarity approaching that of the 1880's had been established again, but this time it was in the parishes in which it should have been:

*Table 6–13*

PARISH DEMOCRATIC VOTE OVER 90 PERCENT, 1900,
WITH AVERAGE NEGRO PERCENT OF POPULATION, 1870–1900
(STATE AVERAGE, NEGRO 49 PERCENT)

| | | | | | |
|---|---|---|---|---|---|
| Tensas | 91% | Pointe Coupee | 74% | Richland | 64% |
| East Carroll | 90% | Caddo | 72% | West Carroll | 60% |
| West Feliciana | 84% | West Baton Rouge | 71% | Rapides | 56% |
| St. Charles | 76% | East Feliciana | 69% | St. Martin | 52% |
| Bossier | 75% | Red River | 68% | St. Bernard | 49% |
| Morehouse | 75% | De Soto | 67% | Jefferson | 45% |

Many of the parishes displaying solidarity were found in territorial clusters—in the plantation areas of the cotton country, up the Mississippi, down the Red River, across the Felicianas, and clustered about New Orleans. Most of these were parishes in which the Negro registration had previously outnumbered the whites and where the plantation remained a dominant force in the economy. These were the home parishes of the Bourbon Democrats, the conservative unreconstructed southern gentlemen. For them, ideoology had become a reality.

Despite the overwhelming victory of the Democrats at the polls and, despite the decreased white registration, the white Republican-Populist fusion carried pluralities for Caffery in Cameron, Ascension, and St. James. Impressive support was also given in many other parishes that had demonstrated Populist tendencies before. The traditionally Whig-Republican sugar bowl provided a sizable Republican vote in backing Caffery on the Republican ticket. The distribution of Caffery support on the Populist side brings into sharp relief the block of hill parishes where, yet, the farmer's voice was heard.

# The Classic Profile
## Average Gubernatorial Winner
## 1900-1904

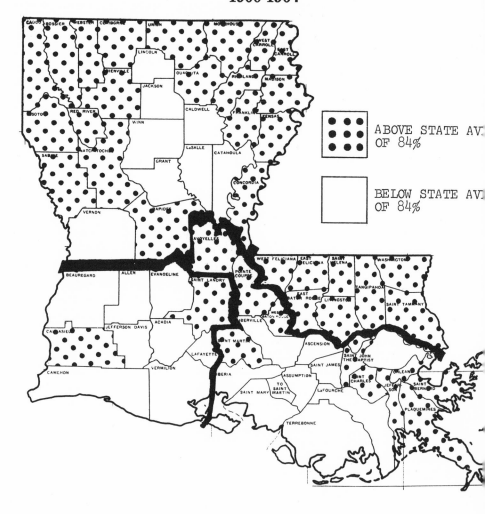

ABOVE STATE AV
OF 84%

BELOW STATE AV
OF 84%

The gubernatorial general election of 1904 was a very one-sided contest. The Republican candidate W. J. Behan, received but 10 percent of the total vote. The count of the votes polled in this election, 54,222, represented a drop of more than 20,000 below the total vote of 1900. What little Republican support remained in Louisiana was concentrated in sugar country. The Republican vote reached as high as 41 percent in Ascension Parish, and in total, there were fourteen parishes which had a Republican vote higher than the state average of 10 percent. Three of the previously strong Populist parishes, Natchitoches, Winn, and Catahoula, registered vestiges of the former protest; people here were not yet willing to let Democratic ascendancy be complete.

But what counted from now on was the Democratic white primary. In the primary that preceded the general election of 1904, the total vote was some 12,000 more than the Democratic total of 60,206 votes in the general election of 1900. Part of this gain came from South Louisiana Democrats who had voted for Caffery then, but were now back in the Democratic camp. The distribution of the support of the winner of the primary, Newton Blanchard, demonstrated the pattern of the new one-party tendency, when a candidate had the endorsement of the New Orleans Choctaws. The prediction of Blanchard's victory might have been the 71 percent of the New Orleans vote which went for him. Part of the highest parish percentages favoring the machine candidate clustered in the Mississippi Delta cotton country and in the sugar country. Democratic success also made inroads in the Central Pine Hills. One student of the period suggested that the surprising support of the Ring candidate here was due to the successful campaign appeals of Martin Behrman, Choctaw leader, who ran for state auditor on the Blanchard ticket.[84] The election of 1904 demonstrated that Louisiana had become a one-party state.

The bulwark of white supremacy, the one-party control of the state which the Bourbons had gained through the act of disfranchisement, now seemed secure. However, a continued internal power struggle is revealed in a study of the voting patterns in Democratic primary

[84] Reynolds, *Machine Politics*, 99.

elections as voters were asked to endorse Bourbon candidates. The power structure, consisting of those who had fashioned the constitutional instrument of 1898, had to be content to compete with such new political expressions as the movement for "good government," while looking back over their shoulders at remnants of the agrarian unrest in the form of alternative candidates representing the hill parishes. The review of tendencies in the early decades of the twentieth century, therefore, is facilitated by bringing together primaries where the machine candidates clearly prevailed (1908 and 1916), and primaries where the good government candidate, together with an alternative candidate from the Hills, provided stiff opposition to the machine (1912 and 1924) (Appendix B, Table 5). In 1920, as the narrative account will develop in the next chapter, the "good government" candidate won outright.

When the one-party primary determined the choice for governor, the variance in the vote became greater. While in the general elections of 1900–1904 the average statewide vote had been heavily Democratic (84 percent), in the primary contests of 1908 and 1916 the vote was not nearly so one-sided, the average support for the winning machine candidate having been 65 percent. Moreover, when the Hills alternative joined good government forces, as in the primaries of 1912 and 1924, the total vote tended to divide almost equally three ways. No such positive assertion may be made about within-state differences in these primary elections, although, of course, Orleans was the foundation of machine support and the location of the support for Hill alternatives is obvious. At the same time, the highest support for good government candidates tended to be seated in South Louisiana.

The Old Regular Democratic machine followed the Bourbon line in 1908, when the incumbent lieutenant governor, J. Y. Sanders, entered the contest for nomination. He had been a law partner of former Governor Foster, unanimously elected speaker of the House in 1900, and had served on the suffrage and election committee at the 1898 constitutional convention. His objective there had been: "Fix it so every white man could vote and no Negro get within a mile of the polls."[85] His

[85] Mary Elizabeth Sanders, "The Political Career of Jared Young Sanders" (Master's thesis, Louisiana State University, 1955), 22.

Bourbon credentials were impeccable, and the machine politicians showed no hesitation in endorsing Sanders; the machine alliance with the Bourbons had become a leading tendency.

In the primary election of 1908, Sanders received 56 percent of the statewide vote; the machine produced a near 10,000-vote majority in New Orleans with which to offset any close margins in the country parishes. The distribution of support in this election approached the classic pattern; Bourbons from the Mississippi Delta parishes in the north, and from sugar country in the south, aligned with the cluster of support about New Orleans. However, the appearance of farmer parishes from western Louisiana within the ranks of the Democrats of this decade gives reason to pause. These former Populist parishes, Vernon and Sabine in particular, participated in the Democratic primaries in support of the machine candidate.

Vernon and Sabine were among a group of parishes that grew rapidly in population between 1890 and 1910.[86] Extensive lumbering operations attracted large numbers of farmers and laborers to them in this period. The population of Sabine, for example, doubled in the period from 1890 to 1910, and that of Vernon tripled. In 1910, the racial composition of the two parishes was 79.0 and 87.6 percent white, respectively. Vernon had shown a 33 percent increase in voter registration in the period from 1897 to 1910. A parish like Vernon enjoyed the lumber boom, but when the mills moved on to fresher forests, leaving a devastated cutover area, farmer and lumber worker became hard-pressed to eke out a bare existence. The result was a turn to radical politics.[87] Louisiana faced change, and the perpetuation of Bourbon control was guaranteed only if the power structure learned how to use it to their own advantage.

If one factor of modernization is industry, and the presence of industry may be measured by the proportion of gainfully employed males not in agriculture,[88] then consider the following:

[86] T. Lynn Smith, *The Growth of Population in Louisiana, 1890–1930* (Louisiana State University, Agricultural Experiment Station Bulletin No. 264 [Baton Rouge, 1935]), 9.
[87] Gradie McWhiney, "Louisiana Socialists in the Early Twentieth Century: A Study of Rustic Radicalism," *Journal of Southern History*, XX (1954), 315–36.
[88] Daniel Lerner, *The Passing of Traditional Society* (Glencoe, 1958), 46.

Table 6–14
PERCENT MALES EMPLOYED, NON-AGRICULTURE,
IN NATION AND STATE, 1870–1960*

|               | 1870 | 1880 | 1890 | 1900 | 1910 | 1920 | 1930 | 1940 | 1950 | 1960 |
|---------------|------|------|------|------|------|------|------|------|------|------|
| United States. . . | 43 | 46 — | 55 | 57 | 65 | 71 | 75 | 78 | 85 | 85 |
| Louisiana . . . . | 35 | 32 | 34 | 36 — | 50 | 57 | 60 | 64 | 80 | 90 |

* Source: Simon Kuznets, *Population Redistribution* (Philadelphia, 1960), II.

Louisiana, traditionally agrarian, began her industrial development fully two decades after the nation did. The rapid spread of lumbering, as well as the discovery of oil and gas, contributed to the relatively large jump in the proportion of males employed in non-agricultural occupations, after 1900.[89]

With winds of change blowing across the state, the machinery being perfected by Bourbon and city Democrats was not unopposed. Cries of "corruption and inefficiency in government" were heard. Opposition was being consolidated to satisfy the urge to reform. The Constitution of 1898 had failed, as would the subsequent one, to fit the processes of government to the temper of the times. Louisiana was experiencing industrial development which would reshape her society, with new groups and new problems requiring satisfactions and solutions. The governor found himself head of an administration largely beyond his control, and one student found that the constitutional convention and the indifferent electorate which voted on the flood of amendments that came in the twentieth century had become the two important governing bodies.[90]

It was at this time that the movement of Progressivism overtook the southern region and found support in Louisiana. Progressivism in the South was a continuance of the previous agrarian unrest, but it was now focused on urban problems.[91] The Progressives seemed particularly anti-corporation, although their middle class concern did

[89] Millet, " 'Imperial' Calcasieu."
[90] James W. Prothro, "A Study of Constitutional Developments in the Office of the Governor of Louisiana" (Master's thesis, Louisiana State University, 1948), 88.
[91] Link, "The Progressive Movement,"

not extend to unionism and social legislation. Progressivism has been defined as an amalgam consisting of: agrarian radicalism, business regulation, good government, and urban social justice reform.[92] As such, Progressivism became a movement for positive government, embracing a public service concept. As adopted in the South it became traditionalistic, individualistic, and set in a socially conservative milieu. The Progressives looked back, as the Populists had done before them, to an agrarian Arcadia.[93]

The year 1912 was a troublesome one for the Bourbons and their machine counterparts as Louisiana found itself caught up in "good government" opposition and backwoods socialism. John M. Parker emerged in state politics in the gubernatorial election of that year.[94] Two years before, Parker had been instrumental in organizing the Good Government League. The League led by Parker, was established to work for a more efficient local government in New Orleans. The move thus paralleled the national scene, where a new rationale of public administration gave impetus to reform movements. In 1910, for example, William H. Taft had established the Commission on Economy and Efficiency in Government. Businessmen got behind it with the slogan: "Let's make government more business-like." Parker meant business, and in 1912, the League put forward a candidate for governor—Judge Luther Hall.

As League candidate, Hall opposed John T. Michel, who was backed by the New Orleans machine. Michel was the incumbent secretary of state and an Old Regular of long standing. The race took on a new dimension, however, when Dr. James B. Aswell resigned the presidency of the State Normal School at Natchitoches and announced his candidacy as an independent. Aswell has been elected state superintendent of education during the adminstration of Governor Blanchard, and he was credited with guiding the progress which was being made in education. The rural people had reason to appreciate what a lack of educational advantages could mean, and

[92] George B. Tindall, *The Emergence of the New South, 1913–1945* (Baton Rouge, 1967), 32.

[93] Tindall, *"Emergence of New South,"* 7.

[94] Spencer Phillips, "Administration of Goveror Parker" (Master's thesis, Louisiana State University, 1933).

# Candidate Pluralities, Gubernatorial Primary
## 1912

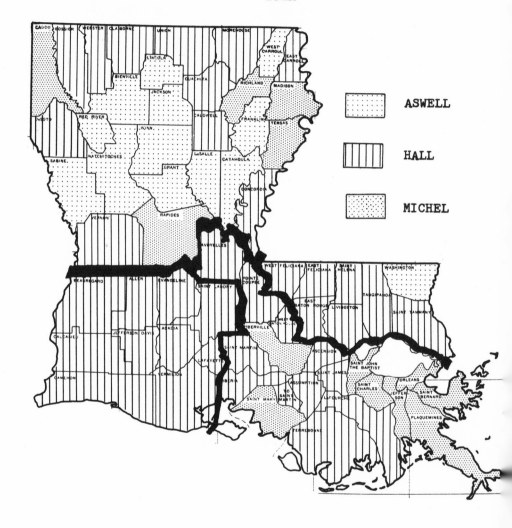

at Natchitoches, Aswell had worked for improvement of rural schools in the Hills. In this election he gained stature by refusing to place himself in the hands of the Good Government League or to withdraw from the race. A Hills alternative was provided.

The race lay between Michel and Hall, although the entry of Aswell was to demonstrate the support that could be had by appealing to the Hill Parishes. Hall won the primary election with 43 percent of the total vote. The machine candidate, Michel, received 37 percent and, even without the candidacy of Aswell, who received 20 percent of the vote, it is doubtful that the machine could have won. For the strength of both Hall and Aswell was found in the country parishes. The machine did manage to keep its strength in the city, when again, the Ring candidate was given a plurality of almost 10,000 votes over the double opposition. The appeals of reform had spread too widely, however, to enable the machine to swing the primary election of 1912 (Map 6-5).

The Old Regular Michel was able to gain pluralities outside of New Orleans in only eleven parishes. The distribution indicated that the Bourbon-machine alliance could still register the old pattern, despite the opposition. In the rural areas, Michel won pluralities in plantation country, in Madison, Tensas, and Richland, and in Iberville, St. Mary, and a cluster of parishes about New Orleans. Rounding out the list were Rapides and Caddo, traditionally planter parishes, where a new urbanism was afoot. In Caddo many plantations along the Red River remained Bourbon and the Bourbon predisposition of Shreveport would become stronger with passing years.

The distribution of parish support for the Good Government candidate was widespread. Nearly all of South Louisiana voted for Hall in a bloc, and he also won pluralities in the parishes along the Arkansas border. The parishes of the Hills, however, gave their plurality support to Aswell. This was not surprising, in the parishes that had produced so recently the strong Populist tendency, where the voter would have been enthusiastic for the one candidate who was a genuine independent. At any rate, the cluster of parishes which gave Aswell his pluralities was the heart of the country of the People's Party.

After the primary election, and before the presidential election of 1912, John M. Parker went over to Teddy Roosevelt and the Bull Moose Republicans. Parker opposed the tariff stand of the Democrats and called for a Louisiana brand of Progressivism. He claimed that the Progressive Party he helped organize in the state was the first white man's party ever established in the South. For Parker, the Louisiana ProgressiveParty stood for: reasonable tariff protection, absolute federal control of the Mississippi River, and white supremacy.[95] Its immediate concern was to line up statewide support for the Progressive candidate for President, Theodore Roosevelt.

The appearance of lumber corporations in the hills and prairies of Central and Southwest Louisiana after the turn of the century brought, not only an increased population of farmers and workers and momentary economic gain, but also the attempt to organize the lumber workers by Socialist groups.[96] When Eugene V. Debs spoke at Winnfield in 1908, the local Socialist Party was well organized and had elected half the officials of Winn Parish. This parish had, only a decade before, taken the lead in the Populist movement. The struggle for social and economic betterment through the use of the ballot was not complete.

With Roosevelt and Debs on the presidential ballot, together with the regular Republican William H. Taft and the Democratic candidate Woodrow Wilson, there is explanation enough for the drop in Democratic support from the average 83 percent in 1900–16, to 77 percent in 1912. (Appendix Table 2) This was contrary to the rather level trend to support the Democrats in nation and region during this period. The 8 percent drop in Democratic support in Louisiana, however, is even more noteworthy in its distribution.

Winn Parish gave almost 36 percent of its vote to the Socialist presidential candidate Debs. Two more parishes, Vernon and West Carroll, voted more than 30 percent for Debs, and Caldwell, Grant, and LaSalle each supported the Socialist with more than 20 percent of the total vote. Where the lumbering industry was important, the Debs vote was high. The top quarter of Socialist support, ranging

[95] Tindall, "*Emergence of New South*," 29.
[96] McWhiney, "Louisiana Socialists."

from 12 to 36 percent, was concentrated in the Hill Parishes as the following will show:

Table 6–15
TOP QUARTER PARISHES FOR DEBS, 1912

|  | Total | North La. Hills | Central Hills |
|---|---|---|---|
| Number of Parishes . . . . . | (16 of 64) | (5 of 8) | (6 of 7) |
| Percent of Quarter . . . . . . | 100% | 31% | 38% |
| Votes for Debs . . . . . . . | (2,921) | (557) | (1,458) |
| Vote as percent of State Total . | 56% | 11% | 28% |

Put this way, 69 percent of the top quarter of Debs support was located within the Hill Parishes, and together these parishes made up 39 percent of the 5,192 votes cast for Debs in Louisiana.

This phenomenon of a rustic radicalism in Louisiana would not be so important had not the very people showing this tendency come from, or resided in, the parishes of Populist protest and had they not been farmers or related to the farmer class. The Farmers' Alliance and the Populist Party had already shown anti-capitalistic, if not outright Socialist, tendencies. As the lumber operators stripped the Louisiana hills, the farmer had grasped the chance to add to his meager subsistence by engaging in lumbering. This may not have increased the level of living of the hill people, for there were many among the farmers willing to work at almost any wage. The farmer thus experienced the "corporation."

The Socialist Party had earlier, in 1904, found more success in urban Louisiana; the first evidence of socialism in Louisiana was the 995 votes cast for Debs in the presidential election of that year. Orleans Parish contributed 48 percent of that vote. But as a student of Louisiana socialism put it, the city radicals were more strictly Marxian socialists, "more given to discussion than to action and by 1912 the farmers and lumber workers had taken over the party."[97] As a result, any possibility of fusion with the more radical International Workers of the World operating in the state was lost. But since urban reform was

[97] *Ibid.*, 321.

a hot issue of the times, it is interesting to see what parishes or candidates did fare well in 1912.

While Louisiana was not to achieve urban status in the census
count until 1950, its major city, New Orleans, had long been chief city
of the South. The nation's population became predominantly urban
between 1910 and 1920, a condition stimulated no doubt by the heavy
internal migrations associated with World War I. It took another
World War to get Louisiana urbanized, but not until 1960 was the
population of the South predominantly urban.

Emerging urban parishes of Louisiana comprised 43 percent of the
total registration of 1908. Twenty-eight percent of the registered
voters resided in New Orleans, while 8 percent and 7 percent, respectively, were found in urban parishes of South and North Louisiana.
At this time, the urban registration in the North made up one-fourth
of the voters in that area, while in the South the urban voters constituted slightly more than one-fifth the registration. Noting these
distinctions, examine the urban vote in the presidential election of
1912, charted on the facing page.

Clearly, Parker's version of Progressivism in Louisiana most
appealed to the urban voter, with over half the statewide Progressive
total of 12 percent coming from New Orleans and nearly three-fourths
from the urban parishes overall. It was predominantly a South
Louisiana vote, with 20 percent (all but 7 percent) of the remaining
country vote coming from ten southern parishes. On the other hand,
while 40 percent of the Republican votes were urban, most of their
votes came from the country as in the past; nearly a third of the
Republican vote was located in five South Louisiana Planter and
Bayou voter type units. The Democratic vote, which made up
77 percent of the state's total, was widely distributed, but a substantial
contribution was provided by New Orleans, whose voters went
80 percent for the machine's choice for President.

Enamored of the pure principles of Progressivism, John M. Parker
decided to run himself in 1916. He was opposed, of course, by the
Old Regulars and Bourbons, whose candidate was Ruffin G. Pleasant.
In 1912, Parker had become an active Progressive and had endorsed
Theodore Roosevelt in his losing fight for national Republican

Table 6-16

URBAN PARISHES VOTE, PRESIDENTIAL ELECTION, 1912

| | Progressives (Roosevelt) | | Republicans (Taft) | | Democrats (Wilson) | | Socialists (Debs) | |
|---|---|---|---|---|---|---|---|---|
| Caddo | 1,129 | | 34 | | 1,946 | | 91 | |
| Ouachita | 48 | | 17 | | 902 | | 113 | |
| Rapides | 110 | | 46 | | 1,334 | | 182 | |
| North Louisiana Urban | 1,277 | 11% | 97 | 1% | 4,192 | 7% | 386 | 8% |
| E. Baton Rouge | 96 | | 46 | | 1,076 | | 41 | |
| Calcasieu | 362 | | 171 | | 2,144 | | 584 | |
| Lafayette | 53 | | 244 | | 646 | | 76 | |
| Jefferson | 97 | | 7 | | 607 | | 27 | |
| South Louisiana Urban | 608 | 9% | 468 | 10% | 4,473 | 7% | 727 | 14% |
| Orleans | 4,965 | 53% | 904 | 29% | 26,433 | 43% | 732 | 14% |
| Total Louisiana Urban | 6,850 | 73% | 1,469 | 40% | 35,098 | 57% | 1,845 | 36% |
| Country Parishes | | 27% | | 60% | | 43% | | 65% |
| Percent of State Total Vote | | 12% | | 4% | | 77% | | 7% |

leadership. In so doing, Parker resigned his position as chairman of the Good Government League, as it was nominally a faction of the Democratic Party. He had voiced his determination to continue fighting for good government in Louisiana. Parker said he had become a Progressive out of respect for Roosevelt: "I am for Roosevelt because I believe he is one of the most active and progressive men in the United States, and does things."[98]

Parker would need to do things if he would win the governorship from control of the New Orleans Ring. The Louisiana Progressives elected the South's only third-party congressman, from Thibodaux, in 1914, and during the fall of 1915, Parker announced his candidacy for governor in Crowley. He advocated a protective tariff on sugar and rice, a stand which should have had sympathetic appeal among oldtime Republicans in Louisiana. He condemned the bosses, called for the abolition of unnecessary offices, and for a short ballot, all proper progressive issues. He also advocated a limited constitutional convention.[99]

An incident from the campaign revealed the forthrightness of Parker, and provided a ploy which would be followed by others in years to come. The New Orleans Protestant Ministers' Association asked three question of the candidates concerning the enforcement of gambling and Sunday laws. With straight face, Pleasant answered that he would enforce the laws under question, and of course, all other laws within his jurisdiction. Parker answered, however, in no such virtuous terms. Where there were regulations on gambling, these would suffice, if followed. Besides, it was a matter for the people to decide, whether they wanted to gamble or not. Anyway, the enforcement of such laws generally was left to local authorities.[100]

There had been mixed feelings concerning the candidacy of John M. Parker. No one wished to doubt the personal qualifications of the man, but it was felt that inasmuch as the Democratic candidate Pleasant had been duly nominated in the party primary, it was a bit unfair for Parker to have nominated himself. To meet this problem,

[98] Phillips, "Governor Parker," 11.
[99] Tindall, *Emergence of New South*, 30.
[100] Phillips, "Governor Parker," 13.

the Progressives held a nominating convention in which Parker was overwhelmingly endorsed. Nevertheless, it was felt that Parker and his ticket were foredoomed to failure. To beat the combined efforts of the established Bourbon Democrats and their New Orleans Ring allies would be singularly difficult. Even if Parker should win, his power of performance would be negligible in the face of a probably hostile legislature. The editorial opinion of the Alexandria *Democrat* adequately summarized the situation:

We are willing to admit that the conditions in Louisiana are bad politically, and there is much room for improvement, but considering the fact which everyone knows that Parker is a man of splendid character, great personal integrity, rugged, honest, and extraordinary business ability, in the event of his election, which nobody for a moment thinks probable, what would he be able to accomplish? He would be absolutely powerless as has been the present governor whom Mr. Parker assisted largely in elevating to the executive chair, and whose honesty of purpose and sincere desire to put into execution plans for the up-building and advancement of the State and all its people have never been questioned by any except his political enemies.[101]

Reformers might be able to capture the governorship, but without friendly support in the legislature, no great reforms would be forthcoming. The platforms and appeal of the Good Government faction of the Democratic Party and the earnestness of the Progressive movement might find widespread support among the electorate, but politics were still dominated by the Bourbons. Control of local parish affairs, and in particular, control of the legislature, was in the hands of the power elite.

In 1916, the Old Regulars and their country allies emerged triumphant. Pleasant received more than 60 percent of the votes, piling up a majority over Parker of about 32,000 votes. New Orleans voters gave Pleasant a majority of 10,000, which apparently had become the Ring's dependable lead. Nevertheless, Parker had gained majorities in sixteen of the state's sixty-four parishes, and the distribution showed Parker's stand had impressed the voters in the sugar and rice areas. The sixteen majority parishes, with the ten more

[101] Quoted in Phillips, "Governor Parker," 11.

in which the percentage vote was above the state average of 37 percent, outlined the borders of French South Louisiana. The resulting pattern looked ever so much like that which would emerge in the parish distribution of votes in the Louisiana elections of 1960.

A number of factors could account for this phenomenon. South Louisianians, slightly less averse to the sins of gambling, may have supported Parker's position on that count. His stand on the tariff may have been widely accepted. Or finally, the Progressive label of 1916 was akin to Republicanism, whose seat of support had ever been in South Louisiana. Parker received his weakest support in the parishes of North Louisiana, along the Mississippi, and along the Arkansas and Texas borders, as if there had been an anti-gambling judgement there.

In other southern states, Progressive leaders gave way to what became known as Dixie demagogues in vain attempt to bring down the Bourbon ascent. In each case the racial theme was touched in an assertion of white supremacy. The Progressives' reforms were aimed at problems brought by urbanism, but few could mistake their fundamental kinship to the conservative Bourbons. And if anyone expected the demagogues to upset the establishment, they found that after the sound and fury, nothing happened. The demagogues made the rural masses feel important, but they had made a class appeal without a class program. "They challenged the conservative hierarchies but made no sustained efforts to destroy them. They built their own machines but only to perpetuate themselves in office, and hence could not raise up a new succession."[102] Although a certain romance still existed in Dixie, a realism introduced to Louisiana politics would bring the Bourbons down.

[102] Williams, *Romance and Realism*, 63.

# CHAPTER VII

# The Rise of "Longism"

### 1. The Progressivism of John M. Parker and Why It Failed

Huey P. Long probably owed part of his success to the failure of John M. Parker to firmly establish his political position against the Bourbons. While by no means a typical "man of the people," Parker had a somewhat progressive program that was different from those of other state politicians up to 1920. The present section will highlight the political program of Governor Parker and attempt to estimate how it fared.

There is a parallel between Parker's campaigns for governor in 1916 and 1920 and Robert Kennon's in 1948 and 1952. Both men lost on their first tries, but in losing discovered specific lessons which helped assure victory in the second attempts. One of these lessons was the necessity of having strong organizations in both New Orleans and the rural areas.

The years 1920 and 1952 were similarly notable for reform campaigns—both candidates were "anti"; anti-Ring in Parker's case and anti-Long in Kennon's. Because the rural vote was close, both men were able to win through sizable victories in New Orleans.

In 1920, John M. Parker was recognized by the Old Regulars as the man to beat, and the campaign between Colonel Frank P. Stubbs and Parker was a bitter one. After twenty years of successful political battles, the Ring had many enemies and was accused of corruption; it was a natural target for a reform candidate. Mayor Martin Behrman, the leader of the Ring, philosophized that "most people remember what you did to them rather than what you did for them."[1] The

---

[1] George M. Reynolds, *Machine Politics in New Orleans, 1897–1926* (New York, 1936), 216.

theme of reform has a long and notable record of usefulness to politicans.

Determined to win the necessary vote in New Orleans, Parker established the Orleans Democratic Association to fight the Ring (Choctaws or Old Regulars). Later, as governor he would withdraw patronage power from the Ring and defeat their candidate for mayor, Behrman, with a candidate of his own choosing. Parker was able to accomplish all this in 1920. However, the Ring made a prompt comeback, and for fairly obvious reasons. In the first place, Parker realized that in order to fight fire with fire he had been forced to organize a machine in many ways no better than the Ring's, and he felt some reluctance to use the very tactics he claimed to be fighting.[2] Also the Orleans Democratic Association had in its ranks many disgruntled Ring men, political opportunists, and reformers. Naturally such a discordant group could not provide a sustained opposition to the Old Regular machine of New Orleans.

In this phase of Louisiana politics, however, it was necessary to organize and to make organization relatively permanent, for with the advent of Democratic supremacy, only the strong and politically wise could hope to wrest control from the Bourbons. They had worked hard and long for their successful domination. So, if it were impossible to beat them without joining them and copying their methods, then join them and beat them at their own game. This was to be part of Huey Long's key to success.

Who supported Parker in his successful defeat of the Ring in 1920 ? (Map 7-1) First of all, there was the organized support in New Orleans, where the city vote favoring the candidacy of Parker constituted 45 percent of the total city vote. The consistent spread of some 10,000 votes in favor of the Ring-backed candidates had been narrowed to 5,000. If workingmen were supporting the Choctaw machine, Parker's gain had come from the support of the more privileged groups in the city. Parker's New Orleans support made up 27 percent of his state-wide total (Appendix C, Table 5), which seemed to be all that good government candidates could get from the city. Another

---

[2] Spencer Phillips, "Administration of Governor Parker" (Master's thesis, Louisiana State University, 1933), 156.

# John M. Parker Vote, 1920

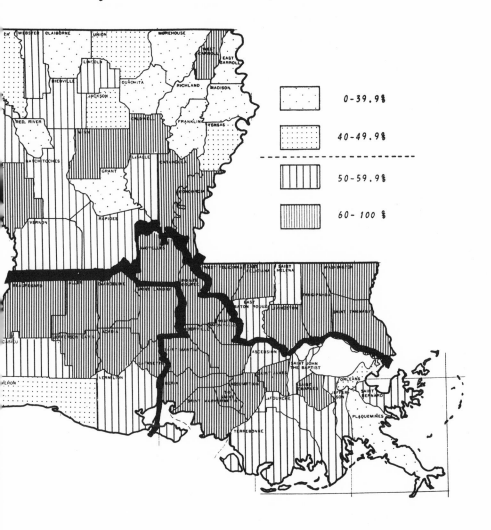

14 percent of the Parker vote had been contributed by the other emergent urban parishes. In fact, Caddo, which was counted urban for the first time by the 1920 Census, went 50 percent Parker. But while the urban parish vote alone appeared to be enough to ensure victory for machine candidates, John M. Parker won in 1920 with considerable rural parish support.

The Parker average state vote was 54 percent and in terms of parish voter type areas, it was clear that his heaviest support had come, as it had in 1916, from South Louisiana units. Parker received his largest country vote in the Third Congressional District, which embraced the heart of the sugar bowl (Map 7–1). His most impressive gains over 1916 came from North Louisiana, which overall averaged 49 percent for Parker, and where the Central Pine Hills support went as high as 60 percent. Huey Long had stumped for Parker in 1920, believing he favored the sort of economic reforms Long had been proposing as Public Service Commissioner. The apparent impact of such a union of progressive good government and Hills farmer sentiment can be found in the distribution of parish votes by percentage interval among voter types, showing where the almost 75 percent of Louisiana parishes carried by Parker were located.

*Table 7–1*

JOHN M. PARKER VOTE, 1920,
BY VOTER TYPE AREAS

| Voter type units | | Number of Parishes | | | |
|---|---|---|---|---|---|
| | 0–39% | 40–49% | 50–59% | 60–100% | (N) |
| So. La. Planter Parishes . . . | — | — | 2 | 6 | (8) |
| Florida Parishes. . . . . . . | — | — | 3 | 5 | (8) |
| Southwest Louisiana . . . . | — | 1 | 2 | 7 | (10) |
| Central Pine Hills . . . . . | 1 | — | 3 | 3 | (7) |
| So. La. Bayou Parishes. . . . | 1 | — | 4 | 3 | (8) |
| North Louisiana Hills . . . . | 2 | 2 | 3 | 1 | (8) |
| Macon Ridge. . . . . . . . | 2 | — | — | 1 | (3) |
| No. La. Planter Parishes . . . | 4 | 2 | 3 | 1 | (10) |
| Urban Area . . . . . . . . | — | 1 | 1 | — | (2) |
| | (10) | (6) | (21) | (27) | (64) |

Against the formidable Parker candidacy, the Bourbons managed to hold on to their traditional seats of support, but even in the North Louisiana Planter Parishes there was defection. The combined appeal of John M. Parker and Huey P. Long was such that Hills and Southwest Louisiana moved into the Parker majority, alongside the southern parishes. Now, the success of the program for which he campaigned so vigorously lay in the hands of the new legislature, which Parker hoped to influence.

Ask some old-timers about John M. Parker, and they will assert that he was the best governor Louisiana ever had; in turn they would scoff the name of Long. Yet, if the measure of success be political longevity, Long managed to perpetuate his position, while Governor Parker failed in his endorsement of a successor in 1924. The test might just as well be the establishment of a constructive program of governmental reforms. Taking the chair of Governor in 1920, Parker was to meet with a postwar mood of sympathy among the electorate in behalf of the principle of reform. The social and economic changes wrought in Louisiana, as elsewhere in America, as a consequence of World War I, meant that whoever became governor must be prepared to solve many practical problems. Moreover, the reaction of puritan morality which gripped the country, after 1918, provided a fertile ground in which to implant a sweeping reform against the corruption of machine politics. The political independence of Governor Parker likewise tended to demonstrate to the voters that the man was more important than the party.

During the campaign, the Parker forces never allowed attention to be diverted from the main issue—that of Ring rule. Their platform has been summed up: The Ring rules New Orleans and rules it badly. If the Ring elects a governor, the Ring will rule the state and rule it badly; therefore, defeat the Ring.[3] This much of the Parker platform was successful, for the time being at least.

Upon the first meeting of the legislature after Governor Parker took office, there were forwarded at regular intervals to the representatives and senators a series of proposals which can be summarized in ten points:

[3] *Ibid.*, 34.

1. Financial program
   a) Severance tax of 2 percent
   b) Inventory of state property
   c) Construction work
2. Good roads
3. Labor legislation
4. Oil and gas laws including ways and means of regulation
5. Political program, including a constitutional convention
6. "Blue Sky" law to protect financial investors
7. Legislation for New Orleans
8. Changes in executive department, including administration of state charitable institutions
9. Cost-of-living aid by encouragement of agriculture, and invitation for business to come to Louisiana
10. Conservation and reforestation.[4]

Important portions, at least, of all ten points were enacted into law during the regular session of the legislature of 1920. Parker got Louisiana out of the mud; he has been called the "gravel roads" governor because of the steps taken under his administration to create a workable, pay-as-you-go highway system in the state.[5] He negotiated a "gentlemen's agreement" concerning the proposed severance tax, and began to build a greater agricultural and mechanical college on a tract of land just south of Baton Rouge. Still more of his program became effective after the Constitution of 1921 was ratified.

In 1913 the legislature had called a limited convention, where the delegates were charged to make provisions concerning the state's bonded debt and to establish a sewerage and water board for New Orleans. The convention was restricted from establishing any article inconsistent with any existing provision and, thus, the convention was nearly powerless. The 1921 convention which followed was ideologically permeated with the spirit of "good government."[6] The resulting document has been called more legislative than constitutional, having become a listing of statutes and amendments, rather than creating a

[4] Ibid., 46.
[5] Garnie W. McGinty, A History of Louisiana (New York, 1951), 250; George B. Tindall, The Emergence of the New South, 1913–1945 (Baton Rouge, 1967), 237.
[6] Charles W. Tapp, "Development of the Constitutional Appointive Power of the Governor of Louisiana" (Master's thesis, Louisiana State University, 1964), 62

substantive instrument. Good government was equated with a narrow view of political action, and as a result the new constitution did include many procedural limitations upon the legislature and the governor, although the latter was left with the broad appointive powers which had been granted in 1879. Logically, Charles Tapp has argued, there was no reason why the delegates who drafted the 1921 constitution should have placed any restriction upon the governor, for political control was still in the hands of the Bourbons. But to them government was a negative force, and they feared it might be used in a positive way.[7]

While for the conservative government is negative, there is no inhibition in the use of the police powers of the state to protect law and order. Louisiana, in the twenties, was not immune to the national temper of reform, nor to the fever of intolerance and here, as elsewhere, the Ku Klux Klan was resurrected.[8] Indeed, the Louisiana Klan was regarded as one of the realm's most important, one of the nation's fifteen strongest.[9] While in Louisiana the Klan was not numerically powerful (about 25,000 listed members), its concern for moral reforms and "native" virtues gave it wide appeal, and support of the Klan gained as it became a potential law enforcer and fraternal order. Whatever ultimate influence the Klan might have had in Louisiana, paradoxically anti-Catholic here as it was elsewhere, was thwarted by the Mer Rouge incident in 1922, where extremist behavior led Governor Parker to call out the militia.

The Klan had determined to "clean up" the old planter parish of Morehouse by raiding stills and other such actions and threatened all those who objected. "The reign of terror reached its climax with the disappearance of two citizens of Mer Rouge, who, the Exalted Cyclops of Bastrop 'officially announced,' would never return, and whose bodies months later came to the surface of Lake La Fourche with marks of beastly torture."[10] It was at this point that the Governor interceded to forestall warfare between the two North Louisiana

[7] *Ibid.*, 65.
[8] Tindall, *Emergence of New South*, Chap. 6.
[9] Kenneth Earl Harrell, "The KKK in Louisiana, 1920–1930" Ph.D. dissertation, Louisiana State University, 1966), iv.
[10] Tindall, *Emergence of New South*, 192.

towns. The violence receded afterwards, but widespread sympathy for the movement and the secrecy and potential terrorism of the "invisible empire" generated much fear within the state.

In Louisiana, the first of the two blows which led to the demise of the Klan was Parker's intervention in the Mer Rouge affair and the legislation he later secured which required the Klan to register its membership rolls with the state. These actions served to reveal the danger of the Klan. The second blow which diminished the Klan's influence in Louisiana was its failure to unite on the candidacy of one man in the 1924 gubernatorial primary election.

Reform makes a popular appeal, and successful reform may whet the appetite for more.[11] The question that remains to be answered, then, is why Parkerism was such a respectable failure? It was said in Governor Parker's behalf that his administration tried to meet the pressing problems of the early twenties, and there did not appear to be anything amiss in the particular steps which Parker had taken. But Parker would have had to make good on his reform of the New Orleans Ring if his administration were to be called a success. In that he failed, and another four years passed before Parker-like programs of reform could be carried out. More than this, however, John M. Parker never seemed to realize that not only the New Orleans machine could be politically evil or corrupt. "The corruptor of politics in the form of privileged business he did not see, or seeing, was unwilling to break its strangle hold. His reforms failed because they were not in reality carried out and because they did not remove the economic causes of machine control."[12]

The Bourbon one-party system had been secured by a ruling elite which consisted of a parish seat governing class made up of the "banker-merchant-farmer-lawyer-doctor group."[13] In his pitiless characterization of its habits and assumptions, Jasper B. Shannon found them as joiners who practiced the "boosterism" of the new South, part of an elite caught between the tradition of agrarian

---

[11] *Ibid.*, 236.
[12] Reynolds, *Machine Politics*, 233.
[13] William C. Havard, "Louisiana and the Two-Party System," *Louisiana Academy of Sciences*, XVI (1953), 78.

gentility and the sanitary conveniences of the emerging industrial order.[14] The Progressive reforms of a John M. Parker may have helped the urban and business interests in alliance with the Bourbon "Whig" parish-seat elite, but in the twenties, the Louisiana population still consisted predominantly of farmers and workers, and their circumstance was as hopelessly depressed as ever.

One significant indicator of the domination by a ruling class, in the American setting, at least, is claimed to be the educational status of a population. On this count, as V. O. Key has demonstrated, Louisiana was at the bottom of the listings, for as late as 1940, 14.8 percent of the rural native white males over twenty-five years of age had not completed a single year of schooling.[15] This is telling evidence of how hard the governing group pressed down. While in Louisiana, the urban white population in 1940 had completed as many or more years of schooling as the national average, the state was rural, and it was the farmer, white as well as black, who suffered educational deprivation. In fact, the 1940 census showed that the gap between the amount of schooling reported by farmers and persons living elsewhere, instead of being lessened, was actually wider than ever. "The white farmer of the state aged 65–70 years in 1940 had received, on the average, 3.3 years of schooling less than had the urban resident in the same age group; farm people aged 20–25 years had received, on the average, 4.2 years less than their contemporaries in the cities of the state."[16]

While the fact that farmers of Louisiana were educationally underprivileged was bad enough, the combined threat of the boll weevil and declining cotton prices in the twenties devastated the economic security of the rural population. The demand for staples in World War I had raised the price of cotton from the low of 4.59 cents a pound in the recession of 1894 to an all-time high of 35.34 cents by 1919. By 1921 cotton was worth only half as much. But, at the same time, the infestation of the boll weevil had reduced cotton production from

[14] Quoted in Havard, "Louisiana and Two-Party System," 44 ff.

[15] V. O. Key, Jr, *Southern Politics* (New York, 1949), 160.

[16] T. Lynn Smith and Louise Kemp, *The Educational Status of Louisiana's Farm Population* (Louisiana State University, Agricultural Experiment Station Bulletin No. 424 [Baton Rouge, 1947]), 26.

a quite large total of 13.4 million bales to 7.9 million bales. One result of the agricultural crisis was that the southern states lost the first chance since the Civil War to accumulate capital and to break the chain of the farmer to the creditor.[17]

A final indication of the depressed status of the "have-nots" in Louisiana can be found in the figures on farm ownership (see Table 6–4, and 6–5). While for two decades (1900–20) the agricultural census had shown that about 45 percent of all farms had been operated by owners, after 1920 a sharp decrease was measured. The farmer could hold the line no more. By 1935, only 36 percent of Louisiana farms were still operated by owners. As the census data is set to show, increasingly more farmers, white and black alike, went down into tenancy after 1920.

Against such a background of social and economic deprivation, the spectacular success of Huey P. Long four years after John M. Parker left office might serve to demonstrate that Parker should have provided more reforms. Indeed, the pent-up demand for public services in Louisiana was such "that the achievement of things accomplished with decorum in other states assumed the form of class struggle in Louisiana and provoked a vituperative hostility on both sides."[18] Where Parker had built gravel roads, Long built concrete roads, and they were good roads, even if only "a few miles were paved in every parish to let the people see the superiority of concrete over gravel."[19] The programs of the two governors paralleled in many respects, but the popular support of the two leaders was singularly different. Long's appeal was more broadly to the masses, whereas Parker, half Republican anyway, had not sufficiently disassociated himself, in the people's eye, from the dominant economic groups of the new Louisiana.

The failure of Parkerism to perpetuate itself rests essentially upon the factor of electoral appeal. While Parker provided an opposition which might have posed a threat to the Bourbon oligarchy, still, voter turnout was low. The total gubernatorial vote numbering

[17] Tindall, *Emergence of New South*, 112.
[18] *Ibid.*, 237.
[19] McGinty, *History of Louisiana*, 250.

143,553 in 1920 had been only a little more than 20,000 above the total in the vigorously contested primary election of 1912, after the total vote had dropped some 9,000 in 1916. (Appendix A, Table 1) A more telling clue to Parker's failure is found in the turnout figures which show that, whereas the percentage of registered voters voting in 1912 had been 80 percent, the proportion had dropped to 55 percent in 1920.

The farmers of the Hills, who were to give Huey Long such strong support, had had definite ideas about the reforms necessary in Louisiana society. The generation that had felt the exhilaration of the movement of the People's Party and had flirted with Socialism had not yet died off. Reform was in the air in Louisiana, but there had been a metamorphosis of progressivism in the South,[20] such that, while the public service and good government impulses were still strong, a drive for moral righteousness and conformity held sway, and a clean-up campaign whose purpose was to perpetuate the domination of the Bourbon or his big-business allies lacked popular appeal in Louisiana. Like the Whigs and their concern for fiscal prudence and efficiency in the previous century, the program of Governor Parker, no matter how good, was doomed. It failed because it was not conceived of and for the "people."

II. *The Rise of Huey P. Long: His Mission and His Legacy*

Forty years and ten gubernatorial elections have passed since Huey P. Long broke the Bourbon rule with his victory in the 1928 primary. The Bourbons had managed to blunt the efforts of the Parker forces and to win big with a machine-backed candidate in 1924 so that, to the power structure, the rise of Long must have been the more startling. The following table will show how stunning indeed the "Long surge" appears, placed along side the testimony of Louisiana's support of the Bourbon ascendancy:

[20] Tindall, *Emergence of New South*, Chap. 7.

Table 7-2

GUBERNATORIAL PRIMARY ELECTION WINNER'S PLURALITY, 1908–67
(WINNER'S PERCENTAGE MINUS THE LOSER'S)

| Year | Bourbon (machine, or anti-Long) | | Other (good government, hill alternative, or Long) |
|------|------|------|------|
| 1908 . . . . | 10% | | — |
| 1912 . . . . | — | (The Bourbon rule) | 6% |
| 1916 . . . . | 46% | | — |
| 1920 . . . . | — | | 8% |
| 1924 . . . . | 16% | | — |
| 1928 . . . . | — | | 16% |
| 1932 . . . . | — | (The Long surge) | 20% |
| 1936 . . . . | — | | 34% |
| 1940 . . . . | 4% | | — |
| 1944 . . . . | 8% | | — |
| 1948 . . . . | — | (Bi-factional | 32% |
| 1952 . . . . | 24% | politics: Long | — |
| 1956 . . . . | — | vs. anti-Long) | 2% |
| 1960 . . . . | 8% | | — |
| 1964 . . . . | — | | 4% |
| 1967 | | 64% | |

(The McKeithen phenomenon)

The Bourbon candidates for governor won three of the five Democratic primary elections that preceded the rise of Huey Long, and did so with convincing margins. The best that good government reformers could do when the machine was under attack was the 8 percent plurality mustered by Parker in 1920. As has been shown above, in both instances when the reformer won, failure to break the machine's control led to an immediate reversion to the dominant pattern of things. In the case of Parker, his substantive program of improved roads, education, and other neglected public functions was substantially thwarted.

The Long surge which commenced with Huey's election in 1928 can be viewed as dramatic evidence of a radical reform movement of which Populist and Socialist protest were the forerunners. The Bourbon anti-Longs, however bitterly they may have fought back, were dealt a crushing defeat, and were ultimately routed by Huey Long's relentless attack and counter-organization in the early 1930's. The result of Long's development of a programmatic and organizational opposition to the Bourbon rule was the development of what Allan P. Sindler has called a relatively persistent "cohesive bifactionalism" within the framework of the Democratic Party in the state.[21] In preliminary, two things must be said of this period: The fact that a governor was constitutionally prohibited from succeeding himself in office and, after Huey's untimely death in 1935, the fact that his brother Earl managed to capture for his own use the Long charisma, both served to guarantee lively competition for the conservative forces of the state.

A number of elements led to a plethora of writing, much of it derogatory, about the "Kingfish"; the convincing victory of Huey Long at the polls, the organizational machinery he constructed, the intense loyalty of his following, the spread of his ideology of "share the wealth" to a national audience, and his unquestioned and unparalleled dominance over the political life of the state of Louisiana. Two recent reviews by Longs' chroniclers and their evaluations of him make it possible to present in outline form some major explanatory characteristics attributed to him:[22]

As Dethloff has pointed out, the most striking thing about the writings on Huey Long is the number of different terms used by any one author to describe a single individual.[23] It can also be shown that the older writings have taken a generally dim view of Long while the newer, or "revisionist" views have been more charitable. It is easy to see Huey P. Long in both good and bad lights. Any complete study of Huey P. Long must address itself to at least the three following questions: How did Huey P. Long rise to power in terms of electoral

[21] Allan P. Sindler, *Huey Long's Louisiana: State Politics, 1920–1952* (Baltimore, 1956).
[22] Henry C. Dethloff, "Huey P. Long: Interpretations," *Louisiana Studies,* III (1964), 219–32; John Adam Moreau, "Huey Long and His Chroniclers," *Louisiana History,* VI (1965), 121–39.
[23] Dethloff, "Huey P. Long," 228.

## Table 7-3

CHARACTERISTICS ATTRIBUTED TO HUEY P. LONG

ADVOCATES OF VIEW*

**Political Factors**

Type of Leader:
- Dictator: 1, 2, 3, 5, 7, 8, 9, 10, 14, 15.
- Demagogue: 1, 2, 8, 10, 17.
- Mass leader: 4, 9, 12, 14, 18.

Motivation:
- Fascist Tendency: 3, 8, 13, 15.
- Lust for power: 13, 14.
- Realist: 9, 12, 14, 18.

**Economic Factors**

Accomplishments:
- Improved things: 1, 12, 16, 18.
- Did nothing, really, to improve: 2, 13, 14.

Ideology:
- Leftist: 11.
- Old America Frustrated: 13.
- Neo-Populist: 9, 18.

**Societal Factors**

Social forces and their resolution: 6, 9, 14, 16, 18.

* 1. Hamilton Basso, *Mainstream* (London, 1944); 2. Carleton Beals, *The Story of Huey Long* (Philadelphia, 1935); 3. Hodding Carter, "Huey Long: American Dictator," in Isabel Leighton (ed.), *The Aspirin Age, 1919–1941*; 4. W. J. Cash, *The Mind of the South* (New York, 1941); 5. Forrest Davis, *Huey Long, A Candid Biography* (New York, 1935); 6. Henry Dethloff (ed.), "Huey Pierce Long: Interpretations," *Louisiana Studies,* III, (1964) and *Huey P. Long: Southern Demagogue or American Democrat,* Dethloff (ed.) (Boston, 1967); 7. John Kingston Fineran, *The Career of a Tinpot Napoleon* (New Orleans, 1932); 8. Harnett T. Kane, *Louisiana Hayride* (New York, 1941); 9. V. O. Key, Jr., *Southern Politics* (New York, 1949); 10. Reinhard Luthin, *American Demagogues: Twentieth Century* (Glouster, Mass., 1959); 11. Donald R. McCoy, *Angry Voices: Left-of-Center Politics in the New Deal Era* (Lawrence, 1958); 12. Daniel M. Robinson, "From Tillman to Long: Some Striking Leaders of the Rural South," *Journal of Southern History,* III (August, 1937); 13. Arthur M. Schlesinger, Jr., "The Messiah of the Rednecks," in *The Politics of Upheaval* (Cambridge, Mass., 1960); 14. Allan P. Sindler, *Huey Long's Louisiana: State Politics, 1920–52* (Baltimore, 1956); 15. Raymond Gram Swing, *Forerunners of American Fascism* (New York, 1935); 16. George B. Tindall, *The Emergence of the New South, 1913–1945* (Baton Rouge, 1967); 17. Robert Penn Warren, *All the King's Men* (New York,

THE RISE OF "LONGISM" 225

support? How did he stay there? What was his political style? What
bothered the earlier chroniclers of Huey Long was his alleged
behavior after he came to power, and his expansion of power and
control. While many works have commented upon the flamboyant
style of this great politician so fascinated by power, only the more
scholarly studies as those by political scientists Allan P. Sindler and
V. O. Key, Jr., and historian T. Harry Williams have been concerned
with finding the social forces which might account for the electoral
support of Huey P. Long. The present work, in an earlier version,
may be said to have pioneered in this direction by testing the possibility
of using the methods of political ecology to trace the continuities or
discontinuities of political tendencies in Louisiana.

There is great merit in Williams' view of Long as a mass leader,
a realist, and as neo-Populist, as seen above. The reason for this can
be found in the analysis of political tendencies which has been
presented up to this point. It was not inevitable that Huey Long
should become so great a figure. The times had demanded a leader in
economic and social reforms, but it didn't have to be a man like
Long, and Louisiana had responded already to the promise seen in
John M. Parker. Huey P. Long came at the right time, and he changed
the times because of what he was. Long was a mass leader who
achieved a charismatic domination of Louisiana as a consequence of
his realistic skill in manipulation of the frustrated demands of
Populism.[24]

With Louisiana dominated by outside corporations and ruled by a
planter-business coalition which relegated economic questions from
the sphere of public discussion, the situation was intensified by
agricultural depression and increased tenancy in the rural parishes
and by failure to obtain remedy through state government. The
social environment was prepared for charismatic acquiescence, and a
dogmatic form was put forth by a leader who personified and inspired
the masses.[25] It could be said that the entire system of pre-Long
Louisiana with its ideological system of white supremacy and economic

[24] Daniel John O'Neil, "A Study in Charismatic Domination" (Master's thesis,
Louisiana State University, 1961).
[25] *Ibid.,* 135.

paternalism had been conducive to an atmosphere of anti-individ-
ualism and, if this is so, "the individualist par excellence, the charismatic leader, would reap the benefits of this atmosphere."[26] Long's
message could be summarized as a castigation of disproportionate
wealth personified by the corporations, and if given the power, Huey
Long promised to lead to utopia.

In the consideration of social forces it is possible to show the manner
in which cleavage and opposition can be resolved, as it was in Louisiana
and other southern states, such that an uneasy equilibrium was
reached in which the Bourbons ruled, the Negro was subjugated, and
the poor and white were inhibited in political action by the binds of
the dogma of white supremacy.[27] The ruling oligarchies found,
however, that demagogues could upset this delicate balance by
"pushing the race button," by mobilizing a responding electorate
through playing upon the fear of the Negro. It is important to note
that Long was not demagogic in this southern tradition. The power
potential was present in Louisiana, as elsewhere, but because of
unique factors in the state's historical experience and in the personal
biography of Huey P. Long, it was used to go in a different direction.
Long mobilized the farmer by working on his pent-up socioeconomic
frustrations. As the journalist James Rorty put it in the thirties,
Huey Long appealed to the century-old hatred of the "red neck"
farmer for the plantation owners and for the new hierarchy of big
business in New Orleans. Longism became a class movement, as to the
farmer and to the middle class of city and town, "Huey posed the
rhetorical question: 'Little man, what now?' and answered for them:
'Every man a king.' "[28]

The farmer had been outnumbered in the Democratic conventions,
and now, in the early 1900's, he was being outmaneuvered in the
Democratic primary elections. The actions of the dominant minority
in taking the ballot from the Negro and in frustrating the poor
and white, to the extent that voting became nothing more than a

---

[26] *Ibid.*, 111.
[27] Perry H. Howard and Joseph L. Brent III, "Social Change, Urbanization, and
Types of Society," *Journal of Social Issues*, XXII (1966), 77.
[28] James Rorty, *Where Life is Better* (New York, 1936), 334.

civic formality, might well have spelled the political doom of the Bourbons. Democracy in Louisiana had become perverted; yet, it has been shown above how the farmer groups tended to respond to the gubernatorial candidacy of what has been labeled a "Hill-alternative." The primary election of 1924 may have presaged the breaking of Bourbon rule.

In 1924, as in 1912 (see Appendix B, Table 5), with one of their own as candidate for governor, voters in the Hill Parishes of North Louisiana responded with majority votes. The 1921 constitution had created a new Public Service Commission upon which Long was making a political name for himself as Railway Commissioner, tilting with the Standard Oil Company and utility corporations, exacting lowered rates for their customers. While he had backed the reformer Parker in the previous election, Long broke with the Progressive forces when Parker had acquiesced over the question of a severance tax upon oil, that important element which in Louisiana came to rest on top of the usual Southern-Bourbon-business domination. Huey jammed the oligarchy hard when he helped enact, in the 1922 legislature, a 3 percent severance tax on petroleum obtained from Louisiana wells.[29]

The success of Huey Long's candidacy was hindered, however, by the intrusion of the Klan issue in the campagin of 1924.[30] For, while Long tried to duck the issue and concentrate upon economic matters, his North Louisiana base tended to make him a regional candidate. Although most Klansmen had backed the machine candidate Henry L. Fuqua, who tried to straddle this issue, the Ku Klux Klan's failure to unite behind one candidate served to hasten its demise in Louisiana. Hewitt Bouanchaud, Governor Parker's personal choice, pledged to outlaw the Klan. With the Klan issue in the forefront, it might be expected that the campaign would center upon the candidate who could best play upon the theme of white supremacy, but, of course, the religious factor cut across the Klan issue, and, in a state where at least half the electorate was Catholic, this cross-pressure inhibited such a tendency. It is instructive

---

[29] Sindler, *Huey Long's Louisiana*, 48.
[30] Harrell, "KKK," 333; Sindler, *Huey Long's Louisiana*, 48–50.

to note that another future governor, Sam H. Jones, also began his statewide political career in 1924, by bucking the pro-Klan sentiment when he supported John J. Robira, the anti-Klan candidate for district attorney in the five parishes at the southwest corner of of Louisiana.[31]

There is still to be considered, though, that one effect of the Klan issue was to call attention to the fact that two Protestant candidates were running against the Catholic one, Bouanchaud. A decided North-South split was apparent, in the parish distribution of the candidates' pluralities. (Map 7–2) While no candidate gained a majority, Bouanchaud led the primary election with 35 percent of the total votes cast, leading in twenty-three parishes, all of them below the North-South line. The machine-backed candidate, Fuqua, ran in second place, with a support of 34 percent, gaining the perennial 10,000 vote edge in New Orleans, leading in Baton Rouge and Lake Charles, and carrying the planter parishes of the delta and Felicianas. In this election, Huey Long, with voter support of 31 percent, carried most of North Louisiana and extended his appeal into the hill-farm and pine flat areas of the Florida Parishes. The impression of regional distribution is further increased by reviewing the success of the three candidates among the Louisiana voter types areas:

*Table 7–4*

FIRST PRIMARY PLURALITIES, 1924,
AND SECOND PRIMARY WINNER BY VOTER TYPE AREAS

| Voter Type | Bouanchaud | Fuqua | Long (N) | Runoff 1924 Fuqua (N) |
|---|---|---|---|---|
| North Louisiana Planter . . | — | 6 | 4 | 10 |
| Macon Ridge. . . . . . . | — | 1 | 2 | 3 |
| North Louisiana Hills . . . | — | — | 8 | 8 |
| Central Pine Hills . . . . . | — | — | 7 | 7 |
| | (7) | (21) | (28) | (28)      (28) |

[31] Personal correspondence.

| | | | | | | |
|---|---|---|---|---|---|---|
| Florida Parishes . . . . . | — | 3 | 5 | | 8 | |
| Southwest Louisiana . . . | 7 | 2 | 1 | | 3 | |
| South Louisiana Planter . . | 8 | — | — | | — | |
| Bayou . . . . . . . . . | 7 | — | — | | — | |
| Urban Area . . . . . . | — | 1 | 1 | | 2 | |
| | (23) | (6) | (7) | (36) | (13) | (13) |
| STATE . . . . . . . . . | (23) | (13) | (28) | (64) | (41) | |

When the results of the second (runoff) primary, in which Fuqua won with 58 percent of the vote cast, are placed beside the first, the regional consistency is clear. Bouanchaud's majorities in the runoff were located in the same twenty-three parishes in which his pluralities were found in the first primary. In the 1924 election, then, the parish distribution of votes shows the profile expected when the issue of religion/race takes precedence over economic/class considerations. This is the "pyramid" profile which was to reappear in the elections of 1960, outlining the boundaries of French-Catholic Louisiana. (see Map 10–1)

The class appeal of Huey Long's campaign is seen in the complete solidarity among the two Hills units and his support in the eastern Florida Parishes. Likewise, the support for Fuqua, outside New Orleans, suggests continuity of the traditional Bourbon planter-business coalition. The tradional cleavage outlining the river "Y" profile appeared in diminished form in the first primary, but in the runoff, despite the fact that Long did not indicate his preference, the Hills went with the Bourbons' man. In the next gubernatorial election the "Y" profile, found in clear outline in 1896, would be in evidence again. While his greatest popularity was still limited to the Hill parishes, Long had run second in fourteen parishes in 1924, all but three of which were in South Louisiana. Longism had a class appeal, and next time he must strengthen his organization and extend his country support into French Louisiana if he was to win.

Huey P. Long did become governor of Louisiana, in 1928, and while he did not win outright in the first primary, so adroitly did he manage to divide his opponents that the opposition declined to enter a runoff. Long's chances had improved when the legislature in 1924

# Candidate Pluralities, Gubernatorial First Primary

# 1924

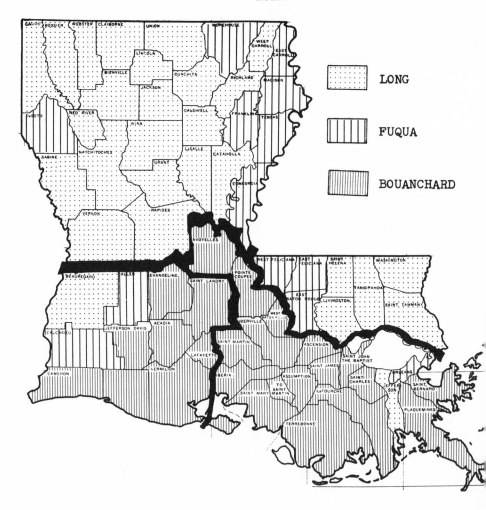

passed anti-Klan measures which effectively removed the religion/race issue. His opposition resembled that of 1924 and Long's candidacy served to divide the country vote so that again the New Orleans vote became critical. In 1924 Colonel John Sullivan's "New Regulars" had backed Bouanchaud, but now he sided with Huey Long, while the New Regulars with Mayor Paul Maloney had gone to the Simpson camp. The Old Regulars had backed the candidacy of Riley J. Wilson, long-time congressman from the Eighth District. The line-up and results of the 1928 gubernatorial primary looked like this:

*Table 7-5*
CANDIDATES AND VOTES, 1928*

| Candidate | Position | Backing | Number | Percent |
|---|---|---|---|---|
| Huey P. Long | Public Service Commissioner | Ewing newspapers, Sullivan | 126,842 | 43.9 |
| O. H. Simpson | Governor upon Fuqua's death | New Regulars | 80,326 | 27.8 |
| Riley J. Wilson | 8th Distict Congressman | Old Regulars | 81,747 | 28.3 |

* Source: Sindler.

The first and last time that Long candidates had the widespread benefit of a good press was in 1928; in fact Huey Long later resorted to printing his own newspaper in order to carry his message to the people. In wooing New Orleans, he promised to bring natural gas to the city and to build free bridges in contrast to the toll-bridge policy of the Bourbons. His proposals did not win New Orleans over (out of 78,387 votes, Wilson's margin over Long was 18,000), but he did get results over the countryside, and Long-built bridges are still in use over rivers and bayous throughout Louisiana.

Outside New Orleans, the vote in opposition to Huey Long was located along the classic fracture line of the rivers and valleys and within the parishes containing Shreveport, Monroe, and Baton Rouge (Map 7-3). Wilson and Simpson carried or led in only seventeen parishes:

*Table 7-6*
MAJORITY OR PLURALITY PARISHES FOR LOSING CANDIDATES, 1928
Wilson                                    Simpson

| Majority (4) | Plurality (4) | Majority (6) | Plurality (3) |
|---|---|---|---|
| E. Carroll | Caddo | E. Baton Rouge | E. Feliciana |
| Madison | Catahoula | Jefferson | Pointe Coupee |
| Morehouse | Orleans | Plaquemines | St. Landry |
| Tensas | Ouachita | St. Charles | |
| | | St. James | |
| | | W. Feliciana | |

Outside planter parishes and the cities, Huey Long, in 1928, gained majority support in thirty-eight parishes and pluralities in nine more as his appeal spread among the rural masses.

The catalytic manner in which the candidacy of Huey P. Long served to mobilize the electorate can be seen by looking at the data on voter turnout in Louisiana after the turn of the century when the Bourbons established their rule. The depressing effects of disfranchisement and the Bourbon domination of the Democratic Party can be seen, as turnout and registration data are tabulated:

*Table 7-7*
GUBERNATORIAL VOTING, TURNOUT, AND REGISTRATION, 1896-1940

| Year | Gubernatorial vote | White voting age | White voting age registred | Percent registered voters voting (turnout) | Percent white voting age registred |
|---|---|---|---|---|---|
| 1896 . . . . | 206,354 | 154,000* | 153,169 | 74% | 86% |
| 1900 . . . | 76,870 | 177,878 | 125,437 | 56 | 70 |
| 1904 . . . . | 54,222 | | 106,360 | 60 | |
| 1908 . . . . | 106,905 | | 152,142 | 69 | |
| 1910 . . . . . . . . . | 240,001 | 152,000 | | 63 |
| 1912 . . . . | 123,408 | | 153,044 | 80 | |
| 1916 . . . . | 114,519 | | 185,313 | 61 | |

* Estimated.

| | | | | | |
|---|---|---|---|---|---|
| 1920 . . . | 143,553 | 564,017 | 257,282 | 55 | 46 |
| 1924 . . . . | 239,529 | | 322,600 | 74 | |
| 1928 . . . . | 288,915 | | 377,246 | 76 | |
| 1930 . . . . . . . . . | | 703,239 | 350,425 | | 50 |
| 1932 . . . . | 379,949 | | 557,674 | 68 | |
| 1936 . . . . | 540,370 | | 641,589 | 84 | |
| 1940 . . . | 553,723 | 899,960 | 701,659 | 79 | 79 |

In the case of Louisiana, two cycles may be traced, the first peaking in 1912 when a three-candidate competition included a "Hill alternative," and the second cycle peaking in 1924 when Huey Long represented the Hills. Even though in 1920 the white registration had increased by 40 percent over that of the previous election, and the increase in the vote was at the rate of 25 percent, the turnout was 25 percent less than it had been in 1912. By 1940, so far as the white population was concerned, the rates of turnout and of registration reached the relatively high averages which have been maintained up to the present time.

Although in 1920, reform Governor Parker had managed to break the succession of machine-backed candidates, it did not seem to stimulate voter registration, for, in fact, of the increase in white registration from 1908 to 1920 (+93,302) 43 percent of it was due to the female registration made possible by the Nineteenth Amendment to the Constitution of the United States. In the next decade, moreover, parishes in North Louisiana actually had shown a loss in the absolute number in white *male* registrants, as these tabulations will show:

*Table 7–8*
WHITE VOTER REGISTRATION

| | State | | North Louisiana | |
|---|---|---|---|---|
| | Male | Female | Male | Female |
| 1920. . . | 211,831 | 45,451 | 49,355 | 7,978 |
| 1930. . . | 237,395 | 113,030 | 44,960 | 19,332 |
| | + 12% | + 149% | − 9% | + 142% |
| 1936. . . | 383,250 | 258,339 | 82,728 | 52,327 |
| | + 61% | + 127% | + 84% | + 171% |

# Huey P. Long Vote, 1928

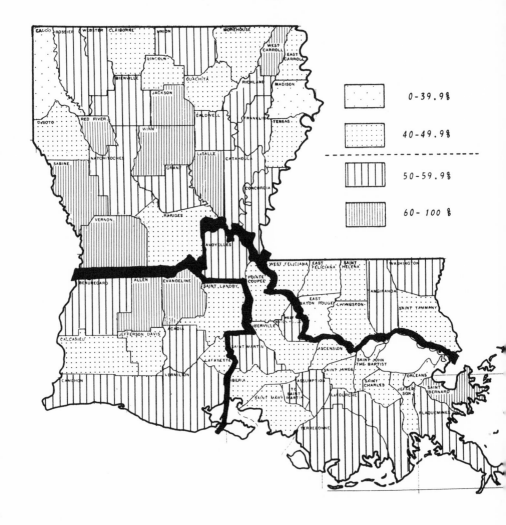

| | |
|---|---|
| ☐ | 0 - 39.9% |
| ▨ | 40 - 49.9% |
| ▥ | 50 - 59.9% |
| ▥ | 60 - 100 % |

Only the large increase (1920–30) in the rate of female registration in North Louisiana, which nearly equaled the state-wide rate of increase, offset the 9 percent loss of male registration there, most of these losses having been recorded in Hill Parishes. The figures for the period 1930 to 1936, however, show North Louisiana male registration 23 percent greater than the state male increase, while female registration was 44 percent greater than the state increase in female registration. Finally, 57 percent of the state male registration increase (1930–36) had been in North Louisiana, while the proportion for females, there, was 36 percent.

Up to the advent of Huey Long, then, the rates of registration increase and voter turnout were both in decline. These findings would seem to support the remarks Seymour Martin Lipset has made confirming the Tingsten thesis that a sudden increase in the size of the voting electorate reflects tensions and serious governmental malfunctions. If democracy requires that every man may vote, then elements within Louisiana society had sought to suppress attempts to meet that requirement. Unlike those European countries where one is automatically registered, participation here is the result of two decisions: to register when the issues are warm and to vote when the issues get hot.[32] If this assertion is correct, in the period 1900–20, a combination of apathy (futility and alienation?) and of power restrictions (governmental policies) worked to reduce political participation in Louisiana. It was as a consequence of what Allan P. Sindler has called the "buccaneering liberalism" of Longism that Louisiana took her place among the states in the practice of political democracy. The Long faction became a vehicle of expression for the depressed farmer class in Louisiana, and a great surge in voter turnout resulted.

Voter turnout had increased almost 100 percent in nearly all areas in 1928 over that of 1920, yet, a significant difference may be found in terms of whom the voters supported. On the one hand, voter strength in the Hills, Macon Ridge, Bayou Parishes, and Southwest Louisiana was behind the candidacy of their own kind of man, Long, while on

[32] Seymour Martin Lipset, *Political Man* (Garden City, 1960), 185, 229.

the other hand, New Orleans and the other urban parishes, and delta planter parishes as seats of planter-merchant domination contained voters in opposition to him. These areas subsequently became the backbone of anti-Long strength. A tabular summary follows:

Table 7-9
LONG MOBILIZATION
VOTER REGISTRATION AND TURNOUT, 1920 AND 1928

| Frequency distribution of Huey Long vote | Year | Registration | Turnout |
|---|---|---|---|
| 16–39% | 1920 | 108,390 | 61,402 |
| (12) | 1928 | 170,935 | 121,437 |
| | | Increase 58% | Increase 98% |
| 40–49% | 1920 | 39,941 | 23,919 |
| (14) | 1928 | 51,063 | 47,415 |
| | | Increase 28% | Increase 98% |
| 50–59% | 1920 | 60,137 | 31,975 |
| (18) | 1928 | 73,260 | 65,334 |
| | | Increase 22% | Increase 104% |
| 60–74% | 1920 | 52,347 | 26,257 |
| (20) | 1928 | 57,446 | 54,731 |
| | | Increase 10% | Increase 108% |
| (N 64) | | | |

Most important of all, it can be seen that the increase in voter turnout in Long areas like the Hills was not the consequence of an increase in registration. The differences in the relation of registration to turnout can be seen in the parishes on either side of the Long majority line. In the high percentage intervals which contained parishes of both North and South Louisiana with a farmer population, *registration increase was small while voter turnout was much greater.* This is in striking contrast to the low intervals of Long support where *turnout had increased as also did registration.* Until Huey P. Long offered his leadership, much of the farmer class, though registered, had stayed home on election day.

The gubernatorial primary election of 1928 broke the Bourbon rule as the appeal of Huey P. Long reached the white farmer class in all sections of Louisiana. With the advent of Long, the white electorate moved from restriction to a more open politics. Evidence is needed to verify the assertion that the success of Longism rested upon the ability to bridge the two Louisianas and gain the support of the lower classes. The analysis may begin with an inspection of the distribution of the Long parish support by voter types, arraying the data in such a way that the Long and anti-Long areas are readily apparent:

*Table 7–10*

HUEY P. LONG VOTE, 1928

PARISH DISTRIBUTION BY PERCENTAGE INTERVALS

| Voter type | 0–39% | 40–49% | 50–59% | 60–100% | (N) |
|---|---|---|---|---|---|
| North La. Planter Parishes | 5 | 4 | 1 | — | (10) |
| Florida Parishes | 3 | 2 | 1 | 2 | (8) |
| South La. Planter Parishes | 1 | 3 | 4 | — | (8) |
| Urban Area | 2 | — | — | — | (2) |
| Macon Ridge | — | 1 | 1 | 1 | (3) |
| South La. Bayou Parishes | — | 2 | 3 | 3 | (8) |
| Central Pine Hills | 1 | — | — | 6 | (7) |
| North La. Hills | — | 1 | 4 | 3 | (8) |
| Southwest La. | — | 1 | 4 | 5 | (10) |
| | (12) | (14) | (18) | (20) | (64) |

The within-state differences are such that the thirty-eight Long-majority parishes are found to bridge North and South Louisiana. Almost all the Bayou voter type parishes join the Hills and Southwest Louisiana areas in majority support for Huey Long. Long sentiment was also found in the parishes along Macon Ridge, which in the first decades of this century were filled with farmer migrants from the Hills. It was the Planter Parishes and Urban Areas which seemingly recognized the potential threat to their interests in Longism.

It will be recalled that another kind of reform candidate, the Progressive John M. Parker, likewise carried parishes in both North and South Louisiana, but now it is possible to show differences in the distribution of the two kinds of opposition to the Bourbon rule. (See Map 7–1):

*Table 7–11*
PERCENTAGE DISTRIBUTION, PARKER PARISH VOTE 1920,
COMPARED TO LONG PARISH VOTE, 1928, BY VOTER TYPE AREAS

Number of Parishes

|  | So. West | | Central Hills | | No. La. Hills | |
|  | − 50% | + 50% | − 50% | + 50% | − 50% | + 50% |
|---|---|---|---|---|---|---|
| Parker | 1 | 9 | 1 | 6 | 4 | 4 |
| Long | 1 | 9 | 1 | 6 | 1 | 7 |

|  | Bayou | | Urban | | Macon Ridge | |
|  | − 50% | + 50% | − 50% | + 50% | − 50% | + 50% |
|---|---|---|---|---|---|---|
| Parker | 1 | 7 | 1 | 1 | 2 | 1 |
| Long | 2 | 6 | 2 | 0 | 1 | 2 |

|  | Florida Parishes | | South Planter | | North Planter | |
|  | − 50% | + 50% | − 50% | + 50% | − 50% | + 50% |
|---|---|---|---|---|---|---|
| Parker | 0 | 8 | 0 | 8 | 6 | 4 |
| Long | 5 | 3 | 4 | 4 | 9 | 1 |

STATE

|  | − 50% | + 50% |
|---|---|---|
| Parker | 16 | 48 |
| Long | 26 | 38 |

While within Southwest Louisiana and the Central Pine Hills, support for the two reformers was constant, Long, understandably, picked up increased support in the North Louisiana Hills and, significantly, Huey Long held his own among the Bayou Parishes. It was within the Parishes dominated by planter interests that Long lost support as compared to Parker, but while Long was able to carry only one North Louisiana Planter Parish, Bossier, he was able to hold his own in four South Louisiana Planter Parishes; West Baton Rouge, Ascension, Iberville, and St. Mary joined the adjacent Bayou Parishes in support of Huey Long. Likewise three parishes in the piney woods east of Baton Rouge remained reform oriented.

In order to show more clearly the association of the farmer class with Longism, the Long vote may be compared with the percentage of farms owned in Louisiana, taking this variable as an indicator of family farm versus plantation areas:

*Table 7–12*
LONG PARISH VOTES, 1928

Number of Parishes

| Percent farms owned 1930 | State | | | No. La. | | |
|---|---|---|---|---|---|---|
| | − 50% | + 50% | (N) | − 50% | + 50% | (N) |
| Low (4–22%) | 17 | 16 | (33) | 9 | 7 | (16) |
| High (34–82%) | 9 | 22 | (31) | 2 | 10 | (12) |

| Percent farms owned 1930 | So. La. | | |
|---|---|---|---|
| | − 50% | + 50% | (N) |
| Low (4–22%) | 8 | 9 | (17) |
| High (34–82%) | 7 | 12 | (19) |

It is significant that parishes low in farm ownership are below 50 percent in support of Long, whereas, parishes high in farm ownership are also high in support of the Long candidacy. This likewise holds for the North Louisiana parishes, but no significance can be attributed to the South Louisiana parish tabulation. When the Long parish vote is controlled by a frequency distribution of percentage farms owned in 1930, association between the two variables and in the expected direction is seen to exist:

*Table 7–13*
LONG PARISH VOTE, 1928,
PERCENT FARMS OWNED, 1930

| Percent farms owned | Average Long vote |
|---|---|
| 70% & Above (4) | 60% |
| 50–69% (11) | 56% |
| 40–49% (11) | 54% |
| 30–39% (11) | 54% |
| 20–29% (14) | 53% |
| 4–18% (13) | 41% |

The profile of Bourbon parish support had been the "Y" formed by the confluence of the Red and Mississippi rivers, and it was found to represent the backbone of the "anti-Long" vote in 1928. Yet, it is possible to find within-parish differences on the ward level in the eleven parishes through and along which the rivers flow in North Louisiana. The ward votes for Huey Long can be shown to differ as between those close to or back from the rivers:

*Table 7–14*
LONG VOTE IN NORTH LOUISIANA RIVER PARISHES, 1928

Number of Wards

|  | Total | | | Red River | | |
|---|---|---|---|---|---|---|
|  | − 50% | + 50% | (N) | − 50% | + 50% | (N) |
| River wards | 32 | 17 | (49) | 15 | 7 | (22) |
| Hill-Back wards | 17 | 25 | (42) | 17 | 22 | (39) |

|  | Mississippi | | |
|---|---|---|---|
|  | − 50% | + 50% | (N) |
| River wards | 17 | 10 | (27) |
| Hill-Back wards | 0 | 3 | (3) |

Again, as was found to be the case with percentage farms owned, the data "fits" the expected cells. That is, in all three cross-tabulations, the number of wards located in the intervals for and against Huey Long constitutes significant relationships; in confirmation of expectation, river wards are anti-Long while hill-back wards are pro-Long.

While the plantation was the predominant influence in all the wards of the Mississippi Delta parishes in 1928, at the same time, its proximity to the hills has meant that the parishes through which the Red River flows contain both a planter and farmer group, and the voting behavior of the population has hence been accordingly influenced. It would make little sense to use the whole of Red River Parish, for example, as a unit of measure when a breakdown of the ward vote may more clearly indicate the underlying conditions of political life. Along the course of the river, plantations are found in sizable number, and in these wards the support of Long was found to be weakest. Away from the river, as the alluvial bottom terrain gives way to hills, the wards in support of Long become more numerous until they merge with the strong upland farmer core of Long strength. The farmer class support of Huey Long in 1928 has been stressed, and the implication has been made that Long's urban support was weak. Since, however, a candidate could not win the governorship solely by the accumulated votes of country farm parishes, it is necessary to search for other categories of the electorate who supported him. While the urban vote in 1928 was consistently anti-Long, control by frequency distribution of all cities with population 5,000 and over in 1930 reveals a significant progression:

*Table 7–15*
LONG VOTE IN LOUISIANA'S MAJOR CITIES, 1928

| Size of city | Average Long vote |
|---|---|
| 400,000 (1) | 23% |
| 20,000–80,000 (4) | 30% |
| 10,000–20,000 (3) | 45% |
| 5,000–10,000 (11) | 40% |
| (N) (19) | 29% |

The smaller the population of a city, the larger the percentage of support for Huey Long tended to be. The extent of this tendency can be seen here:

*Table 7–16*
LONG VOTE PERCENTAGES, 1928,
BY URBAN AND RURAL CATEGORIES

| Category | Average Long Vote |
|---|---|
| Orleans Parish | 23% |
| Cities of 5,000 & over | 29% |
| parish seats | 43% |
| Urban parish seats | 49% |
| Rural parish seats | 36% |
| Rural vote (state total minus parish seats votes) | 56% |

The conservatism of country towns has been pointed out above (page 218) and the anti-Long sentiment of parish seats is outstanding. But this is not all, for when the average Long vote in the Parish seats of Hill voter types is compared with those within the North Louisiana Planter voter type unit, the comparison is all the more striking—48 percent in the Hill parish seats and only 28 percent in Planter Parish seats. The same relationship holds in South Louisiana, where the parish seat votes in Bayou and Southwest Louisiana voter type areas average 54 percent in support of Huey Long, while the average support of parish seats in Planter and Florida Parish areas falls to 43 percent.

One final example of the differential support for Huey Long, representing a potential labor support for Longism, consists of the distribution of votes in the 1928 primary election by types of wards in New Orleans.

*Table 7–17*
PERCENT SUPPORT FOR 1928 CANDIDATES
BY SOCIOECONOMIC STATUS WITHIN TYPES OF WARDS

| Type of ward | Wilson | Simpson | Long |
|---|---|---|---|
| Upper (13, 14, 16) | 44% | 38% | 15% |
| Middle (6, 7, 8) | 54 | 30 | 16 |
| Lower (1, 2, 3, 10, 11) | 48 | 19 | 33 |
| City (17 wards) | 49% | 28% | 23% |

In New Orleans, the ward-based representation in the state legislature made the city's voters easy to organize. Moreover, the historical development of New Orleans tended to produce natural areas clearly delineated by their social and cultural characteristics. With the data presented here, three types of wards are roughly outlined, ranging from upper, to middle, to lower class. The upper set embraces the "up-town" university section of New Orleans, long known as the "silk-stocking" wards. The lower extreme includes the "Irish Channel" and can be thought of as the core of working-class New Orleans, particularly in the late 1920's, although today this area is becoming predominantly Negro in residential characteristic. The in-between set ranges from Esplanade Ridge toward City Park and across the middle-class reaches of Gentilly.

Wilson, with the organizational support of the Old Regular Choctaws, was able to score heavily across the range of wards, although his poorest showing was found to be in the upper-class area. Simpson, with the support of the "good government" elements in the city, predictably drew his heaviest vote from upper-class wards and his lightest from the working-class areas. Long drew his heaviest support from the lower-class areas and received a uniformly poor vote in the upper and middle sections. While Huey Long failed to carry the cities where there were social groupings whose economic and political sympathies were part of the old Bourbon complex, a clear differential in urban voting behavior was apparent. The tendency among workers to support candidates with programs closer to their interests than those of the dominant minority was obvious, and Long's following in working-class districts of New Orleans and other cities became clearly visible.

The gubernatorial victory of Huey P. Long in the Democratic primary election of 1928, then, was class based. Frustrated Populist tendencies made up the sociological basis of Longism. Results of elections of such a crisis nature indicate the presence of a latent consensus which might lead to further concerted action at the polls. Protest had been registered concerning the actions leading to Secession. A reaction of political solidarity occurred among the farmers of the hills in the 1880's. The farmer found voice to protest his frustrations in the Populist movement during the economically depressed 1890's and even flirted with Socialism in the decade beginning with 1910. The rise of Huey Long was therefore no political accident; and it is more than coincidence that Winn Parish, the boyhood home of Huey Long, should have been the center of Populist and Socialist sentiment and a later stronghold of Longism. With the rise of Huey Long the political balance in Louisiana tipped in favor of the farmer class. Although Long's organization had reached others such as urban workers and gained their support, the core of his strength remained among the farmers.

Coefficients of rank correlations have been computed between the parish vote for Huey Long in 1928 and the Socialist presidential and Populist gubernatorial votes previously.

*Table 7–18*
PARISH RANK ORDER CORRELATIONS OF SELECTED ELECTIONS

|  |  | Populism 1896 | Debs 1912 | Huey Long 1928 |
|---|---|---|---|---|
| State | 1896 |  | + .365 | + .621 |
|  | 1912 |  |  | + .400 |
| North Louisiana | 1896 |  | + .573 | + .612 |
|  | 1912 |  |  | + .856 |

These are taken to confirm the continued presence of a planter-farmer cleavage which analysis of the ecological panel in Chapter Five had traced. There, the presence of apparent geographic correlations from election to election was pointed out, such that a continuity in regional distribution of the parish vote within Louisiana is found. In almost every crucial election two areas emerged, one characterized by a concentration of plantations, the other by a concentration of family farms. Discussion revealed a general consistency between the Secession issues of 1860–61 and the Populist uprising culminating in the 1896 gubernatorial election. In verifying this consistency it was impossible to resort to statistical analysis due to the fact that the parish boundary lines changed quite radically between the two elections. Thus for these two elections it is necessary to rely upon the geographic coincidence alone in checking consistency. The geographic seat of planter domination in both periods described the "Y" profile which has been characteristic of population distribution in Louisiana.

After viewing the cartographic distribution of parish votes for the Populist election of 1896 and the Debs vote of 1912, it is not surprising that a positive correlation of .365 should be found between Populism and Socialism. However, this coefficient accounts for slightly less than

10 percent of the variance between the two election parish arrays, which means that a great deal of variation remains unexplained. That even this much correlation exists is surprising, considering the number of variables that might be involved. What happend in the parish voting behavior can be shown with a set of simple contingency tables:

*Table 7–19*

POPULIST PARISH VOTE, 1896

Number of Parishes

| Socialist parish vote, 1912 | State | | | No. Louisiana | | |
|---|---|---|---|---|---|---|
| | − 50% | + 50% | (N) | − 50% | + 50% | (N) |
| Low 0–4.9% | 14 | 15 | (29) | 5 | 2 | (7) |
| High 5–36.0% | 15 | 15 | (30) | 10 | 11 | (21) |

| Socialist parish vote, 1912 | So. Louisiana | | |
|---|---|---|---|
| | − 50% | + 50% | (N) |
| Low 0–4.9% | 9 | 13 | (22) |
| High 5–36.0% | 5 | 4 | (9) |

No significant relationship exists among the lows and highs, statewide, since there is an almost equal distribution of parishes among all the cells. The parish distributions do reveal an important regularity on the within-state level, such that ten North Louisiana parishes, which had been low in Populist support, shifted to high Socialist support and, inversely, thirteen South Louisiana parishes which had been high in the Populist support which bridged the areas shifted to low support of the Socialist, Eugene Debs. The Catholicism dominant in South Louisiana, which would be expected to be generally anti-Socialist, must have influenced the distribution of the Socialist vote. On the other hand, many farmers in the uplands had come to work part-time in the lumber industries to augment their meager farming incomes, and, hence, a shift would be expected here in the direction of increased Socialist support. Indeed the coefficient of correlation of +.573 for the North Louisiana association between Populist and Socialist votes is in confirmation of this. The strongest support of the

Socialists, as shown above (page 204) was concentrated in those parishes where lumbering had become a major activity.

The most striking geographic correspondence exists between the Populist vote of 1896 and the 1928 Huey Long vote. When these two votes are subjected to statistical analysis, a correlation coefficient of +.621 is discovered. No more of the variance is accounted for in this case by correlation of the rank-order of parishes in North Louisiana, but when the parish data are distributed in contingency tables, in all three sets (state, North and South Louisiana) significant relationships exist in the distribution of lows and highs:

*Table 7–20*
POPULIST PARISH VOTE, 1896

Number of Parishes Populist

| Long parish vote 1928 | State | | | North Louisiana | | |
|---|---|---|---|---|---|---|
| | − 50% | + 50% | (N) | − 50% | + 50% | (N) |
| − 50% | 20 | 6 | (26) | 9 | 4 | (13) |
| + 50% | 14 | 19 | (33) | 5 | 9 | (14) |

| Long parish vote 1928 | South Louisiana | | |
|---|---|---|---|
| | − 50% | + 50% | (N) |
| − 50% | 11 | 2 | (13) |
| + 50% | 9 | 10 | (19) |

The planter-farmer cleavage appears uniformly in the low Populist-Long and high Populist-Long cells. Most striking is the shift from low Populist to high Long in all three sets of tables. In devotion to Populism and to Huey Long, the people of the uplands joined those of the French lowlands.

In both 1896 and 1928 the opposition to the farmer movements lay in the river bottoms of the Red and the Mississippi. There would seem to be no negative factor here to distort the consistency of the voting behavior save to the extent that farmers who lived in the Mississippi area had increased in number by 1928 and voiced the resentment of farmers elsewhere. The Long faction also gained support in the northwest corner of the state, where plantation influence and presence of a large Negro population exerted pressure upon the farmer. By 1928 the farmers of this area, too, had joined the protest. Long's appeal likewise drew support from the bulk of French Louisiana which had not been wholly for Populism.

The positive correlation between the 1912 Socialist presidential vote and the 1928 Long primary vote was expected and can be explained on the same basis as the Socialist-Populist correlation. Again the solid farmer area supporting Long matches the core of the Socialist support, as the increase in the coefficient when the North Louisiana parish rank orders are compared tends to show. It may well be asked why the state correlation is not as strong as that between Populism and Long. The main answer seems to be the nature of the two appeals. Farmer and part-time laborer evidently found in Huey Long the same hope they had found in Gene Debs. The difference was that Long's appeal was much wider than Debs's. This can be shown by again sorting out the data within contingency tables and by noting that in the relationship between the lows and highs of Socialist and Long votes, only that of North Louisiana is significant:

*Table 7–21*
SOCIALIST VOTE, 1912

Number of Parishes Socialist

| Long parish | State | | | No. Louisiana | | |
|---|---|---|---|---|---|---|
| vote 1928 | − 50% | + 50% | (N) | − 50% | + 50% | (N) |
| − 50% | 16 | 11 | (27) | 6 | 6 | (12) |
| + 50% | 14 | 20 | (34) | 0 | 15 | (15) |

| Long parish | So. Louisiana | | |
|---|---|---|---|
| vote 1928 | − 50% | + 50% | (N) |
| − 50% | 10 | 5 | (15) |
| + 50% | 14 | 5 | (19) |

In the uplands, all the high Long parishes had come from an attempted organization of labor in a state and a period when there was no traditional labor vote. The main variation in the two votes occurred in French Louisiana which was relatively untouched by the Socialist appeal, but it was in this area that Huey Long gained much of the added support which brought him the governorship.

It was, then, the farmer-lumber worker element of the population which contributed to the continuity of support in the elections that have been analyzed above. In Populism and the promises of Huey Long the people of the uplands and the French lowlands believed they had found deliverance from planter-merchant rule. The opposition to the Bourbon-Democrat, which had been dormant for more than a quarter century, had become manifest. The strong reaction of the Bourbon was to be expected, as Huey Long's election ended single-class political domination in Louisiana.

Huey P. Long was a master politician, and his political ideology, if Long actually had one, was in the tradition of Populism as it had been experienced in his native hills. Intentionally or otherwise, Long made corporation domination his constant target. Once having scored victories for the "people" as railroad and public service commissioner, he demonstrated his political acumen with controversial activities which kept his name constantly on the lips of Louisianians. Long had successfully opposed vested interest, and he ran on his record.

Long became governor of Louisiana in 1928 on an "anti" platform; but it was not the worn platform of anti-Ring, anti-corruption, and anti-inefficiency-in-government which made him so popular and gave Long his support from the people. The hill folk from whose ranks Huey himself emerged might not be aware of the economic and legal subtleties behind exploitation by corporation interests. But a politically frustrated and economically destitute farmer-worker class could understand what the championing of Huey Long was all about when he demanded protection of the "people's" rights and the establishment of public utility rates and tax relief designed to keep more money in their pockets. Long chose his targets carefully in his political fights against the domination of vested interests. When it was said that Huey was fighting the Bourbons and absentee corporation interests like Standard Oil, the farmer of the hills knew what Long was doing.

The ideology of "share our wealth" was perhaps economically unworkable, but the simple program of thirty dollars per month old age pension for citizens over sixty years of age, the limitation of poverty and working hours, a balanced agricultural production which prevented price-lowering surpluses, and the taxation program which would destroy big fortunes was something the lower classes in Louisiana and elsewhere could readily appreciate. The appeal was disarming, since Long buttressed it with liberal quotations from the Bible and the great leaders of all time.[33] Huey Long had a record of stepping on the toes of the powers that be, and there was no reason for the people to believe he would not be successful in making "every man a king" if he were elected governor.

Lack of legislative support did not deter Long from carrying out his program. He was well versed in traditional statehouse maneuvers, and he rewarded the legislator who voted right with the plums of patronage for satisfying the constituents back home. His Bourbon enemies tried to destroy Long in 1929 with nineteen general articles of impeachment, but in this fight for his political life, Huey Long brought forth the round robin statement signed by fifteen senators in his support which was more than the one-third necessary to block the proceedings in the legislature. Long managed to get his program through and to penalize the opposition. He was successful in gaining control of and decentralizing the boards and commissions of the state government. His enemies and the intellectually articulate were severely critical of Long's methods, but Carleton Beals, although he deplored Long's "dictatorship," justified his actions in this situation.[34]

Huey Long insured the establishment of his program in the state, and no Louisiana governor since 1928, as no president since Roosevelt, has felt it expedient or wise to throw out the general pattern of reform. Long made a public record to which his partisans pointed with pride.[35] Property assessments were reduced by some 20 percent. Huey Long distributed more than half a million free schoolbooks to public and parochial students alike in the amount of more than half a million. At free night schools 175,000 illiterates over twenty-one years of age learned to read and write. Long raised Louisiana State University to an institution with a first-rate academic rating and where enrollment

[33] Huey P. Long, *Share Our Wealth* (Washington, D.C., 1935 ?).
[34] Carleton Beals, *The Story of Huey Long* (Philadelphia, 1935), 92.
[35] *Time*, Oct. 3, 1932, 10–11.

was increased from 1,500 to 5,000. The Long highway program was responsible for 2,500 miles of new paved roads, 6,000 miles of new gravel roads, and numerous bridges. He built the $5,000,000 state capitol, the $150,000 executive mansion, and the state university's school of medicine in New Orleans. The charity hospital program was increased to care for some 1,800 patients per day, and mental hospitals were generally improved. Regardless of the cost and who was to pay, Huey P. Long established a record of achievement that was tangible and durable.

CHAPTER VIII

# The Long Era, 1928–1956
# Bifactional Politics?

1. *How Huey P. Long Broke the Bourbon Rule*

The impact of Huey P. Long and his successors upon the electorate was such that a distinct political tendency was structured. The Long era began with Huey's bid for the governorship in 1928 and lasted thirty-two years, or through his brother Earl's second full term as governor which began in 1956. But it did not end there altogether; the pattern of Long support still held through the gubernatorial primaries of 1963–64. The distinctiveness of the Long tendency led political observers to declare that in Louisiana a cohesive bifactionalism had been established in this deepest South one-party state.[1] This section will trace the Long tendency in terms of its electoral composition and consider the question of bifactionalism.

The question is whether Longism caused Louisiana to become bifactional—Long versus anti-Long. Was politics already bifactional or did the Long surge so open Louisiana society that a mass politics ensued in which a succession of Long candidates took on the field? The initial surge had lasted through three elections (Table 7–2), followed by the election of two anti-Long administrations. "Uncle" Earl, unable to succeed himself because of constitutional prohibition, which he vainly tried to overcome, began an alternation with anti-Longs in the primary election of 1948. Even though the national concern over civil rights had brought the race issue back into Louisiana politics by 1960, the gubernatorial winner in 1964 was John J. McKeithen. With the backing of a significant portion of traditional Long supporters, including the late "Uncle" Earl's wife Blanche, McKeithen could be called at least "half a Long."

[1] V. O. Key, Jr., *Southern Politics* (New York, 1949); Allan P. Sindler, *Huey Long's Louisiana: State Politics, 1920–1952* (Baltimore, 1956).

It was Allan P. Sindler who investigated the proposition that bifactional rivalry had become an alternative to two-party competition in Louisiana,[2] but even this account hedges in its estimation of the extent to which Longism was representative of bifactionalism as such, in its more inclusive details. The analysis is focused upon the period from 1928 to the elections of 1952. Effective bifactional politics should tend to discourage personal and localistic followings outside the state's political dualism. Yet, in Louisiana, the practice developed of making the first primary a free-for-all, a testing of the popularity of favorite sons who may or may not be able to deliver their followings to an indicated choice between the bifactional candidates in the second runoff primary. Sindler shows conclusively that the supposed personal followings turn out to be limited in terms of transferability and concluded: "The fact that the run-off primary influence of the losing candidate in the first primary is overshadowed by the orientation of his followers toward the bifactional system supports Louisiana's claim to possession of *something like* a two-party system."[3] It was found that local issues were relatively uninfluenced by state politics and that bifactional organization in terms of ticket systems and legislative control approached completeness only during the period of the personal domination of Huey P. Long. His contribution, according to Sindler, was to inject clarity and order into the confusions of one-party politics.[4]

A more recent study has shown that, even in his heyday, Huey Long's domination of the legislature was far from complete and the example is used of highway disbursements to show that Long's technique followed the hallowed traditions of American politics and patronage more than that of the dictator.[5] Huey was moderate in his use of highway funds to punish enemies or reward his friends, and Edward F. Renwick concluded that Long spent money where it would do the most good in terms of support from the state's voters.

[2] Allan P. Sindler, "Bifactional Rivalry as an Alternative to Two-Party Competition in Louisiana," *American Political Science Review*, XLIV (1955), 641–62.
[3] *Ibid.*, 653, emphasis added.
[4] *Ibid.*, 662.
[5] Edward F. Renwick, "The Longs' Legislative Lieutenants" (Ph.D. dissertation, University of Arizona, 1967).

Such a finding does not, of course, take anything away from the skill or virtuousity of the Longs in relationship to their legislatures. Thomas V. Garcia extended this sort of investigation to the relationship of bifactionalism to voting behavior on constitutional issues.[6] In particular the issue of the "blue ribbon" boards first established under the administration of Sam H. Jones is examined because it provides a clear distinction between the Longs and the anti-Longs, the one inclined to social reforms by means of a strong executive, the other advocating governmental reforms through a reorganization of institutions and activities. Garcia found that the voting results in gubernatorial primaries when compared with results on constitutional board issues demonstrate that factional support was transferred to the issues. What such studies show more than anything else is how the so-called bifactionalism is more a function of patterns of voting support than legislative or party control. It reflects the traditional cleavage of the haves and have-nots, a conservative-liberal division.[7]

In the electoral contests, it can be seen that when Longism wins, it tends to win big, while when the anti-Long opposition wins in off years, it tends to win with small margins. The following table traces this variance in Long support among the parishes:

*Table 8–1*

VARIANCE IN LONG SUPPORT

|  |  | Number of Parishes | | | |
|  |  | 0–39% | 40–49% | 50–59% | 60–100% |
| Populism | 1896 | 12 | 12 | 9 | 26 |
| Parker | 1920 | 10 | 6 | 21 | 27 |
| Bourbon | 1924 (2nd) | 19 | 4 | 4 | 27 |

[6] Thomas V. Garcia, "The 'Blue-Ribbon' Boards—A Case Study of Bifactionalism in Louisiana Politics as Reflected in Voting Behavior on Constitutional Issues" (Master's thesis, Louisiana State University, 1964).

[7] William C. Havard, "Louisiana and the Two-Party System," *Proceedings of the Louisiana Academy of Sciences*, XVI (1953).

| Long      | 1928 Won | 11 | 15 | 17 | 21 |
|-----------|----------|----|----|----|----|
| "         | 1932 Won | 7  | 13 | 25 | 19 |
| "         | 1936 Won | —  | 2  | 15 | 47 |
| "         | 1940 Lost| 9  | 32 | 18 | 5  |
| "         | 1944 Lost| 18 | 26 | 17 | 3  |
| "         | 1948 Won | 1  | 1  | 4  | 58 |
| "         | 1952 Lost| 25 | 28 | 7  | 4  |
| "         | 1956 Won | 3  | 10 | 19 | 32 |
| Davis     | 1960     | 9  | 14 | 4  | 37 |
| McKeithen | 1964     | 11 | 9  | 7  | 37 |
| McKeithen | 1967     | —  | —  | 1  | 63 |

Except in 1952, when the Longites were divided among themselves, it can be seen that when the Long candidate won, most of the sixty-four parishes were located in the intervals of support above 50 percent. When the opposition won, the variance was great, as most of the parishes shifted to the intervals of support on either side of 50 percent. These figures, together with the ones tabulated on page 222, may be taken as benchmarks for the analysis of the Louisiana elections of the Long era which will be made below. (See also Map 7-3)

To account for the phenomenon of Longism, it is necessary to find where lies the Long support. Through the voter type areas the tracing of political tendencies is made manageable by comparing within-state differences in voter support among ecological clusters of parishes. In this manner, the emerging pattern of Longism is readily linked to the profiles of parish voting behavior the previous analysis has revealed. A crucial question, however, is whether or not the voter type units actually do describe patterns which are statistically significant. Having found already that the parish distribution of Long support in 1928 correlates in telling manner with that of Populism in another era of Louisiana politics, to know that to compare percentage votes for Long candidates by voter type areas from 1928 to 1956 is to measure meaningful relationships adds an extremely useful summary devise to the analysis of the Long era. The table on page 255 lists the appropriate percentages:

Table 8-2

PERCENT VOTE FOR LONG CANDIDATES, 1928–56, BY VOTER TYPES

| Unit | 1928 | 1932 | 1936 | 1940 | 1944 | 1948 | 1952 | 1956 | Mean | Average Deviation |
|---|---|---|---|---|---|---|---|---|---|---|
| North La. Hills | 59 | 53 | 67 | 51 | 47 | 73 | 49 | 61 | 57 | 7.5 |
| Central Pine Hills | 62 | 52 | 65 | 55 | 54 | 73 | 49 | 68 | 60 | 7.2 |
| Macon Ridge | 57 | 66 | 72 | 56 | 48 | 78 | 43 | 58 | 60 | 9.2 |
| North La. Planter | 38 | 57 | 62 | 43 | 36 | 66 | 35 | 52 | 49 | 11.0 |
| South La. Planter | 46 | 53 | 62 | 44 | 41 | 63 | 47 | 62 | 52 | 7.7 |
| Florida Parishes | 47 | 54 | 59 | 46 | 47 | 60 | 37 | 58 | 51 | 6.7 |
| South La. Bayou | 57 | 60 | 76 | 53 | 47 | 76 | 38 | 50 | 58 | 10.3 |
| Southwest La. | 61 | 47 | 66 | 46 | 49 | 65 | 40 | 58 | 52 | 7.6 |
| Urban Area (New Orleans, Jefferson) | 26 | 73 | 75 | 54 | 50 | 66 | 34 | 41 | 51 | 16.0 |
| STATE AVERAGE | 44 | 57 | 67 | 48 | 46 | 66 | 39 | 51 | 52 | 8.3 |

Tests used: Kruskal-Wallis one way analysis of variance (H = 51.76 w/8df p < .001)
Kendall Coefficient of Concordance ($\chi$ = 19.008 w/7df p < .05)

It can be seen that in most of the voter type units—those pro-Long as well as those anti-Long—the average deviation is quite small. In other words, there is a consistency in the percentage support of Long candidates, election by election, within each voter type cluster of parishes when compared to its mean percentage vote for the entire period. Subsequent analysis will explain the seeming exceptions in the voting behavior of the North Louisiana Planter Parishes, Southwest Louisiana, and the Urban Area.

In seeking political tendencies it is more important to trace patterns of voting behavior than internal consistency. The following table outlines the Long majorities by voter type units:

*Table 8–3*
LONG MAJORITIES BY VOTER TYPES, 1928–56

| Voter Type | 1928 | 1932 | 1936 | 1940 | 1944 | 1948 | 1952 | 1956 |
|---|---|---|---|---|---|---|---|---|
| No. La. Planter | — | Long | Long | — | — | Long | — | Long |
| Florida Parishes | — | Long | Long | — | — | Long | — | Long |
| So. La. Planter | — | Long | Long | — | — | Long | — | Long |
| Urban Area | — | Long | Long | — | — | Long | — | Long |
| Southwest La. | Long | — | Long | — | — | Long | — | Long |
| Macon Ridge | Long | Long | Long | Long | — | Long | — | Long |
| So. La. Bayou | Long | Long | Long | Long | — | Long | — | Long |
| No. La. Hills | Long | Long | Long | Long | — | Long | — | Long |
| Central Hills | Long | Long | Long | Long | Long | Long | — | Long |

Test: Cochran's Q (Q = 36.5 p < .001)

As was expected, two distinct patterns of support for Long candidates can be found. Here are the planter and urban parishes aligned against the united farmer parishes of North and South Louisiana. As with the voter type percentages, the seeming exceptions, together with an explanation of why planter and urban units would vote for Long candidates at all, will be forthcoming. But first, with significance found and pattern confirmed, the same data will be used to compute a series of linear correlations which will make it possible to determine the direction which voting behavior takes, election by election, among the voter type areas.

*Table 8-4*

PRODUCT-MOMENT CORRELATIONS FOR LONG CANDIDATES,
1928–64, BY VOTER TYPE AREAS PERCENT VOTE FOR LONG CANDIDATES*

| | 1932 | 1936 | 1940 | 1944 | 1948 | 1952 | 1956 | 1960 | 1964 | 1967 |
|---|---|---|---|---|---|---|---|---|---|---|
| 1928 | −.618 | .055 | .432 | .390 | .510 | .656 | (.772) | .258 | (.792) | −.500 |
| 1932 | | .684 | .540 | .080 | .047 | .293 | (−.737) | −.014 | .135 | .159 |
| 1936 | | | (.743) | .103 | .655 | −.199 | −.573 | −.177 | −.091 | .278 |
| 1940 | | | | (.746) | (.775) | .209 | −.076 | .145 | .339 | .462 |
| 1944 | | | | | .339 | .270 | .029 | −.137 | .100 | −.170 |
| 1948 | | | | | | .353 | .021 | .409 | .606 | .154 |
| 1952 | | | | | | | (.842) | .178 | .397 | −.264 |
| 1956 | | | | | | | | .070 | .488 | −.483 |
| 1960 | | | | | | | | | (.901) | (−.737) |
| 1964 | | | | | | | | | | (−.760) |

* Coefficients in parentheses are significant at .05 level or less.

257

The correlation matrix tabulated below shows association as well as direction in voting behavior. That is, while the signs show whether the distribution of percentage Long support by voter type in one election will vary in the same or opposite direction in another, at the same time, the amount of the coefficient will show the degree of relationship that can be measured in percentage support as between one election and another. It is possible to find out which elections appear to be important indicators of the Long tendency (Table 8–4). Although the unevenness in the degree of association among the Long elections can be accounted for only in terms of the circumstances surrounding each one, it is possible to see that for two elections, 1940 and 1956, a number of others correlate at a level of statistical significance. That is to say, the distribution of Earl Long percentage support among the voter types in 1956 describes a pattern quite similar to the percentage support of Long candidates in 1928 and 1952, while the Earl Long support in 1940 resembles that for Long candidates in 1936, 1944, and 1948. Of course the negative sign for the 1956/1932 coefficient of correlation indicates a reversal of the predominant tendency. The degree of relationship measured in each of these elections explains over 50 percent of the variance therein. That is, as reference to the table of Long percentages by voter types will show by way of example, in the "scatter" for the elections of 1956 and 1928 (Earl and Huey Long at each end of the twenty-eight-year period), the hard core of Long support can be found in the similarity of percentages for farmer units:

*Table 8–5*

A COMPARISON OF LONG SUPPORT, 1928
AND 1956, BY FARMER VOTER TYPE AREAS

| Unit | 1928 | 1956 | Difference |
|------|------|------|------------|
| No. La. Hills | 59 | 61 | + 2 |
| Central Hills | 62 | 68 | + 6 |
| Macon Ridge | 57 | 58 | + 1   d = − 1 |
| So. La. Bayou | 57 | 50 | − 7 |
| Southwest La. | 61 | 58 | − 3 |

While the difference among farmer units turns out to be negligible, within the remaining planter-urban units the difference in the percentage support for Huey as compared to Earl amounted to an accumulation of 66 percent.

Another less conventional way of trying to find which of the elections in the correlation matrix for the Long era are the more typical is to accumulate, for each of the eight elections, the explained variance (computed as the square of the coefficient of correlation) and calculate the average:

*Table 8–6*

ACCUMULATED EXPLAINED VARIANCE FOR EACH ELECTION
LONG ERA CORRELATION MATRIX

| Election | Accumulated Explained Variance 1928–56 | Average Explained Variance |
|---|---|---|
| 1940 | 2.237 | 32% |
| 1956 | 2.182 | 31% |
| 1928 | 2.010 | 29% |
| 1936 | 1.830 | 26% |
| 1932 | 1.778 | 26% |
| 1948 | 1.532 | 22% |
| 1952 | 1.506 | 21% |
| 1944 | 0.914 | 13% |

Put this way, again the elections of 1940 and 1956 appear as the ones that most consistently depict, in their relationship with the others, the pattern of Longism, while 1928 averages out a close third. In the first and second of these elections, Earl Long was the standard-bearer, while, of course, in 1928 it was Huey Long. The middle range, where average explained variance amounts to 25 percent, is filled by the elections of 1932 and 1936, representing the surge of Long support which broke the Bourbon rule in Louisiana. In 1948 Earl Long had made a comeback after eight years of anti-Long reform while in 1952 the Longs themselves were divided and only for the wartime election of 1944 does explanation really "wash out." Thus alerted to the general pattern of voter support in the Long era, it will be possible to provide more perspective in a brief narrative analysis of Louisiana politics in this period.

II. *Long Candidates and Their Opposition*

With the governorship won and impeachment at the hands of the Bourbons averted, Huey P. Long set about consolidating his position. In 1930 Long set his sights on the United States Senate and in the primary election of that year easily beat the congressional incumbent of thirty-two years, Joseph E. Ransdell, getting 57 percent of the total votes cast and carrying fifty-three parishes with majorities. With typical manipulative flourish, Long managed, then, to maneuver Alvin King, president pro tempore of the Senate into the governor's chair, thus securing his control of the state. In 1932 the Longs offered a full ticket of nine candidates for state office, and Huey chose his longtime supporter Oscar K. Allen of Winn Parish to head it. But while the entire Long slate was swept into office, the distribution of voter support was somewhat different from that of 1928.

*Table 8–7*

DISTRIBUTION OF PARISH LONG SUPPORT, 1932, BY VOTER TYPES

| Unit | Number of Parishes 0–39% | 40–49% | 50–59% | 60–100% | Change in Number of Parishes above 50% over 1928 |
|---|---|---|---|---|---|
| North La. Planter | 1 | 1 | 4 | 4 | + 7 |
| Florida Parishes . | — | 3 | 3 | 2 | + 2 |
| South La. Planter | 1 | 2 | 2 | 3 | + 1 |
| Urban Area . . . | — | — | — | 2 | + 2 |
| Southwest La. . . | 3 | 2 | 4 | 1 | — 4 |
| Macon Ridge . . | — | — | — | 3 | + 1 |
| South La. Bayou. | — | 3 | 2 | 3 | — 1 |
| North La. Hills . | — | 2 | 6 | — | — 1 |
| Central Pine Hills | — | 2 | 4 | 1 | — 1 |

What has to be explained is the negative coefficient of .618 computed for the relation between voter type percentage support of the Long candidate in 1928 and 1932. The victory margin of 57 percent had been the same as in Huey's successful senate bid two years previously, but the changed direction can best be explained in terms of two observations: (1) In 1932 the New Orleans machine backed the Long candidate, and (2) the "friends and neighbors" influence of the only serious opposition to O. K. Allen in South Louisiana. The Choctaw-Long alliance can be seen as moving the traditional Bourbon areas of Orleans and the Planter Parishes toward acceptance of the Long candidate. Together this increment of voter support would have been enough for Long to hold off the field; the resulting influence upon distribution of voter support was such, however, that while the Planter Parishes produced majorities for the Long candidate, the degree of majority support in the Hills fell away. The other influence affecting the pattern of Long support was the candidacy of Dudley J. LeBlanc, Public Service Commissioner and advocate of the old age pension. The election results, after Dudley and Huey had swapped observations concerning the benefits of the pension plan to the Negro population, showed that LeBlanc gained his greatest relative strength in his own section of the state. Indeed, his greatest inroad on Long support was found to be in Southwest Louisiana, which as a unit had dropped from 61 to 47 percent in support of the Long candidate in 1932.

It is not possible to approach the 1936 gubernatorial election without considering two things: (1) Huey P. Long's alleged tyranny; and (2) his martyrdom. The brief period of three years after the 1932 election was the time in which Long, having consolidated his position, exercised the great powers latent in the office of governor in Louisiana, found his mass charisma held national attention, continued to promise social reforms at home, and offered to "share the wealth" of America. Louisiana appeared to like it, and why would the nation not accept the notion of a welfare state as well? It is somewhat ironic to find that Allan P. Sindler and other interpreters of Long saw in his program of reforms a panacea cynically put together to win votes, especially so after at least half of what Sindler claimed to be the essence of Long's program,[8] including old age pensions, farmer crop subsidies, and minimum wages has since been enacted into federal law. (Of course the national program aimed to get votes, too.) Huey P. Long had put together a program, a political package, aimed at furthering his success at the polls, but what has often been missed is that almost all the ingredients could have come from Huey's exposure to the Populism and backwoods socialism which had flourished in his native hills.[9] This is not to say, however, that by the time of his assassination in 1935, Huey's control of Louisiana had not become dictatorial. But with martyrdom, the permanence of the reform appeal of Longism might be guaranteed.

The strong role of the executive in Louisiana government has been stressed in this study. The legislature, throughout most of the state's history, has been secondary to the governor; the governor has been expected to do things when elected. On the local level, especially in South Louisiana, the politicians, planters, lawyers, sheriffs, and priests traditionally acted as spokesmen for the French-speaking people who were unable to articulate their interests and needs. In this milieu, is it so surprising that a Huey Long could rise to political power, and acting the role of the strong man, perpetuate his political program? The Whig philosophy that the people should be ruled merged with the Jacksonian belief that the people should rule. In Longism the people saw everything to gain.

Yet, if traditionally the role of the executive was a major one in Louisiana government, the dogmas, if not the spirit, of Jacksonian Democracy were perpetuated.[10] The expanding functions of government were scattered among numerous holders of fragments of the executive power at the very time that rising industrialism and urban growth made demands of a stronger or more centralized executive. Once this had happened, who could gather again the pieces of executive authority except the strong man? Government by bureaucracy became the accepted pattern, and the electorate decided whether

[8] Sindler, *Huey Long's Louisiana*, Chap. 4.
[9] T. Harry Williams, *Huey P. Long* (New York, 1967), 11.
[10] James W. Prothro, "A Study of Constitutional Developments in the Office of the Governor of Louisiana" (Master's thesis, Louisiana State University, 1948), 99.

direction would be through their representative, the governor, or through the indirect action of boards. Opinion was split on this matter.

Longism, like the New Deal, brought more people to the polls than had ever voted previously, and the Long candidates got the larger part of this increase in ballots. Huey Long was sponsoring state reforms (as Franklin Roosevelt was doing nationally), and the people registered their satisfaction upon election day. By the election of 1936, not only had the tendency of Longism become established, the people of Louisiana registered their strongest approval. Richard W. Leche had been given over two-thirds of the record vote of more than one-half million; the same year, President Roosevelt gained the electoral votes of every state but Maine and Vermont. In the jockeying for position[11] which followed the death of Huey P. Long, South Louisiana and New Orleans supporters of Huey managed to secure the nomination of Leche for governor and added the Long name to the ticket by backing the sometimes dissident brother Earl for lieutenant governor. The Kingfish's men hoped that they could perpetuate political power for themselves, routinizing the charisma of the fallen leader by drawing upon the patterned voter support of Longism.

The election of 1936, then, became the peak of the Long surge that had scattered the Bourbon Democrats in disarray. Even so, variation in the pattern of voter support was such that, while a relatively high + .684 coefficient of correlation can be computed for the elections of 1932/1936, the relationship of 1936 with the "classic" pattern of 1928 is hardly discernable (+ .055). In the election-by-election figures, down the face of the correlation matrix, it is to be expected that some degree of continuity will be found, but the "washing out" effect in this case is seen to follow from the extremely high Long percentages of support among the voter type areas and the fact that only two parishes had less than majority support. Richard W. Leche had gained 67 percent of the vote statewide, and only in the Florida Parish unit did the Long support fall below 60 percent. In this election, however, even the unit's anti-Long bastion of East Baton Rouge had gone Long by 51 percent.

[11] The formal and informal procedures of Louisiana elections lend easy analogy to horse racing (see Chapter 10 below).

Louisiana gained an unenviable reputation for political corruption as, in 1939, the national press featured the "scandals" Federal prosecutors had uncovered. The heirs of Longism had become spoilsmen on a grand scale, as Huey predicted they would if he were not around to ride herd on them.[12] Charges of income-tax evasions resulted in the conviction and imprisonment of the Governor and other state officials and it was thought the house that Huey built had come tumbling down.

Yet, in the hotly contested election of 1940, the reform faction barely managed to secure victory, with 52 percent of the votes cast. The lower classes had not forgotten what Longism had done for them, and the middle-class elements of the social stratification of Louisiana at this time, so crucial in the outcome of future elections, were not yet present in sufficient number. The traditional farmer-planter cleavage remained in the agricultural economy and the farmer class showed its strong tendency to support the Long candidate, Huey's brother Earl, who had become acting governor when Leche went to jail, and who now had the chance to employ the charisma of his name.

Both planter and businessman still held such economic influence that a sizable opposition to Longism might have been mustered within the electorate. Yet, the growing industrial capacity of Louisiana was bringing, not only class elements whose political tendencies augmented the old Bourbon complex which might create a new power base, but also an increasing labor vote which would show a political tendency more sympathetic to Longism. Even though Labor organization had not made appreciable inroads on Louisiana,[13] a large potential bloc of voters was present. Farmers and laborers voted for Earl Long in such numbers that Longism was almost perpetuated in 1940, when he received a vote of over a quarter of a million in the runoff, representing 48 percent of the total.

Many groups, despite the cost in taxes, had registered satisfaction concerning the increased state services which Longism had provided.

---

[12] T. Harry Williams, "The Gentleman from Louisiana: Demagogue or Democrat," *Journal of Southern History*, XXVI (1960), 3–21; Sindler, *Huey Long's Louisiana*, 128.
[13] Alex S. Freedman, "The Social Aspects of Recent Labor Union Growth in Louisiana" (Master's thesis, Louisiana State University, 1950).

No reform group could take this away and still hope to be supported at the polls. The fact of the matter is that in 1940 the new administration under the new governor, Sam H. Jones, had no intention of turning back the clock, but rather, meant to clean up corruption and administer the state bureaucracy more efficiently.[14] Jones, a lawyer from Lake Charles was a liberal in his own right who had admired the progressivism of John M. Parker. The old dominant minority had been forced to use extreme measures in their ascendancy after 1896 through the vehicle of the great disfranchisement; this was an error that Jones recognized. The people, tired of the old order, had found a champion who would establish something new, as the following excerpt from Jones's first legislative message on May 20, 1940, attests:

I occupy a unique position in Louisiana political life. I am a liberal who has consistently opposed the out-going regime because of its tendency towards dictatorship; because of unconstitutional and undemocratic methods used, and because of the many flagrant vices evident in the system used by it. To me these were paramount issues because the methods used were destructive of democracy itself. But, I believe in benefits and services on a safe and sane basis. I have had the audacity to say that the regime which commenced in 1928 came about as a result of the faults, defects, and omissions of the administrations which preceded it.

The principal reason for the revolutionary changes of 1928 was that the great masses of the people were being forgotten. In opening my campaign on September 21, 1939, I said:

I am not unmindful of the causes and effects in the political world, and of the affairs of the state. The present regime, at its inception, was ushered in because of the sins and faults and defects of a preexisting group. Many thousands of Louisianians were ready for a change which would dig up by the roots the power then entrenched and give it to the people—benefits of which they were justly entitled. Among these were many thousands as honest, sincere, and conscientious as can be found in the state of Louisiana. Among these was my own father, who hated with holy fervor, all that smacked of corrupt politics.[15]

[14] Robert H. Weaver, *Administrative Reorganization in Louisiana* (Louisiana State University, Bureau of Government Research [Baton Rouge, 1951]).
[15] *Louisiana Senate Journal*, 10th Reg. Sess., 23.

There was nothing in the stance of Sam H. Jones, then, to indicate any desire to close Louisiana politics, again. In fact, it can be seen that the outcome of the runoff primary election made it one of the closest in Louisiana history, indicative of an extremely open, or competitive situation. Seventy-nine percent of the registered voters had turned out, and the total vote of 553,723 had topped that of the previous election by over 13,000. With the future of Longism on the line, the election of 1940 could be expected to reflect the hard core of Long support, and this has been confirmed in the above analysis of the Long correlation matrix. While the distribution of Long support by voter type unit in 1940 correlates to a significant degree with that of the preceding election, it can be seen that the association tends to hold for the elections of 1932 and 1928 as well, a consequence of the stability of the ecological pattern. Most important of all, however, is the manner in which parish support is arrayed in frequency distribution in the four percentage intervals:

*Table 8–8*

LONG SUPPORT BY VOTER TYPE, 1940

| Unit | 0–39% | Number of Parishes | | |
| | | 40–49% | 50–59% | 60–100% |
| --- | --- | --- | --- | --- |
| North La. Planter . . . . . . | 2 | 6 | 2 | — |
| Florida Parishes . . . . . . . | 2 | 5 | 1 | — |
| South La. Planter . . . . . . | 1 | 6 | 1 | — |
| Urban Area . . . . . . . . . | — | 1 | 1 | — |
| Southwest La. . . . . . . . . | 2 | 5 | 3 | — |
| Macon Ridge . . . . . . . . | — | — | 3 | — |
| South La. Bayou . . . . . . . | 1 | 4 | 1 | 2 |
| North La. Hills . . . . . . . | 1 | 3 | 2 | 2 |
| Central Pine Hills . . . . . . | — | 2 | 4 | 1 |

In the total distribution of parish support, the smallest number in the entire Long era appeared at the extremes, below 40 percent and above 60 percent: nine parishes and five parishes, respectively. In other words, in the hotly contested election of 1940, which followed the Louisiana scandals, over three-quarters of the parishes clustered in the two percentage intervals about 50 percent in their support of the Long candidate. While thirty-two parishes had supported Long in the interval of 40–49 percent, only eighteen parishes had registered support for Long in the majority from 50–59 percent, but this set of parishes had included Orleans, 55 percent of whose 141,923 voters had gone for Long. It is interesting to note the extent to which a decade of Long politics had effected the differential voting behavior of socioeconomic categories in New Orleans, as the Long candidate scored heavily in lower- or working-class wards:

*Table 8–9*

PERCENT SUPPORT FOR CANDIDATES, 1940, IN NEW ORLEANS
BY GROUPS OF WARDS, BY SOCIOECONOMIC STATUS

| Type of Ward | Earl Long | Sam Jones |
| --- | --- | --- |
| Upper | 38% | 62% |
| Middle | 58 | 42 |
| Lower | 72 | 28 |
| City | 55% | 45% |

The vote tended to break even in the middle classes, but the lower-class category was, of course, the unit of numbers.

Among the voter type units the classic profile is revealed where the Planter Parishes supported Sam Jones, but with most of such parishes clustered in the interval of just below 50 percent. While the farm parishes of North Louisiana tended to hold to the pattern of Longism, in the South the "friends and neighbors" influence can be seen, together with what must have been echoes of the older Progressive tendency. But, in the Bayou Parishes of Plaquemines and St. Bernard, already in evidence was the block of support which boss Leander Perez could contribute. Overall, it can be said that the vote in 1940 meant, not a reflection of Long-anti-Long opposition, but a willing urge to go along with the precedent and the promise of reform.

The administration of Sam H. Jones did not turn back the clock of social development. It established a system of Civil Service for state employees and what were called blue ribbon boards, the appointed members of which were to supervise the administration of state services with economy and efficiency. While stressing governmental reforms, it is noteworthy that Governor Jones did not substantially alter the pattern of spending established by the Longs, as a brief look at a comparison of administrative budgets will show:

*Table 8–10*
TRENDS IN STATE GOVERNMENT FINANCES*

| Adminis-tration | Average Yearly Administrative Budget ($ in millions) | Authorized (Increase) | Authorized Bonded Debts (1930–50) | (Purpose) |
|---|---|---|---|---|
| 1916 | $6.8 m. | — | — | |
| 1920 | 16.4 | 10.0 | — | |
| 1924 | 22.9 | 6.5 | — | |
| 1928 | 34.9 | 12.0 | $80,000,000 | (Hwys., Bldg.Capital) |
| 1932 | 51.9 | 17.0 | 80,000,000 | (Hwys., refunding) |
| 1936 | 72.5 | 20.6 | 35,000,000 | (Hwys.) |
| 1940 | 84.2 | 11.7 | 15,000,000 | (Hwys., Improvements, Institutions) |
| 1944 | 95.5 | 11.3 | 38,000,000 | (Hwys., Improvements, Institutions) |
| 1948 | 208.0 | 112.5 | 65,700,000 | (Vet. Bonus, LSU) |
| 1952 | 416.3 | 208.3 | — | |
| 1956 | 569.8* | | | |

* Actual expenditure.
* Source: State Auditor's Report; *Financial Statements*, Dept. of Administration; *Tax Commission, Budget Recommendations*, 1918–20 to 1938–40.

This list of figures is taken to show the general increase in governmental services characteristic of the country as a whole in response to the complexities of the twentieth century. But in Louisiana, it can be seen that each successive reform governor from Parker in 1920 through Jones in 1940 called for budgeted expenditures double that of his predecessor. To continue the pattern, the 1948 Earl Long administration's average budget was two and a half times more than that of 1940, and Robert Kennon, in 1952, produced a budget twice as high as the previous administration's. The billion dollar budgets of the 1960's give evidence of the continuing prosperity of Louisianians, but the foregoing discussion points to the conclusion that it is necessary for the elected officials to be *willing* to increase the taxation upon which any dramatic increased expenditures are based. The Longs appeared preeminently willing not only to increase taxes but also to float bond issues with which to finance capital improvements; and all subsequent governors have seen fit to follow suit. In this fact there is more than a hint of explanation for the alternation in office between the Longs and the opposition. The "neo-Parkerism" of the Jones administration indicated that the realism injected into politics by Huey P. Long had been continued, as the ins and outs each concerned themselves with solving the state's problems.

As election time came in 1944, Governor Jones found it difficult to get a candidate who would hold the chair until he was eligible to run again; it was finally agreed that James H. (Jimmie) Davis, public service commissioner from North Louisiana, was his man. Davis, the folk singer-composer, was, as the farmer in his native northeast Louisiana would say, "a good ole country boy." But this did not mean that Jimmie was without political acumen, and he settled what problems arose and presided over a state in which wartime prosperity brought increasing surplus revenues. Since these revenues had not found their way into new programs by the end of Davis' administration they provided for the welfare spending which Earl Long would commence in 1948.

If 1940 was the most typical election in terms of the voter type distribution of Long support, 1944 must be seen as the least, except for the high degree of continuity found in the statistically significant coefficient of correlation computed between it and 1940 ($+$ .746). First primaries, in the new competitive Louisiana politics became sorting out contests as increasingly more candidates, serious, nuisance, or otherwise, vied for a position in the runoff, in which, it should be noted, the Long candidate always was present. In an open struggle for power, candidates professing the Long banner tended to diffuse the voter support, raising the question of what would have happened if the so-called Long faction had remained united. The following chart shows how things worked out in 1944:

*Table 8–11*

CANDIDATES AND VOTES

FIRST PRIMARY GUBERNATORIAL ELECTION, 1944

| Candidate's Home Base (Voter Type) | Long Candidates | | | Opposition | | |
|---|---|---|---|---|---|---|
| | Name | Vote Percent | Number Parishes Plurality | Name | Vote Percent | Number Parishes Plurality |
| North | | | | Davis | 34.9 | 34 |
| Louisiana | | | | Caldwell | 7.2 | — |
| Florida | Morgan | 27.5 | 11 | | | |
| Parishes | Morrison | 15.9 | 11 | Lanier | 0.3 | — |
| Southwest | Clements | 4.3 | 2 | Moseley | 1.5 | — |
| Louisiana | LeBlanc | 8.4 | 6 | | | |
| | | 56.1 | 30 | | 43.9 | 34 |

Despite the wishes of supporters of Longism from North Louisiana parishes, the main Long pretender had to be Lewis Morgan, former Sixth District congressman and minor Longite, whom the Choctaws and New Orleans Mayor Robert S. Maestri backed. His chances seemed to improve when Earl K. Long, always the realist, agreed to run for lieutenant governor on the ticket. The first primary returns put Morgan ahead in New Orleans and throughout the range of Hills. Jimmie Morrison, Sixth District congressman since 1942, had run well for governor in 1940 and in his own bailiwick by carrying pluralities in seven parishes, and this time was able to extend his support in South Louisiana to include eleven parishes. Ernest Clements had been conservation commissioner under Governor Leche and a state senator before that, but this early supporter of Longism managed pluralities only in his native Allen Parish and adjacent Beauregard. Dudley LeBlanc, perennial candidate from Lafayette, rounded out the list of Long candidates; although in the past LeBlanc had his differences with the Longs regarding the extent to which the coverage of welfare measures should go, now he hitched his political wagon to the Long star. His support came, as it had previously, from his home base area.

Among the Long opposition the most formidable gubernatorial candidate was Jimmie Davis, who used widespread newspaper support to cut into Long strength in North Louisiana. His thirty-four-parish plurality is evidence enough of that. Beyond his home base Davis carried eleven South Louisiana parishes, including urban Jefferson and East Baton Rouge. Other candidates for governor included Lee Lanier, editor of a country newspaper in Amite; Vincent Mosely, a "nuisance" candidate hailed by some as an independent from Opelousas; and Sam Caldwell, mayor of Shreveport, who was hurt badly by Davis' candidacy. In sum, the list of Long candidates accumulated a majority of the votes.

In the runoff, Jimmie Davis won by the close margin of 54 percent, carrying majorities in 44 parishes, but ahead of Morgan by only 33,313 statewide, and thus the keen competition shown in the 1940 election continued. In fact, in the final outcome, the number of parishes in the 40–60 percent intervals decreased from 50 to 43, moving downward to join parishes in the 0–39 percent interval of Long support. The pattern of Davis success can be seen in the distribution of support among the voter type units, thus providing a means of finding where the voting support for the candidates in the first primary went:

*Table 8–12*

LONG CANDIDATE SUPPORT BY VOTER TYPE AREAS

1944 RUNOFF

| Unit | Number of Parishes | | | |
|------|------|------|------|------|
| | 0–39% | 40–49% | 50–59% | 60–100% |
| North La. Planter . . . . . . | 8 | 2 | — | — |
| Florida Parishes . . . . . . . | 3 | 2 | 2 | 1 |
| South La. Planter . . . . . . | 3 | 5 | — | — |
| Urban Area . . . . . . . . . | 1 | — | 1 | — |

| | | | |
|---|---|---|---|
| Southwest La. . . . . . . . . | — | 7 | 3 | — |
| Macon Ridge . . . . . . . . | — | 2 | 1 | — |
| South La. Bayou . . . . . . . | 2 | 4 | 1 | 1 |
| North La. Hills . . . . . . . | 1 | 4 | 3 | — |
| Central Pine Hills . . . . . . | — | — | 6 | 1 |

The main tendency to be found here is the drift away from Long support in North Louisiana among planter and hill areas. Only the parishes in the Central Hills held firm to the Long pattern. While in the south and west defection was likewise to be found, most of the parishes there stayed within the 40–49 percent interval of Long support. The Longs had failed a second straight time to stem the tide of reform, but as indicated above, at the end of the wartime administration of Jimmie Davis, trends seemed to point to another surge of Longism.[16]

In 1948 the Longs made a decided comeback, with Earl K. Long running for governor, supported and aided by his nephew Russell, Huey's son and heir to the political magic of the name.[17] Three other candidates had entered the race, although it was widely believed that a runoff would find Long pitted against Sam H. Jones again. Jimmie Morrison, the congressman from the Florida Parishes, was running again, but the dark horse was Judge Robert Kennon. Politically unknown at this time, the Webster Parish judge posed as a veterans' candidate and appealed to the Long opposition, who opposed "High Hat" Sam Jones's alleged close connections with big business.

Jones had the advantage of being the administration candidate, but the fact that he had, by and large, the support of industrial interests counted against him with the broad layers of the lower classes. Long led easily in the first primary, receiving 42 percent of the total votes cast. In the runoff he directed his political invective toward Sam Jones while proposing an ambitious welfare program. Earl's endorsement at the polls was overwhelming, and he beat

[16] Sindler, *Huey Long's Louisiana*, 207.
[17] Rudolf Heberle and Alvin L. Bertrand, "Factors Motivating Voting Behavior in a One-Party State," *Social Forces*, XXVII (1949), 349.

Jones with 65 percent of the vote cast and gained majorities in all but two parishes. Once again the swing of parishes to the top percentage interval of Long support, this time constituting fifty-eight of the sixty-four parishes, created a distribution of support among the voter type areas which, like 1936, does not correlate highly with the pattern of other elections. Nonetheless, 1948 shows significant association with 1940, and measures relatively high with 1936 and 1928.

The results of the first primary had forecast clearly who the eventual winner would be. Long gained heavy support in almost all of the Hill parishes and in eight of the South Louisiana French parishes. His strongest opposition was seated in the urban parishes, such as East Baton Rouge, Calcasieu, and Caddo. Likewise, certain of the Planter parishes in the Mississippi Delta showed considerable opposition to Earl Long. Yet, analysis on the ward level, as had been carried out for Huey Long's vote in 1928 above, (page 240) will show that increased populations in backwater settlements during the thirties had swelled the farmer votes and that the Long candidate got many of them:

*Table 8–13*
RED RIVER AND MISSISSIPPI DELTA PARISHES
EARL LONG VOTE BY WARDS, 2nd PRIMARY, 1948

|  | Below 50% | Above 50% |
|---|---|---|
| Red River Wards |  |  |
| River | 14 | 18 |
| Hill | 5 | 24 |
| Miss. Delta Wards |  |  |
| River | 11 | 6 |
| Back | 3 | 10 |
| Total Wards |  |  |
| River | 25 | 24 |
| Hill-Back | 8 | 34 |

It can be seen along the Red River and within the Mississippi Delta that in the twenty years since 1928 the Long tendency had remained strong among the farmer wards, and had even spread into the wards along the rivers, where the planter predominated.

Sam Jones, weak in his home parish of Calcasieu, found his main backing in the more urban areas about New Orleans and Baton Rouge. Kennon's support was seated for the most part about Shreveport, Monroe, and the hills near his native Webster. However, Kennon also proved surprisingly strong in Lake Charles and Baton Rouge, and in the southern section of bayou and planter country, a forecast, perhaps of things to come. Jimmie Morrison scored heavily in his native Florida Parishes, as he had consistently done. With Long's strong initial support, and the decided shift of Morrison's support in his favor, Long had no trouble in the runoff primary.[18]

Continued postwar prosperity and Earl's promised veterans' bonus considered, perhaps it is not so surprising that another Long surge occurred at the polls. What is surprising is how Long, in New Orleans, was able to carry even middle-class wards against the candidacy of Sam Jones:

*Table 8–14*
PERCENT SUPPORT FOR SECOND PRIMARY CANDIDATES, 1948,
IN NEW ORLEANS BY GROUPS OF WARDS BY SOCIOECONOMIC STATUS

| Type of Ward | Earl Long | Sam Jones |
|---|---|---|
| Upper . . . . . | 37% | 63% |
| Middle . . . . . | 70 | 30 |
| Lower . . . . . | 72 | 28 |
| City . . . . . . | 63% | 37% |

Compared to the New Orleans class vote in 1940 when the two candidates had faced each other (Table 8–9), it can be seen that while lower-class and upper-class wards had virtually the same proportion of votes, in the middle-class wards Long made deep inroads where previously he had more nearly broken even in voting support.

It will be recalled that not until the census count of 1950 was the

18 Heberle and Bertrand, "Factors Motivating Voting Behavior," 346.

Louisiana population considered an urban one. In fact, Louisiana population changed rapidly from predominantly rural to urban as a consequence of the wartime boom in the economy.[19] For the urban proportion of the population had remained nearly stationary in the 1930 and 1940 counts (40 and 41 percent, respectively), but in 1950, 55 percent of all Louisianians resided in urban areas. The rapid growth of the Louisiana population was associated with the rise of lesser cities to urban prominence, particularly the industrialized areas of Shreveport, Monroe, Alexandria, Baton Rouge, and Lake Charles, so that we can, after 1950, speak of the parishes that contain them, together with Orleans and Jefferson, as Urban Parishes. In 1950 these seven urban-industrial parishes contained almost half the state's population (47 percent) and what is more important, almost as many voters: 45 percent of the total votes in the second primary of 1948 were cast in the Urban Parishes, and Long had received 62 percent of them. While, as has been mentioned above, labor organization had not become particularly strong, in the 1948 elections there can be little doubt that the Long margin in the urban-industrial parishes was due to labor's support.[20]

While Huey P. Long and his successors, including his brother Earl, managed to couple farmer and laborer into a following whose combined support became difficult to overcome, ultimately, nearly half a century after disfranchisement, politicians would have to meet the issue of the Negro vote. When the United States Supreme Court denied the legality of the white primary in the 1940's, Negro voter registration in Louisiana had been very slight (886 in 1940), and was centered in New Orleans where the rudiments of a Republican Party organization had been maintained. But by 1948, the number of Negro voters registered (28,177) was something to be reckoned with, if elections were close. Since the Louisiana Negro's greatest benefits had come through the Long version of welfare legislation, their increased registration could hardly be bad news for Longism. And

[19] Bardin H. Nelson, "The Impact of War on Population Redistribution in Louisiana" (Master's thesis, Louisiana State University, 1943).

[20] See my "Voting Behavior in Baton Rouge," *Proceedings of the Louisiana Academy of Science*, XV (1952), 84–100.

although it might be called expediency for the Longs to encourage Negro registration, the Longs had never before made political capital out of the race issue.

It can be suggested then, that the reappearance of the Negro in Louisiana politics was a consequence of tacit approval, if not downright encouragement from white politicians. An obvious association exists between Long incumbency in the governor's office, or the presence of a Long factional candidate in a gubernatorial primary election, and an increase in Negro voter participation. The reemergence of the Negro in Louisiana politics cannot be evaluated, as Professors Fenton and Vines have pointed out, simply through observing the statewide "averages" of Negro participation. They say that an important characteristic of Negro registration in Louisiana is the extreme range of variation to be found among the several parishes.[21] What then, are the underlying elements supporting increasing Negro registration and voting, and how are these associated with the reciprocities of political behavior? The study mentioned above provides part of the answer. Taking into consideration such factors as (1) the presence of a plantation economy (2), the effect of Negro-white population balance within the parishes, or (3), the effects of urbanism, the single most important finding concerning Negro registration in Louisiana was the association of it with the religio-cultural variable.[22] Fenton and Vines feel that the French-Roman Catholic subculture of South Louisiana sustains a more permissive attitude toward the Negro. This important study investigated Negro registration through 1956. After that, strong resistance against Negro suffrage developed until 1959 when Governor Earl K. Long was fighting before the legislature to preserve civil rights for the Negro in Louisiana.[23]

The initial increase in Negro registration took place in urban and Catholic New Orleans, where Negro organizations pressed earliest for Negro suffrage in the state.[24] As a matter of fact, members of

[21] John H. Fenton and Kenneth N. Vines, "Negro Registration in Louisiana," *American Political Science Review*, LI (1957), 704.
[22] *Ibid.*, 713.
[23] A. J. Liebling, *The Earl of Louisiana* (New York, 1961), 28, a perceptive account of the occasion.
[24] Fenton and Vines, "Negro Registration," 711.

the Negro community competed among themselves to claim credit for leading in this civil rights issue. Leaders of segments of the New Orleans Negro community moved to put Negro registrants upon the lists,[25] and by 1946, this city with 4,822 new voters contained 64 percent of the total Negro registration of the state. The upsurge of Negro registration continued in other urban parishes and in South Louisiana, although of the total of 28,177 new voters, nearly half of them were registered in the city. The first truly sizable numerical gain occurred in the period from 1948 to 1952 (28,177 to 107,844), when Earl Long sat in the governor's chair and attempted to maintain control of state political affairs with his hand-picked candidate in the latter year. These numerical gains in Negro registration curve upward with spectactular rates of increase through 1952, at which time the pace seemed to slacken until the total reached a maximum of over 161,000 in 1956, when "Uncle Earl" Long swept back into office with a first primary majority.

Subsequent analysis will trace Negro voting behavior in more detail, but at this point it is necessary only to determine the general direction of the tendency. While in New Orleans the success of reform Mayor deLesseps S. Morrison was built upon an electoral foundation that included Negroes and upper whites, in state politics at this time the vote in Negro precincts did not appear to be a bloc vote:

*Table 8–15*
NEW ORLEANS NEGRO VOTE, IN SELECTED PRECINCTS
SECOND PRIMARY, 1948

|  | Earl Long | Sam Jones |
|---|---|---|
| Ward 10, Precincts 14–15–16–17 and | 2,025 | 511 |
| Ward 11, Precincts 11–23–13–14 | 80% | 20% |

By the time of the 1952 gubernatorial primary elections nearly one-half the people of the state lived in the seven urban and industrial

[25] Sindler, *Huey Long's Louisiana,* 256–61.

parishes. Two-fifths of Louisiana Negroes had migrated to these seven parishes by 1950, and in most cases, Negroes made up nearly a third of these parishes' populations. In 1952, the Negro voters there represented 63 percent of the total Negro voters who had registered. It would no longer be possible to unite rural Louisiana against New Orleans, or the latter with a portion of the former. The increase of population in urban centers had created a larger working class and a new middle class whose favor at the polls must be won. Likewise, the class structure of the rural parishes had changed. The farmers were generally more secure, better educated, and more prosperous than ever before. If the class position of the rural or urban dweller had been altered and generally improved, so the subtle psychological process of identification might work in the direction of alliance with the older status groups of power and prestige. The predispositions of the old Bourbon Democrat might remain in force, reinforced through the aspirations of social mobility among members of the new emergent middle class.

Of the nine gubernatorial candidates in the Democratic primary of 1952, only five were given serious consideration, although Dudley J. LeBlanc counted himself in the running again. The results of the election indicated that Louisiana politics still could be understood in terms of the Long and anti-Long cleavage.[26] Yet, the campaign brought out clearly the fact that more than the old political battle with the former symbols was involved, since every leading candidate considered himself an independent[27] Once again it is clear that if the Longs had been united, the swing to the opposition might have been averted, but their disunity at election time seems to have become a predictable characteristic, particularly because of Earl Long's continued political ambitions.

Although the reform administrations of 1940 and 1944 had left much of the bureaucracy of Longism intact, the 1948 administration of Earl Long proved to be four years of higher taxes and heavy

[26] Rudolf Heberle, George A. Hillery, Jr., and Frank Lovrich, "Continuity and Change in Voting Behavior in the 1952 Primaries in Louisiana," *Southwestern Social Science Quarterly*, XXXIII (1953), 328–42.

[27] New Orleans *Item*, 1951–52. This paper ran weekly columns printing views and reports of the candidates, most of whom claimed "independence."

*Table 8–16*

CANDIDATES AND VOTES

FIRST PRIMARY GUBERNATORIAL ELECTION, 1952

| | Long Candidates Votes Cast | | Parish | | Opposition Votes Cast | | Parish |
|---|---|---|---|---|---|---|---|
| | Number | Percent | Plu- ralities | | Number | Percent | Plu- ralities |
| Spaht | 173,987 | 23 | 23 | Kennon | 163,434 | 21 | 16 |
| Boggs | 142,542 | 19 | 3 | McLemore | 116,405 | 15 | 13 |
| Dodd | 90,925 | 12 | 3 | LeBlanc | 62,906 | 8 | 6 |
| | | | | Others (3) | 11,535 | 2 | 0 |
| | 407,454 | 54% | 29 | | 334,280 | 46% | 35 |

spending.[28] "Welfare statism" was given its greatest boost in Louisiana at the same time the national trend was to turn away from the dangers of "creeping socialism." The observant politician might detect that the new middle class was among those most sensitive to this trend. Whereas the state total spending of the last year of the Davis administration had amounted to $170 million, it rose to $336 million during the 1950–52 fiscal period. In 1950, Earl Long alienated many of his own followers when, encouraged by the resounding victory of his nephew Russell in his bid for a full-term Senate seat, Earl persuaded his legislature to hold a constitutional convention in which his administration would be granted a second consecutive term.[29] The heat of opposition to this move was so great that the legislature called off the convention, and the after-effects continued in a rejection by the electorate of a giant bond issue which Earl had hoped to float. Earl Long's attempted power grabs led to loss of support from his lieutenant governor, Bill Dodd, and alienated his nephew, Senator Russell Long. Earl was clearly of the old school of Longism, but Russell seemed to be from a different classroom. A columnist pointed to Russell's good standing in the Senate and to the cynical summation of a wag who felt that "education is the ruin of a demagogue."[30]

[28] New Orleans *Item*, May 11, 1952, p. 1.
[29] Sindler, *Huey Long's Louisiana*, 231–32.
[30] New Orleans *Item*, July 25, 1952; Doris Fleeson, p. 9.

At any rate, the Earl Long administration was going out of office, but benefits seemed to be here to stay, and the action of the candidates in 1952 indicated they considered themselves on uncertain ground on which they had to feel their way, to play safe and be independent. Dudley J. LeBlanc's appearance in the 1952 gubernatorial race marked his third try and fitted the temper of the year. LeBlanc had become a successful manufacturer of Hadacol, a patent medicine, and this time his approach was, "It is time to elect a businessman to run the biggest business of them all, the government of the state of Louisiana."[31]

Also a candidate was Robert Kennon, who had run in 1948, and who that same year had faced Russell Long in a race for an unexpired term in the United States Senate (receiving 49 percent of the vote). Throughout the 1952 governor's campaign he claimed that the other candidates were appropriating his platform which was the first to be announced and which grew out of his judgment of the temper of the people. The platform had a twelve-point program of pledges:

· Continuance of $50-a-month old-age assistance.
· Businesslike administration of affairs of highway commission through establishment of a board.
· Repeal of two cents additional gasoline tax enacted in 1948.
· Improvement of public health.
· Removal of state institutions from political control by creating boards.
· Prison reform.
· A modern parole system.
· Preservation of home rule.
· Constitutional civil service.
· Availability of voting machines in every voting precinct.
· Bringing of new industry to Louisiana.
· Encouragement of agriculture and making an effective team of farmer, businessman, and banker.[32]

Much of Kennon's program could be seen as a blend of Longism and the previous reforms of Sam Jones, and the essential difference

[31] New Orleans *Item*, Oct. 28, 1951, p. 20.
[32] New Orleans *Times-Picayune*, Jan. 17, 1952, p. 1.

between the programs of another candidate, Carlos Spaht, and Kennon appeared to be that Kennon presented his platform with the promise of a businesslike administration. Louisiana was experiencing an unprecedented prosperity, and who but the businessman had made this possible? Spaht was dedicated to the task of carrying on the program of Longism, but this now smacked of machine politics and the welfare state. This sort of government, it was claimed in this states' rights state, would parallel Trumanism on the national scene. Against this, Kennon proffered an administration whose virtue would be self-righteousness and whose watchword would be efficiency.

Perhaps the Kennon program was not so much different from past reforms, yet, Kennon made his strongest appeals in the urban areas of the state, and did not make the effort that other candidates did in the rural areas. Robert Kennon, it appeared, was up on his political know-how. The people of Louisiana had come to accept the good of Longism as an inevitable function of modern government. No one dared take it away. Kennon, then, gave the impression that he was a man of the people, the people of the 1950's.

The third major opposition to the Long candidates came from James McLemore, the candidate who proved to have the most conspicuous class appeal. The election results showed that his support was definitely drawn from planter areas. A businessman, McLemore was an avowed independent and his campaign headquarters started a "citizens'" revolt which was peculiarly akin to the term "crusade" which was used later the same year in the presidential campaign. Toward the end of the campaign he declared that there was a swing to his candidacy, and the 15 percent of the vote he received indicated that he was correct. He appealed to prestige and power groups and the new middle class, linking his candidacy to what was termed a revolt against the "Truman-Socialism" debacle in Washington. Like other conservatives, McLemore was careful to state that he was not against welfare, for every needy citizen should get assistance, but the political padding must go. McLemore was the heir apparent to the 1948 Dixiecrat movement, which he obviously sought to tap.

In his campaign for the gubernatorial nomination, Hale Boggs stated that the state legislature should be more than the governor's rubber stamp. He called for an improved old-age pension program, a salary raise for school teachers to meet cost-of-living increases, rebuilt and widened highways, and the attraction of commerce and industry to Louisiana. He would maintain Longism, but he opposed Earl Long.

A respected member of the U.S. House of Representatives, Boggs drew the support of Senator Russell Long who with apparent sincerity, charged that his Uncle Earl had "mansionitis." When it was charged that Boggs was actually Earl's candidate, by the anti-Longs, the conservative Shreveport *Times* denounced the claim and openly endorsed Boggs.

William Dodd, the estranged lieutenant governor of the Long administration, accepted the program of Longism as well, but he fought the power grab, and since he had government experience, his election, he said, would ensure a smooth transition in the office. Dodd felt that taxes could be reduced even under the type of administration the people were now experiencing. He made many friends in the state, especially among the growing labor unions. Yet, his campaign talks gave the impression that he was trying to convince himself that he was a frontrunner in the race.

District Judge Carlos Spaht was Earl Long's choice to succeed to the governorship, but he was chosen only after Long had tried to persuade others to run. Spaht pointed out that most of the opposition said they would retain all benefits of the present state administration and at the same time promised multiple tax reductions. This, he said, was always a good trick if it could be done. Whether Earl Long and his political allies or Spaht and his personal friends wrote the Long platform of 1952, it was written in such a way to meet the challenge of the Long opposition. It too would be carried out constructively, and with the humanitarian touch traditional of Longism. Lest there be any danger at all of more power grabs (and to counter the Kennon pledge of more blue ribbon boards), Spaht endorsed the establishment of an advisory council in order to make the new Long administration the most incorruptible and productive.

If it were true that the two judges who became the front runners had similar platforms, then what was Kennon doing with a program like the Longs? Kennon might well have considered himself the heir to the reform administrations of the 1940's, for his position, like theirs, could not be radically different from that of the administration in office. No wholesale removal of any Long-endorsed practice was suggested. Welfare aid must be continued, the institutions were to be furthered, the state prison Angola was to be improved, and home rule preserved. The difference was that Kennon pledged to continue services and at the same time cut taxes. Being an independent with no previous record in government, Kennon could more easily make his promises sound legitimate.

Longism had been the political creed of the small people, the farmer, the worker, and the small businessman, whose traditional support was firmly seated. In 1952, the die-hards, the farmers of the hills, remained loyal to the tradition, but even here the area of support had shrunk.[33] The clear-cut profile of farmer class opposed to planter and business interests was blurred. The voting behavior of Macon Ridge affords a good example as the cotton farmers of Franklin and Richland parishes, many of whom had come from the hills, supported Spaht in the first primary but endorsed Kennon in the runoff with between 52 and 58 percent of the vote. The farmer class itself was divided, as it had been in the 1880's, only now, good times had brought the farmer security and a newly enjoyed status, and he looked further up the class ladder for his political identification.

Spaht's support had come from Long country, while LeBlanc and Dodd turned out to be favorite son candidates and failed to gain much support outside their home territories. The crucial battle of this 1952 election was fought in the urban parishes. Kennon proved to be the candidate with the best organization, and his city vote made the difference. He had claimed that with thirty thousand New Orleans votes in the first primary, victory would be his; more than thirty-three thousand Kennon votes were counted. In the second primary the urban appeal of Kennon was overwhelming, for in the seven urban-industrial parishes, the electorate had favored his candidacy with

[33] Heberle, Hillery, and Lovrich, "Continuity and Change," Figures 1 and 2.

POLITICAL TENDENCIES IN LOUISIANA

65 percent of the parish totals. Moreover, the contribution of these seven parishes to the total state vote of Kennon was 49.8 percent, almost half the entire Kennon support.

Spaht, on the other hand, gained but 42 percent of his second primary support in the urban areas, scoring handily only in the parishes of the Central Hills. It was this support which provided what little association has been found to exist between the elections of 1948 and 1952 (+ .353).

In fact, the Long disunity in 1952 was such that a low point for the Long era had been reached in the number of parishes in which the Long candidate secured a majority vote (eleven):

*Table 8–17*
LONG CANDIDATE VOTE, SECOND PRIMARY, 1952,
BY VOTER TYPE AREAS

| Unit | Number of Parishes | | | |
| | 0–39% | 40–49% | 50–59% | 60–100% |
| --- | --- | --- | --- | --- |
| North La. Planter | 7 | 3 | — | — |
| Florida Parishes | 5 | 3 | — | — |
| South La. Planter | 1 | 4 | 2 | 1 |
| Urban Area | 2 | — | — | — |
| Southwest La. | 4 | 6 | — | — |
| Macon Ridge | — | 3 | — | — |
| South La. Bayou | 4 | 3 | — | 1 |
| North La. Hills | 2 | 2 | 3 | 1 |
| Central Pine Hills | — | 4 | 3 | — |

For the first time, Macon Ridge and Southwest Louisiana provided no parish majorities for Long, and in the North Louisiana and the Central Pine Hills the decrease of support is easily seen.

Yet, the continued potency of a Long united front is obvious; also obvious is the difficulty of following a Long incumbent. The combined "Long" group of Spaht, Boggs, and Dodd polled 54 percent of the votes cast in the first primary, more than enough to win. But it was precisely here that the continuity in voting behavior was disrupted.

The intrafactional quarrel had weakened its chances. This point was clearly made in a study which tried to identify the six leading candidates in terms of Long-Opposition cleavage. "The geographic distribution of Kennon's support in 1952–II corresponds more closely to that of Jones' support in 1948–II than Spaht's support in 1952–II does to Long's in 1948–II."[34] If Boggs and Dodd support was added successively to that of Spaht and correlated with the Spaht second primary strength, it was found that as the strength of other candidates was added to the Spaht support, the correlation coefficients declined rather than increased (they increased in the case of Kennon), suggesting that *part* of the Dodd and Boggs vote went to Kennon in the second primary.

The most significant phenomenon in 1952 was the increasing Negro participation in the political battle,[35] for the number of Negroes registered to vote had reached 107,884, more than three times what it had been in 1948. Registered in large numbers in the urban areas and the rural French parishes, the Negro once more became an important factor in political success. Since the Negro as a class category had tended to support Longism, his appearance might be essential to that political program. For as the traditional Long support diminished in the rural parishes, the new support from the Negro would be a possible key to future Louisiana politics.

One previous study of urban voting behavior has been published using Baton Rouge as a crucial case,[36] and it will be useful to summarize the findings presented there and to project the analysis of voting behavior to the 1952 elections. Before 1960 it was not possible to make computations of socioeconomic characteristics of a statistical nature for Baton Rouge because of the lack of census tract data. However, the city did lend itself to a delineation of social ecological areas. In the terminology of urban ecologists there were "natural areas" within the city, setting apart sections on a residential basis as predominantly "worker" or "business-professional" areas. The ecological pattern of Baton Rouge was quite clear and afforded the

[34] Heberle, Hillery, and Lovrich, "Continuity and Change," 335.
[35] *Ibid.*, 339.
[36] Howard, "Voting Behavior in Baton Rouge."

opportunity to draw conclusions concerning the voting behavior of various class elements of the population, on the precinct level.

In the 1948 elections it was found in Baton Rouge that Earl Long was an also-ran in the first primary, due to the earlier episodes of Huey Long's fight with the Standard Oil Corporation which maintained a huge refinery in the city. Jimmie Morrison had polled strong support in worker precincts, while Robert Kennon was a strong second choice in both worker and business-professional precincts—a forecast of 1952, perhaps. In the second primary, the worker precincts shifted to the support of Long, whereas Jones had gained large majorities in the areas of business class predominance. It was believed that in the showdown, the workers considered Long to be a lesser evil than the businessman's candidate Sam Jones.

The Negro had little or no voice in the 1948 election, but it is necessary to isolate this element of voters in making a class analysis of 1952 voting behavior. The precincts have been lumped into three general categories, based upon the predominance of some residential groupings. Not all Negroes are workers, but the majority who live in distinctly Negro areas are wage earners; and of course there are Negroes who live in predominantly white precincts, even. Analysis will proceed with a look at the tendencies of the "Negro worker," the "white worker," and the "business-professional-white" (upper white) precincts. It must be remembered at all times that these categories are not mutually exclusive.

In the 1952 first primary, the group of Negro precincts clearly showed a preference for Long candidates; Kennon and McLemore together were a choice of only 17 percent of the Negro voters. At the other end of the social pyramid, the upper white precincts showed a much greater proportion of support for those two candidates. Even so, the three Long candidates shared 48 percent of the choices of this unit. Here, it may be contended, the lower range of the unit, the white collar category of voters, tended to show a more decided leaning toward the Long candidates. The white worker precincts gave heaviest support to the candidacy of Kennon, 52 percent, with the other candidates splitting the remainder.

In the runoff, the Negro unit demonstrated again the preference for

*Table 8–18*
VOTING PERCENTAGES IN ECOLOGICAL AREAS
OF BATON ROUGE, 1952 PRIMARIES

FIRST PRIMARY:

| Type of Precinct | Spaht | Boggs | Dodd | Kennon | McLemore | Total |
|---|---|---|---|---|---|---|
| Negro Worker | 39 | 15 | 30 | 14 | 3 | 100% |
|  | 23 | 11 | 28 | 4 | 3 |  |
| White Worker | 13 | 17 | 13 | 52 | 5 | 100% |
|  | 24 | 37 | 35 | 47 | 24 |  |
| Upper White | 21 | 17 | 9 | 39 | 14 | 100% |
|  | 53 | 52 | 37 | 49 | 73 |  |
| Total | 100% | 100% | 100% | 100% | 100% |  |

SECOND PRIMARY:

| Type of Precinct | Spaht |  |  | Kennon |  | Total |
|---|---|---|---|---|---|---|
| Negro Worker | 75 |  |  | 26 |  | 100% |
|  | 33 |  |  | 5 |  |  |
| White Worker | 26 |  |  | 74 |  | 100% |
|  | 29 |  |  | 46 |  |  |
| Upper White | 34 |  |  | 66 |  | 100% |
|  | 38 |  |  | 49 |  |  |
| Total | 100% |  |  | 100% |  |  |

the Long candidate, although Kennon gained more support here than the combined Kennon-McLemore vote of the first. The fact that the groupings are not mutually exclusive might be cited in explanation of this shift. In the upper white precincts, Kennon must have picked up Long first primary support as well as McLemore, while his most surprising support came from the white worker precincts, reversing the proportions of the Negro precincts. Yet, it was pointed out that in 1948, only in the second primary did the Long candidate gain worker votes in any number.

Looked at the other way, in terms of the proportionate amount of support each candidate received from the three precinct units, it is clear that McLemore gained his greatest support from the upper white elements. Both Boggs and Kennon emerged as candidates with upper white and white worker support, but little Negro support, while Dodd's following paralleled more closely the proportions of Spaht's support, marking him as more the Long type of candidate. In the runoff Spaht appeared to draw support from each class grouping in nearly equal proportions. Of course, Spaht's showing in the upper white precincts was to be expected due to his many social connections in these areas. Still, he obtained only about one-fifth of the vote cast in these precincts in the first primary. One striking conclusion which may be made is that the Negro support tended to serve as an index of the Long identification of the candidate.

Earl K. Long came back himself in 1956 and gained a majority of 51 percent in the first primary. In the eight elections from 1928 through 1956 this marked the fifth gubernatorial race won by Long candidates and their third won by a majority in the first primary. Thus despite scandal, crudeness, and counterappeals on behalf of respectability, the electorate returned again to the "buccaneering liberalism" of the Longs.[37] In this alternation, the Longs, it has been shown, have had the better of it, winning with greater margins and supported by a larger number of hard-core parishes. Of the two election victories since World War II, however, they were both won by "Uncle Earl," the "last of the red-hot poppas."[38] Investigation will show that the heavy support from Negroes (161,410 were registered) contributed to Long's margin of victory.

Earl Long's accomplishment of carrying pluralities in every parish except Orleans is all the more remarkable inasmuch as he disavowed use of the new-fangled TV and carried on a traditional grass-roots stump campaign, a performance at which, of course, he had no peers. "Chep" Morrison, the bright young reform mayor of New Orleans, and his Crescent City Democratic Organization with which he had beaten the Old Regulars since 1946, was the major opposition, but his plurality in the city was a scant 2,017 votes more than Earl Long received. James McLemore ran again, but he slipped badly compared to his 1952 showing, no doubt hurt by the candidacy of Francis C.

---

[37] Sindler, *Huey Long's Louisiana*, the title of chap. 8.
[38] Brooks Read and Bud Hebert, editors and narrators, *The Voice of Earl Long* (Baton Rouge, News Records, Inc., 1961).

Grevemberg, chief of state police under the Kennon administration and respectable foe of gambling who later was to run for governor under the Republican banner. The Kennon administration's candidate had been Frederick T. Preaus who fared badly outside North Louisiana and the urban areas.

*Table 8–19*

CANDIDATES AND VOTES

FIRST PRIMARY GUBERNATORIAL ELECTION, 1956

| Long Candidate | | | Opposition Candidates | | |
|---|---|---|---|---|---|
| Votes Cast | | Parish | | Votes Cast | Parish |
| Number | Percent | Plu-ralities | | Number | Percent | Plu-ralities |
| Long 421,681 | 51% | 63 | Morrison | 191,576 | 24% | 1 |
| | | | Preaus | 95,955 | 12% | — |
| | | | Grevemberg | 62,309 | 8% | — |
| | | | McLemore | 48,188 | 5% | — |

The 1956 election is associated most consistently in its relationship with the others in the correlation of percentages by voter type areas since 1940. The Earl Long support was highest in the areas said to depict the pattern of Longism.

*Table 8–20*

LONG SUPPORT BY VOTER TYPES, 1956

| | Number of Parishes | | | |
|---|---|---|---|---|
| Unit | 0–39% | 40–49% | 50–59% | 60–100% |
| North La. Planter . . . . . . | 1 | 3 | 4 | 2 |
| Florida Parishes . . . . . . . | 1 | 1 | — | 6 |
| South La. Planter . . . . . . | — | — | 3 | 5 |
| Urban Area . . . . . . . . . | — | 2 | — | — |
| Southwest La. . . . . . . . . | — | 2 | 4 | 4 |
| Macon Ridge . . . . . . . . | — | — | 2 | 1 |
| South La. Bayou . . . . . . . | 1 | — | 5 | 2 |
| North La. Hills . . . . . . . | — | 2 | 1 | 5 |
| Central Pine Hills . . . . . . | — | — | — | 7 |

The Hills had swung back to the high percentage interval of support for the Long candidate in 1956 as had most of the Florida Parishes where farmer and worker resided. The traditional Long bridge to South Louisiana was seen again in the support of parishes in the Bayou country and in the Southwest Parishes. The Long support in the South Louisiana Planter Parishes deserves comment. In the parishes through which the Mississippi River flows southeastward from Baton Rouge, a substantial increase in the number of industrial plants had appeared by 1950, when census data could be used to show a large increase in the worker category of the labor force. Together with increased Negro voter registration in these parishes, this new element in the electorate in the Planter Parishes tended to be pro-Long.

A sampling of Negro precincts within Louisiana cities reveals that Earl Long most likely did receive the bulk of this bloc of votes. In the northern part of the state, the Long candidate was favored by some 80 percent in the Negro precincts of Monroe, while significantly, the runner-up was Morrison with 15 percent support. In Baton Rouge, where the Long candidate had been highly favored in 1952, the predominantly Negro precincts had voted Long by 68 percent while again, "Chep" Morrison was able to hold second place with 21 percent. Finally, in New Orleans, where Morrison had built his successful reign as mayor upon a support consisting of upper white and Negro votes, Earl Long was able nevertheless to get 45 percent of the vote in the Negro precincts (and 25 percent in upper white precincts).

If the parish voter type distribution of percentages in 1956 is characteristic of the profile of Longism (Map 8–1), then the use of a number of variables in cross-tabulation with the Earl Long vote may provide a summary of tendencies at this point of time in the Long era. If the pattern of Longism was a combination of farmer and worker, Negro and white, Protestant and Catholic, and North and South Louisiana voter categories, then the distribution of parishes high in Long support would be expected to divide *both* high and low on the incidence of such variables as percent urban, percent Negro registration, percent Catholic, and ratio of workers to self-employed.

# Average Long Candidates Vote, Eight Gubernatorial Primary Elections, 1928-1956

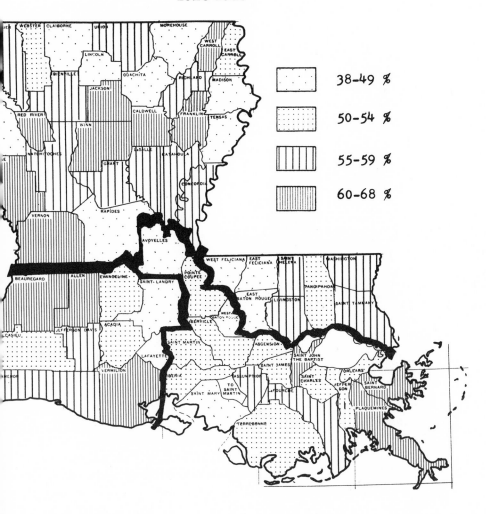

38-49 %

50-54 %

55-59 %

60-68 %

Such a finding would confirm the bridging effect of Longism, and its importance can be shown by considering the cross-tabulation of parish percent Catholic and Negro registration by North and South Louisiana, where cleavage is the outcome:

*Table 8–21*

DISTRIBUTION OF PARISHES BY PERCENT
CATHOLIC AND PERCENT NEGRO REGISTRATION
BY NORTH AND SOUTH LOUISIANA*

|  |  | Percent Catholic, 1956 | | |
|---|---|---|---|---|
|  |  | Low (0–34.9%) |  | High (35–99%) |
|  | Low (0–13.9%) | +++++ +++++ +++++ +++++ | 00 00 | 00000 00000 |
| Percent Negro Registration, 1956 |  |  |  |  |
|  | High (14–40%) | ++++ +++ | 00 + | 00000 00000 00000 00000 |

* O = South Louisiana Parishes (N 36).
  + = North Louisiana Parishes (N 28).

Put this way, it is possible to see the cleavage between North and South Louisiana in terms of Negro registration and percent Catholic (20 North low-low as against 20 South high-high), as well as the relationship between Catholicism and Negro voter registration. When, however, percent Long is compared with percent Catholic in this manner, a quite different pattern is found (Table 8–22).

Now, Catholic and non-Catholic parishes alike join in support of the Long candidate. Similar distributions are to be found in comparing the relationship between the other variables mentioned above and the Long support. These may be summarized by focusing upon the the two cells which contain the parishes with high Long percentages, which number fifty one, and determining the lows and highs from the other axis (Table 8–23).

*Table 8–22*

DISTRIBUTION OF PARISHES BY PERCENT
LONG VOTE AND PERCENT CATHOLIC
BY NORTH AND SOUTH LOUISIANA*

|  | | Percent Long Vote, 1956 | |
|---|---|---|---|
|  | | Low (0–49%) | High (50–100%) |
| Percent Catholic 1956 | Low (0–34.9%) | +++  0 ++ | +++++  000 +++++  00 +++++ +++++ ++ |
|  | High (35.99%) | 0000 000  + | 00000 00000 00000 00000 000 |

\* O = South Louisiana Parishes (N 36).
 + = North Louisiana Parishes (N 28).

*Table 8–23*

DISTRIBUTION OF PARISHES IN THE TWO HIGH
(MAJORITY) LONG CELLS

| Cell Combination | Number of Parishes | | Total |
|---|---|---|---|
|  | North La. | South La. | (N) |
| High Long Low Negro Registration . . . . . . . . . | 15 | 9 | (24) |
| High Long High Negro Registration . . . . . . . . . | 6 | 21 | (27) |

| | | |
|---|---|---|
| High Long Low Worker Ratio. . . . . . . . . . . . 13 | 14 | (27) |
| High Long High Worker Ratio. . . . . . . . . . . . 9 | 15 | (24) |
| High Long Low Urban. . . . . . . . . . . . . . 15 | 16 | (31) |
| High Long High Urban. . . . . . . . . . . . . . 8 | 12 | (20) |

The rather complete balance between North and South Louisiana in regard to the low and high incidence tends to hold for each variable but urbanism, where the thirty-one low urban may be taken not as an exception but as indicative of the rural Long support.

The significance of the parish distributions found in this set of tables lies in the consideration that if either race or religion should reenter Louisiana politics, the North-South bridge of the Longs would be broken. North Louisiana would separate from South in its parish distribution of voting percentages in the race-religion cleavage pattern which had been seen in the 1924 second primary. This was exactly what happened in the 1960 elections, as subsequent analysis will show.

# CHAPTER IX

# The Issue of Civil Rights
# and Presidential Elections

*1. The Louisiana Version of The "Solid South," 1900–1944*

The Bourbon ascendancy had been predicated on the denial of civil rights to the Negro, and thus, a tendency to support the Democratic Party became an indicator of the South's defense of white supremacy. By the 1960's, however, it was the *lack* of such support in presidential elections which could be used to represent the defensive reaction of the southern region toward the egalitarian demands of the nation. The South no doubt would have preferred to remain a closed society, and while in Louisiana politics had been opened by the impact of Longism, for the most part it did not extend to presidential politics. The thesis to be defended here is that, in presidential elections, Louisiana voters registered their preference for that party or candidate most likely to allow the South to avoid change.[1]

According to C. Vann Woodward, the South has now experienced two "reconstructions."[2] Hindsight has seen the pattern of events which constituted the first, but the outcome of the second, which began in 1954, is not yet clearly in view. Still, striking parallels are apparent. After the first, "redemption" was followed by efforts to build a "new south" on industrial foundations. The region built up a bulwark of white supremacy through the device of compulsive voting for the Democratic Party in what became known as the "Solid South." Since the Supreme Court's school desegregation decisions, however, the South has not been able to strike bargains for any more

[1] Perry H. Howard and Joseph L. Brent III, "Social Change, Urbanization, and Types of Society," *Journal of Social Issues*, XXII (1966); Howard, "The New Electorate in the South," paper read at Symposium on Southern Politics, Louisiana State University in New Orleans, Feb. 18, 1967 (lithograph).

[2] C. Vann Woodward, *Origins of the New South* (Baton Rouge, 1951), provides the grounds for the comparison.

redemptions from a determined nation. Rather, it has innovated numerous devices such as the White Citizens' Council movement, revival of the Klan, and delaying tactics in the courts to keep its "way" intact. Once more the call for a new industrialized South is heard, but at the same time, voters in the region have registered an increasingly conservative (non-Democratic Party) vote.

In Louisiana the historical reaction appeared to be more thoroughgoing than in the southern region. This has been shown in Appendix A, Table 2, where in the five presidential elections from 1900 through 1916, while Louisiana Democratic support averaged 34 percent above that of the nation, it was even 23 percent higher than the regional support. This pattern is seen to hold until the fateful election of 1948. In the earlier period, even the Progressive and Socialist flirtations were not so serious that any Louisiana parishes fell below 50 percent in Democratic support, and to view the figures is to be convinced:

*Table 9–1*

PRESIDENTIAL DEMOCRATIC PERCENTAGES, 1900–64

| Election Year | Percent Turnout | State Percent | Number of Parishes | | | |
|---|---|---|---|---|---|---|
| | | | 0–39% | 40–49% | 50–59% | 60–100% |
| 1900 | 52% | 79% | — | — | 6 | 58 |
| 1904 | 50 | 89 | — | — | — | 64 |
| 1908 | 49 | 85 | — | — | 1 | 63 |
| 1912 | 51 | 77 | — | — | 7 | 57 |
| 1916 | 50 | 86 | — | 6 | 1 | 57 |
| 1920 | 49 | 69 | 5 | 9 | 2 | 48 |
| 1924 | 38 | 76 | 1 | — | 8 | 55 |
| 1928 | 57 | 76 | — | — | 2 | 62 |
| 1932 | 48 | 93 | — | — | — | 64 |
| 1936 | 51 | 89 | 1 | — | 1 | 62 |
| 1940 | 53 | 86 | — | — | — | 64 |
| 1944 | 48 | 81 | — | — | — | 64 |
| 1948 | 45 | 33 | 48 | 11 | 3 | 2 |
| 1952 | 62 | 53 | 6 | 9 | 30 | 19 |
| 1956 | 58 | 40 | 33 | 18 | 13 | — |
| 1960 | 70 | 50 | 31 | 9 | 3 | 21 |
| 1964 | 73 | 43 | 33 | 9 | 13 | 9 |

The depressing effect of Bourbon rule can be seen in the relatively low percentage turnout of registered voters in these presidential elections. Until 1952, when it began to rise and parallel that of gubernatorial elections for the first time since the Civil War (Appendix A, Table 1), turnout hardly averaged 50 percent. Through the election of 1912, only remnants of the previous South Louisiana Republicanism were present, as but a few parish votes failed to array in the top interval of Democratic support. The "bulge" that began to appear in the intervals below 50 percent in 1916 and continued into the 1920 election was produced by South Louisiana parishes within which sugar remained the number one staple and where tariff considerations were important. In 1913, the tariff legislation of the Wilson administration was not protective enough for the Louisiana sugar interests, and the expected reaction in anti-Democratic support can be seen.

Republican opinion in Louisiana was peculiarly sensitive in the year 1920. The Progressive-Republican Parker had been elected governor with strong backing in South Louisiana, and in the presidential election Harding had been given majorities in fourteen parishes in Planter, Bayou, and Southwest voter type areas. A Republican vote as high as 75 percent had been recorded in Iberia Parish. In this election, only the Solid South carried for the Democrats in the electoral college. While the Democratic candidate had stood on the Wilson record, a war-weary electorate defeated him. Harding, as one journalist observed, had been elected "by disgust."[3] In Louisiana, reviving the old Whig concern for self-interest in the sugar country, was the subtle question of tariff. Not long after gaining office, the Republicans repudiated Democratic demands for free trade with exhausted Europe and in 1922 established tariff rates higher than ever before in our history.[4] This was good reason for the sugar interests to exhume and reassert old tendencies in 1920.

The Republican bulge began to recede in 1924, and the next election showed the Democratic solidarity which helped to give the South its political name. Yet, in the 1928 election, while all but two parishes

---

[3] Quoted in John D. Hicks, *The American Nation* (Boston, 1945), 547.
[4] Samuel E. Morison and Henry S. Commager, *The Growth of the American Republic* (New York, 1937), 532.

had Democratic votes of 60 percent and over, and the statewide average of 76 percent had been almost identical with that of the preceding election, important within-voter-type differences could be found. The clue to this might have been that in 1928 the turnout of registered voters had climbed 38 percent from the election before to a relatively high 57 percent. It is necessary to determine to what the electorate had responded in 1928.

The presidential election of 1928 had posed a delicate problem for the South, and in Louisiana the party leaders were running scared.[5] Sam Jones, then a young assistant district attorney, had been asked to campaign in the Protestant areas of the state. Democrats felt they could not vote for Alfred E. Smith, a Catholic urbanite (the Wet-Dry issue cut across this as well), and yet if they did not, their common white front would be breached. The resulting vote revealed that there were many "Hoovercrats" throughout the South, but their distribution was distinctive. Almost without exception those southern states (six) with the highest proportions of Negroes within the population polled a decisive Smith vote, while the other five went Republican. This might not be quite true, for as some of the Texans liked to put it: "We didn't go Republican; we just went Baptist."

It is not enough to show that in the sixteen parishes with Negro populations outnumbering the white, Smith was given a majority. The significant aspect of the Smith vote in Louisiana was that the parishes in the southern Catholic-and-French region contributed the greatest majorities, in striking contrast to the previous election:

*Table 9-2*
PRESIDENTIAL VOTE, 1924 AND 1928,
BY NORTH AND SOUTH LOUISIANA

|  | 1924 | | | 1928 | | |
|---|---|---|---|---|---|---|
|  | Total | Democrat | Percent | Total | Democrat | Percent |
| North Louisiana | 31,572 | 25,891 | 82% | 57,056 | 40,703 | 72% |
| South Louisiana | 90,379 | 67,327 | 74% | 158,777 | 123,952 | 78% |
| Total State | 121,951 | 93,218 | 76% | 215,833 | 164,655 | 76% |

[5] Personal correspondence with Sam H. Jones.

While the Democratic support in North Louisiana dropped by 10 percent, in the rest of the state it was increased by 4 percent. Even the planter parishes with large Negro populations polled a smaller vote for Smith than had been given to Davis in 1924. Put another way, the increase in the number of votes in support of the Democrats was 58 percent in the North and 85 percent in the South. Still the impact of the Smith candidacy was such that relatively more total votes were cast in 1928 than in the previous election in North Louisiana (84 percent more as compared to 77 percent for South Louisiana). Hence it is safe to say that within the state the cultural differential was more important than the racial composition of the population, and the fact that the Republican tendency had lingered in South Louisiana makes the Smith vote of 1928 all the more telling.

Louisiana led region and nation in support of the presidency of Franklin D. Roosevelt. In the four New Deal elections, solidarity prevailed; only two parishes had Democratic support below 60 percent in the entire period. After 1928, North Louisiana voter types again led South Louisiana, when for example, Central Pine Hills voted 96 and 87 percent respectively in 1932 and 1936 compared to the South Louisiana Bayou area votes of 87 percent:

*Table 9-3*

DEMOCRATIC PRESIDENTIAL PERCENTAGES BY VOTER TYPE, 1924-64

| Unit | 1924 | 1928 | 1932 | 1936 | 1940 | 1944 | 1948 | 1952 | 1956 | 1960 | 1964 |
|---|---|---|---|---|---|---|---|---|---|---|---|
| North La. Planter | 83 | 73 | 94 | 92 | 82 | 76 | 28 | 48 | 30 | 25 | 18 |
| Macon Ridge | 83 | 76 | 98 | 91 | 88 | 77 | 42 | 61 | 34 | 29 | 13 |
| North La. Hills | 91 | 77 | 97 | 91 | 89 | 73 | 25 | 54 | 33 | 23 | 20 |
| Central Pine Hills | 81 | 70 | 96 | 87 | 88 | 73 | 34 | 57 | 35 | 30 | 27 |
| Florida Parishes | 85 | 68 | 93 | 88 | 88 | 82 | 33 | 57 | 49 | 41 | 36 |
| Urban Area | 78 | 84 | 94 | 92 | 88 | 83 | 31 | 52 | 39 | 50 | 48 |
| Southwest La. | 71 | 77 | 93 | 89 | 84 | 83 | 40 | 57 | 48 | 69 | 57 |
| South La. Planter | 65 | 86 | 86 | 86 | 83 | 87 | 39 | 64 | 48 | 73 | 59 |
| South La. Bayou | 64 | 88 | 78 | 78 | 84 | 86 | 16 | 48 | 38 | 62 | 50 |
| State Average | 76 | 76 | 93 | 89 | 86 | 81 | 33 | 52 | 40 | 50 | 43 |

In the 1940 election, the state's north and south differences flattened out but by 1944, it can be seen that once again, North Louisiana had fallen below South in percentage support of the Democratic candidates. For reasons which will be brought out below, the 1944 election thus anticipated the great hiatus in Democratic support which can be seen to have occurred in 1948 (Table 9–4).

Voting behavior in presidential elections describes two patterns when majority support is traced by voter types, as in the case for gubernatorial support in the Long era. Here, however, the patterns do not emerge until after the 1956 election, and now the cleavage is one of North-South Louisiana rather than farmer-planter. When the differential support for Roosevelt in 1944 is recalled, though, this finding is not so surprising, nor is the manner in which 1944 appears to be the key election in the series from 1924 through 1964, when the Democratic support by voter types area is subjected to correlational analysis (Table 9–5).

The rank-ordered array of Democratic percentages by voter types for the election of 1944 correlates most consistently high with the others in the matrix, but in a negative direction for earlier elections and positively for later ones. As expected, the percentage distributions of 1944 and 1928 show marked association, since in both elections, North Louisiana parishes were lower and South Louisiana parishes were higher in Democratic support, which for the earlier elections was contrary to the predominant North Louisiana support. But for the elections after the pivotal 1944, each one correlates positively and in increasing degree of association, for now South Louisiana Democratic support began to predominate.

Furthermore, it can be shown that while the earlier and later sets of elections are highly associated among themselves, there is little association at all between the correlation of earlier with later. Of course, this is the statistical result expected after finding the two patterns of voter type support for the elections of this period. These regularities are quite apparent when the average explained variance for each set of elections is computed (explained variance taken as the square of each correlation coefficient) (Table 9–6).

## Table 9-4

### DEMOCRATIC PRESIDENTIAL MAJORITIES BY VOTER TYPES, 1924-64

| Voter Type | 1924 | 1928 | 1932 | 1936 | 1940 | 1944 | 1948 | 1952 | 1956 | 1960 | 1964 |
|---|---|---|---|---|---|---|---|---|---|---|---|
| North La. Planter | Dem. | Dem. | Dem. | Dem. | Dem. | Dem. | — | — | — | — | — |
| Macon Ridge | Dem. | Dem. | Dem. | Dem. | Dem. | Dem. | — | Dem. | — | — | — |
| North La. Hills | Dem. | Dem. | Dem. | Dem. | Dem. | Dem. | — | Dem. | — | — | — |
| Central Pine Hills | Dem. | Dem. | Dem. | Dem. | Dem. | Dem. | — | Dem. | — | — | — |
| Florida Parishes | Dem. | Dem. | Dem. | Dem. | Dem. | Dem. | — | Dem. | — | — | — |
| Urban Area | Dem. | Dem. | Dem. | Dem. | Dem. | Dem. | — | Dem. | — | Dem. | — |
| Southwest La. | Dem. | Dem. | Dem. | Dem. | Dem. | Dem. | — | Dem. | — | Dem. | Dem. |
| South La. Planter | Dem. | Dem. | Dem. | Dem. | Dem. | Dem. | — | Dem. | — | Dem. | Dem. |
| South La. Bayou | Dem. | Dem. | Dem. | Dem. | Dem. | Dem. | — | — | — | Dem. | Dem. |

Cochran Q Test: ($Q = 69.4$ $p < .001$)

*Table 9–5*

RANK ORDER COEFFICIENTS OF CORRELATION
PRESIDENTIAL ELECTIONS PERCENT DEMOCRATIC
BY VOTER TYPE AREAS, 1924–64

|      | '24 | '28    | '32   | '36    | '40    | '44    | '48   | '52    | '56    | '60    | '64    |
|------|-----|--------|-------|--------|--------|--------|-------|--------|--------|--------|--------|
| 1924 | —   | −.690* | .718* | .558*  | .600*  | −.690* | −.050 | .118   | −.400* | −.183  | −.174  |
| 1928 |     | —      | −.145 | −.126  | −.090  | .700*  | −.146 | −.115  | −.134  | .550*  | .600*  |
| 1932 |     |        | —     | .637*  | .637*  | −.164  | .236  | .308*  | −.163  | −.178  | −.177  |
| 1936 |     |        |       | —      | .297   | −.145  | .084  | −.144  | −.147  | −.162  | −.160  |
| 1940 |     |        |       |        | —      | −.143  | .043  | .145   | .090   | −.139  | −.129  |
| 1944 |     |        |       |        |        | —      | .250  | .360*  | .617*  | .917*  | .891*  |
| 1948 |     |        |       |        |        |        | —     | .861*  | .207   | .283   | .050   |
| 1952 |     |        |       |        |        |        |       | —      | .358*  | .285   | .183   |
| 1956 |     |        |       |        |        |        |       |        | —      | .642*  | .748*  |
| 1960 |     |        |       |        |        |        |       |        |        | —      | .933*  |
| 1964 |     |        |       |        |        |        |       |        |        |        | —      |

* Significant at .05 level or less.

*Table 9–6*
AVERAGE EXPLAINED VARIANCE, PRESIDENTIAL ELECTIONS,
RANK ORDER CORRELATIONS BY VOTER TYPE

|          | Earlier<br>1924–40 | Later<br>1948–64 |
|----------|--------------------|------------------|
| 1924–40  | 27.8%              | 5.5%             |
| 1948–64  | —                  | 29.6%            |

Correlations of voter type distributions of Democratic support in 1944, 1960, and 1964 produce the greatest explained variance in reflection of the shift of Democratic support to South Louisiana (49,43, and 40 percent respectively). On the other hand, 1924 produces the third greatest amount of explanation, an average of 42 percent. This election typifies the earlier pattern of Solid South Democratic support. There remains, then, the task of trying to trace the shifting pattern of Democratic support as well as to explain how each set of elections in the correlation matrix is indicative of the continuing southern concern for the complex of states' rights and civil rights.

Louisiana and the other southern states could not remain unaffected by the continued ascendancy of the New Deal, drawing its chief support as it did from a coalition which depended increasingly upon the backing of organized labor and urban minorities. Likewise, the war emergency allowed even more federal controls to be exercised by the administration, and the ceiling prices on tobacco and cotton were unpopular with southern farmers. The whole array of wartime discontent had included insistent Negro demands for elimination of discrimination within the armed forces as well as without, and altogether reinforced the winds of southern conservatism. Governor Sam Jones had declared in 1943 that the Democratic support known as the Solid South was a political booby trap and that the region had gotten better treatment from the Republican Party.[6] A cry for rejection of the New Deal was echoed a year later by the Shreveport *Times* which alleged that President Roosevelt had spoken the name "Demo-

[6] George B. Tindall, *The Emergence of the New South, 1913–1945* (Baton Rouge, 1967), 724.

cratic Party" for the first time in twelve years during the course of the campaign, having previously referred to the "New Deal" or "We."[7] It went on to encourage the election of Mr. Dewey, for the sake of preserving the constitutional republic. There was little surprise, then, in the 1944 presidential election results which showed decreased Democratic support throughout the South.

The Louisiana reaction in 1944 produced the lowest Democratic percentage since 1928, and in North Louisiana, all but four of the twenty-eight parishes exceeded the Republican state average of 19.3 percent. The factor which hastened the defection of this most solid of southern states appeared to be the hassle which developed in the Democratic State Central Committee over the issue of having presidential electors pledge support for the Roosevelt-Truman ticket. It led to the dropping of three electors who refused to pledge and prompted the Shreveport *Times* to lead a protest in North Louisiana which culminated in the relatively high Republican vote in the November election. It is for this reason that the movement of Republican tendency to North Louisiana at this time should be taken as an index of protest rather than as a harbinger of the emergence of any two-party tendency. Still, as the correlation between 1944 and 1928 can be taken to show, a conservative reaction took place in North Louisiana. Of the twenty-four parishes there with percentages above the state average, eight of them ranged from 30 to 39 percent, while another six ranged from 25 to 29 percent. Winn Parish led the state with a Republican vote of 38.6 percent. Here was a conservative protest vote in an area with a tradition of radical dissent.

While it may have been difficult to discern at that time, a new direction was taken as the South sought to maintain its traditional identity. One student of presidential politics in the South, Jasper B. Shannon, foresaw in the summer of that year what was happening, and he wrote: "As the presidential year of 1948 moves toward its fateful decisions, the role of the South appears less and less nationally significant. . . . A Truman victory could only spell a long period of continued bickering in the party with the likelihood of southern

[7] Shreveport *Times*, October 29, 1944, p. 14.

Democrats becoming a smaller and smaller tail to the Democratic kite. . . . The traditional South looks in vain for avenues of escape."[8]

## II. *The Search for Alternatives to the Democrats, Since 1948*

In the face of impending change, state party organization increased in importance as a potential arena for political maneuvers. If the national Democratic Party could nominate candidates for the presidency whose liberal background was distasteful to southern politicians, it might be possible to put the weight of state party machinery behind other than Democrats. That this was possible in Louisiana followed from the fact that in each presidential election year members of the Democratic State Central Committee were chosen during the primaries in January and February when gubernatorial candidates were also chosen, and that the central committee controlled the selection of delegates to the national Democratic convention as well as determination whether to endorse the national ticket, afterward.[9] It followed, also, that the state central committee tended to accept the lead of a new administration in Baton Rouge. Thus, the sensitive relationship of party organization (local-state-national) may remain latent, as it did through the early decades of this century up into the New Deal elections, only to become important when, as in 1944, the seeds of revolt were sown. With characteristic initiative, conservative Democrats, beginning in 1944–48, saw in the central committee the means of frustrating federal moves to modernity. The local party became an important aspect of the state's part in the presidential election process and the question arose as to whether Louisiana voters would have free choices in quadrennial Novembers.

If the maintenance of states' rights (and white supremacy) could no longer be accomplished through support of the Democratic Party, then the South would look for other vehicles. The radical swing of all but five Louisiana parishes out of the majority Democratic

---

[8] Jasper B. Shannon, "Presidential Politics in the South," *Journal of Politics*, I (1939), 488–89.

[9] L. Vaughan Howard and David R. Deener, "Louisiana," in Paul T. David, Malcolm Moos, and Ralph M. Goldman (eds.), *Presidential Nominating Politics in 1952: The South* (Baltimore, 1954), III, 278.

percentage intervals in 1948 is indicative of such a search. Yet, it has been reported that, up until the surprise move by the Democratic State Central Committee on September 10, which joined Mississippi, Georgia, and South Carolina by making the Dixiecrat slate of J. Strom Thurmond and Fielding Wright the official nominees of the state party, the Truman-Barkley ticket would carry Louisiana.[10] After all, the welfare liberal Earl K. Long had earlier in 1948 engineered the comeback of Longism by carrying every parish but two in his runoff campaign against the conservative Sam Jones.

Governor Long, however, had remained neutral on the question of the merit of the Dixiecrat movement, which had grown from the refusal of delegates at the Democratic Convention at Philadelphia to soften President Truman's civil rights stand (southern opposition actually hardened it in the platform). He was motivated, at least in part, by the wish to avoid any controversy which might hurt the chances of his nephew Russell Long's winning the Senate seat being contested by Robert Kennon.[11] Conservative leaders such as Sam Jones and Leander Perez, representing the new economic forces of oil and gas interests (instead of the old cotton-rice-sugar complex),[12] however, managed to complete the coup which denied Truman a place on the ballot. Democratic National Committeeman W. H. Talbot, who had vacillated on his stand, finally came out for the Dixiecrats, complaining about "Truman's cold war against the South," but Fifth District Congressman Otto E. Passman led a visitation to the Governor and said that in fairness, Truman should be on the ballot, even though he, Passman, supported the Dixiecrats.[13] Governor Long then called a twelve-day special session of the legislature to revise the ballot. A closed-door conference which included Senator Allen Ellender, central committee chairman Henry C. Sevier, and Leander Perez fashioned a compromise which provided for the placement of the Truman-Barkley Ticket on the ballot. Ironically, in retaliation to the conservatives perhaps, Earl Long used the occasion to persuade

[10] V. O. Key, Jr., *Southern Politics* (New York, 1949), 341.

[11] Allan P. Sindler, *Huey Long's Louisiana: State Politics, 1920–1952* (Baltimore, 1956), 220.

[12] Howard and Deener, "Louisiana," 266.

[13] Shreveport *Times*, Sept. 21, 1948, p. 1.

the legislature to abolish the Civil Service Commission which had been erected in the administration of Sam Jones.

These maneuvers made for exciting political reading, yet, as has been commented upon above, interest and turnout for presidental elections tended to lag far behind that of the gubernatorial contests where, no doubt, the voter felt his ballot really counted. The impression of general disinterest in the outcome of the 1948 presidential election gained from a scanning of state newspapers is confirmed by the turnout figures which show that, while registration in 1948 had reached an all-time high of nearly 925,000 and a turnout of 71 percent of these potential voters had occurred in the gubernatorial contest, in the presidential election only 45 percent of the voters turned out, the lowest percentage since 1924. The rapid turn of events in Louisiana, which suddenly gave voters the chance to participate in the Dixiecrat revolt had given the electorate four options: (1) stamp the Democratic Rooster for States' Rights (49.1 percent); (2) vote the Truman-Barkley ticket (32.7 percent); (3) vote Republican (17.5 percent); or (4) stay at home. (The Progressive Party candidacy of Henry A. Wallace which received 0.7 percent of the vote hardly counted.)

The Dixiecrats found no widespread consensus for the wisdom of their revolt from the national Democrats, and while Governor Thurmond had asserted at a Shreveport rally in late October that his party would claim 142 electoral votes, in the end they got the thirty-eight electoral votes from the four states of Alabama, Louisiana, Mississippi, and South Carolina, the last three of which had entered the Dixiecrats as the Democratic nominees. If the time-honored device of southern conservatives to span economic class cleavage by appeals to racial anxieties was expected to work in 1948 in Louisiana, the outcome in the vote was difficult to discern. North Louisiana parishes, for example, highest in state Republican support in 1944, would be expected to be solidly states' rights in 1948. Yet Map 9–1 (page 310) shows that such was not entirely the case. In fact, the 1948 presidential election is difficult to explain in terms of parish voter pattern.

The solid, regular Democrat support in Southwest Louisiana is not so surprising, but that in the heart of traditionally Republican sugar country is (tideland oil issue ?). Surprising, too, is the Democratic holdout of planter parishes in Northeast Louisiana. Otherwise, except for the Democratic defection in the Hills, apparent in 1944 as well, the parish distribution of States' Rights support does suggest a hint of the traditional Bourbon "Y" profile. Only a hint, for as the following figures will show, the most important result of the 1948 election can be seen to be the continuation of the North-South split which began in the previous election and which was to continue to be the case (Table 9–7).

While the location of parishes that provided Republican support above the state average shifted from North in 1944 to South Louisiana in 1948, nevertheless, the continuance of protest is found in the northern support of the Dixiecrats above the state average in an equally large number of parishes. But, at the same time, nearly two-thirds of South Louisiana parishes likewise supported the Dixiecrats and in both North and South a number of parishes could be found which remained loyal to the national Democrats. Still, the somewhat greater number in South Louisiana helps to explain the positive association (+.250) between 1944 and 1948 Democratic votes found in the correlation matrix presented above.

One searches in vain for a clear pattern of voter response in the 1948 presidential election, except for the emergent North-South division. Subjecting the States' Rights vote to further analysis, even the most expected relations hold only at the extremes.

"If," in the classic statement of V. O. Key, "the backbone of the Solid South is the black belt, the loyalists of 1928 would be expected to be the rebels of 1948."[14] Clearly enough, of the parishes with a Negro population over 55 percent, all seven had Dixiecrat majorities in the 60 percent and above interval. But the relationship weakens rapidly, as of the thirty-one parishes with a Negro population above 35 percent, only twenty-three had Dixiecrat majorities, and almost one-third of them were distributed in the 50 to 59 percent interval. And on the other extreme, of the thirty-one parishes with the smallest proportions of Negroes within the population, over two-thirds (twenty-one) had

[14] Key, *Southern Politics*, 329.

## Table 9–7

### Number of Parishes above State Average for Selected Parties, 1944–60, by Voter Type Areas

| (N) Unit | 1944 Rep. 19.3 | 1948 StRt 49.8 | 1948 Rep. 17.5 | 1948 Dem. 32.4 | 1952 Rep. 47.0 | 1956 StRt 7.2 | 1956 Rep. 53.3 | 1956 Dem. 39.5 | 1960 StRt 21.0 | 1960 Rep. 28.6 | 1960 Dem. 50.4 |
|---|---|---|---|---|---|---|---|---|---|---|---|
| (10) North La. Planter | 8 | 7 | 1 | 3 | 7 | 10 | 3 | 1 | 9 | 10 | — |
| (8) North La. Hills | 7 | 8 | — | 2 | 4 | 8 | 3 | 2 | 7 | 7 | — |
| (3) Macon Ridge | 2 | 2 | — | 3 | — | 3 | — | — | 3 | 3 | — |
| (7) Central Pine Hills | 7 | 6 | — | 3 | — | 6 | 2 | 2 | 6 | 7 | 1 |
| (28) North La. Total | (24) | (23) | (1) | (11) | (11) | (27) | (8) | (5) | (25) | (27) | (1) |
| (8) Florida Parishes | 3 | 6 | 2 | 4 | 1 | 2 | 2 | 7 | 8 | 1 | — |
| (2) Urban Area | — | 1 | 1 | 1 | 1 | — | 2 | 1 | 2 | — | 1 |
| (8) South La. Planter | — | 3 | 3 | 6 | 1 | — | 2 | 7 | — | 1 | 8 |
| (7) South La. Bayou | 2 | 6 | 5 | — | 4 | — | 4 | 5 | 2 | — | 7 |
| (10) Southwest La. | 2 | 4 | 3 | 6 | 3 | — | 2 | 9 | — | 1 | 9 |
| (36) South La. Total | (7) | (20) | (14) | (17) | (10) | (2) | (13) | (28) | (12) | (3) | (26) |

# Presidential States' Rights Vote, 1848

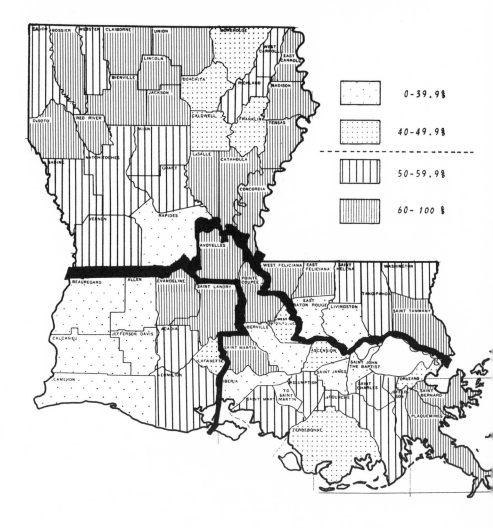

*Table 9–8*

NUMBER OF PARISHES BY PERCENTAGE INTERVALS,
STATES' RIGHTS, 1948, AND PERCENT NEGRO, 1950,
NEGRO REGISTRATION, 1948, AND PERCENT URBAN, 1950

|  |  | 0–39%<br>(11) | 40–49%<br>(9) | 50–59%<br>(20) | 60–100%<br>(24) |
|---|---|---|---|---|---|
| 1950<br>Percent Negro<br>Population |  |  |  |  |  |
| Over 55% | (7) | — | — | — | 7 |
| 45–54.9% | (10) | 3 | 2 | 1 | 4 |
| 35–44.9% | (14) | — | 3 | 6 | 5 |
| 25–34.9% | (15) | 2 | 3 | 5 | 5 |
| 15–24.9% | (11) | 4 | 1 | 5 | 1 |
| Under 15% | (7) | 2 | — | 3 | 2 |
| Parishes<br>with Negro<br>Registration |  |  |  |  |  |
| Some | (33) | 9 | 5 | 14 | 5 |
| None | (31) | 2 | 4 | 6 | 19 |
| 1950<br>Percent<br>Urban |  |  |  |  |  |
| 50–100% | (8) | 3 | 3 | 2 | — |
| 30–49.9% | (19) | 2 | 2 | 7 | 8 |
| 0–29.9% | (20) | 3 | 3 | 7 | 7 |
| None | (17) | 3 | 1 | 4 | 9 |

Dixiecrat majorities. In a comparative analysis of black-belt voting behavior in North Carolina, Mississippi, and Louisiana, William D. Morgan found that Louisiana must be considered a deviation, since, while North Louisiana parishes confirmed the Key thesis, South Louisiana black-belt parishes did not.[15]

With as many as 28,177 Negroes registered to vote by 1948, even though this number constituted but 3 percent of the total registration, the presence of some registered Negroes rather than none in a parish might be taken as an indicator of moderation. New Orleans contained almost exactly half of the total, while almost one quarter of the registered Negroes resided in the urban parishes of Caddo, Ouachita, Rapides, East Baton Rouge, and Calcasieu. The remaining 27 percent were distributed mostly in South Louisiana (20 percent) and in the northern parishes (6 percent). Still, only one more than half the parishes (thirty-three) had "allowed" Negroes to register to vote in 1948, but the relationship to States' Rights support showed an almost equal number of parishes with Dixiecrat majorities regardless of the presence of Negro registration.

Finally, it might be expected that opposition to the States' Rights movement would be strongest in the urban parishes and again, at the extremes, this is found to be true. Of the eight parishes with 50 percent or more of the population in urban residence, only two had Dixiecrat majorities. These were Caddo and Rapides, and in subsequent elections it was found that the North Louisiana urban areas followed (or led?) the regional tendency toward conservatism. On the other end of the frequency distribution, of the sixteen parishes with no urban population, twelve of them had States' Rights majorities. In the two middle intervals, however, twenty-nine out of thirty-nine were in the Dixiecrat majority.

Altogether, the seven urban-industrial parishes had contributed over one-half the total votes cast in the presidential election of 1948 (53 percent). But the urban voters, who were moving in increasing numbers from the country, were not immune to revolt, either, as here the Dixiecrats also led the list, if at a slightly reduced percentage support:

---

[15] William Davis Morgan, "A Comparative Analysis of Black-Belt Voting Behavior in Three Southern States: Presidential Elections, 1948–1964" (Master's thesis, Louisiana State University, 1966).

*Table 9–9*

SEVEN URBAN-INDUSTRIAL PARISH PRESIDENTIAL PERCENTAGES, 1948

|  | State Average | Seven Urban Industrial Average |  | Urban Proportions State Totals |
|---|---|---|---|---|
| States' Rights | 49% | 43% | — | 46% |
| Truman | 33 | 35 | — | 57 |
| Republican | 17 | 21 | — | 64 |
| Progressive | 1 | 1 | — | 84 |

At the same time, slightly less than half the total number of Dixiecrat votes had come from the seven urban-industrial parishes. With organized labor and Negro groups working for Truman, it is not surprising to see that more than half of the Truman support came from the urban parishes. Nor could the bulk of the Progressive vote have come from elsewhere, as the Wallace brand was assuredly not kin to the traditional position in Louisiana. What is most important, perhaps, is to note the urban base of the Republican vote in this election, reflecting a more typically urban response to "Trumanism." Indeed, while urban Republican strength swelled, until in 1956 its support constituted 56 percent of the urban vote, in the 1948 election the urban proportion of the total Republican vote was the greatest of the eight elections in the twenty-eight year period, 1932–60.[16] In the same period, the Urban Democratic proportion of the state total was also the largest of all in 1948, but at the same time this election marked the lowest urban support the Democratic Party had received. Rounding out the major options, of the three times the States' Rights Party was on the ballot (1948, 1956, and 1960) its greatest urban proportion of the state total was reached in the election of 1960.

Taking the study of precinct voting in Baton Rouge mentioned above as illustrative, another dimension of voting behavior may be added, one increasingly important in analysis since in 1950 the

[16] Rudolf Heberle, William C. Havard, and Perry H. Howard, *The Louisiana Elections of 1960* (Baton Rouge, 1963), 59.

census counted the state's population predominantly urban in residence. In 1948, on the precinct level, where voters from similar socioeconomic categories were present, it was clear that the liberal/ conservative split in gubernatorial politics continued in the presidential election. In fact, these categories voted quite clearly according to expectation. It is possible to trace the association among the precinct votes for gubernatorial candidates places on a liberal to conservative continuum and to link these with the precinct votes for the presidential candidates:

*Table 9–10*

POSITIVE RANK ORDER CORRELATION COEFFICIENTS BY PRECINCTS
BETWEEN CANDIDATES IN 1948 GUBERNATORIAL PRIMARY
AND PRESIDENTIAL ELECTIONS IN BATON ROUGE*

| | First Primary | | | | |
| | "Liberal" | | | "Conservative" | |
| | Morrison | Long | . | Kennon | Jones |
| **Second Primary** | | | . | | |
| Long | + .940 | + .541 | . | — | — |
| Jones | — | — | . | + .538 | + .919 |
| **Presidential** | | | . | | |
| Truman | + .899 | + .378 | . | — | — |
| Thurmond | — | — | . | + .354 | + .364 |
| Dewey | — | — | . | + .238 | + .720 |

* Source: Howard, "Voting Behavior in Baton Rouge," *Proceedings,* Louisiana Academy of Sciences, XV, August, 1952.

Baton Rouge had been, of course, an anti-Long stronghold, and though the recent trend to urban industrialization within Louisiana had certainly brought an increasingly larger working class vote, in Baton Rouge it had not appeared to be a strong Long vote. Rather, Baton Rouge labor supported Long candidates only when there was no other acceptable choice. Hence, the correlations above show that Earl Long must have picked up most of the first primary support of

Congressman Jimmie Morrison and that the labor vote went Democratic in 1948. On the other hand, increasing numbers of white-collar and upper-class white voters, favoring the anti-Long Kennon or Jones candidacy, chose between Thurmond and Dewey in the presidential election, with the greatest Republican sentiment in precincts wherein businessmen and professionals resided:

*Table 9–11*
1948 PRESIDENTIAL VOTE IN BATON ROUGE
RESIDENTIAL AREAS*

|         | Business and Professional | White Collar | White Labor |
|---------|:---:|:---:|:---:|
| Truman  | 28% | 39% | 51% |
| Thurmond | 39 | 41 | 36 |
| Dewey   | 33 | 20 | 13 |

* Source: Heberle and Howard, "Ecological Analysis of Political Tendencies in Louisiana," *Social Forces*, vol. 32, May 1954.

Thus it could be said that conservatives in Louisiana were in rebellion not alone against the liberalism of the national Democratic Party. They had been against the local radicalism of the Longs, as well,[17] and now, an opportunity presented itself to see how far they could go while the Longs were straddling the States' Rights issue, caught on the defensive, as it were. Obvious inroads among Long voters can be inferred from the voter type rank-order correlation coefficient of +.544 for the association between the Long first primary percentages in 1948 and those for the Dixiecrats. At the same time a negligible association of +.025 has been computed between the Long percentages by voter types and those for the regular Democrats. Contrary to the logic of the Long tendency, then, a significant number of parishes supported the Dixiecrats in 1948 while no such distribution could be found for Truman-Barkley support:

[17] William C. Havard and Robert F. Steamer, "Louisiana Secedes: Collapse of a Compromise," *The Massachusetts Review*, I (1959), 139.

Table 9–12
THE LONG TENDENCY AND PRESIDENTIAL VOTING, 1948

Number of Parishes

|  | Long First Primary | | |  | Long First Primary | |
|---|---|---|---|---|---|---|
|  | Below 50% | Above 50% |  |  | Below 50% | Above 50% |
| Below 50% | 16 | 5 |  | Below 50% | 31 | 28 |
| States' Rights |  |  |  | Truman-Barkley |  |  |
| Above 50% | 19 | 24 |  | Above 50% | 4 | 1 |

It can be concluded that the results of the 1948 presidential election turned significantly on the question of leadership, and that the conservatives had made the most from the failure or inability of the Longs to take a stand on the presidential election consistent with Longism.

With the Longs taking sides, with a swing back of thirty-nine parishes to the majority columns as compared to the fourteen in the panic of 1948, and with a comfortable statewide majority of 53 percent for the Democratic candidate, the results of the 1952 election led this author and others to the perils of generalizing from a single case.[18] A seeming liberal/conservative cleavage was found which joined Long/Democrats opposite anti-Long/Republicans. At the same time, a widely accepted view claimed that the urban-industrial development of the South would inevitably liberalize in the direction of two-party politics. The study *Presidential Politics in Louisiana, 1952*,[19] however, by focusing upon pre-convention campaigns and both national

---

[18] The first edition of the present work; Rudolf Heberle and Perry H. Howard, "An Ecological Analysis of Political Tendencies in Louisiana: The Presidential Elections of 1952," *Social Forces*, XXXII (1954), 344–50; Havard, Heberle, and Howard, *Elections of 1960*.

[19] L. Vaughn Howard and David R. Deener, *Presidential Politics in Louisiana, 1952* (New Orleans, 1954).

conventions as well as the ensuing presidential election battles, provided a perspective from which no such easy parallels could be drawn. A review of what happened when the Democratic Party faced the race problem is instructive in this respect: (1) In 1944 presidential electors in Louisiana refused to pledge loyalty to the Roosevelt-Truman ticket; and, (2) In 1948 the Democratic State Central Committee in revolt gave the rooster symbol to the Thurmond-Wright ticket. In 1952, the Democrats of Louisiana had three chances to revolt:[20] (1) At the Chicago convention over the "loyalty oath"; (2) When the Democratic State Central Committee gave Stevenson the rooster; or, (3) When Democratic factional machines determined to stay with Stevenson. But in 1952, no revolt took place, although, as narrative account and analysis will bring out, the political atmosphere was charged with possibilities.

The resounding defeat of the Long forces in the 1952 gubernatorial primaries has been recounted above. Here it is important to emphasize the position of strength the new governor, Robert F. Kennon, would bring to the spring organizational meeting of the Democratic State Central Committee. The Kennon forces dominated the preceedings and were able to elect Vice-Chairman N. B. Carstarphen of Shreveport to the post of chairman. The next order of business was to oust from their positions as national committeemen former Governor Earl Long and his cohort, Miss Mary Evelyn Dickerson. The last order of business for the Kennon forces was the selection of the national convention delegation, and this was accomplished in a manner which provided that several powerful political figures would be insured selection by taking advantage of the rule charging the state central committee with the responsibility for "election or selection." The method adopted enabled central committeemen from each congressional district to choose two delegates with one full vote each and two alternates, while the central committee would complete the delegation by choosing eight delegates at large with one-half vote apiece. The selection method produced a delegation in which 'Kennon men" had

<hr>

[20] Howard and Deener, *Presidential Politics*, 97.

the majority, as six of the eight district committees chose delegates
either positively blessed by Kennon or not opposed by him.[21]

*Table 9–13*

DISTRICT DELEGATES TO 1952 DEMOCRATIC NATIONAL CONVENTION

Kennonites:

1st District: Leander Perez of Plaquemines Parish, a leading States'
Righter in 1948;
Louis J. Roussel, a New Orleans oil and real estate man and
a Kennon backer.

2nd District: Mayor deLesseps Morrison of New Orleans;
Frank B. Ellis of New Orleans, Earl Long's replacement
as national committeeman.

4th District: Governor Kennon himself;
Sherwood Loe of Shreveport.

5th District: Henry C. Sevier of Tallulah, former chairman of the state
central committee;
Claude Harrison, businessman and a longtime supporter of
Kennon from Monroe.

6th District: J. W. Sanders of Baton Rouge;
Jesse H. Cutrer, Jr. of Bogalusa.

Non-Kennonites:

3rd District: After an attempt by Kennon foes to unseat delegates chosen
favorable to Kennon, in the final outcome the Governor's
men were the following:
Otis Bourg of Houma;
C. C. Burleigh of Franklin.

7th District: W. J. Cleveland of Crowley, a friend of Earl Long;
Former Governor Sam H. Jones of Lake Charles.

The Democratic State Central Committee completed the delegation on April
17th by selecting the delegates-at-large who were:
Senator Allen J. Ellender
Senator Russell B. Long

[21] *Ibid.*, 68–69.

N. B. Carstarphen, chairman of the central committee
Loney J. Autin of Jefferson Parish
Henry E. Linam of Shreveport
R. H. Crosby, Jr., of De Ridder
John W. Olvey of Shreveport
Clifton L. Ganus of New Orleans

This "all-star" delegation would be led to the Chicago convention by Governor Kennon, who had been elected chairman. L Vaughn Howard and David R. Deener have suggested that the Louisiana delegation was both united and potentially divided.[22] It was united by a number of concentric circles of common interest, as it were, which included: (1) a core of Kennon supporters; (2) a continuance of anti-Truman sentiment; and (3) commitment to the position of States' Rights. Even here it was possible to find two factions grouped about Frank Ellis, on the one hand, and Leander Perez and Governor Kennon on the other. The delegation had potential points of division in the presence of a number of political "feuds" which included: (1) Leander Perez versus Sam H. Jones; (2) Governor Kennon versus Jones; and (3) Kennon versus Senator Russell Long. With this group typical of what other southern states were sending to Chicago, it is understandable that the National Democratic Committee had some uncertainty about how to handle the southern delegations. The loyalty oath issue raised by the resolution of Senator Moody of Michigan to adopt temporary rules requiring that each delegation be bound by the actions of the convention promised to produce political fireworks.

The issue proved sticky for the Louisiana delegation since, in its April 17th meeting, the central committee had passed a resolution to the effect that the Democratic Party and voters of Louisiana would not be bound to support or vote for the nominees of the national convention. Moreover, the feelings of Governor Kennon for the Republican alternative, as well as Judge Perez' plans for active support of Eisenhower in the event of a walkout, were public information. Thus it was that the National Democratic Convention became the

---

[22] Howard and Deener, "Louisiana," 281-82.

stage upon which "real" Democratic support and hidden Republican sympathies would be unveiled. Governor Kennon became increasingly adamant in his refusal to accept the requirements for seating the Louisiana delegation, while Russell Long and Frank Ellis urged acceptance of a compromise loyalty oath. Ellis had found that a "simple declaration" from the Louisiana delegation would be acceptable to the credentials committee, and he managed to persuade all the delegation but Leander Perez to agree. But this occurred while Kennon was absent, and when he returned he ruled the compromise out of order and had the delegation reverse itself. This action led to Ellis' resignation, which was refused by the delegation.

When the roll call on nominations for the presidential candidate began, Louisiana, South Carolina, and Virginia were without portfolio. Governor Battle stated that under Virginia rules the nominee must be on the state ballot, and this led to a vote on seating Virginia's delegation. It was at this time that Senator Long got the floor to declare that he, personally, was willing to accept the loyalty oath, stating that "I am willing to stake my entire political career on the principle of letting the people of my state vote."[23] The credentials committee then accepted Long's statement and ruled that any others who so declared would be allowed to vote, at which time Louis Roussel and Loney Autin joined Long, and together they cast all twenty Louisiana votes in favor of Virginia being seated. This action put the dissidents in an awkward position should the three delegates continue to vote for the Louisiana delegation and likewise took the steam out of any threatened walkout. Thus, "Louisiana avoided walking out or perhaps being kicked out of the Chicago convention." but "disagreements between various segments of the delegation itself resulted from the experience at Chicago, and these were carried back to Louisiana."[24]

Back home, the state central committee on August 20 gave the rooster emblem to the Stevenson-Sparkman ticket, but only after the Perez faction was given heavy opposition from the list of those who favored Governor Stevenson. Louis Roussel came back from Chicago split from the Kennon faction and declared himself willing

[23] Howard and Deener, *Presidential Politics*, 76.
[24] *Ibid.*, 77, 80.

to take the fight to give the rooster symbol to Stevenson and Sparkman to the United States Supreme Court if necessary. Loney Autin and W. J. Cleveland joined Roussel in agreeing that Stevenson should have the support of the Louisiana Democratic Party. When the central committee convened, Frank Ellis joined the list of supporters of Stevenson as did former Governor Earl Long who quipped that "Truman can't anymore control that man than the man in the moon."[25] In awarding the Democratic rooster to the Stevenson-Sparkman nominees, the central committee held that this was in no way an endorsement of the ticket. Thus the way was left open for individual Democrats to declare *"J'aime Ike"* if they wanted to.

There was plenty of opportunity for the Democrats to stray as the Republican Party, under the active leadership of John Minor Wisdom, was using the Eisenhower candidacy as the means to build a two-party politics in the state. Americans for Eisenhower was organized by the new-guard Republicans on a bipartisan basis and succeeded in forming effective electioneering machinery, particularly in the urban parishes. Among the Ike supporters were Sam Jones, Rufus Fontenot, state collector of revenue, and C. C. Aycock, speaker of the Louisiana House of Representatives. While Adlai E. Stevenson ran practically unaided by the official party organization, Frank Ellis served as state campaign manager, and most of Mayor Morrison's ward chairmen of the Crescent City Democratic Association worked for Stevenson, although the mayor himself made no public endorsement. Senator Russell Long and Congressman Hale Boggs sat on the platform when Stevenson spoke in New Orleans, offsetting somewhat the absence of Governor Kennon (who later appeared with General Eisenhower during his visit to Louisiana). The Democrats lacked the ready supply of money available to the Republicans, but this liability was made up to some extent by the support of Earl Long and the work of his followers in support of the Illinois governor. Thus the Democrats had the endorsement of many liberals who had been associated with Longism and whose political names were known by Louisiana voters. That the election would result in a vote cast on

[25] *Ibid.*, 83.

class lines was clearly evident as one inspected the difference in financial backing and in the choice of local party headquarters throughout the state.

In reviewing the results of the campaign and the election, in which the Democratic candidate Adlai E. Stevenson received 53 percent of the total vote cast, marking up to this time the greatest percentage turnout (62 percent) in all save one presidential election (1868) in the state's history, it could be said that Stevenson's victory in Louisiana had been *a triumph of the principle of party loyalty.*[26] While race was not yet an issue, it was implicit in the distaste for the Fair Employment Practice Commission stance of Truman. Louisiana's interest in the tidelands oil settlement likewise became part of the appeal of Eisenhower. Yet, in the outcome of the 1952 presidential election, the Louisiana Democratic Party seemed to have recovered from the panic of 1948 and on the surface seemed more liberal than before. For the support of the Democratic candidate among the voter types followed the classic pattern of Longism (A voter type rank order correlation coefficient of +.667 between the 1952 Long second primary and Democratic support has been computed):

*Table 9–14*
PRESIDENTIAL DEMOCRATIC SUPPORT BY VOTER TYPES, 1952

Number of Parishes

| Unit | 0–39% | 40–49% | 50–59% | 60–100% |
|------|-------|--------|--------|---------|
| North La. Planter | 2 | 3 | 5 | — |
| North La. Hills | 2 | 1 | 2 | 3 |
| Macon Ridge | — | — | 1 | 2 |
| Central Pine Hills | — | — | 4 | 3 |
| Urban Area | — | — | 2 | — |
| South La. Bayou | 1 | 2 | 4 | 1 |
| Florida Parishes | 1 | — | 4 | 3 |
| Southwest Louisiana | — | 2 | 7 | 1 |
| South La. Planter | — | 1 | 1 | 6 |
| | (6) | (9) | (30) | (19) |

[26] *Ibid.*, 97.

The reason for this can be found by inspecting the top percentage interval, where the location of the nineteen parishes distributed therein are found to be almost equally in North and South Louisiana. The same can be said of the parishes in the 50–59 percent interval, so that something of a reversal of the regional split of the two previous presidential elections occurred, although the high degree of association in the distribution of parish Democratic support in 1948 and 1952 (+.861) attests to continuity in the pattern of rank order percentage support by voter type. The incipient split found in 1944 was still there in 1952. Even in this Democratic year, North Louisiana Planter and Hill parishes maintained the tendency to revolt.

The predominant farmer parishes which formed the core of the support of Longism with few exceptions strongly supported the candidacy of Stevenson. Yet, the crucial point in the 1952 presidential election was found to be within the cities of Louisiana. The support of the two presidential candidates tended to break even in urban areas, and the Negro vote (over 100,000 had been registered prior to the November presidential election), which was found to be united and in high turnout, in the end proved to be the deciding factor in giving the Democrats a bare majority. Where predominantly Negro precincts could be spotted, the Democratic support was found to be solid. A "colored box" in Merryville, Beauregard Parish, near the Texas border, contained 116 ballots favoring Stevenson and 2 for Eisenhower. Negro precincts in Baton Rouge and New Orleans had votes of over 90 percent in favor of the Democrats, and with turnout participation ranging from 70 to 88 percent.[27]

The ballot count on the ward level allowed analysis to seek significant areas of support for the two presidential candidates (Table 9–15). The vote in the seven urban-industrial parishes was even, the Democratic candidate favored by only 50.9 percent. Nearly half the state vote was cast there so that the Democratic differential must be located elsewhere. In New Orleans, the vote was split almost evenly, also, but in the larger urban places the Republican candidate gained the

[27] *Ibid.*, 96.

advantage, while in the smaller urban places the Democratic vote more than made up for this.

*Table 9–15*

THE PRESIDENTIAL VOTE OF WARDS IN 1952

| Wards | | Republican Vote | | Democratic Vote | |
|---|---|---|---|---|---|
| Group | Number | Number | Percent | Number | Percent |
| New Orleans | 17 | 82,572 | 48.7 | 89,999 | 51.3 |
| Urban Places over 10,000 | 16 | 87,133 | 52.1 | 79,916 | 47.9 |
| Urban Places 2,500-9,999 | 52 | 49,626 | 46.4 | 57,245 | 53.6 |
| Rural Wards | 447 | 84,591 | 46.4 | 97,867 | 53.6 |
| State Total | 532 | 306,925 | 47.0 | 325,027 | 53.0 |

In the larger cities of Louisiana there was a regional difference in the support given the Republican candidate. Cities located in the parishes listed in the Republican column recorded a high Eisenhower vote. Even where the parish went Democratic, as in Calcasieu, Rapides, and East Baton Rouge, the city vote of Lake Charles, Alexandria, and Baton Rouge respectively, was higher in support of the Republican Party than the parish average. The total ward counts for smaller cities gave the Democratic candidate 54 percent of the vote. It was thought that perhaps the larger cities or towns in this group may have been more inclined to the Republicans, but when ranked according to size of population there was no telling difference. There was still some tendency for these urban wards to register a higher Republican vote than in surrounding rural wards, but the lack of a large middle- or upper-class population and the presence of more small businessmen and laborers with close ties to the farmers worked as factors, for the vote in the remaining rural wards was the same as for the wards containing small urban places. There was consistently more Democratic support away from the larger urban places, indicative perhaps of the traditional political tendency of the farmer class.

On the precinct level it is possible to analyze the voting behavior of different layers of the social class structure of the electorate. This has been done for the three major cities of New Orleans, Shreveport, and Baton Rouge, using sample precincts categorized on the basis of census tract data, as Negro, white labor, and upper white:[28]

*Table 9–16*

DEMOCRATIC PERCENTAGES, 1952, IN SAMPLE
PRECINCTS BY SOCIOECONOMIC CATEGORIES*

|  | Negro | Upper White | White Labor |
|---|---|---|---|
| New Orleans . . . . . . . . . . | 81% | 24% | 58% |
| Shreveport . . . . . . . . . . . | 92 | 15 | 35 |
| Baton Rouge . . . . . . . . . . | 93 | 26 | 61 |

* Source: Howard and Brent, "Social Change, Urbanization, and Types of Society," *Journal Social Issues*, XXII, January 1966.

The tendency of upper whites to become "presidential Republicans" is readily apparent in 1952, while at this time white labor (by far the majority of urban voters, numerically) paralleled the labor vote elsewhere in finding its economic interests served by, and showing its 60/40 preference for, the Democrats. The Negro category displayed its decided preference of the Democratic nominee in 1952 as well. Finally it should be noted that both categories of white precincts in Shreveport displayed the conservative voting behavior becoming characteristic of North Louisiana.

Using Baton Rouge data on the 1948 presidential vote in residential areas it is possible to show that the desire to turn away from the Democratic Party continued to prevail in 1952:

[28] Occupation data for each census tract was categorized so that a manual-non-manual break could be made. This material was analyzed in the summer of 1964 under a Louisiana State University Faculty Research Grant.

*Table 9–17*
VOTING BEHAVIOR IN RESIDENTIAL AREAS
OF BATON ROUGE: 1948 AND 1952 COMPARED*

| Precincts | 1948 Republican- States' Rights Percentages Combined | 1952 Republican Percentage |
|---|---|---|
| Business and Professional . . . . . . . . . . | 72% | 68% |
| White Collar . . . . . . . . . . . . . . . | 61 | 49 |
| Labor (White) . . . . . . . . . . . . . . . | 49 | 39 |

* Source: Heberle and Howard, "Ecological Analysis," *Social Forces*, XXXII, May 1954.

In these figures, the tendency to prefer any alternative to the Democratic Party is found, particularly on the part of the more economically well-to-do. White collar workers tended to support the Republican candidate in 1952, also, but here there was more falling away from the 1948 stand than occurred among upper-class categories. The Democratic tendency of white labor in these voting figures shows how up until 1952, at least, the race issue had not replaced the bread and butter issue of labor.

It is possible to take one further step in the isolation of leading tendencies through presentation of a correlation table showing the relationships between the vote for Eisenhower and that for candidates in the 1952 gubernatorial election, computed with percentage support by wards:

*Table 9–18*
PRODUCT-MOMENT COEFFICIENTS OF CORRELATION
BETWEEN VOTE FOR EISENHOWER AND LEADING
GUBERNATORIAL CANDIDATES BY WARDS, 1952

| | Liberal Long Candidates | | | | . . . | Conservative Long Opposition | | |
|---|---|---|---|---|---|---|---|---|
| | Spaht II | Spaht I | Dodd I | Boggs I | . Kennon I | LeBlanc I | Kennon II | McLemore I |
| Eisen- hower: | −.470 | −.317 | −.288 | −.053 | . +.011 | +.030 | +.470 | +.532 |

The relationship between voting in state and national elections was a consistent one in 1952. Liberal and conservative tendencies within the electorate show stability in expression of voter choices, and a continuity of the Bourbon Democratic sentiment is revealed, found in the pattern of McLemore support. The relatively high coefficient of correlation between the States' Righter James McLemore and Eisenhower support indicates that the two candidates were backed by similar portions of the electorate. With the exception of the Kennon second-primary vote, itself swelled by the votes of McLemore supporters, there is a general blurring of association in the support of gubernatorial candidates and the Republican candidate. Yet, there is definite direction of association indicated, opposite for the two categories of candidates. The Kennon support of the second primary consisted of voters bent on moving away from the center toward the political right. Kennon's post-primary climb onto the Eisenhower bandwagon must have seemed a pleasing gesture to those with a conservative inclination. The negative correlations between Eisenhower and Long candidates were expected, and it is interesting to see that, except for Boggs, the degree of association, although negative, is greater than on the conservative side.

Rank order computations of coefficients of correlation did show on the parish level what had been suggested by ward-level analysis. A line of affinity of out-and-out Eisenhower support with the Kennon and McLemore backing and with the Dixiecrat defection of 1948 is found to exist:

*Table 9–19*

RANK ORDER COEFFICIENTS OF CORRELATION BETWEEN
THE VOTE FOR EISENHOWER AND SELECTED CANDIDATES
AND ELECTIONS, BY PARISHES

| Eisenhower | Kennon II | + .614 |
| Eisenhower | McLemore I | + .518 |
| Eisenhower | Kennon I | + .132 |
| Eisenhower | Dixiecrat 1948 | + .395 |

This tendency, the unity of support of the traditional dominant minority, remained strong. It was more than coincidental that some of the highest Republican support in Louisiana was found within the rural areas where the Negro tended to outnumber the whites in the population. It became clear during the campaign that the Dixiecrats of 1948 would find it expedient to swing to the Republican Party. This was not a vote to ensure a solid Democratic Party in Louisiana, nor even a move towards two-party politics. It was a continuing revolt aimed at keeping political dominance.

One final cross tabulation may depict the consequence of the support of Stevenson by elements of Longism. This has to do with tracing the presidential voting behavior of the parishes as distributed in the intervals of second primary Long Candidate support:

*Table 9–20*

LONG SUPPORT AND PRESIDENTIAL SUPPORT, 1952

Number of Parishes

| Long Candidate | | Democratic Percentages | | | |
|---|---|---|---|---|---|
| Second Primary | | Below 50% | | Above 50% | |
| Percentage Intervals | | North La. | South La. | North La. | South La. |
| 0–39% | (24) | 6 | 6 | 3 | 9 |
| 40–49% | (29) | — | — | 12 | 17 |
| 50–59% | (6) | 1 | — | 3 | 2 |
| 60–100% | (5) | — | 1 | 3 | 1 |
| | | (7) | (7) | (21) | (29) |
| | (64) | | (14) | | (50) |

Three points will be made regarding these figures. In the first place, it is quite noticeable that the Republican majority parishes are to be found almost exclusively in the lowest percentage interval of Long support. The second point to make is that while the Longs had been routed by the Kennon forces in all but eleven parishes, the degree of support for the Long candidate had not fallen below the 40–49 percentage interval in twenty-nine parishes, and in all of these, the Democratic presidential candidate had gained a majority. The final point has to do with the continued evidence of the bridging between North and South Louisiana in 1952.

A shift of but twenty thousand votes to Eisenhower would have reversed the Democratic margin of victory (38,102), for although the Republicans lost, they amassed the largest number of votes in Louisiana history. One study has shown that disunity had weakened the Republican chances when old guard party members, in resistance to the new leadership organized by John Minor Wisdom, had established "Republicans for Eisenhower" in answer to the Wisdom-backed "Americans for Eisenhower." The Republicans themselves had offered a number of reasons for "Ike's" defeat in 1952 including: (1) the Negro vote; (2) Democratic factional organizations; and (3) Governor Kennon's organization did not go "all out."[29] This appears to be an objective analysis of what happened, as the high degree of Democratic support by Negro voters has been traced above, and comment has been made on how both the Crescent City Democratic Organization and the Old Regulars in New Orleans, as well as Longites everywhere, had endorsed and worked for Stevenson. Governor Kennon found he had to compromise in order to pass his administration's constitutional amendments which were also to be voted on in the November election.

After the defeat in 1952, Governor Stevenson, as titular head of the party, succeeded in starting harmony moves among the national Democrats which included overtures to the Southern conservatives.[30] In Louisiana these actions served to reinforce the degree of unity which had prevailed in the presidential campaign, and demands began to be made to punish those Democrats who had backed Eisenhower. At the August, 1954, meeting of the Democratic State Central Committee Governor Kennon received a shattering blow when Camille Gravel was elected a national committeeman to replace Frank Ellis instead of Robert A. Ainsworth, the choice of the Governor. Some found Earl Long's hand in this, since Gravel was a Long supporter who had twice acted as Earl's campaign manager in the Eighth Congressional District.

[29] Howard and Deener, "Louisiana," 276–78.
[30] Howard and Deener, *Presidential Politics*, 104–105.

In the summer of 1956 the stage was set for a rerun of the 1952 Stevenson-Eisenhower contest, and in Louisiana, National Committeeman Camille Gravel exuded confidence that this time Stevenson would double his previous margin of victory. He reasoned that chances were better because the National Democratic Party had been courting Louisiana. "Never before," Gravel said, "has Louisiana had the recognition from the national party it has now and never before has the national party been so fully accepted by Louisiana Democratic leaders."[31] This time Stevenson would have the united support of all Democratic factions, and Gravel's list included Earl Long, Russell Long, Mayor deLesseps Morrison, Senator Ellender, Frank Ellis, and seven congressmen. John Minor Wisdom did not share Gravel's view and countered that Eisenhower would get a strong silent vote to overcome the effect of Louisiana's political machines in the hands of professional Democratic politicians. The Republican leader proved to be correct in his statement that "contrary to professional politicians there is more Louisiana enthusiasm for Ike today than four years ago."[32]

Equally as optimistic, but hardly as accurate, was the estimation of Robert G. Chandler, an executive of the newly formed States' Rights Party with local headquarters in North Louisiana. He thought that his party would carry the Fifth District by two-to-one over both major parties. For there was consternation everywhere regarding the effects of the 1954 Supreme Court ruling on school desegregation, and now the States' Rights Party in Louisiana could be said to provide an alternative to both Democratic and Republican Party stands on civil rights. Already politicians were plotting resistance such as the move by the Louisiana Legislature, with prodding from Willie Rainach, North Louisiana chairman of the House Un-American Activities Committee and one of the architects of the White Citizens Councils movement in Louisiana, to outlaw the state NAACP organization. The wave of anti-Trumanism which had swept Louisiana into the States' Rights column in 1948 and the sentiments which allowed

---

[31] Baton Rouge *Morning Advocate*, Oct. 28, 1956, Sec. A, p. 1.
[32] *Ibid.*, Oct. 28, 1956, Sec. A, p. 1.

Eisenhower to carry the Fourth District in 1952 were expected to bring success to the States' Righters again, in 1956.

At the same time, their leaders were predicting that sizable numbers of Negro voters would defect from the Democrats and support the President. A. P. Tureaud, state attorney for the outlawed NAACP, estimated that at least 30 percent of the Negro vote would swing to Eisenhower, while in Baton Rouge a Negro newspaper editor declared that the Negro might give Ike a second chance on implementing the Supreme Court school decision.[33] For reasons of his own, state Senator Willie Rainach remained uncommitted, expecting, perhaps, that the strong States' Rights sentiment being claimed for North Louisiana would keep the state safe from the Democrats.

The knowledgeable political commentator Margaret Dixon had concluded that the forthcoming election might go down in Louisiana political history as one of the toughest in the long list of stormy battles of the ballot box.[34] For not only were some saying that the Republicans would win in the face of the Democratic solidarity, what with the reports of the Negro vote swinging back, but, also, the campaign found Governor Earl Long silent. This unusual stance on the part of the Governor was said to follow from his intense desire to pass a number of constitutional amendments to further his administrative program and to call a long-needed constitutional convention.

The outcome of the election on November 6 found Eisenhower the winner with a majority of 40,550 votes (329,047 Republican, 243,977 Democratic and 44,520 States' Rights); he had gained 53 percent of the total vote cast, which was the highest percentage obtained by any presidential candidate in Louisiana since 1944. The Republican victory was hailed as marking the reality of a two-party system, and John Minor Wisdom thought that Republican registration would go up in Louisiana. From the other side Camille Gravel found three reasons why the predicted Democratic victory did not materialize: (1) The personal popularity of the President; (2) The defection of the Negro vote to Eisenhower; and (3) The heavy burden of state

[33] Baton Rouge *Morning Advocate*, Nov. 4, 1956, James McLean, Sec. A, p. 4.
[34] Baton Rouge *Morning Advocate*, Nov. 4, 1956, "Capital Beat," Margaret Dixon, Sec. B, p. 7.

issues.[35] While a majority of voters rejected the Democrats again, they also handed Earl Long one of the worst defeats he had suffered by turning down the call for a constitutional convention almost four to one (274,000 to 73,000). It was reported that many feared the Governor was attempting a power grab, reacting to his behavior in the past legislative session when "Uncle Earl" roamed up and down the aisles trying to pass his tax bills. Long had been frustrated by the preceding administration which had managed to sponsor and pass a constitutional amendment requiring a two-thirds vote in each house of the legislature to increase existing taxes or levy new ones.[36]

As the Republicans carried Louisiana in the 1956 presidential election, the Democrats failed to get a majority vote in any of the nine voter types, just as had happened in 1948 (Table 9-3). Still, as can be seen in the correlation matrix (Table 9-5) the distribution of Democratic support by voter types in 1956 does not associate highly with that for 1948 (+.207), and only barely at the level of significance with the distribution of 1952 (+.358). Rather, it is with the percentage distribution of support in pivotal 1944 that the 1956 results show more affinity (+.617). In fact, the 1956 pattern of Democratic support by voter types remained relatively consistent with that of the next two elections, so that it will be useful to try to trace the profile of decreasing Democratic fortunes in 1956.

The leading tendency in the 1956 presidential election, after the Democrats had carried parishes in both North and South Louisiana in the preceding election, was to be found in the reappearance of the regional split which had been discovered earlier for 1944 and 1948 (Table 9-7). Only this time, while North Louisiana leaned heavily toward States' Rights as an alternative to the Democrats, three-fourths of South Louisiana parishes maintained Democratic support above the state average of 40 percent, even though thirteen parishes had Republican percentages above the state average of 54 percent. But while the regional difference in Democratic support was a noticeable tendency, the crucial element in the 1956 election was the

---

[35] Baton Rouge *Morning Advocate*, Nov. 7, 1956, James McLean, Sec. A, p. 4.
[36] For greater detail see Havard, Heberle, and Howard, *Elections of 1960*, 35 ff.

heavy Republican support to be found in the urban-industrial parishes of the state.[37]

For the first time in Louisiana political history, the urban parishes carried a majority vote for the Republican Party, (56 percent) and amassed a total of 194,815 Eisenhower votes, which was 8,627 more than the record Stevenson got in 1952 when Democratic unity and the Negro vote prevailed. But this urban consensus did not hold in subsequent presidential elections, when the urban parishes of South Louisiana went Democratic and those in the northern part of the state remained Republican. In 1956, however, it is easy to see in looking at urban precinct votes how the Negro voters helped the Republicans:

*Table 9–21*

DEMOCRATIC PERCENTAGES IN SAMPLE NEGRO PRECINCTS IN 1956

|  | 1956 Percent | Percent Less than 1952 |
|---|---|---|
| Shreveport | 65% | − 27% |
| New Orleans | 43% | − 37% |
| Baton Rouge | 29% | − 64% |

Of course the impact of this shifting vote is predicated on the assumption that a sizable number of the more than 161,000 Negro registered voters went to the polls, as they had done in the previous election. The Negro leadership had said that that the Democratic Party organization had taken a lot for granted if they had counted upon the Negro vote. A. P. Tureaud explained the shift of Negro voters to the Republican column as a protest vote against a hostile legislature and its segregation laws, and that it was difficult to reconcile the likes of Adlai Stevenson and Willie Rainach in the same party.[38]

While in 1952 the pattern of Longism, even in defeat, correlated highly with the pattern of Democratic victory (+.667), the 1956 association of Long and Democratic percentage support by voter

[37] *Ibid.*, Table 3.
[38] Baton Rouge *Morning Advocate*, Nov. 6, 1956, James McLean, Sec. A, p. 4.

types had washed out (—.158). In the light of what was to come as a result of increasing concern over the issue of desegregation, the most pertinent thing which could be said was that while in 1956 the influence of Longism was still the "bridging" of North and South Louisiana parishes, in presidential politics, North Louisiana had gone anti-Democratic Party for good. This can be shown in a cross tabulation of gubernatorial and presidential percentages by parishes, North and South:

*Table 9–22*

DISTRIBUTION OF PARISHES BY PERCENT
LONG VOTE AND DEMOCRATIC VOTE, 1956

| | | Percent Long Vote | |
| | | Low (0–49%) | High (50–100%) |
|---|---|---|---|
| | Low (0–49%) | +++++ 00000<br>+ 0 | +++++ 00000<br>+++++ 00000<br>+++++ 00000<br>+++++<br>++ |
| Percent Democratic Vote | | | |
| | High (50–100%) | 00 | 00000<br>00000<br>000 |

O = South Louisiana Parishes (N 36).
+ = North Louisiana Parishes (N 28).

Fifty parishes had Long majorities in the 1956 gubernatorial election, and these were distributed almost evenly between North and South Louisiana (twenty-two and twenty-eight). On the other hand, it is apparent that no such bridging effect obtained in regard to presidential election behavior as all twenty-eight North Louisiana parishes were anti-Democrat.

The resistance to federal encroachment upon the "southern way of life" was not left entirely up to the electorate and their voting response in presidential elections. A new turn was seen after the Supreme Court decision of 1954 called for the desegregation of public schools "with all deliberate speed" in the form of the white citizens' council movement which volunteered to help local and state officials to put up resistance. As was manifest in the South as a whole, the moderate found himself without a voice. The Louisiana Legislature, most of whose members had campaigned as staunch segregationists, proceeded to fashion blueprints of resistance to desegregation, independent from Governor Long's leadership. One important part of the design was to be the purge of registration lists. The consequence of this was twofold: in the first place, between 1956 and 1958 more than 31,000 Negro names were dropped from the registration rolls, more than half of these from North Louisiana parishes, over 5,000 from Ouachita Parish alone;[39] secondly, racism was brought back into Louisiana politics, weakening the foundation of the Long faction. The purge was most effective where segregation attitudes were most rigid, untempered by such factors as Catholic religious orientation or the urbanism as in New Orleans where the Negro community had countered with the establishment of "registration schools" in which Negro college youth instructed their elders in the techniques of successful registration.

The United States Commission on Civil Rights reported in 1961 on its investigation of voting in Louisiana and summarized the techniques of the purge as follows:

1. The use of constitutional law and supplemental statute in which stringent qualifications for voting were maintained.
2. Denial where parish registrars of voters feel not even the need to use legal subterfuge to prevent the Negro from registering.
3. The non-permanent registration practice followed in at least sixteen (rural) parishes where every four years voters must reregister.
4. Purges and challenges which allow any two bona fide voters to question by affidavit the right of a person to be registered.
5. Slowdown techniques which tend to discourage the potential Negro voter from making the effort to register.

[39] Havard, Heberle, Howard, *Elections of 1960*, Table 2, Appendix G.

6. Threats of reprisal, which, of course, always have been effective outside the urban areas of the South.[40]

While the decline in Negro registration was in fact short-lived, it was only in New Orleans and the South Louisiana area, however, that the 1960 figures topped those of 1956. In North Louisiana, urban as well as rural, the political climate remained "conservative" and attitudes toward Negro registration rigid. Many aspiring candidates admitted favoring segregation and called attention to the evils of the Negro bloc vote.

The final collapse of moderation before the growing forces of segregation could be seen in the action of the Democratic State Central Committee on October 8, 1958, when it managed to oust Camille Gravel from his post as national committeeman.[41] He had been reelected for a full four-year term in 1956, and at the San Francisco convention, and afterwards, Gravel had championed the mild civil rights plank of the Democratic Party. More serious from the standpoint of the segregationists, perhaps, was the position of Gravel on the Supreme Court's school decision. Gravel claimed the segregation issue was "morally wrong" and "legally settled." For over a year Governor Long had been able to prevail upon the central committee to leave Gravel alone. It had appeared that his policy "of moderation through indirection was vindicated, and that he had tacitly added to this usual practice a 'sufficient rope' method of dealing with the anti-Long segregationist leadership."[42] But when Camille Gravel backed a candidate for Congress against one supported by Governor Long in September 1958 (and defeated Earl's choice), the jig was up. Now Governor Long interposed no longer, and the segregationists' desire to get rid of Gravel prevailed despite the national committee's action to uphold him in his post.

Havard and Steamer argued that by failing to protect Gravel against the Central committee Governor Long gave up his opportunity to act

[40] United States Commission on Civil Rights, "Report of Sub-Committee on Voting for State of Louisiana," (Washington D. C., 1961).
[41] Havard and Steamer, "Louisiana Secedes," 144.
[42] Ibid., 143.

as broker between national and state organization—"a brokerage which had enabled him to serve both groups in the interest of moderation." The subsequent and more widely publicized events in the last year of Earl Long's administration tended to jeopardize the entire structure of the Long organization, "thereby further weakening its capacity to stave off extremist racial policies."[43] The thirty-two years during which realism had been injected into state politics by the thrust of Longism was ended.

[43] *Ibid.*, 144.

# CHAPTER X

# Recent Louisiana Politics

## 1. The Elections of 1960 and 1964: Race and Religion

Fourteen years after what Southerners called "black Monday," May 17, 1954, the date of the Supreme Court's historic school integration ruling, it was estimated that 80 percent of the South's Negro children were still untouched by the edict.[1] But in 1960, when Federal Judge Skelly Wright of the Eastern Louisiana District ordered Orleans Parish schools to begin desegregating on September 7, few dared predict the outcome of the federal insistence on change. Among those more certain had been the avowed segregationists such as Judge Leander Perez and State Senator Willie Rainach whose foresight had led to the establishment of a legislative joint committee on segregation.[2] Such leaders had succeeded already in outlawing the NAACP in the state and had turned their attack upon voter registration procedures in an attempt to purge the rolls of unqualified Negroes (and whites) and to harass would-be Negro registrants.

It has been claimed, in retrospect,[3] that Earl Long experienced the series of personal catastrophes in 1959, which brought him and the state extremely unfavorable national press coverage, in conjunction with or even partly as a consequence of the outburst of racially oriented politics. Long had finally collapsed on the floor of the legislature while arguing for the passage of a bill designed to forestall a purge of the voting rolls in various parishes by a committee of staunch segregationists, perhaps culminating a period of working fatigue combined

---

[1] Baton Rouge *Morning Advocate*, May 17, 1968, Sec. A, p. 7.

[2] Edward L. Pinney and Robert S. Friedman, *Political Leadership and the School Desegregation Crisis in Louisiana*, (New York, 1963), Eagleton Institute Cases in Practical Politics, No. 31.

[3] A. J. Liebling, *The Earl of Louisiana* (New York, 1961).

with a generally poor physical condition. Placed under psychiatric care in a private hospital in Texas by his family, and then removed to a mental institution in Louisiana, "Uncle Earl," with his usual flourish, extricated himself by removing the state director of hospitals and the head of the hospital at which he had been detained and putting sympathetic officers in their places. The traditionally anti-Long press in Louisiana had a field day at the expense of the Governor in reporting and commenting on these events, and the local support for Long state-wide candidates began to crumble.

With the approach of the 1959 state primary election, the tide of Longism ebbed to its lowest point since the scandals twenty years before. The most serious difficulty lay in the fact that, unlike his brother Huey, Earl Long maintained his organization largely in his head. Earl had tried to make sure that no other Long adherent got into position to endanger his primacy. He had his quarrels but then consequently made up with politicians both in and out of the Long camp. Huey, on the other hand, was never concerned about balancing off potential internal threats to his leadership. He apparently felt himself able to maintain complete control by means of a thoroughly organized machine (often with two leaders in a given parish watching each other). Huey combined the obsessive loyalty of his followers with his own ability to out-manipulate and get rid of a threatening defector. As a consequence of this difference, the entire Long faction, as an organization, was much more vulnerable in 1960 than it had been after the death of Huey and perhaps even after the 1939 scandals.

The disruption of Longism, brought on by the racial issue, resurrected the time-honored strategy for segregation—a solid white unity. The opposition had been led to answer the Long emphasis on action programs, building physical assets such as roads and bridges, increasing services in education and economic security by stressing sound administration. The white citizens, therefore, were afforded the privilege of political choice based upon economic issues. Now, for the first time since 1924, the issue of being "soft on race" intruded. And for the first time since 1896 the Negro, per se, became an issue in Louisiana gubernatorial politics. In 1896 the concern was the potential of a Negro-Populist fusion, while sixty-four years later the rhetoric took the form of the "Negro bloc vote" and its affinity to to the candidacy of the liberal, New Orleans Mayor "Chep" Morrison. DeLesseps S. Morrison had gained the reputation of being a highly successful reform mayor with liberal tendencies on labor and race relations. He had built his Crescent City Democratic Association (CCDA) and perpetuated his tenure since 1946 by putting together a coalition of upper white and Negro voters. As it turned out, this fact, together with his Roman Catholic faith, rendered Morrison vulnerable to attack by the segregationists on the statewide level. A solid white front in North Louisiana might be used to offset the more moderate acceptance of Morrison in South Louisiana. Still, even with the entrance of Willie Rainach into the race as the segregationist candidate (Earl Long had said a candidate couldn't win in Louisiana on the one issue of race), no one was certain of the outcome.

In addition to Morrison, who as a first-time candidate for governor against Earl Long in 1956 had run well, especially in South Louisiana parishes, and Rainach, whose potential as the segregation candidate was unknown, there were two Long and one anti-Long candidates in the 1959 first primary, as well as six "nuisance" candidates (all of whom together could not be expected to get more than 2 or 3 percent of the total vote). The designated Long candidates, with Earl Long himself as running mate for lieutenant governor, (and barely failing to make the run-off) was James A. Noe from Monroe, inactive in statewide politics for many years, but a Long stalwart from the thirties. He claimed to be running to redeem the name Long and to prevent the repeal of programs consistently fostered by Longism. The other Long candidate was the perennial candidate, William J. Dodd, periodically estranged but never wholly alienated from the Longs. The candidate of those who might be called the traditional anti-Longs (made up of the parish-seat elite and their allies, particularly the major industrial combinations of the state) was former governor Jimmie H. Davis. His stock in trade had been his ability to make his stand of "peace and harmony" appealing to the voters by creating the perfect image of a man to be trusted and one whose intense calm was calculated to bring rational balance into the political life of the state.

By the December 5, 1959 first primary, three issues dominated the election, all of which threatened to destroy the electoral foundation of Longism, as each candidate tried to fill the political vacuum created by the weakened Long organization. First, there was the liberalism represented by deLesseps S. Morrison which gave him a basis for support beyond New Orleans in other urban industrial parts of South Louisiana. Government-reform idealists and urban liberals were attracted to his cause and, of course, the Negro voter was expected to support Morrison as well. Even in South Louisiana, however, the traditional anti-Long forces could be expected to make inroads on Morrison's "respectable" support by charging him as being a spendthrift liberal. Closely related to the liberalism issue was, secondly, the urban-religious question. Morrison's Catholic, Gallic, South Louisiana urbanism was antipathetic to the fundamentalist, Anglo-Saxon, Populist ideology of the piney hills, whatever may have been the affinity of their respective outlooks on economic questions. Finally, on the third issue, race, Rainach posed as the premier guardian of the southern way of life, claiming that Noe, Dodd, and Morrison were soft on the issue and that Davis would be ineffectual. All the candidates had asserted their opposition to integration but the question remained as to how vulnerable the first three were on the issue and to what extent the rural vote could be diverted to Rainach.

The first primary vote indicated the effect of these factors on the traditional pattern of Longism and portended the North-South Louisiana cleavage that appeared in the runoff. It is clear from these figures that, as was the case in 1956, the Morrison support was regional. In fact, 89 percent of the Morrison vote (which had made up 34 percent of the total) was located in South Louisiana parishes. Since in 1956 there had been no runoff in which the test could be made, it was difficult to tell whether this was his bedrock support on which Morrison could build a second primary victory or something near his maximum ceiling. The candidacy of Jimmie Davis showed a nearly equal drawing power, proportionally, in both regions of the state, although 70 percent of his total vote was found in South Louisiana. While Rainach received the highest

*Table 10–1*
CANDIDATES AND VOTES, 1959, FIRST PRIMARY

|  | TOTAL | MORRISON | DAVIS | RAINACH | NOE | DODD |
|---|---|---|---|---|---|---|
| North Louisiana | 219,000 | 30,310 | 64,156 | 72,779 | 35,126 | 16,629 |
|  | 100% | 14% | 29% | 33% | 16% | 8% |
| South Louisiana | 599,692 | 248,646 | 149,395 | 70,316 | 62,528 | 68,807 |
|  | 100% | 42% | 25% | 12% | 10% | 11% |
| STATE TOTAL | 818,692* | 278,956 | 213,551 | 143,095 | 97,654 | 85,436 |
|  | 100% | 34% | 25% | 17% | 13% | 11% |

* Excluding 23,917 "other" votes.

percentage vote in North Louisiana, the extent of the segregation sentiment is measured, perhaps, in the observation that his total vote was divided almost equally between North and South. The degree of Long support slippage in this election is seen in the Noe vote, which in North Louisiana exceded "Chep" Morrison's by less than five thousand.

The greatest significance of the first primary, 1959, lay in the fact that for the first time since 1924 a Long candidate failed to win outright or gain a spot in the second primary. This is portrayed in tabular form when the rank order of support for candidates by region is presented:

*Table 10–2*
RANK ORDER OF CANDIDATE SUPPORT IN NORTH
AND SOUTH LOUISIANA, 1959

|  | State Total | North Louisiana | South Louisiana |
|---|---|---|---|
| Morrison . . . . . . . . . . . . . . | 1 | 4 | 1 |
| Davis . . . . . . . . . . . . . . | 2 | 2 | 2 |
| Rainach . . . . . . . . . . . . . | 3 | 1 | 3 |
| Noe . . . . . . . . . . . . . . . | 4 | 3 | 5 |
| Dodd . . . . . . . . . . . . . . | 5 | 5 | 4 |

The Long candidate Noe only came close in North Louisiana, while the segregationist Rainach led in North Louisiana and drew enough support for third place in South Louisiana. The ultimate significance of this pattern in affecting the second primary can be suggested from a look at the rank order distribution of candidate support among Baton Rouge precincts.

*Table 10–3*

RANK ORDER OF CANDIDATE SUPPORT 1959
BY ECOLOGICAL AREAS OF BATON ROUGE

|  | Upper White Precincts | White Labor Precincts | Negro Precincts |
|---|---|---|---|
| Morrison . . . . . . . . . . . . | 1 | 2 | 1 |
| Davis . . . . . . . . . . . . . | 2 | 1 | 4 |
| Rainach . . . . . . . . . . . | 3 | 4 | 5 |
| Noe . . . . . . . . . . . . . | 4 | 5 | 2 |
| Dodd . . . . . . . . . . . . | 5 | 3 | 3 |

Now it is plain that the advantage in the second primary should go to Davis, inasmuch as his candidacy was given greatest support among the most numerous voter category, white labor. Morrison's lead is seen to follow the pattern of his New Orleans success, a coalition of upper white and Negro voters in what has been called elsewhere the "Atlanta solution" to the challenge of change.[4] The third place support in upper white precincts in Baton Rouge gained by Willie Rainach might also be construed as a potential advantage to Jimmie Davis, for obviously Davis needed only segregationist support together with that of North Louisiana former Long voters (which may have become one and the same) to win his second term as governor of Louisiana.

The location of the major support for each candidate by voter type areas serves to broaden the analysis further. In Table 10–4 the top quarter of parish support is traced and the proportion which the

[4] Perry H. Howard and Joseph L. Brent III, "Social Change, Urbanization, and Types of Society," *Journal of Social Issues,* XXII (1966), 82.

top quarter for each candidate represented of his total vote is computed.

*Table 10–4*

TOP QUARTER PARISH SUPPORT FOR CANDIDATES, 1959,
BY VOTER TYPE AREAS

|  | Morrison | Davis | Rainach | Noe | Dodd |
|---|---|---|---|---|---|
| Total State |  |  |  |  |  |
| Percent* 100% . . . . . . | 33 | 25 | 17 | 12 | 10 |
| Percent |  |  |  |  |  |
| Top Quarter of Total. . . . | 66 | 20 | 32 | 25 | 44 |
| Top Quarter By Voter |  |  |  |  |  |
| Types Number of Parishes |  |  |  |  |  |
| North La. Hills (8). . . . . | — | 1 | 6 | 4 | — |
| Central Hills (7) . . . . . . | — | 2 | — | 7 | 1 |
| Macon Ridge (3) . . . . . . | — | 2 | 1 | 1 | — |
| North La. Planter (10) . . . | — | 5 | 8 | — | — |
| South La. Planter (8) . . . . | 7 | — | — | 1 | 4 |
| South La. Bayou (8) . . . . | 5 | 2 | — | — | — |
| Florida Parishes (8). . . . . | — | 3 | 1 | 2 | 4 |
| Southwest La. (10) . . . . . | 2 | 1 | — | 1 | 7 |
| Urban Area (2) . . . . . . | 2 | — | — | — | — |
| (64) | (16) | (16) | (16) | (16) | (16) |

* Including "other" votes.

Not only was Morrison the most regionally based candidate in 1959, but also fully two-thirds of his total vote was concentrated in sixteen South Louisiana parishes which included Orleans and Jefferson and the heart of French Louisiana. On the other extreme it can be seen that both Davis and Noe bridged North and South Louisiana with the sixteen parishes of their top quarter of support and that it made up but 20 and 25 percent respectively of their state total votes. Two of Davis' South Louisiana parishes were St. Bernard and Plaquemines, showing where segregationist Leander Perez had put his money. The Rainach major support came from Hill and Planter parishes where unregistered Negroes made up high proportions of the total population. Dodd's support had come predominantly from South Louisiana parishes where he enjoyed support from organized labor. Altogether, the pattern which emerged in 1959 indicated a cleavage between North and South Louisiana that seemed less related to the socioeconomic clash of interests that had formerly prevailed than to the issues of race and religion with some admixture of rural-urban antipathy.

There were significant differences between the Louisiana of 1960 and what Huey Long found three decades before in 1930, yet Longism had been built on a coalition of farmers and laborers, and while there were fewer of the former there were more of the latter. Table 6–15 shows that, taking the percent males employed in non-agriculture as an index of modernization, while the nation began her industrial development takeoff by 1890, fully two decades before Louisiana, by 1930 the comparative figures were 75 percent for the nation against 60 percent for the state. The impact of World II was such, however, that the gap between the two narrowed, and in 1960 the state was relatively more industrialized than the nation, with 90 percent of the males employed in non-agriculture compared to 85 percent for the nation.

These figures would mean more, perhaps, if analysis was shifted somewhat to a comparison of the composition of the labor force of the nation and state in the period being surveyed.

*Table 10–5*

PERCENT OF LABOR FORCE IN MAJOR OCCUPATION
GROUPS, NATION AND STATE, 1930–60*

| Census | Agriculture | | Manual | | White Collar | |
|--------|------|------|------|------|------|------|
| Year | U.S. | La. | U.S. | La. | U.S. | La. |
| 1900 | 48% | 55% | 35% | 32% | 17% | 13% |
| 1930 | 20 | 36 | 51 | 43 | 29 | 21 |
| 1940 | 17 | 32 | 50 | 44 | 33 | 24 |
| 1950 | 10 | 8 | 53 | 59 | 37 | 33 |
| 1960 | 6 | 6 | 49 | 56 | 45 | 38 |

* Source: U.S. Census.

Taking the labor force as a whole rather than focusing upon the male category, nation and state can be seen to match on the low percentage of workers which the mechanization of agriculture has rendered necessary.[5] The manual columns, however, show that in industrialization, Louisiana had overtaken and remains ahead of the nation. In regard to the white collar category, an indicator of complexity and bureaucratization, the national proportion is greater.

Indeed, during the 1944 administration of Jimmie Davis, state leaders became so concerned to maintain the industrial impetus the war had brought that a tax exemption industry inducement program was pushed. The following table summarizes the success of the program in terms of new jobs created for each succeeding administration, starting with the single year 1947 at which time the current series of data was first recorded.

*Table 10–6*
NEW JOBS CREATED UNDER LOUISIANA TAX-EXEMPTION
INDUSTRY INDUCEMENT PROGRAM, 1947–67,
DURING SUCCESSIVE POLITICAL ADMINISTRATIONS*

| Administration | New Jobs (in Thousands) | Percent of Total |
|---|---|---|
| Davis 1947 | 13.4 | 11% |
| Long 1948–51 | 21.2 | 17 |
| Kennon 1952–53 | 18.3 | 15 |
| Long 1956–59 | 24.3 | 20 |
| Davis 1960–63 | 17.0 | 14 |
| McKeithen 1964–67 | 28.3 | 23 |
| | 122.5 | 100% |

* Source: La. State Dept. Commerce and Industry.

These figures depict a broken line trend, overall, but by 1960 industrial expansion in Louisiana was a well established tendency. The greatest

[5] Alvin L. Bertrand, *Agricultural Mechanization and Social Change in Rural Louisiana* (Louisiana State University, Agricultural Experiment Station Bulletin No. 458 [Baton Rouge, 1951]).

expansion of new jobs in any one year occurred in 1947, with second place going to 1956 with 11,795 new jobs and with the third most successful year being 1966 with 11,055 new jobs. The relatively low number of additional jobs added in the years of the Kennon administration may be accounted for by the national economic recession of 1953–54, while it is interesting to speculate the extent to which the furor over desegregation during the 1960–63 Davis administration depressed expansion in those years.

Stephen L. McDonald has traced the growth of the economy of Louisiana in the period 1947–59 and showed that it was greatest in South Louisiana.[6] That is to say, besides the urban parishes throughout the state, the greatest increase in job opportunities, higher incomes, and population growth took place in the southern part of the state. This can be pinpointed by considering pertinent data compared by voter type areas (Table 10–7). Fully every parish which had shown population loss in 1960, except adjacent Avoyelles, was located in North Louisiana. Moreover, they were apart from the urban parishes there, all of which showed population gains above the state average in the same period. Still, over three-fourths of the parishes showing population gain were located in South Louisiana, most significantly in Planter and Bayou voter type areas. Areas of population loss and gain are obviously closely associated with the development of new job opportunities and, in turn, with figures for median income.

In this reporting period, the attraction of new industry to North Louisiana was falling far behind that of the rest of the state. North Louisiana's share of new jobs (1950–59) had amounted to but 16 percent of the total and, aside from the increased jobs in the three urban parishes (7.9 percent) the balance was located in North Louisiana Hill Parishes adjacent to the Shreveport area and the Arkansas border. The South Louisiana share of new jobs (83 percent) was weighted in favor of the urban parishes there which altogether attracted 49 percent of the state total. It was in this period that the

[6] Stephen L. McDonald, *Growth and Fluctuations in the Economy of Louisiana,* *1947–1959* (Louisiana Business Bulletin, XXIII, No. 1, Division of Research, College of Business Administration [Baton Rouge, 1961]).

*Table 10–7*

POPULATION GAIN AND LOSS AND NEW JOB OPPORTUNITIES
IN NUMBER OF PARISHES BY VOTER TYPE AREAS

|  | | Population Loss 1950–60 | Population Gain 1950–60 above State Average* | Percent of State Total New Jobs 1950–59* |
|---|---|---|---|---|
| North La. Hills | (8) | 5 | — | 4.3 |
| Central Pine Hills | (7) | 6 | — | 1.2 |
| Macon Ridge | (3) | 3 | — | 1.0 |
| North L. Planter | (7) | 4 | 2 | 1.4 |
| Caddo | (1) | — | 1 | 4.0 |
| Ouachita | (1) | — | 1 | 3.7 |
| Rapides | (1) | — | 1 | 0.7 |
| South La. Planter | (8) | — | 5 | 15.0 |
| South La. Bayou | (8) | 1 | 6 | 10.0 |
| Florida Parishes | (7) | — | 2 | 6.0 |
| E. Baton Rouge | (1) | — | 1 | 14.8 |
| Southwest La. | (8) | — | — | 3.0 |
| Calcasieu | (1) | — | 1 | 6.6 |
| Lafayette | (1) | — | 1 | 1.6 |
| Jefferson | (1) | — | 1 | 11.0 |
| Orleans | (1) | — | — | 14.7 |
|  | (64) | (19) | (22) | 100% |

Percent of Statewide
Total New Jobs 1950–60          0.4%            82.0%

Median Income Family
and Unrelated Individuals,
1960                           $1,920          $3,779

* Source: PAR and State Department of Commerce and Industry.

expansion of industry occurred which began to line the Mississippi with plants from Baton Rouge south beyond New Orleans in Plaquemines Parish. South Louisiana Planter and Bayou voter type areas contained the nine parishes involved, and 60 percent of all new jobs 1950–59 were established therein.

This all too brief sketch of shifting population and economic development in the emerging new Louisiana has been made in order to provide a bench mark from which to attempt to assess the outcome of the 1960 second primary. In terms of traditional Louisiana politics there were almost as many incongruities in the second as in the first primary. The New Orleans *Times-Picayune* noted that the issues were segregation, labor, and respectability, with religion and sectionalism playing somewhat lesser roles. In point of fact the segregation issue became the really dominant verbal issue, but there were whisper campaigns which insinuated that there was a relation between this issue and the religious and urban factors. Davis was careful himself to avoid the use of any strong language on the race question but his co-campaigners, especially after Rainach agreed to throw his support to Davis, cast aside all restraints. For reasons of their own, the state leadership of the AFL-CIO gave its support to Davis, and with the spokesmen for respectable organized labor behind them the Davis forces began to associate Morrison's labor support with what was called the Hoffa-dominated Teamsters Union, thereby stigmatizing his relation with labor without fear of isolating themselves from the bulk of the labor oriented voters. Jimmie Davis continued calmly and with simple sincerity to plead for a restoration of peace and harmony in the state while his backers hammered at race and labor with a ruthless intensity unusual even in Louisiana politics.

Given the absence of a Long candidate in the runoff and knowing what occurred in the first primary, it is possible to formulate a number of hypotheses regarding the outcome of the second primary. The Davis vote would be expected to be higher in parishes where Catholic percentage was low. Likewise, since the association between registration and religion was found to be high (in the analysis of the 1956 election in Chapter 8), the Davis vote should be higher in parishes where the percent Negro voter registration was low. As an indicator of population loss, the percent of population sixty-five years and over can be used, since this figure is a function of both the birth rate and consequent youthfulness of the population as well as the number of people in working age categories (eighteen through sixty-four years of age) who move where the jobs are. In this case it could be hypothesized that the higher the Davis vote the higher the percent aged in a parish. These three indicators may also be considered as rough equivalents of a North-South Louisiana division among the array of parishes.

Three more variables which might be used as indicators of the difference between the Davis and Morrison vote are the percent urban, percent new jobs established by the industrial development program of the state, and the worker ratio—the proportion of private wage and salary workers to those self-employed among the non-agriculture labor force. While in all three cases it would be expected that the Davis vote was higher in parishes where the incidence of these variables was low, yet the association cannot be so clear cut inasmuch as the distribution of these characteristics among the parishes does not depict so sharp a regional division.

To anticipate the discussion of the results of the second primary, then, a number of statements are tabulated indicating for the majority Davis parishes (N41) the number expected to be associated with the variables enumerated above, and placed beside the actual outcome.

*Table 10–8*
HYPOTHESES CONCERNING EXPECTED ASSOCIATION
OF MAJORITY DAVIS PARISHES, 1960, AND SELECTED VARIABLES

| Of Majority Davis Parishes (N 41): | Number of Parishes | |
| --- | --- | --- |
| | Expected | Observed |
| 90% will be Low Negro Registration | 37 | 30 |
| 90% will be Low Percent Catholic | 37 | 33 |
| 75% will be High Percent Aged | 31 | 26 |
| 75% will be Low Percent Urban | 31 | 23 |
| 75% will be Low Number New Jobs | 31 | 20 |
| 60% will be Low Worker Ratio | 25 | 24 |

Observed/expected tendency ratio = 81%

Jimmie H. Davis won the 1960 second primary by receiving 54 percent of the 901,791 total vote cast with a solid 75 percent of the North Louisiana vote coupled with 46 percent support in the

# Average deLesseps S. Morrison Gubernatorial
# Second Primary Vote, 1960 and 1964

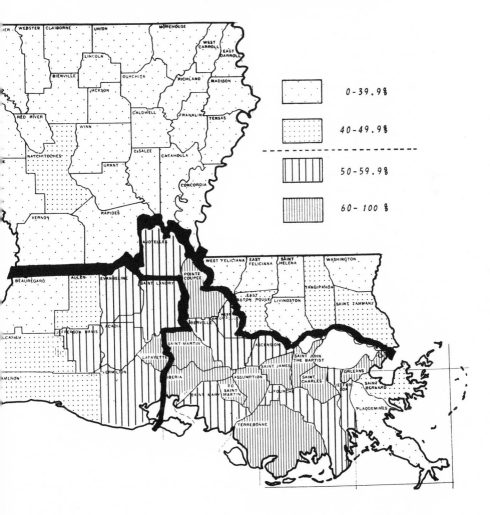

rest of the state. He carried the Florida Parishes and cut into Southwest Louisiana beyond the limits of the very strongest Morrison parishes. (Map 10–1)

*Table 10–9*
DAVIS VOTE, 1960, SECOND PRIMARY BY VOTER TYPE AREAS

|  |  | Average Percent | Number of Parishes | | | |
|---|---|---|---|---|---|---|
|  |  |  | 0–39% | 40–49% | 50–59% | 60–100% |
| North La. Hills | (8) | 86% | — | — | — | 8 |
| Macon Ridge | (3) | 86 | — | — | — | 3 |
| North La. Planter | (10) | 81 | — | — | — | 10 |
| Central Pine Hills | (7) | 64 | — | 1 | — | 6 |
| Florida Parishes | (8) | 58 | — | — | 2 | 6 |
| South La. Bayou | (8) | 49 | 3 | 3 | — | 2 |
| Southwest La. | (10) | 47 | 2 | 4 | 2 | 2 |
| Urban Area | (2) | 42 | — | 2 | — | — |
| South La. Planter | (8) | 37 | 4 | 4 | — | — |
|  | (64) |  | (9) | (14) | (4) | (37) |

In this election the Hill parishes showed a solidarity reminiscent of that of the 1880's, while of all North Louisiana it was the Central Pine Hills (the Long heartland) whose parish average was the lowest in support of the old Long opposition, Jimmie Davis. With Davis carrying a bloc of parishes by 70 to 90 percent and Morrison a smaller cluster of urbanized, Catholic, and more heavily populated parishes by 50 to 70 percent, it was obvious that this was not sufficient for the latter to win.

In the urban industrial parishes of the state the vote broke even, with Davis taking 50.8 percent of the 419,537 votes (comprising 47 percent of the total vote cast) for an urban lead of 7,368. Morrison received 60 percent of the Orleans Parish vote and 55 percent of neighboring Jefferson Parish, but in the periphery of the industrial strip (and areas likewise less heavily Catholic) such as Baton Rouge and Lake Charles, he slipped badly. Another feature of this second primary that gives some indication of the influence of the intrusive and emotionally compelling racial and religious antipathies was the fact that the total vote in the second primary increased by 57,744 over that of the first primary and precinct checks indicated that the overwhelming proportion of the increase must have gone to Davis. One final observation concerning the distinctiveness of this election which seemed to spell the demise of the voter pattern characteristic of the Long era has to do with the lack of association found in the correlation of this election with previous ones by voter types (See Table 8–4). There is virtually no association between the voter type distribution of votes for the 1956 and 1960 election (+.070).

It is possible, now, to test more thoroughly the stated hypotheses regarding the Davis vote and its association with a number of explanatory variables. First of all, the state's sixty-four parishes will be grouped in percentage intervals from low to high for each variable, and the Davis percentage of the total vote at each level will be computed. This is done in the following table.

*Table 10–10*
JIMMIE H. DAVIS PERCENTAGES OF TOTAL VOTE
SECOND PRIMARY, 1960, IN LOUISIANA PARISHES
CLASSIFIED BY PERCENT CATHOLIC, NEGRO REGISTRATION,
AGED, NEW JOBS, AND WORKER RATIO

| Percent Intervals From Low to High | 1956 Percent Catholic | 1960 Percent Negro Registration | 1960 Percent 65 Years & Over | 1960 Percent Urban | 1950–59 Number New Jobs | 1960 Worker Ratio |
|---|---|---|---|---|---|---|
| 1 | 88 | 83 | 50 | 75 | 74 | 65 |
| 2 | 80 | 70 | 55 | 56 | 61 | 68 |
| 3 | 55 | 62 | 68 | 64 | 68 | 62 |
| 4 | 38 | 41 | 81 | 57 | 51 | 60 |

The expectation of association between the Davis vote and the first three variables is borne out with remarkable regularity as the greater the incidence of the variable within a parish grouping, the lesser (or greater as in the case of percent aged) the percentage Davis support. It will be noted that Davis' only losses occur within the most Catholic and Negro parishes while, conversely, only within the parishes with least aged does the Davis vote approach less than a majority. These findings tend to confirm the north-south split which, it was suggested above, had characterized the 1960 election.

The degree of regularity in movement from low to high tends to blur with the variables of urbanism, new jobs, and worker ratio. While a range of from 18 to 23 percent exists between low and high in each set, to group the parishes this way is to make Davis appear to carry a majority at each level. But Morrison was expected to carry a majority at precisely the high level of incidence of these variables in groups of parishes. If correspondence between these variables and the Davis vote does not seem meaningful then perhaps it will be when the index of race is included. Then one will see that the change indicated by these variables did not necessarily bring new liberal political tendencies to Louisiana politics.

To pursue the question of the importance of race in effecting the outcome of the election of 1960, it is possible to compute the Davis percentages in those parishes which are low and high on the variable in question as the percent of Negro registration is made to vary.

*Table 10–11*

JIMMIE H. DAVIS PERCENTAGES OF TOTAL VOTE
SECOND PRIMARY, 1960, IN LOUISIANA PARISHES
LOW AND HIGH PERCENT URBAN, NEW JOBS, AND
WORKER RATIO CLASSIFIED BY PERCENT NEGRO REGISTRATION

| Percent Negro Registered | | Low (0–49) Percent | High (52–100) Urban | Low (0–232) Number | High (240–7,655) New Jobs | Low (33–72) Worker | High (73–117) Ratio |
|---|---|---|---|---|---|---|---|
| 0–4 | (17) | 85 | 81 | 87 | 81 | 87 | 82 |
| 5–10 | (18) | 73 | 59 | 71 | 66 | 67 | 70 |
| 12–17 | (14) | 60 | 50 | 55 | 55 | 59 | 44 |
| 20–42 | (15) | 41 | 41 | 44 | 40 | 41 | 41 |

These figures mean that the Negro variable discriminates more than the other three in producing variation in the Davis vote. That is to say, in parishes where relatively few Negroes are registered (generally a measure of resistance on the question of racial desegregation) the support for the segregationist candidate is high regardless of either low or high incidence of the other variables being manipulated in the analysis and, of course, vice versa. In 1960 the effect of the race issue was strong enough to push the Davis majority up into the third level, leaving the Morrison majority a function of racial moderation and coincident with high percent Catholic population.

The 1959–60 gubernatorial primary elections, then, were disruptive of the pattern of Longism, which had bridged North and South Louisiana with a coalition of farmer and labor voters, a cleavage which pitted North against South, Protestant against Catholic, and rendered race the primary issue in the place of economic realities. Perhaps Earl Long understood better than most that a four-year term of a relatively inactive and conservative administration would create the kind of situation for which his appeals were ideally suited. He had always played down the race issue (after all there were 150,000 Negro votes in the state), and he could assume that this issue furnished but a limited amount of mileage for political travel in the face of recent national developments.

In point of fact, Earl Long's victory in the congressional primary in the Eighth District in the heart of the hills within nine months of the second primary was an indication of the shrewdness of his calculations. If he had not died immediately following that congressional race, in which he won over a young, conservative incumbent who had beaten the Long-endorsed candidate only two years before, few observers would have doubted that "Uncle Earl" would have been the odds-on favorite to rebuild his machine sufficiently to challenge for the governorship in 1964. As it happened, the death of Earl Long left a tremendous hiatus—in a sense deliberately created by Earl himself—in the leadership of the Long faction. Meanwhile, the voting behavior in state elections had come to parallel that of recent presidential elections in Louisiana and the revival of racism and the intrusion of religious and cultural xenophobia carried over in toto to the 1960 presidential election in the state.

The Democrats, who had lost Louisiana to Eisenhower the last time out, were optimistic again with the nomination of Senator John F. Kennedy, a Roman Catholic, as the standard bearer. Frank

Ellis was named state campaign manager for the party. The Republicans, who had nominated incumbent Vice-President Richard M. Nixon as their candidate, were hopeful of perpetuating the conservative tendency by taking Louisiana again, and had named Republican National Committeeman George W. Reese to help put Nixon across. The prospects were clouded, however, by the entrance of the States' Rights Party, whose campaign manager in the state was David C. Treen. Many foresaw that if the conservative vote was split, a candidate as attractive to South Louisiana voters as Senator Kennedy might end up the winner of Louisiana's ten electoral votes as a plurality.

This expectation was narrowly averted as the Democratic Party received a majority, 50.4 percent of the record high total of 807,891 votes cast. The Republicans ran second with 28.5 percent, and the States' Rights Party received the rest, 21.1 percent. At the same time, with the conservative vote split, the extent of the Kennedy margin over his nearest competitor was a substantial 21.9 percent. In this election the incipient North-South Louisiana split, foreshadowed in presidential elections since 1944 and manifest in the recent gubernatorial contests, emerged in stark relief.

*Table 10–12*

KENNEDY VOTE, 1960, BY VOTER TYPE AREAS
WITH COMPARATIVE PERCENTAGES OF THE OTHER CANDIDATES

| | | Average Percent | | | Number of Kennedy Parishes | | | |
|---|---|---|---|---|---|---|---|---|
| | | Dem. | Rep. | St. Rt. | 0–39% | 40–49% | 50–59% | 60–100% |
| North La. Hills | (8) | 23 | 40 | 27 | 8 | — | — | — |
| Macon Ridge | (3) | 29 | 33 | 38 | 3 | — | — | — |
| North La. Planter | (10) | 25 | 41 | 35 | 9 | 1 | — | — |
| Central Pine Hills | (7) | 30 | 42 | 28 | 7 | — | — | — |
| Florida Parishes | (8) | 41 | 21 | 39 | 3 | 5 | — | — |
| South La. Bayou | (8) | 62 | 17 | 21 | 1 | 1 | 1 | 5 |
| Southwest La. | (10) | 69 | 22 | 8 | — | 1 | 1 | 8 |
| Urban Area | (2) | 50 | 27 | 52 | — | 1 | 1 | — |
| South La. Planter | (8) | 73 | 17 | 10 | — | — | — | 8 |
| | (64) | | | | (31) | (9) | (3) | (21) |

As the percentage distribution of the Kennedy vote indicates, either the voters liked him a great deal or disliked him, and at the same time, the negative parishes are found among North Louisiana voter type areas while the positive Kennedy parishes are found to the south. The Florida and Bayou Parishes provide the buffer, and here the parishes of East and West Feliciana, St. Helena, and the Perez dominated parishes of Plaquemines and St. Bernard produced pluralities ranging from 44 to 65 percent States' Rights. As previously pointed out, the Longs, with traditional North Louisiana Hills support, never had taken an extreme stand on segregation. It is instructive to note, therefore, that while the North Louisiana parishes were to become strongholds of white supremacy, nevertheless there still remained, in 1960, remnants of the former liberalism. Indication of this is found in parishes along Macon Ridge together with the Central Hills, all of which in the presidential election registered the closest approximation of any parishes to an even three-way split of the vote.

The expression of voter sentiments in the elections of 1960 was extremely stable, as can be indicated from the quite high rank order coefficient of correlation of Morrison and Kennedy percentages by voter type areas (+.936). The distribution of the vote in 1960 likewise showed affinity with other elections, such as 1928 (+.550) and 1944 (+.917) where the Democratic support had likewise been seated in South Louisiana (Table 9–5). The question that remains to be answered is, however, given the similarity between the two candidates, why did Kennedy win while Morrison lost?

If it is assumed that the Kennedy vote came substantially from Catholics, Negroes, and labor, then the differences in the geographic distribution between the Kennedy and the Morrison vote furnish a clue to the puzzle of Kennedy's victory and Morrison's defeat when both had very similar assets as well as handicaps, including well-organized and well-financed campaigns, attractive public personalities, liberal attitudes on the race issue (in Morrison's case at least at the outset), urban backgrounds and Catholic religious affiliations. A glance at the two tables which summarize the second primary and presidential votes (Tables 10–9 and 10–12) will show that while the average percent support by voter types could be arrayed in almost identical order, in every case but the Florida Parishes and the Central Hills, the Kennedy support was several percentage points higher than that for Morrison. This can be shown by accumulating North and South Louisiana average percents for each candidate. Thus in North Louisiana the Morrison total was 83 as compared to 107 for Kennedy while to the south the accumulated totals were 267 for Morrison and 295 for Kennedy.

One explanation of the percentage lead of Kennedy over Morrison has to do with the differential support of labor. Taking ecological areas of Baton Rouge as representative, with the city being in the forefront of industrial expansion and with substantial numbers of both Catholic and Protestant voters, the difference in support of the candidates stands out. While Kennedy received 51 percent of the vote in white labor precincts, Morrison received but 35 percent. Multiplied by 60, roughly the proportion of this category of voters to the total, it is plain that Kennedy enjoyed about a three to two advantage. Of course this is only to state a tendency as, after all, the state averages were quite close, 50.4 percent for Kennedy and 47 percent for Morrison, and the gap quickly closes as one observes that in white labor precincts in New Orleans the support was almost identical, 54 percent for Kennedy and 55.1 percent for the hometown candidate, Morrison.

Regardless of the extent of the increment of white labor votes in the Kennedy support, religion and race proved to be the key variables in determining the direction of the presidential vote in Louisiana, just as was found to be the case in the gubernatorial elections. This has been verified by Bernard Cosman[7] who found that for the religious factor, the Democratic percentage in 1960 followed the rise in each level of Catholicism, while the inverse was true for the Republican vote. In 1956, however, no such variation could be found. In regard to the racial factor, Cosman found that whereas voting behavior in the least Catholic parishes varied with the size of the nonwhite population, the presence or absence of Negroes in the Catholic parishes did not

[7] Bernard Cosman, "Religion and Race in Louisiana Presidential Politics, 1960," *Southwestern Social Science Quarterly*, XLIII (1962), 237.

seem to have been an important determinant of voting tendencies. Religion seemed related to racial tolerance as measured by the greater number of Negroes registered to vote in the Catholic parishes.[8]

These generalizations are confirmed in a set of frequency distributions constructed to allow comparison with the regularities in voting behavior found for the gubernatorial second primary (Tables 10–10 and 10–11)

*Table 10–13*

JOHN F. KENNEDY PERCENTAGES OF TOTAL VOTE PRESIDENTIAL, 1960,
IN LOUISIANA PARISHES CLASSIFIED BY PERCENT CATHOLIC,
NEGRO REGISTRATION, WORKER RATIO

| Percent Intervals from Low to High | 1956 Percent Catholic | 1960 Percent Negro Registration | 1960 Worker Ratio | Percent Negroes Registered | Low 33–72 Worker | High 73–117 Ratio |
|---|---|---|---|---|---|---|
| 1 | 27 | 22 | 48 | 0–4 (17) | 22 | 24 |
| 2 | 30 | 44 | 45 | 5–10 (18) | 48 | 40 |
| 3 | 53 | 52 | 46 | 12–17 (14) | 56 | 54 |
| 4 | 73 | 70 | 45 | 20–42 (15) | 63 | 62 |

Once again it was found that for each level of increase in percent Catholic or Negro registration the vote percentages increase accordingly, but that there is no such correspondence found between worker ratio and the vote. And again when the worker ratio was divided into low and high sets of parishes, as the Negro registration increases, the percentage Kennedy support increases. The continuity in voting behavior between gubernatorial and presidential election is borne out then, except that for each variable and at each level of increase, the Kennedy support is some 10 percentage points above the comparable figures for the Morrison vote.

In summary it may be said that Kennedy and Morrison had support from almost identical categories of voters, except that Morrison received considerable backing from business interests but not from

---

[8] John H. Fenton and Kenneth N. Vines, "Negro Registration in Louisiana," *American Political Science Review*, LI (1957), 713.

labor, while Kennedy was largely opposed by businessmen and their associates but had the backing of organized labor. And, of course, both candidates received support from Catholics and met opposition from Protestants and from segregationists.

This rather extended analysis of the 1960 elections is justified because the political tendencies which emerged at that time continued, in large part, to manifest themselves in subsequent elections. The Davis administration almost immediately had faced the problem of the desegregation of public schools in New Orleans, and the segregationists made the most of it, urging the governor to call special sessions of the legislature in which the attempt was made to build a legal bulwark against desegregation. This is the subject of an able case study of political leadership and the school desegregation crisis by Edward L. Pinney and Robert S. Friedman, who made the point that in Louisiana, where the office of the governor is such a strong one, it seemed out of place somehow for the governor to acquiesce to the demands of the legislature.[9] It is true that concessions were made to the militant segregationists in the form of packages of segregation legislation, yet dramatic shows of resistance such as those made in Arkansas, Mississippi, and Alabama were conspicuously absent in Louisiana. The Davis administration seemed open to the interpretation of being a holding or containing action in which nearly all the latently explosive issues were kept latent and nearly all of the groups who might have exploited these issues tactically were held in check. Throughout his term of office the Governor had been publicly reticent, but showed exceptional skill in acting, and at times in refusing to act, to keep major issues in as near a state of suspension as the necessities of public affairs would admit.

Charles W. Tapp has shown that the disruptive trends introduced into Louisiana politics in the elections of 1960 were affirmed in the 1963–64 gubernatorial elections.[10] This appeared to be the case despite the eventual election as governor of an ostensible Long candidate, for the racial issue had remained heated and, the candidates

---

[9] Pinney and Friedman, *Political Leadership*, 8.

[10] Charles W. Tapp, "The Gubernatorial Election of 1964: An Affirmation of Political Trends," *Louisiana Academy of Sciences*, XXVII (1964).

vying for position did not campaign on the traditional issues. Rather than the charges and countercharges of excessive spending, patronage and graft against the Longs, or the "do-nothingism" and favoritism toward vested interests of the opposition, the candidates attacked or defended the Kennedy administration, the Supreme Court, and federal authority in general. All these were easily seen as factors related to the race issue.

Each of the major candidates conceded top position in the first primary to "Chep" Morrison, who had decided to make the run for a third straight time, something of a record in Louisiana politics. The strategy became one of finding the issues and getting the support which would enable the candidate to capture the number two spot and thus become the candidate to defeat Morrison again in the runoff. The lineup of candidates seemed familiar enough as a split in the remnants of the Long forces produced two candidates: John J. McKeithen and Gillis Long. The former enjoyed the active backing of Mrs. Blanche Long, wife of the late "Uncle Earl," whose legislative floor leader McKeithen had been in 1948. McKeithen had gone on to become Public Service Commissioner in North Louisiana, the position from which both Huey Long and Jimmie Davis went to the governorship. Gillis Long, a young lawyer with a private practice in Washington, D.C., and experience as counsel for a congressional committee, had won the seat for Louisiana's Eighth Congressional District in 1962. A distant cousin of Senator Russell Long, Gillis had received his wholehearted endorsement after Russell decided against running himself, partly due, no doubt, to the legislature's failure to endorse a constitutional amendment in 1962 which would have allowed a governor to succeed himself with another four-year term.

A familiar figure on the anti-Long side was former Governor Robert F. Kennon who enjoyed the backing of business and industrial interests and whose known views on race and states' rights meant that at least some of the segregationists would back him. The fifth of the major candidates, State Superintendent of Schools Shelby Jackson was the other dyed-in-the-wool segregationist, who counted on his strength among teachers and professional educators to give him a base from which to expand his support.

The assassination of President Kennedy two weeks before the date of the primary produced an unknown effect on the outcome of that election. Its immediate effect was to require several of the candidates to radically alter their campaign strategy, as Kennon, Jackson, and McKeithen had been running hard against the "feds" in general and the Kennedys in particular. McKeithen had claimed that Washington had two candidates in the gubernatorial race, Gillis Long and Morrison; Morrison at that time was serving as the Kennedy-appointed Ambassador to the Organization of American States. Morrison, and to a lesser degree Long, could expect to gain whatever benefits might accrue from the tragedy.

Results of the first primary gave Morrison an identical percentage point lead (33 percent) as the first primary results in 1959. His closest rival was McKeithen with 17 percent of the total vote cast, much less than Davis had gained in 1959 (29 percent). Long (15 percent) missed gaining the second spot by a tantalizing less than twenty thousand votes, while but ten thousand votes behind Long was Kennon (14 percent) and the "soaring eagle" Shelby Jackson landed fifth with 12 percent of the total vote.

By the statistical method of quartile rankings it is possible to determine those parishes which exhibited the highest degree of affinity with the various candidates. A comparison of the Morrison support in both 1959 (Table 10–4) and 1963 reveals that the presence of this candidate served to crystalize the electoral forces on something other than the traditional pattern structured by thirty years of Longism. In both first primary elections, "Chep" Morrison received 66 percent of his total parish support among the sixteen of his top quarter. This contiguous set of parishes stretched from Pointe Coupee on the north to Iberia on the west, Lafourche and Jefferson on the south, and Orleans to the east. The pattern was identical for the two elections except that in 1963 Morrison lost St. Landry and Lafayette from the Southwest voter type area but gained East Baton Rouge from the Florida Parishes set and Ascension in the South Louisiana Planter Parishes. The amazing stability of Morrison support remained statewide (33 percent both time) and regionally as well. Morrison lost but 1.1 percent in his North Louisiana total and 1.5 percent in South Louisiana (14.0 to 12.9 and 42.0 to 40.5 respectively).

*Table 10–14*

TOP QUARTILE PARISH SUPPORT FOR MAJOR CANDIDATES, 1963,
BY VOTER TYPE AREAS

|  | | Morrison | McKeithen | Long | Kennon | Jackson |
|---|---|---|---|---|---|---|
| State Totals | | | | | | |
| Number | | 299,700 | 157,304 | 137,778 | 127,870 | 103,949 |
| Percent | | 33 | 17 | 15 | 14 | 12 |
| Percent | | | | | | |
| North La. | | 12.9 | 22.0 | 12.9 | 22.3 | 22.1 |
| South La. | | 40.5 | 15.6 | 16.0 | 11.1 | 7.5 |
| Percent Top Quarter of Total Vote | | 66 | 26 | 24 | 34 | 27 |
| Top Quarter by Voter Types Number of Parishes | | | | | | |
| North La. Hills | (8) | — | 1 | 2 | 5 | 5 |
| Macon Ridge | (3) | — | 3 | — | 2 | 2 |
| North La. Planter | (10) | — | 2 | — | 7 | 4 |
| Central Pine Hills | (7) | — | 6 | 2 | — | 1 |
| Florida Parishes | (8) | 1 | 2 | 3 | 1 | 4 |
| South La. Bayou | (8) | 5 | — | 2 | 1 | — |
| Southwest La. | (8) | — | 2 | 4 | — | — |
| Urban Areas | (2) | 2 | — | — | — | — |
| South La. Planter | (10) | 8 | — | 3 | — | — |
| | (64) | (16) | (16) | (16) | (16) | (16) |

McKeithen received his highest degree of support among the parishes within and adjacent to the Central Pine Hills in a diagonal line running from West Carroll on Macon Ridge to Beauregard Parish in the Southwest. At first glance this would seem to confirm his affinity to Longism, yet in reality McKeithen's top quarter support was a composite of the parishes found in Davis' and Noe's top quartile support in 1959. Thus three-fourths of the parishes in McKeithen's top support (thirteen of sixteen) had also been high in Davis or Noe support: four from Davis', five from Noe's, and four parishes which had been in both the Davis and Noe top support.

While Gillis Long had hoped to draw upon traditional Long support in North Louisiana, percentage-wise he ended up tied with Morrison for last place there, with but four parishes of his top quarter of support. Otherwise the top Gillis Long support was drawn rather equally from among South Louisiana voter type areas, in parishes that have traditionally backed Long candidates. Long cut into Morrison's strength in predominantly French parishes and where organized labor made up a sizable proportion of the electorate. In fact, Long was runner-up to Morrison in fourteen parishes. Gillis Long had cultivated a folksy style that was meant to be and has been compared to that of Earl Long at his best. At the same time, he had a breadth of political experience denied most home-grown politicians and had managed to attract backers ("young men for Gillis Long") from a potentially new element in Louisiana politics—a rising class of young business and professional men whose call for a new look in Louisiana politics is similar to a development that has taken place nationally. There had seemed to be a potential tendency here which might have created a new base in South Louisiana for the liberalism of Longism, and had it not competed with the Morrison style and lost its chance as the Negro vote went solid in backing "Chep" Morrison, quite likely Gillis Long would have entered the runoff.

The two candidates on the most conservative end of the array of candidates, Kennon and Jackson, tended to split the vote between themselves in North Louisiana, where their upper quarter parishes were located. Jackson, however, had also gained support in four Florida Parishes while Kennon's top quarter included East Feliciana and Plaquemines parishes. Jackson had carried plurality votes in a total of thirteen parishes which had been second only to the twenty-six carried by Morrison, while Kennon had carried pluralities in but ten parishes. Kennon had been runner-up in seven of the parishes of Jackson pluralities while Jackson was also runner-up in seven of the parishes won with a plurality by Kennon. Quite obviously, had the conservative and segregationist vote been united behind one candidate, he would have made the runoff. Kennon would have had the better chance because of fears of business and industrial interests that Jackson's extreme position on racial matters would damage the state's economic development.

Like 1959, then, the Morrison support was seated in South Louisiana French country and whatever the alignments which obtained for the other candidates, it was obvious that Morrison simply attained the maximum ceiling he had reached before. Kennon and Jackson took the top spots held by Davis and Rainach in North Louisiana in 1959, while to the South, Gillis Long took the second place position which had belonged to Jimmie Davis. McKeithen, in winning the number two spot statewide, found himself in the third position in both regions of the state. Still, it was obvious that the political cards were stacked against Morrison as McKeithen would easily receive the bulk of the Kennon and Jackson votes in a showdown against Morrison.

*Table 10–15*

McKeithen Vote, 1964, Second Primary by Voter Type Areas

| | | Average Percent | Number of Parishes | | | |
|---|---|---|---|---|---|---|
| | | | 0–39% | 40–49% | 50–59% | 60–100% |
| North La. Hills | (8) | 80 | — | — | — | 8 |
| Macon Ridge | (3) | 89 | — | — | — | 3 |
| North La. Planter | (10) | 77 | — | — | — | 10 |
| Central Pine Hills | (7) | 82 | — | — | — | 7 |
| Florida Parishes | (8) | 58 | — | 1 | 1 | 6 |
| South La. Bayou | (8) | 54 | 4 | 2 | 1 | 1 |
| Southwest La. | (10) | 51 | 1 | 2 | 5 | 2 |
| Urban Area | (2) | 34 | 2 | — | — | — |
| South La. Planter | (8) | 36 | 4 | 4 | — | — |
| | (64) | | (11) | (9) | (7) | (37) |

In point of fact, with the disruptive tendencies of 1959 remaining in evidence, McKeithen won the governorship in the 1964 second primary by receiving 52.2 percent of 944,066 votes cast, and carrying forty-four parishes to the forty-one carried by Davis four years previously. McKeithen had gained majority support in all the parishes carried by Davis but one, East Baton Rouge (which went for Morrison), and carried three more than Davis, Acadia, Evangeline, and Vermilion. The distribution of the McKeithen support by voter types was almost a carbon copy of the 1960 Davis vote (Table 10–9). While the coefficient of correlation between average percent Davis and McKeithen by voter types was a high +.901, as a manifestation of McKeithen's being at least "half a Long" his majority support was extended into Southwest Louisiana as was shown above.

John J. McKeithen was not through campaigning, as the state Republican organization which had intermittently offered statewide tickets mounted opposition with the candidacy of Shreveport business-man Charlton Lyons. Modern day Republicanism in Louisiana had been extended from the single concern with presidential politics beginning around 1952 and, particularly in the Shreveport area, efforts had been made to build a grass-roots party organization.[11] Lyons charged McKeithen with being the machine candidate, voiced the need for a two-party politics, and claimed the Republican chances for bringing a real change for the better in Louisiana government were good. Political pundits advanced the opinion that the Democratic nominee gave Lyons unnecessary advantage by taking his candidacy seriously, but McKeithen's energetic campaign for the March 3, 1964, general election of governor proved his evaluation to be correct. The remarkable political intuition of Governor McKeithen, of which this was an example, will be discussed in the following section.

Increased Republican strength across the state was seen as election time approached. The urban tendency towards increased Republican sentiments was already there to build upon. This was coupled with the bitterness engendered by the recent gubernatorial primaries which led segments of the "Chep" Morrison and Gillis Long forces, to say nothing of the Bob Kennon and Shelby Jackson people, to work

[11] Kenneth N. Vines, *Two Parties for Shreveport* (New York, n.d.), Eagleton Institute Cases in Practical Politics.

openly for Lyons.[12] To combat this threat to party unity, McKeithen in late February announced a number of provisional appointments which included persuading Morrison to head a crash program for new industry and Shelby Jackson a program on Americanism. Kennon was reported to have turned down a similar position. McKeithen also managed to get shelved a fight in the state central committee between segregationist and loyal Democrats over a so-called free presidential electors plan. The Democratic nominee stumped the state in an effort to get out the vote and reversed the charges of machine politics. His nomination had been the result of choices on the part of close to one million Democratic voters, while Lyons had been hand-picked by the few men who sat on the Republican State Central Committee. As McKeithen put it, he had won his Democratic nomination for governor in two tough primaries over "giants of Louisiana public life," while his Republican opponent merely used a postage stamp.[13] McKeithen added that he remained uncommitted and uncontrolled and that with little organization and less newspaper support he had been backed by the people, to whom the next four years would be dedicated.

In the general election, Democratic nominee, John J. McKeithen beat back the strongest Republican challenge in almost a century by gaining 61 percent of the more than 725,000 votes cast, only 200,000 short of the record total in the heated second primary. Lyons gained far more votes than the 83,000 polled by Francis Grevemberg in 1960 against Governor Davis, and as was to be expected, scored his heaviest gains in the urban areas. He won big in Shreveport but fared less well in such urban centers as Baton Rouge, Lake Charles, and New Orleans. The general profile of Lyons support can be seen in the quartile distribution of his vote by voter type areas (Table 10–16). Both candidates had professed to be for segregation, but in the planter and hill parishes in the northwest corner of the state, where Willie Rainach had counted his greatest support, the affinity with the Republicans proved greatest. The five Louisiana parishes Lyons

[12] *Morning Advocate*, February 2, 1964, "Capital Beat," Margaret Dixon, Sec. B, p. 5.
[13] *Morning Advocate*, February 21, 1964, Sec. A, p. 4.

*Table 10–16*
CHARLTON LYONS, GENERAL ELECTION, 1964,
QUARTILE DISTRIBUTION OF PARISH VOTE BY VOTER TYPE AREAS

|  |  | Average Percent | 7–22% | 23–30% | 31–42% | 43–71% |
|---|---|---|---|---|---|---|
| North La. Hills | (8) | 39 | — | 2 | 3 | 3 |
| Macon Ridge | (3) | 25 | 1 | 1 | 1 | — |
| North La. Planter | (10) | 44 | — | — | 5 | 5 |
| Central Pine Hills | (7) | 22 | 5 | 1 | 1 | — |
| Florida Parishes | (8) | 27 | 4 | 1 | 2 | 1 |
| South La. Bayou | (8) | 27 | 2 | 4 | 1 | 1 |
| Southwest La. | (10) | 31 | 2 | 4 | 1 | 3 |
| Urban Area | (2) | 44 | — | — | — | 2 |
| South La. Planter | (8) | 29 | — | 5 | 2 | 1 |
|  | (64) |  | (14) | (18) | (16) | (16) |

carried were Bossier, Caddo, Claiborne, DeSoto, and Lincoln. The Perez stronghold in the opposite corner of the state, however, held the line most solidly for McKeithen. Superficially, Lyons' Republicanism seemed to be the "new" presidential type which has been accounted for as a radical search for an alternative to the modernity of the national Democrats. Superficial parallel with the traditional pattern of Longism is also seen in the manner in which Central Pine Hill and Florida Parishes fell in the lowest quarter of conservative Lyon support. The place where the Lyons vote most nearly followed expectation, however, was in the urban parishes where, aside from the parishes already mentioned above, Lyons received his greatest support.

A number of factors can be listed which in combination, perhaps, explain the positive association between Morrison and Lyons urban South Louisiana votes. These include the traditional anti-Long urban vote, moderates alienated by McKeithen's use of the race issue and his attack on the national administration, increasing urban Republican sentiment, and Morrison supporters bitter that their candidate—seemingly incapable of losing just weeks before—had experienced his third and perhaps last defeat. (Later in the summer Mr. Morrison met untimely death in an airplane crash.)[14]

Table 10–17
LYONS AND MORRISON PERCENTAGE VOTE IN URBAN PARISHES

|  | Morrison | | Lyons |
|  | 1960 | 1964 | 1964 |
| --- | --- | --- | --- |
| Orleans | 57 | 64 | 44 |
| Jefferson | 55 | 61 | 43 |
| East Baton Rouge | 45 | 55 | 48 |
| Lafayette | 67 | 62 | 45 |
| Calcasieu | 43 | 49.7 | 44 |
| Rapides | 35 | 37 | 37 |
| Ouachita | 25 | 23 | 40 |
| Caddo | 27 | 28 | 71 |

There was little consistency overall, with the Lyons support and that of other elections:

Table 10–18
RANK ORDER COEFFICIENTS OF CORRELATION BETWEEN LYONS, 1964,
AND SELECTED ELECTIONS BY VOTER TYPE AREA PERCENTS

|  | Morrison | Eisenhower | Johnson |
|  | 1964 | 1956 | 1964 |
| --- | --- | --- | --- |
| Positive: | .525 | .258 | .185 |

| States' Rights 1960 | Goldwater 1964 | Stevenson 1956 | States' Rights 1948 | Kennedy 1960 | McKeithen 1964 | Nixon 1960 | Average Long 1928–56 |
| --- | --- | --- | --- | --- | --- | --- | --- |
| Negative: | | | | | | | |
| .052 | .075 | .092 | .100 | .425 | .508 | .675 | .732 |

The Lyons pattern of support among the voter types showed paradoxical affinities such that while the highest positive association was

[14] Tapp, "Election of 1964." 85.

found to be with the Morrison support in the recent second primary, an almost equally as high negative association existed between Lyons and Kennedy support. Nixon's 1960 support associates but slightly higher negative than does McKeithen's second primary support and the average support for Longism. There was more association, and positive at that, between the Johnson than between the Goldwater support in 1964. The Lyons vote was a strange interlude in a series of elections in which a pattern of cleavage had appeared, dividing North and South Louisiana in general over the question of race, but with enough segregation sentiment in South Louisiana parishes to affect the balance.

In the direction of state affairs Louisiana voters had chosen to stay with the kind of leadership to which they were accustomed, reassured, no doubt, that they were safe on race either way. It had been demonstrated, however, that a Republican vote could be mobilized, and the state organization of that party saw the chance to exploit the potential in the forthcoming presidential election. Many asserted the day of two-party politics had come when in November Senator Barry Goldwater swept the state's ten electoral votes. But with nominal Democrats such as the incumbent secretary of state and the lieutenant governor backing the Republicans, (Governor McKeithen sat out the election, but later claimed he was one southern leader who did not back President Johnson) and with Louisiana only one of five Southern states which joined Arizona in support of Goldwater, an answer to the question of what the vote meant must now be sought.

As racial tensions increased in the early 1960's and as dissatisfaction with the manner in which Presidents Kennedy and Johnson implemented civil rights legislation gripped the white electorate in the Deep South, the segregation issue was easily exploited in local and state elections, and with a candidate who declared himself champion of southern states' rights, it was more susceptible to exploitation at the presidential level. "White electorates in the Deep South responded much as their grandfathers would have. They voted for what they perceived to be the 'candidate of the southern white man.'"[15] The

---

[15] Bernard Cosman, *Five States for Goldwater* (University, Ala. 1966), 62.

empirical evidence of this is found in the Goldwater support which followed the line of counties outlining a "total crescent" ranging from South Carolina, through Georgia, Alabama, Mississippi, and into the parishes of North Louisiana.[16] It was perfectly clear to everyone, including the voters, that this vote was the continuation of protest, a compulsion almost to seek to support that which held most promise of perpetuating the identity of the traditional South, manifest since 1948.

President Johnson, the Democratic candidate for reelection, received but 43 percent of the 896,293 total votes cast in a Louisiana presidential race which provided the highest percentage turnout of registered voters (73 percent) since 1868. Almost 100,000 more voters cast ballots in 1964 than in the 1960 election. Louisiana joined her sister states of the old Confederacy in providing 62 percent of the counties of the United States carried by Goldwater. Their distribution was pronounced in Louisiana, however, as Goldwater swept North Louisiana with the same solidarity Republican and States' Rights had enjoyed last time, while Johnson carried twenty-two parishes in South Louisiana. (Map 10–2) In fact the 1964 presidential election results in Louisiana correlate significantly with each of the preceding elections discussed in Chapter 9 where the northern parishes of the state had supported other than the Democrats while the southern parishes tended to support the Democratic Party with majority votes (Table 9–5). Thus the Johnson support by voter type areas showed affinity with the Democratic vote in 1928 (+.600), 1948 (+.891), 1956 (+.748), and the most recent Kennedy vote, in 1960 (+.933).[17]

The remarkable stability in the pattern of voting behavior since 1960 could be seen in the parish distribution of the Johnson vote in comparison with that for his counterpart Kennedy in the previous presidential election (Table 10–12).

[16] Perry H. Howard and Joseph L. Brent III, "Social Change, Urbanization, and Types of Society," *Journal of Social Issues*, XXII (1966), 80.

[17] Compare William Nolan Kammer, "Louisiana's Electoral Alignments and the Presidential Vote in 1964," *Southwestern Social Science Quarterly*, XVIII (1966), 127–35.

# Presidential Democratic Vote, 1964

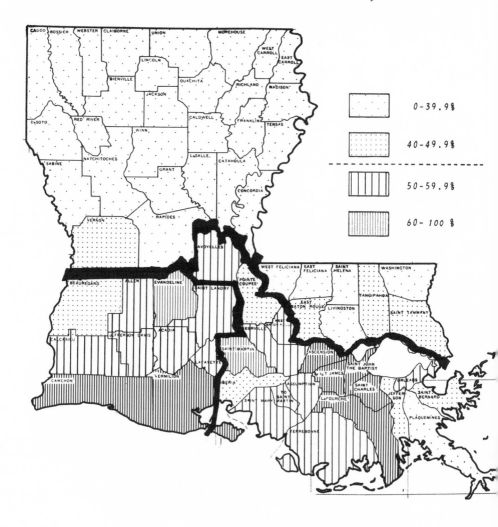

*Table 10–19*

JOHNSON VOTE, 1964, BY VOTER TYPE AREAS

| | | Average Percent | Number of Parishes | | | |
|---|---|---|---|---|---|---|
| | | | 0–39% | 40–49% | 50–59% | 60–100% |
| North La. Hills | (8) | 20 | 8 | — | — | — |
| Macon Ridge | (3) | 13 | 3 | — | — | — |
| North La. Planter | (10) | 18 | 10 | — | — | — |
| Central Pine Hills | (7) | 27 | 6 | 1 | — | — |
| Florida Parishes | (8) | 36 | 5 | 3 | — | — |
| South La. Bayou | (8) | 50 | 1 | 2 | 3 | 2 |
| Southwest La. | (10) | 57 | — | 1 | 6 | 3 |
| Urban Area | (2) | 48 | — | 1 | 1 | — |
| South La. Planter | (8) | 59 | — | 1 | 3 | 4 |
| | (64) | | (33) | (9) | (13) | (9) |

With the exception of two voter type areas, North Louisiana Hills and Macon Ridge, the rank order of average percents was the same for 1960 Kennedy and 1964 Johnson support. The two exceptions swapped ninth and seventh place as all voter units recorded lower percentage Democratic support in 1964. The effect of this is seen in the tendency of South Louisiana parishes to move into the 50–59 percent interval in 1964 whereas the number of majority parishes decreased but two. Still this was enough to push the Morrison-Johnson rank order coefficient of correlation by voter type average percents downward (+.840) from the Morrison-Kennedy association (+.936).

Bernard Cosman has pointed out that aggregationist studies as well as survey research agree that in southern urban areas the multi-class solidity of the region's presidential vote has given way to class cleavage.[18] But Cosman questioned whether the Republican vote would continue to parallel the socioeconomic differentials (as has been shown above for Louisiana) among a racially aroused metropolitan electorate, and his answer was that, as in Birmingham, the Goldwater candidacy all but eliminated polarization of the vote along class lines.

[18] Cosman, *Five States for Goldwater*, 82 ff.

Much the same pattern has been reported for Louisiana cities,[19] although here the similarity among upper white and white labor precincts was not so great, and the general level of Democratic support since 1952 had remained higher. This may be explained as being a reflection of the more liberal atmosphere of Louisiana politics as a function of leadership in the Long era.

*Table 10–20*
PERCENTAGE REPUBLICAN VOTE IN SHREVEPORT AND NEW ORLEANS, 1952 AND 1964, BY TYPE OF PRECINCT

|  | SHREVEPORT | | New Orleans | |
|  | Upper White | White Labor | Upper White | White Labor |
|---|---|---|---|---|
| 1952 | 15% | 35% | 24% | 58% |
| 1964 | 13 | 19 | 37 | 41 |
| Difference | − 2 | − 16 | + 13 | − 17 |

According to expectation, however, while in 1952 the difference between upper white and white labor support in Shreveport and New Orleans was in the range of 20 and 34 percent, respectively, in 1964 the class differential was but 6 and 4 percent. Much the same convergence can be demonstrated by computing the percentage Eisenhower and Goldwater votes in urban and rural wards for North and South Louisiana.

*Table 20–21*
EISENHOWER, 1952, AND GOLDWATER, 1964, PERCENTAGES OF TOTAL VOTE CAST IN URBAN AND RURAL WARDS IN NORTH AND SOUTH LOUISIANA

|  | Eisenhower | | Goldwater | |
|  | Urban | Rural | Urban | Rural |
|---|---|---|---|---|
| North Louisiana | 56.3% | 44.4% | 76.3% | 79.4% |
| South Louisiana | 47.7 | 39.3 | 47.0 | 47.4 |

[19] Howard and Brent, Table 2, p. 81.

In 1952 the Republican tendency was not so pronounced since the Long leadership supported the candidacy of Governor Stevenson and, at that time, the Eisenhower support was clearly more an urban phenomenon. In 1964, however, with Governor McKeithen refusing to take sides, not only was the Republican support higher in North than South Louisiana, but also the urban-rural difference was almost eliminated.

As Cosman put it in summary statement: "A politics of section, whether based on race or some other shared interest, tends to bring together men of all social strata in a single political party. . . . In 1964, the Deep South vote polarized around race."[20] So it was in Louisiana in the elections of 1960 and 1964.

## II. The McKeithen Phenomenon*

John J. McKeithen's gubernatorial career has been unprecedented. Beginning as something of a dark horse[21] he campaigned successfully through two heated primaries and a general election hotly contested by the Republicans. He led a legislature willing to implement his campaign promises and busied himself with upgrading the image of Louisiana in order to accelerate the attraction of new industry. He confronted the race issue head on and bluntly declared that in Louisiana there would prevail law and order. In fact, the most important action of Governor McKeithen has been the apparent manner with which he intended to use the great power inherent in the office of governor in Louisiana. That power would be used, not to perpetuate the inhibiting structure of white supremacy, but to solve the problems attendant upon Louisiana's rightful place in twentieth-century America. Something of the nature of this phenomenon may be gained by reviewing the campaign tactics of John J. McKeithen.

The literature on the techniques of campaigning for office within the modern democratic state is sparse and scattered, for the art has

* With Joseph B. Parker.

[20] Cosman, *Five States for Goldwater*, 90.

[21] See the somewhat inaccurate estimation in William C. Havard, Rudolf Heberle, and Perry H. Howard, *The Louisiana Elections of 1960* (Baton Rouge, 1963).

been nurtured on the local level and within the traditions of party organizations. Not until the advent of television has this hallowed know-how been threatened with destruction as the newest media of mass communication changed the rules of the game, making it possible for the candidate to appear simultaneously in the living rooms of all those who choose to keep the set on.

The 1960 presidential campaign TV debates dramatically revealed the import of the image the candidate could project through this medium. It was in the same year that TV became significant statewide in Louisiana, although even then, only the "cosmopolitan" candidate, the late "Chep" Morrison made major use of it. In the 1956 campaign "Uncle Earl" Long avoided the contraption altogether, reached the voters from the stump in the traditional manner, and romped home in the first primary. But by 1964 television had found its way into virtually every rural hamlet, and the test was made to see whether candidates would be able to translate the old-time campaign techniques to the now ubiquitous medium.

Louisiana politics has frequently captured the attention of the nation through mass communication media. While many journalistic observers continue to be woefully lacking in their perceptiveness of the essence of the political process in this southern state, they have accurately discerned that politics takes on the characteristics of a "state religion" in Louisiana. In his amusing and insightful treatment of the late Earl K. Long's career, A. J. Liebling compared Louisiana's political style to that of the Mediterranean littoral and Latin America. In terms of the intensity with which the political game is played, there is little doubt that Liebling's analogy was appropriate. This intensity carries the drive of a mass politics, in the case of Louisiana on a rural populist basis, where, as the winning candidate in 1964 remarked in populist egalitarian rhetoric that his election proved that any mother's son could become governor of Louisiana.

Since political factions, unlike political parties, tend to be based on loyalty to an individual or small group of individuals, they are often ephemeral. Passing the mantle of the leader is not easy, especially when candidates for that leadership are numerous. Part of the interest in Longism stemmed from the continuity that such a political family was able to fashion amidst adversity. Now that "Uncle Earl" was dead, and with no Long candidate in the runoff in 1960, the question on the lips of Louisiana politicians was what would happen in 1964?

Senator Russell B. Long, son of Huey and nephew of Earl, was heir apparent to the Long leadership. Russell is in looks, speech, and political philosophy a toned down version of his flamboyant father. At thirty, he was elected to the Senate. After his 1948 election to an unexpired term, he had no difficulty in holding his Senate seat in three subsequent elections. Upon the death of Robert Kerr in 1962, Long became the second ranking Democrat on the powerful Senate Finance Committee and when Chairman Harry Flood Byrd, in his seventies and in poor health, finally stepped down, Long became the chairman. Under the Johnson administration Russell Long became Senate whip. Furthermore, the folkways of the Senate could allow him to remain committee chairman as long as the Democratic Party is in the majority or as long as he lives—in either case, under normal circumstances, a good while.

In spite of his seniority in the Senate, Russell Long seriously considered running for governor in 1963. Political gossip reported that he dismissed the idea after a proposal to remove the state constitutional prohibition upon a governor serving more than one consecutive term failed to pass the legislature in 1962. When it became apparent that Russell would not run, the Long forces began an intensive search for a good candidate.

It is hardly an exaggeration to say that the race for governor in Louisiana begins four years before the election. The governor is in effect a "lame duck" from the outset of his term, and would-be contenders cast a covetous eye upon the office, for the Louisiana governorship is one of the strongest among the fifty states. On the day after the Democratic runoff primary, the unsuccessful contenders begin mapping their strategies for next time. The loser in the second primary is severely handicapped because at least three or four candidates defeated in the first primary have gotten a thirty-day lead on him. This is not to mention a number of other potential gubernatorial candidates who had run for lesser offices such as lieutenant governor, attorney general, or state superintendent of education. In

Louisiana politics as in horse racing (with which the analogy is close) a strong runner in the field frequently scares away many of the competitors, who move to lesser races.

For three years this shuffling period continues. Numerous "loners" break off from their respective packs to take a chance at making a name for themselves. Most officials elected statewide automatically consider themselves gubernatorial material. The short ballot movement had little success in Louisiana where there are ten executive offices, other than governor, filled by the electorate of the entire state. There are always a number of hopefuls in the state legislature as well as mayors, the state's congressional delegation, and the state judiciary. Talking about one's candidacy for governor is easy and inexpensive and, moreover, it is fun and ego-building, a game that takes only one to play.

The last year prior to the qualifying date is a period of more serious milling. The number of potential candidates shrinks to a numerically impressive group of twenty or so. The search for support, especially financial, becomes very intense at this stage. A number of potentials face reality and decide either to "drop down in money" and run for lesser state offices on the ticket of one of the other candidates, or to hang on in their present offices and wait for another chance. When this process is completed, there are five or six serious contenders, plus three or four "nuisance candidates" who run for fun. The filing fee for governor in 1964 was only $250.

After the death of Earl K. Long in 1960 and the colorless and seemingly fumbling administration of Governor Jimmie H. Davis, it became apparent that the 1964 election would be a real "horse race" with Long supporters attempting to engineer a comeback and the opposition out to capitalize on the disarray of the Long forces. With Russell Long out of the running most observers felt it could be anybody's race.

Two candidates were in the running early. Former Governor Robert F. Kennon (1952–56) never stopped running after his election in 1952. He was ineligible to succeed himself in 1956, and he felt the time was not right in 1960; but he maintained his contacts around the state, and as a moving force in the Democrats-for-Eisenhower movements in 1952 and 1956, he was in the political limelight. Kennon was recognized as a strong segregationist, a states' rights spokesman, and promoter of a right-to-work law. He was regarded as a "good gum-shoe politician" effective as a stump campaigner and handshaker in small, face-to-face settings. But his inability to communicate effectively via the medium of television in a state that had experienced the expansion of the urban labor force in the twelve years since his last campaign left many questions about his chances. Kennon loomed as the strong contender within the anti-Long entries during the shuffling period.

The next candidate out was Public Service Commissioner John J. McKeithen, who announced his intention to seek the governorship shortly after Earl Long's death. McKeithen was a protege of Earl Long, serving as Long's floor leader in the House of Representatives from 1948 to 1952. In the latter year, he ran for lieutenant governor on the Long-endorsed ticket of Spaht-McKeithen which met defeat in the runoff primary. Two years later McKeithen was elected to his present position from the district which Huey P. Long once represented and where Huey had made his reputation by fighting oil companies and railroads on behalf of the "little man." McKeithen followed his example, choosing the Southern Bell Telephone Company as his target. He was instrumental in establishing the rate for pay phones at five cents.

McKeithen had his problems. Though he had been a candidate for statewide office in 1952 he did not gain great prestige from the race. At that time he was a thirty-three-year-old state representative running on Earl Long's selected ticket in a campaign in which Earl was the dominant figure. In addition, McKeithen hailed from one of the most sparsely populated parishes in the state, and he represented the smallest of Louisiana's three public service districts. Furthermore, Russell Long was cool to the McKeithen candidacy. One characteristic of Long leadership had been its reluctance to share control with those who do not bear the Long name. Moreover, a public opinion poll conducted a year before the election by a potential gubernatorial candidate did not augur well for McKeithen's candidacy. After seeing the results of the poll, Senator Long and many of the

Long stalwarts began to look to other quarters for a Long standard
bearer. They did not have to look far.

In the 1962 congressional elections another Long had made his debut
in Louisiana politics. Gillis W. Long, Russell's fifth cousin, was
elected to Congress from the Eighth District. Gillis Long graduated
from Louisiana State University Law School and went to Washington
to seek his political fortune. After Earl Long's death in 1960, he
returned to his home in Alexandria and began to set the stage for a
race for the congressional seat. In the campaign he demonstrated he
had profited from his behind-the-scenes participation in several
of Uncle Earl's political battles. A vigorous campaigner, he developed
a most effective brand of folksiness on the stump. Upon defeating
the incumbent and another opponent with impressive ease, Gillis
Long immediately became gubernatorial material.

Knowing the rules of the game, Gillis did not discourage talk of
his possible candidacy. Sources close to him contended that Long
was reluctant to seek the governorship so early in his political career
because he felt his chances for success would be increased by serving in
Congress three terms before making a run for the governor's office in
1968. However, he was easily convinced that the should enter the race.
In May of 1963 Senator Russell Long announced his support for
Gillis, and he was "off and running." His candidacy severely divided
the Long camp, and both Gillis and John McKeithen fought for
leadership of Longism.

Division within the Long camp was paralleled by division among
the opposition. DeLesseps Morrison confused the issue by making
it known that he would be in the "parade to the post." Morrison had
proved his ability as a "sprinter," but left some doubts about winning
the distance race. Hardly out of his World War II army uniform,
Morrison was elected mayor of New Orleans in 1946 on the wave of
a reform movement. From that time forward he was to occupy a
politically enviable position in the city. He retained the image of
reformer who had defeated a decadent political machine which had
dominated New Orleans politics for half a century. At the same time
he built a well-oiled machine of his own, the Crescent City Democratic
Association, which retained an aura of respectability.

The last three of Morrison's four elections as mayor of New Orleans were accomplished with relative ease. His success was the result of such factors as ample financial backing by economically influential persons of the community, his organization support, his image as a reformer among the middle classes, and the increased Negro voter registration. He had run for governor in 1956 and was defeated overwhelmingly by Earl Long. But being defeated by Earl Long was not such a disgrace; quite a few others had suffered the same fate. Running again in 1960 he led the field in the first primary but lost the runoff for the reasons enumerated above. The folklore of Louisiana politics warns that a two-time loser is wasting his time in running for governor again. Many political observers felt that Morrison would be overwhelmed by the prevailing norms, especially when he faced the rather dismal task of raising the approximately one million dollars required for a serious campaign for governor.

The field of candidates continued to grow with the entry of Shelby M. Jackson, state superintendent of education. Jackson had been elected first to the education post in 1948 and during his fifteen years in the office became one of the political powers to be reckoned with. He had contemplated making the race for governor in 1956 and 1960 but decided at the last minute to run for superintendent instead. It is probable that he never intended to run for governor on these occasions, but wanted to be in a strong bargaining position vis-a-vis the other candidates for governor when they selected the people to run on their tickets. If that had been Jackson's plan it had been a tremendously successful one.

Other factors pushed Jackson into the race. After the desegregation decision in 1954 he made a serious claim, (along with a cast of thousands) for the leadership of the racist forces. Since the schools have been the main target of the desegregation suits, his claim to be "one thousand percent for segregation" seemed creditable, not because of success in his resistive efforts, but on the basis of his vocal resistance (at that time talking a good segregationist line appeared more important than substantive achievement), and the fact that he was often the named defendant in desegregation suits. In 1960 Jackson was cited for contempt of court and given a suspended sentence by

Federal District Court Judge J. Skelly Wright. Almost immediately thereafter he claimed to be suffering an attack of asthma, and with help of some logical gymnastics he blamed this on the "usurping, dictatorial federal government" and, claiming he would go to jail in defense of "our Southern way of life," he went to the hospital instead. Adding to his segregation appeal Jackson jumped on the "anti-Communist" bandwagon during 1960–61 and instituted programs of instruction in "Communism versus Americanism" in high schools and colleges under the jurisdiction of the state board of education. Commonists (the colloquial expression), were held to be synonymous with "nigger-agitators." Finally, it could be observed that William J. Dodd, another political power in the state and at that time serving as president of the elected state board of education, announced for the position of superintendent.

In 1964 there were two "semi-serious" candidates in the race. Louis J. Michot, a state representative from Lafayette, made known his intentions to run early in the summer of 1963. In the state legislature he had earned a reputation as a reform advocate and as a moderate on the race issue. His moral courage in fighting the "massive resistance" forces in the abortive special sessions of the legislature in 1960–61 was a source of encouragement to moderate forces in Louisiana. Though not very well known beyond his home parish, he looked like a potentially serious threat as a candidate with a reform image. His lack of financial resources doomed him to the status of a semi-serious candidate.

The other semi-serious candidate was Claude Kirkpatrick, state director of public works. Kirkpatrick had served twelve years in the Louisiana House of Representatives and in 1960 had been one of Jimmie Davis' district campaign managers. He was appointed to his present job by Governor Davis and immediately began running for governor. His post, however, did not provide a good jumping-off spot and he too was plagued by a lack of money. Kirkpatrick and Michot were running outside their class and never challenged the pace setters.

Gubernatorial elections in Louisiana always provide a source of comic relief, and some of this entertainment comes from the "nuisance candidates." In this election there were three. Wilford L. Thompson of Zachary did little or no campaigning, but the other two were in the thick of it. Perennial candidate Roswell Thompson was a New Orleans taxi driver whose claim to fame was as chairman of the Society for the Preservation of Southern Traditions. He promised to maintain (or reestablish) segregation in the schools by placing goon squads (though he did not give them this name) in each integrated school to "scare the niggers out." A newcomer was Hugh E. Lasseigne, a Baton Rouge salesman who had been an ardent fan of President Kennedy. He claimed segregation was a problem to be solved but not an issue in the campaign. His frankness and open admission that he did not have a chance made him an interesting candidate and occasionally the most intelligent sounding man in the lot. Lasseigne was present at inauguration ceremonies on May 12, 1964; he was selling umbrellas to a crowd caught unexpectedly in a summer cloudburst.

About eighteen months prior to an election the potential candidates begin to be carefully looked over at the courthouse squares, country stores, and especially by economically influential persons who will be financing the big race. The pace of the potential candidates quickens at this point; they appear at more and more civic gatherings, make more public statements, and do considerable negotiating with local political figures, and begin to line up their tickets. During this stage they are reluctant to announce what everybody knows they are: candidates for governor.

Another piece of folklore of Louisiana politics has it that a candidate should not start running too early. Timing is reputed to be a delicate matter, a candidate should not announce too soon, nor make too many stump speeches and TV appearances too early. At the same time, a candidate should not wait too late. All of this means relatively little in the concrete; after the election every self-styled political pundit in the state will tell how the winner had a perfect sense of timing, making all the right moves, and how his opponent made one mistake after another.

According to prevailing customs, McKeithen erred in making known his intention to run for governor more than two years prior to the election. He began to campaign on a full-time basis a year prior to the election. He made the courthouse circuit and appeared at every meeting to which he could wrangle an invitation. All the "experts" were saying he was setting his pace too fast and that he would be a "too much too soon"candidate who would fade when the real run began. Jackson, Kennon, Morrison, and Long set a slower pace, reserving their strength while McKeithen was out "shaking the bushes" for votes.

The Fourth of July is the more or less official start for campaigning in Louisiana. The town of Ville Platte in famous Cajun country sponsors a "speaking" which most candidates participate in. Many were there in 1963, though Gillis Long and John McKeithen were elsewhere. They had attended the dedication of a monument to the memory of Earl K. Long at Winnfield. Morrison, speaking at Ville Platte, talked about his role in the fight against communism in the Western Hemisphere, as Kennedy's Ambassador to the Organization of American States. He appeared tired from his travels between Washington and Louisiana, his speech was dull, and he seemed out of touch with the Louisiana political scene.

Gillis Long was involved in the action of the United States Congress during the months of July and August, and his absence from the Louisiana scene proved to be a serious setback to his campaign. He urgently needed to expose himself to the Louisiana voter and relied upon TV to overcome the fact that he was relatively unknown. He handled the medium effectively and shaped his program around "jobs and education," stressing that unemployment was high in the state and that the way out was an accelerated education program. While this was a good program upon which to run, it turned out to be too much a "bread and butter" issue, and, like motherhood, it was something all other candidates came to endorse. In his first major TV appearance Gillis Long sounded like a racial moderate, stating that the race question could not be settled in the streets and that as governor he would maintain law and order. He did not belabor the issue at great length at any point in the campaign, stating at several points that he would deal with issues he could do something about. Avoidance of the race issue, it should be noted, was generally interpreted in Louisiana as an indication that the candidate was a moderate.

Former Governor Robert Kennon pitched his campaign in a conservative, segregationist tone. His great claim to fame was his bolting of the Democratic Party in 1952, and in his speeches he blasted the national Democratic Party as a socialist body and made President Kennedy the target of his most venomous remarks. He sponsored statewide TV programs under the title "Kennon vs. the Party." Kennon had the support of Congressman Otto E. Passman, who had earned his reputation as an opponent of foreign aid and as a frequent Democratic Party critic, as well as support from Congressman Joe Waggoner, a segregationist from the Fourth Congressional District. Frank Voelker, Chairman of the State Sovereignty Commission (the official segregation agency of the state) and a potential candidate up to the qualification date, became Kennon's campaign manager.

Kennon's campaign was somewhat unique. Having served as governor he assumed that he had an edge over the other candidates and did not attend many of the meetings at which all the other candidates appeared as a panel, until late in the campaign. The former governor did not handle the TV medium effectively and after a few appearances early in the race he used it very sparingly. But Kennon had other things going for him. He got the endorsement of Leander Perez, the boss of Plaquemines Parish and one of the most extremist and powerful segregationists in the state.

Kennon did not have sole claim to the leadership of the segregationist forces, however, as Shelby Jackson was in the race to stay and pitched his campaign almost totally on the racial issue. It was soon obvious that he would do serious damage to Kennon by taking a sizable share of the conservative vote. He received the support of many of the most vocal segregation leaders. Late in the campaign several of the candidates questioned Kennon's segregationist credentials since he had, after all, supported President Eisenhower, the man who appointed Earl Warren to the Supreme Court and who sent the troops to Little Rock, Arkansas. It was revealed that Kennon had stated Warren would make a great Chief Justice. This was a damaging blow to the claims of the former governor, and he became regarded as a sort of left-wing segregationist, while Jackson could claim to be untainted.

John J. McKeithen floundered for the issues in August and September. In his early TV appearance he had proposed that the state finance the care of cemeteries, promised to campaign against "smut literature," and that he would institute a system whereby any citizen could get a brief session with the governor on particular days. This was not a very impressive program, but he found another issue. He set out to establish himself as the real opposition to the incumbent administration of Governor Davis. He branded himself as an "uncontrolled" candidate and set out to pin the "controlled" label on his major opponents—controlled by Washington, the monied interests, or the Davis administration. His attack was not very subtle, but it was effective in counterposing him against a rather unpopular governor. He ran frequent one-minute "spots" on TV which ended with "Clean Up the Mess in Baton Rouge." McKeithen was carving out for himself a reform image.

Reformers in Louisiana have enjoyed some political success, but they have generally been obsessed with the form of government, stressing civil service and administrative efficiency. The Longs had been rather successful in fighting the reformers by pushing their own kind of reform in the shape of "benefits"—charity hospitals, welfare payments, school lunches, free schools books, low college tuition and toll-free bridges. McKeithen set out to combine the image of the Long progressive with that of the reformer. He did this quite effectively, with the help of his opponents and some of the large daily newspapers. He was accused of doing irreparable damage to the state by having voted for a number of tax increases as a Long floor leader in 1948. McKeithen was able to turn back this attack most effectively. He acknowledged his guilt in voting the tax increases and went on to explain the programs these taxes had financed and to claim a very sizable share of the credit for these programs—free school lunches, old age pensions, veterans' bonuses, and others. In Louisiana where the "welfare state" had become a way of life, these were programs that had benefited a majority of Louisiana voters. The criticism by his opponents and the newspapers, especially the *Times Picayune* ("Uncle Earl's favorite target) was a great boost to his campaign.

McKeithen's campaign manager was the widow of Earl K. Long, Mrs. Blanche Long. Her position in the campaign gave credence to his claim as the leader of the Louisiana Longs. He accused Gillis and Russell of being the "Washington Longs." In bedrock Long country McKeithen advertisements always had at the bottom, "This political advertisement paid for by Mrs. Earl K. Long, Campaign Manager." In areas where the Longs were never very popular, McKeithen played up his reform "uncontrolled" image and made no mention of his Long connections. Here his advertisements were "Paid for by so and so, City Campaign Manager of McKeithen."

To be all things to all men, McKeithen needed one more image, the segregationist image. The Longs had been racial moderates and had in fact come under attack for allowing too many Negroes to register to vote and for providing too many benefits to Negroes. McKeithen had been part of this, and he was in danger of being branded as too weak in defending segregation. But not for long, as he established himself as a "100 percent segregationist" and an opponent to "federal intervention." At the same time, however, McKeithen was careful to stress that he was not a "hater." McKeithen's three images, reformer, Longite, and segregationist, covered just about all the possibilities and he coalesced the three in such a way as to reduce their contradictory features. Flexibility was the hallmark of his campaign. He had set his aim at second place in the first primary and adapted his campaign to that aim. Once in the second primary, he could play up any one, any two, or all three of his images, depending upon whom his opponent might be. Retrospectively, this strategy was brilliant.

McKeithen needed the momentum he had gained from his vigorous first primary race as he faced "Chep" Morrison, who again had far outdistanced the field in the number one spot. A good many political observers thought the runoff all but decided when shortly after the first primary, McKeithen was discovered conferring one night in the state's new million dollar mansion with Governor Davis. He had been driven to and from the meeting by Wilson P.

Abraham, the contractor friend of the Governor. Continuing to show his political adroitness, however, McKeithen turned the discovery of the meeting with the man whose administration had been one of his chief targets in the first primary campaign to his own advantage. This was done in a TV confrontation January 2, 1964, at which time a panel of television newsmen questioned the two candidates.[22]

McKeithen denied flatly that he had visited Governor Davis to make any deal, pointing out how inconsistent that would be with his first primary position. Rather, he said matter of factly, his meeting with Davis was arranged by mutual friends who were concerned about the bloc vote. This had to do with the charge that the registered Negroes in the state had allegedly voted solidly for Morrison, a charge which McKeithen repeated but admitted he could not prove even though the facts all pointed to that conclusion. McKeithen felt the bloc vote was a frightening thing and that he wanted to call the attention of the Governor to it and to seek any help Davis could give on the matter. Under further questioning McKeithen had admitted that he had solicited the vote of Negroes previously. He said he appealed for all votes, white and black, but that this bloc vote for Morrison was something else.

There was nothing in this to hurt McKeithen's chances among a good many voters, but then he turned the tables and questioned what Ambassador Morrison was doing traveling on an eighteen hour trip to Washington while he was making his trip to Baton Rouge. McKeithen was able to add the country boy image to the three with which he won second spot in the first primary. In all innocence he answered Morrison's explanation that he was on army business at the pentagon by saying that he was just an old country boy who had a lot to learn and that just imagine, the pentagon (spoken penagon) was open twenty-four hours a day. Here was the city slicker being outsmarted by the hayseed in a state whose rural traditions lingered on. Whatever really may have transpired at the governor's mansion, it was noted that Governor Davis worked steadily and effectively to aid McKeithen, doing what Earl Long used to do by con-

---

[22] *Morning Advocate*, January 3, 1964, Gibbs Adams, Sec. A, pp. 1, 4.

tacting political leaders all over the state to round up votes for McKeithen.[23]

Perhaps the final maneuver which enabled McKeithen to out-distance Morrison was accomplished by his aids. He had been joined by his running mate from 1952, Carlos Spaht, no longer a judge, and by Mary Evelyn Parker, who quit her job as state welfare commissioner to help McKeithen. She proved to be one of his most valuable allies, for her television attacks upon Morrison's lack of leadership in allowing Baton Rouge, Lake Charles, and other Louisiana cities, let alone Houston, Texas, to surge ahead of New Orleans in industrial and port expansion in the years he had been mayor, were counted by many as a large part of the credit for McKeithen's election.[24]

Emerging as victor by some forty thousand votes in the Democratic Primary, John J. McKeithen looked cautiously over his shoulder at Charlton Lyons, his Republican opponent in the general election. During most of the twentieth century, Republican parties in the southern states have operated as elite patronage clubs, with little effort being made to increase party membership since this would increase the number among whom federal patronage would have to be distributed. The Louisiana Republican Party generally had tried to offer a candidate for the governor's stake, but this was realistically regarded by both Republicans and Democrats as an exercise in futility. As the national Democratic Party has taken a stronger position on the issue of civil rights, the uneasy alliance that shaped the party had been brought under a heavy strain in the states of the Old Confederacy. The Republicans fell heir to a fast track which they did little or nothing to create and upon which they have not run well.

In 1952 the crusading war hero, General Eisenhower, brought a breath of fresh air to southern Republicanism. In Louisiana he missed by a hair's breadth in 1952, and in 1956 this same genial man—the father image—broke the ancient barrier and won in Louisiana. But,

---

[23] *Morning Advocate*, January 19, 1964, "Capital Beat," Margaret Dixon, Sec. B, p. 5.

[24] *Morning Advocate*, May 12, 1964, Inaugural Section, Margaret Dixon, p. 2.

as could be concluded from the analysis of presidential politics in Louisiana in Chapter 9, shadow was not substance.

To develop a genuine two-party system, the Republicans would have to start fielding a stable of entries rather than depending upon a pacer. It would require hard work and bitter disappointment. There would have to be voter registration drives and candidates for elective positions across the board. In such a process there would be a strong possibility that many "Republicanocrats" (Democrats who consistently cross over to vote for a Republican in presidential elections) would not be anxious to give up their privileged sanctuary in the Democratic Party where they enjoy the benefits of access to local office holders. Southern Republicans have been caught in a dilemma— should they offer candidates for offices from the White House to justice of peace or should they be satisfied with aiming for the presidency alone? It appears that the Louisiana Republicans, despite some local efforts in urban areas like Baton Rouge and Shreveport, have followed the latter course. Rather than take the long road they have chosen the shorter one of trying to capitalize on Democratic deserters to elect a President and refuse to worry over Congressional, state and local offices.

After false starts on other occasions, in 1964 the Republicans moved decisively toward severing the umbilical cord which had tied them to their past. This time they had a candidate who was not running for the exercise. Charlton Lyons not only had money (and sources of money) required to make a campaign, he also had fire in his sixty-nine-year-old eyes. An enthusiastic Goldwater supporter, he had quit the Democratic Party after the 1960 Presidential Nominating Convention because he felt the 1960 party platform was a "blueprint for socialism." As a real live conservative he appeared in a strategic position to pick up support from among traditional anti-Long voters who had the marks of Republicans running under the colors of the Democratic Party. Additionally, the disheartened Morrison "true-believers" might turn on McKeithen with a vengeance—even the Negroes, who certainly could find little to like in Lyons's political philosophy, might even the score with McKeithen.

But McKeithen proved to be a skilled politician, and he had been campaigning for governor for well over a year. Now he could see only one more hurdle between himself and the governor's mansion. Persons who had observed him for several years had come to appreciate his political savvy and few could doubt that his political intuitions would fail him at this late date. It was soon apparent that this indefatigable compaigner had suffered no loss of political vision.

McKeithen began the last furlong of the home stretch by saying that he knew Mr. Lyons was a well-respected, distinguished—but elderly—gentleman, and outstanding citizen in his community. He regarded Lyons as a very tough opponent and declared that he would campaign vigorously. Having come through a grueling race within the Democratic primaries in which he earned a reputation as a "street fighter" with deadly aim for the political jugular of opponents, his first move had been to heal the Democratic wounds by a number of well-chosen appointments. He sounded sincere when he said that he would not seek political vendetta, contending that he intended to seek the help of friends and enemies alike in making Louisiana first in everything. Perhaps the only exception was the support McKeithen gave another distant Long relative, Speedy Long, in winning the congressional seat in the Eighth District later that summer and thus removing a political base from Gillis Long.

McKeithen continued to be complimentary to Mr. Lyons, but it was difficult not to see the bulge of his tongue in his cheek, as he referred to Lyons as his "honorable elderly opponent." McKeithen had made a brief trip to the western states (the exact location was not revealed) and returned to say that he had kept his ear to the political ground and from what he could hear Rockefeller would in all likelihood get the Republican nomination for President and that it almost seemed certain that Lyons' hero, Goldwater, did not have a chance. Lyons soon indicated that he had a thin political skin and was something of a novice in the political game. He grabbed the bait—hook, line, and sinker—wasting no time in vowing that he would not support Rockefeller if he got the nomination.

Lyons brought in the Hollywood charmer Ronald Reagan for a three day political road show for Louisiana audiences. Like the fabled "Hadacol" medicine salesman of days past, Reagan was involved in entertaining and selling. His "medicine" was prescribed for the cure of a disease he called "Fabian socialism" or sometimes in layman's language "liberal welfare philosophy." He said he was going down the line for Goldwater. McKeithen soon indicated that he had some acting ability of his own. He let loose a blast that might not have won him votes, but one that certainly won him respect from loyalist Democrats. He referred to Lyons's out-of-state troupe as an invasion of carpetbaggers. It was difficult to appreciate the irony of this label until the personages of the entourage are described. Included, along with Reagan, were Rubel Phillips, a Republican segregationist who had fared well in the Mississippi gubernatorial election; James Martin, an Alabama Republican of similar position who came within fractions of defeating Senator Lister Hill whom he had accused of being too soft on the race question; and the Republican National Committee chairman, Congressman William Miller.

Of Reagan, McKeithen said, "I would suggest specifically to Mr. Reagan that he return to Hollywood and do something about the standing immorality and communism that flourishes in that city. They bring John Birchers in one week left wingers the next."[25] In anticipation of Phillips' intended visit to Louisiana, McKeithen warned, "We are preparing to attack him when he crosses the state line by all means known to modern political warfare." With a sense of political humor that one who loves the game of politics could well appreciate, he told the press, "We Louisiana Democrats are determined to repel this second invasion by the carpetbaggers."[26]

Some reporters interpreted McKeithen's statements as signs he was worried by the strength of his Republican opponent while others felt he was making a strategic error and actually boosting Lyons's cause. Perhaps he was worried, and it is quite likely that he was giving unnecessary publicity to his opponent, but in either case he seemed to be having a really good time. McKeithen is a political pro who enjoys political fights, especially those in which he has the upper hand. He had it in this election, and if he was not having fun he certainly knew how to endure misery and appear to enjoy it.

[25] New Orleans *Clarion Herald*, February 2, 1964, p. 1.
[26] New Orleans *Times-Picayune*, February 4, 1964, p. 1.

John J. McKeithen was said to have been schooled under the tutelage of Earl K. Long; he was an apt student.

Rain marred the inauguration of John J. McKeithen on May 13 1964, the first time in thirty-two years of the quadrennial ceremonies. The McKeithen umbrella went up, symbolic, it turned out, of the new Governor's continuous attempt to build a consensus, Louisiana style. During the general election campaign McKeithen had vowed it was time to seize the opportunity to stop factional bickering within the state, to end the bitterness of the past, and to get the state going. "We know," McKeithen said, "we have problems in Louisiana and we know that Louisiana people can solve these problems."[27] In his inaugural address under the umbrellas, McKeithen called for a new Louisiana and let it be known that he intended to attempt to solve the problem of good government, looking at it as a positive force and as a dynamic instrument of society. Government would be used to take full advantage of Louisiana's natural resources. McKeithen went on to declare that "all of our people now understand that they must walk hand in hand into the future in full cooperation with business and with industry."[28]

The consensus which was to be built by Governor McKeithen can be seen as a function of a number of outstanding features of his administration which at once depended upon chance but more importantly upon extraordinary political acumen. In the summer of 1964, McKeithen found himself without major Democratic opposition since Gillis Long had lost his seat in Congress and deLesseps S. Morrison had lost his life in a tragic airplane accident. The legislature had considered and failed to pass on a constitutional amendment in 1962 which would have allowed an incumbent governor to succeed himself in a consecutive second term. In this political vacuum the talk of a two-term amendment was renewed, and the ground work was laid for its eventual passage by the legislature and referral to the electorate in the November, 1966, general election.

The issue of gubernatorial succession had been tied by the Governor himself to the issue of the powers of the governor's office. It was held

---

[27] *Morning Advocate*, February 16, 1964 (UPI), Sec. A, p. 1.
[28] *Morning Advocate*, May 13, 1964, Sec. A, p. 10.

that the former must follow from a reduction of the latter, and to that end, Governor McKeithen appointed a committee headed by former Governor Sam Jones to study the powers of Louisiana governors. Several Jones Committee recommendations were submitted to the people along with the two-term amendment, the most important ones being a reduction of the vast appointive powers of the governor and providing the possibility of "veto sessions" of the legislature. The only major objections to the two-term amendment had been raised by Gillis Long, who cogently argued that given the power of the governor (regardless of passage of Jones Committee recommendations), it would be impossible to marshal the support and find the financial backing needed to effectively oppose the candidacy of an incumbent. Gillis Long's arguments tended to fall on deaf ears as many charged "sour grapes," and still more held to the rather undemocratic position that to defeat the two-term amendment would guarantee another term for the now unpopular Jimmie H. Davis. (How, if Davis were so unpopular, we shall never know.) The McKeithen consensus expanded as the electorate endorsed a second term for the Governor by a sizable 70 percent of the total vote cast in an election McKeithen had said would be a vote of confidence in his administration.

The Governor was successful in the two-term maneuver, which compounded the consensus he had gained in his handling of the racial unrest which threatened the paper mill city of Bogalusa in the Klan-ridden Florida Parishes. In the racially hot summer of 1965, a showdown seemed certain between local members of the Klu Klux Klan on one side and the Congress of Racial Equality, aided by the armed and militant Deacons for Defense and Justice, led by A. Z. Young, a former president of the local Negro union, on the other side.[29] Crown Zellerbach took over the paper mill in 1965 and admitted reluctance to mix into local traditions which date back to the industry's founding in Bogalusa in 1906. While the company denied discriminatory practices and admitted the legacy of unequal employment practices through inertia, its main problem stemmed from continued

[29] *The National Observer*, July 26, 1965, Jude Wanniski, p. 9.

automation which reduced the number of jobs available. The Bogalusa Mayor, Jesse Cutrer, whose initial claim to fame had been to be thrown out of Louisiana State University in 1935 for writing editorials for the student newspaper critical of Senator Huey P. Long, had worked diligently for racial harmony. Negro voter registration was no problem and moderate leadership of the Bogalusa Voters League, a Negro group, had been able to win improvements for the colored community. Now Bogalusa citizens were at gun-point.

A group of moderate citizens had invited former Arkansas Congressman Brooks Hays, a liberal, to discuss the Civil Rights Act of 1964, but when the Klan objected strongly, the mayor used his office to cancel the invitation in the hopes of avoiding trouble. *The Nation* however, got wind of the deal and "exposed" Bogalusa as "Klantown U.S.A." which in turn sparked CORE into its attempt to gain equal rights for Negroes in the city and made it an armed camp. In these circumstances, the men who control the destiny of the state during peaceful times, the business and political leaders, wondered if they could keep the unrest of Bogalusa from spreading. Their Committee for a Better Louisiana met with the Governor to chart a statewide course for civil rights. McKeithen had tried twice and failed to get a thirty-day cooling off period from Bogalusa Negroes. Now the Governor announced intentions to name a biracial committee which would be charged to find "that path of nonviolent adjustment to the Federal civil rights legislation that Mayor Cutrer had been seeking."[30]

Governor McKeithen made it clear that it was his intention to use the powers of his office to stand firm for law and order. He authorized the Louisiana Commission on Human Relations, Rights and Responsibilities and staffed it with permanent council. In making the announcement McKeithen made the practical statement, "We all are going to continue to live here in Louisiana and so we have got to learn to get along with each other." Compared to the rhetoric used by many Southern politicians, this was the voice of moderation. Two summers later, when the prevailing calm was threatened, Governor McKeithen repeated his position on civil rights disorders in words that

[30] *The National Observer*, July 26, 1965, Jude Wanniski, p. 9.

were sure to appeal to many of the state's voters when he said that violence would not be tolerated from anyone, and if rioting, looting and fire bombing occurred, a lot of persons would be shot.[31]

Citizen committees to work on the solution of critical statewide problems were used quite successfully by Governor McKeithen, and up to a point, the technique promised to work even for the thorny problem of union-management racketeering, which is alleged to be widespread in the capital city area. Another committee was formed, the Labor-Management Commission of Inquiry, which in 1967 and 1968 held a number of hearings concerning an alleged teamster union-private contractor conspiracy. The whole issue has been clouded by possible links to the "mobster" influence which in 1967 *Life* magazine charged against the McKeithen administration. *Life*'s allegation that telephone calls from racket figures such as Carlos Marcello were made to a former McKeithen aid, Aubrey Young, gave the Governor's major opponent, Congressman John R. Rarick, his most potent issue in the upcoming gubernatorial primary.[32]

Despite the large Klan support Rarick received when he ousted Jimmie Morrison from his House seat held for twenty-four years from the Sixth District, and the seeming potency of the rackets issue, the McKeithen concensus held. The Governor won his second term with an unprecedented Democratic primary support of 80.6 percent of the record-breaking 1,037,102 total votes cast. The prediction of Gillis Long was confirmed as the McKeithen umbrella covered the state. In only one parish, West Carroll (56 percent), did McKeithen fail to gain as much as 60 percent support. Although he received a majority in all the parishes, McKeithen's strongest support came from South Louisiana. Of the sixteen parishes of his upper quarter, fourteen came from this area which, of course, reversed the seat of greatest McKeithen affinity in the first primary of 1963. Eight of those parishes appeared in Rarick's top quarter parish support, but in no case did McKeithen's upper quarter in 1963 repeat in his strongest area of support in 1967.[33]

---

[31] *Morning Advocate*, April 9, 1968, Wayne Owens (AP), Sec. A, p. 5.

[32] *Morning Advocate*, October 29, 1967, Bill Neikirk (AP), Sec. A, p. 18.

[33] Public Affairs Research Council, "Democratic Primaries, 1967," *PAR Analysis*, No. 146 (Baton Rouge, 1964).

Shortly after the primary election quadrennial rumblings were heard from the state Democratic Central Committee where loyalist chairman, Edward Carmouche of Lake Charles was ousted and replaced, by backers of Alabama's George Wallace, with staunchly conservative Arthur C. Watson of Natchitoches. The vote of the 117-man committee, which followed the lines of the newly reapportioned legislative districts, is instructive:

*Table 10–22*
NUMBER OF DEMOCRATIC CENTRAL COMMITTEE
VOTES FOR ARTHUR C. WATSON, DECEMBER 28, 1967

|  | North Louisiana | South Louisiana | State Totals |
|---|---|---|---|
| For | 35 | 30 | 65 |
| Against | 3 | 46 | 49 |

With three members absent, the resulting vote outlines clearly the continued pattern of North-South Louisiana cleavage. The actions of the central committee are considered to be significant.[34] When there has been such upheaval within the state committee, it is found that voters have reacted exactly the same way and have swung to the Republicans or to the States' Rights position. How Louisiana voters will tend in the next few years will turn on future actions in the up to now remarkable career of Governor John J. McKeithen.

[34] *Morning Advocate*, April 9, 1968, Wayne Owens (AP), Sec. A, p. 5.

# CHAPTER XI

# The Future of Louisiana Politics

## I. *Political Tendencies and Types of Society*

Methods of political ecology have been used to trace regularities through time in the vote of the Louisiana electorate. Continuity and change have been found, reflecting the underlying social structure and characteristics of what may be called the *political culture* of the state. The effects of these variables upon political tendencies (votes) have been demonstrated. The narrative and analyses carried on in the chapters above show how a political constitution (ground rules) affect behavior over time and how a strong executive relates to a particular population at given socioeconomically conditioned times.

This study has tried to show how political tendencies can serve as indicators of what the vote means. Many students have concluded from the three decades of survey research of voting that the vote reflects very little of rational consideration but follows from more unpredictable emotional responses.[1] The Louisiana story at least lends credence to the view of V. O. Key, Jr., that the electorate's behavior at the ballot box is "responsible."[2] Taking the broad perspective, Key concluded that people vote for the candidate or party which takes the stand on issues that best serve the electorate's definition of political preference in given times and places. If this is true, then strategy calls for identification of the issues in a given election which relate to interests or cleavages and the voting tendencies which manifest them.

---

[1] W. G. Runciman, *Social Science and Political Theory* (Cambridge [Eng], 1963), chap. 5.

[2] V. O. Key, Jr., *The Responsible Electorate* (Cambridge, 1966), 7-8; see also the position of Anthony Downs, *An Economic Theory of Democracy* (New York, 1957), 335-61.

In this study (Chapter Two), a number of interests or cleavage lines were identified (Table 2-2) as providing the focus about which politics was carried on. If politics has to do with the expression or limitation of conflict,[3] it was suggested that the two important variables subject to analysis as the study proceeded would be the degree of *suffrage* and *representation*. While significant changes were found to have occurred in the ebb and flow of suffrage limitation, it turned out that regarding representation, change was more apparent than real.

In antebellum politics, representation was controversial because control of the legislative affairs rested in the hands of a planter-merchant elite whose slaveholdings provided an apportionment largely in their favor. This circumstance was seen as influential in leading Louisiana out of the Union in 1861. Yet, subsequent equalization of representation during Reconstruction and after, including the recent reapportionment under the Supreme Court's "one-man, one vote" formula seemingly provided little effective autonomy for the legislature. It remained dominated, if not outright controlled, by the governor, the power of whose office is almost as extremely great as ever, continuing to provide vast potentials for patronage as well as many invitations to corruption.

One overall historical characteristic of the American South (shared by the subunit Louisiana) had to do with the continuing quarrel over the prerogatives of an elite in placing limitations on suffrage as against the egalitarian movement in its logically opposite direction—unlimited access to the suffrage. Thus Seymour M. Lipset has demonstrated that while the national American value system included orientation to achievement and equalitarianism in mutually supportive combination, the American South, to the extent it has stressed ascription and elitism has constituted a major source of instability of the national political system. Lipset held that the South "was retained in the nation only by force, and down to the present it does not have a stable democratic polity. To the extent that its citizens have felt the pull of the dominant

---

[3] E. E. Schattschneider, *The Semisovereign People* (New York, 1960), for a representative view.

value system, the South has always found it difficult to build an integrated regional social order on its own."[4]

But that is not all. America as the "First New Nation" was founded through the efforts of European settlers who had carried with them particular aspects of the general European historical experience. Louis Hartz has called these *fragments* of European culture brought to and developed in the New World in a three-stage process: "The extrication from Europe, the atrophy of the future, and the unfolding of the fragment potential."[5] Hartz's thesis is deceptively simple: specific migrant groups carried with them different *fragments* of the European cultural whole for adaptation in various colonizing areas. Thus, it turned out, the American *fragment* was a liberal bourgeois (mass?) one, whereas, by way of contrast, that of French Quebec or Latin America was a *fragment* providing a feudal structure (communal?).

Hartz showed how the notion of *fragments* opened possibilities for comparative analysis by contrasting the manner in which North and South America handled the Indian and Negro populations. In accomodating such social *difference*, whereas the feudal *fragment* yielded a low position within the hierarchical structure of a communal society, *the liberal fragment could not do likewise.* For, as Hartz has cogently argued, within the liberal tradition in the United States there was room for no concept of class or hierarchy. The liberal tradition emphasized the demand for equality. The stress on equality meant that either the Indian or the Negro were equal, or somehow they must be excluded. Such a condition quite obviously provided a potentially explosive situation, for what happens when such a society abolishes slavery, for example, and by definition the slave is now instantaneously equal?

The power of Hartz's analysis is magnified when the American South is considered, for it was at once two societies, where both the feudal and liberal *fragments* were present in the form of the plantation (communal) and the farm (rural mass). Thus, Southern experience can be seen as one of successive accomodations to an endemic

---

[4] Seymour Martin Lipset, *The First New Nation* (Garden City, 1967), 246.
[5] Louis Hartz, *The Founding of New Societies* (New York, 1964), 24.

antagonism or cleavage between what Lipset called the elitist view on the one hand and the egalitarian view on the other. But consider further that in Louisiana this circumstance was exaggerated by the even more elitist preferences of its early settlers, and there is urgent occasion for trying to link leading political tendencies as found in this study with variables which might serve as empirical indicators of types of social order.

At least two kinds of order are implied in the discussions of Lipset and Hartz above. One type of social order is hierarchical, where people hold social positions placed along a scale of superiority-inferiority and where such difference is admitted and legitimated.Let this be labeled *communal*, and its opposite, the kind of order which is egalitarian, where all positions are subject to competition, *mass*.

The type of society labeled *communal* can be seen to result from a *vertical* (inequality) order concerning the existence of which there is a general *consensus*. On the other hand the *mass* condition will be one in which the logical opposite, a *horizontal* order (equality), predominates and where not consensus but competition and *conflict* prevail. If the variables thus identified are used in cross tabulation then it is apparent that there will be two further cells to identify as to type of order. These will be labeled *plural* and *total*.[6]

*Table 11–1*

A MODEL OF TYPES OF SOCIETY

|  | Consensus | Conflict |
|---|---|---|
| Vertical | COMMUNAL | TOTAL |
| Horizontal | PLURAL | MASS |

[6] The usefulness of working with a model of four kinds of society has been acknowledged widely by political sociologists. It makes possible to assert that the extension of political suffrage has accompanied the great historical shift from communal to plural (and/or) mass conditions. See William Kornhauser, *The Politics of Mass Society*, (Glencoe, 1959); Erik Allardt (ed.), *Cleavages, Ideologies, and Party Systems* (Helsinki, 1964); Stein Rokkan (ed.), *Approaches to the Study of Political Participation* (Bergen, 1962); Reinhard Bendix and Stein Rokkan, "The Extension of National Citizenship to the Lower Classes," paper prepared for Work Session I, Fifth World Congress of Sociology, Washington, D.C., 1962.

It has been asserted elsewhere[7] that this model of types of order (society) is inclusive and exhaustive of the possibilities and that the model has great explanatory power as a "covering principle." Yet, it can be admitted readily, such a model at this stage, without appropriate linkage to empirical reality, is too formalistic. There is urgent need to find variables which link type of order with empirical indicators of social regularities.

So far, a promising lead may be found in the basic social process of differentiation, or more precisely the question of how *difference* is handled in society, groups, or social relations. Such a variable may be quite meaningful on the political level, as has been intimated in Table 2–3, where the question of how *difference* in regard to *suffrage* was explored tentatively. Disregarding the cross-tabs therein (which ultimately relate to those presented above in Table 11–1), the following kinds of suffrage possibilities can be suggested:

*Table 11–2*
A FOURFOLD TABLE OF *Difference* APPLIED TO THE QUESTION OF SUFFRAGE

| NOT ALL | ALL EXCEPT OTHER |
|---|---|
| Admit difference exists, and legitimate | recognize difference, and eliminate |
| (only people like us should vote) | (only our kind of people should vote, discourage all others) |

| ALL AND OTHER | ALL |
|---|---|
| Recognize difference, and legitimate tolerance procedures | Deny difference exists (relative normlessness) |
| All kinds of people should be encouraged to vote | (Every man for himself) |

Seen in this way, difficulties with the notion of mass society can be clarified as well as drawing its distinction from plural tendencies in the social order. The two types share in common horizontal differ-

---

[7] Perry H. Howard and Joseph L. Brent III, "Social Change, Urbanization, and Types of Society," *Journal of Social Issues*, XXII (1966), 73.

entiation, the conditions of equality. But while the characteristic of the plural tendency is to recognize difference and tolerate it, the mass tendency denies difference in the assertion of the equality of all. The plural order thus rests upon a consensus which has as its object the assertion of equality and affirms the *responsibility* to maintain it. In the mass condition, which is characterized by relative "norm-lessness" in Howard Becker's sense,[8] the intention is conflict. But if conflict is directed toward other individuals, Hobbes's "war of all against all" results. However, conflict may have as its object anything that does not invoke consensual relations with other human beings such as an unexploited continent, dollars, mobility in an expanding economy.[9] Conflict becomes externalized by the theoretically atomized individuals of the horizontal order. All seek rights and power competitively won under conditions of equality of opportunity.

It is considered essentially correct to assert that the great transition in Western societies from communal to modern conditions was double-pronged. That is, two separate conditions and accompanying notions of society emerged, the one stressing toleration of difference (plural) as free-standing voluntary associations asserted their autonomy against the communal order, the other stressing the competition of different but equal units (mass).[10] The former may be associated with the development of democracy in the political sphere and the limitation of political power against the private sector, while the latter may be associated with the individual competition for gain in the open market place. The often used metaphor "massification" tends to blur the distinction made above as it is somehow concluded that since modern machine production is achieved by mass techniques and advertised to customers by mass communication and purchased in mass consumption that modern industrial societies are *mass*.[11]

[8] Howard Becker, "The Normative Reaction to Normlessness," *American Sociological Review*, XXV (1960), 803–10.

[9] This notion is drawn from the book by David Potter, *People of Plenty: Economic Abundance and the American Character* (Chicago, 1954).

[10] Robert A. Nisbet, *Community and Power* (New York, 1967), for a characteristic view of this position.

[11] On the illogic of this construction see Joseph Fichter, *Sociology* (Chicago, 1957). The concept of mass in this sense is accepted by Alvin L. Bertrand, "The Emerging Rural South: A Region Under 'Confrontation' by Mass Society," *Rural Sociology*,

But this construction (and many political scientists tend to use it when they speak of "pluralistic" behavior to mean countervailing powers or competition) overlooks the fact that American political democracy establishes *plural procedures* (tolerance of difference) and that the "mass" is rather found in the economic sphere of behavior. Both Robert A. Dahl and E. E. Schattschneider show the plural aspect of American society having developed from the communal, and that plural procedures must be understood as being the public domain where conflict is muted by consensus, since members of society establish the rules and limits of legitimate conflict.[12] At the same time the United States is also a mass society in its many private spheres, as in the mass consumer market where the individual competes with others in making private choices. This does not mean to deny, however, that mass techniques have not been used increasingly by politicians since the advent of television.

The importance of this discussion is scored by the insistence of scholars such as Lipset who find that the United States was in reality a mixed society (plural *and* mass in the terms developed above), while the southern region, as a variant, had tended to manifest communal-plural-mass tendencies. In the South, as elsewhere, plural commitments followed the establishment of state constitutions in general patterned on the national model, but with the South a planter elite yielded only as much to the plural condition as required, while the yeoman farmer mass sought entrance into the elite by becoming slaveholders and lacking that, in populistic fashion sought more equality through access to cheap lands and increased suffrage. When the relations between the handling of difference in suffrage in Louisiana and observed variance in voting tendencies are explored, it is possible to use them as indicators of periods of Louisiana political history. It is reasonable to declare that when variance is high and different parties each share close to 50 percent of the total vote cast,

---

XXXI (1966), 449–51; a study which does not find the indicated trend but the possibility that differences between urban and rural may be increasing is Norval D. Glenn, "Massification Versus Differentiation: Some Trend Data From National Surveys," *Social Forces,* XLVI (1967), 172–80.

[12] Robert A. Dahl, *Pluralist Democracy in the United States* (Chicago, 1967); Schattschneider, *The Semisovereign People.*

competition is great and, counterwise, when variance is low a party gains a considerable share of the total vote (or little if, as in this study, the general focus has been on the Democratic Party vote) that consensus is great. However, it can be determined only by historical investigation of the issues that are present, as well as the factors of suffrage limitation and turnout in specific elections, whether tendencies within the sets of what are called closed (communal and total) and open (plural and mass) notions of order obtain. The following tabular summary, therefore, is an attempt to demonstrate the association between variance and suffrage within the time span of Louisiana politics:

*Table 11-3*

VARIANCE IN VOTE (PRESIDENTIAL AND GUBERNATORIAL
DEMOCRATIC AVERAGES) AND SUFFRAGE DIFFERENCE

| Low Variance | High Variance | Suffrage Qualifications | Suffrage Difference | |
|---|---|---|---|---|
| | Ethnicity 1812–32 | White males 21 years & over | "Not All" (trend toward plural tendency) | C O M M U N A L |
| | Two-Party 1834–56 (52%) | | | |
| Gubernatorial 1860 (62%) | Presidential 1860 (15, 45, 40%) | | | |
| | Secession 1861 (54%) | | | |
| | Reconstruction 1865–76 (52%) | White & Black males 21 years and over | "All" | M A S S |

Democratic                                              "All with blacks
Solidarity                                              intimidated"
1879–92
(67%)

------------------------------

                    Populist Defeat                    "All"
                    1896
                    (56%)

------------------------------

Presidential                    White males 21    "All except other"   T O T A L
Democratic                      years & over
Solidarity                      White males &
1900–44                         females 21 years
(82%)                           and over (1920)

------------------------------

Bourbon Rule Long Candidates    White and Black   "All and Other"    P L U R A L
1900–24       1928–56          males and females
(62%)         (54%)            21 years & over
------------------------------  (1944)

Natural diversity of interests in Louisiana is manifested in close
votes regardless of suffrage qualifications, except when the total
tendency was exerted in the denial of difference. The genealogy of
Louisiana political parties was shown to rest upon what was made of
the rich physical potentials—upon the interests of sugar and cotton
producers as well as differences in the composition of the population
between the southern and northern parishes of the state. In the
competition for political power French cane planters became Whigs
in opposition to "American" cotton planters who brought their
Democratic Party preference with them as they settled the Florida
Parishes and North Louisiana. But socioeconomic factors helped to
bring together cotton planter and cane Whig in the decades leading
to Secession, in opposition to the farmer classes with their Jacksonian
Democratic tendency. Herein emerged a pattern of voting behavior
which followed the river "Y" system, representing the political
tendency within the most fertile areas of Louisiana, given over to the
plantation slaveocracy.

Not all cotton planters were Whigs, and not all North Louisiana was of the planter class, for, on the lands away from the natural levees and in the uplands, increasing numbers of yeoman farmers joined in support of the Democratic Party. These were joined by Cajun and Creole farmers of the South Louisiana bayous and back country who likewise registered this political preference, although they sometimes followed the persuasion of the planters. A Whig state until 1842, Louisiana, from that time until the Civil War, showed a numerical majority for the Democrats, although in this period of two-party competition the vote most often divided close to 50 percent.

Then as now, Orleans Parish contributed from 20 to 25 percent of the total state vote, and within the city of New Orleans resided a working class—many foreign-born Irish, German, or French— susceptible to the appeal and patronage of the Democratic Party. Yet, although the worker class in the city and the farmer classes in the country made up a majority of the state's voters (despite the limitations of suffrage), this bloc of Democratic support merely contributed to the maintainance of the status quo. Louisiana was governed by "gentlemen," since effective political power rested upon property, and planters had plenty in the presence of slaves who counted in representation but could not vote. There was in reality no party vehicle through which the latent community of yeoman farmer and worker could be used in furtherance of *their* claims in Louisiana society. Groups of great influence (planters in alliance with commercial interests) were opposed by groups of great number (farmers of Hills and Bayou Parishes together with workers of cities and towns).

As the North agitated against slavery, those cotton planters who had found repose in Whiggery discovered that now their interests were protected by the Democratic Party, and in 1860 for the first time a Democratic solidarity of above 60 percent (62 percent) was produced in a gubernatorial election by the forces of John Slidell. It did not hold in the presidential election when a three-way split occurred, and as the issue of Secession became a burning one in Louisiana, sugar planters, city workers, and yeoman farmers displayed a potential community of interests, since none had anything to gain from following the Democrats out of the Union. Tragedy followed, as a failure of parties occurred in the 1850's with the southern Whigs foundered on the reefs of slavery and the Democratic Party in Louisiana split by the factional struggle between the forces of Slidell and Soulé. In this situation, with convention delegates apportioned in favor of the Planter Parishes, the drift to Secession and war became inevitable.

If there had been a chance for moderate elements to continue the lively political competition that had prevailed before the war and to strike a blow for those who had previously been dominated, groupings in both the North and the South by their actions destroyed this possibility for Louisiana. In the Radical Reconstruction of the Republicans the freedman became a political pawn. The same basic cleavage which had produced the antebellum high variance in the vote reappeared, only now the former slaves formed a group of number if not of influence. The Republicans used the freedman to advantage against the Democratic voters, who were comprised of cotton planters and merchants allied now with the farmers of the uplands who asserted their ancient political prejudice. In this struggle, where no limitations on suffrage were made, the South Louisiana sugar planters had given the Republican Party support out of economic (tariff and patronage) considerations, and the carpetbaggers managed to count enough Negro ballots to eke out some close victories at the polls.

After Redemption, for the first time in Louisiana political history, the support of both gubernatorial and presidential Democratic candidates was found in the 60–100 percentage interval as the Democratic Party learned to coerce and use the Negro as the Republicans had done before them. This can be seen as the forerunner to the tendency of Democratic solidarity which would come to prevail in twentieth-century Louisiana. It found its roots in the aspiration of a new class of planters and merchants that emerged from the successful economic reconstruction constituted in the "New South," which in Louisiana meant the survival of the plantation system with the placement of the Negro in new bonds of tenancy. White farmers joined the Democratic Redeemers after 1876 in asserting white supremacy opposed to Black Republican rule. But now the basic alignment of support for the Democracy could be shown to rest once again in the river bottoms, the seat of planter domination.

The anomaly of this picture was the near-100-percent solidarity of voter support in the 1880's coming from the farmer parishes of the uplands. Economic reconstruction meant not only the survival of the plantation system but also that farmer groups became committed to its furtherance. Entering commercial agriculture by concentrating his labor upon one crop (cotton) and ensnared in the crop-lien credit system, the farmer lost his self-sufficiency. It was in this condition, when in years of poor crops or low prices, white farmers faced competition from Negro labor and the threat of a drift into tenancy, that their fears rendered them susceptible to the dogma of white supremacy as advocated by the Bourbons bent upon political domination.

There emerged, however, a difference within the farmer groupings, as loss of farm ownership and consequent tenancy was far less prevalent in the heart of the Hills than in the parishes bordering the Planter areas and grouped along the Arkansas state line. The upland farmer, previously more self-sufficient, had more to lose than the farmer in the river bottoms, where tenancy was already predominant. In this state of affairs farmer groups dropped Democratic solidarity in behalf of white supremacy and sought a more effective alignment in the Populist-Republican Fusion of the nineties. The agrarian protest forced the end result of Democratic redemption to be an answer to the question of *which whites* should rule.

It might be granted by most whites that the Negro should be shown his "place," but the spectacular successes of the Fusion now threatened the continuance of planter-merchant domination. Within the Fusion was found much the same grouping which stood in 1860 without party or vehicle of protest. Disgruntled sugar planters, upland and South Louisiana farmers, and the hounded Negro stood momentarily successful in the nineties only to be frustrated again by the ascendant Bourbons. The gubernatorial election of 1896 became a political watershed statewide, as the presidential election did nationally. In Louisiana the Democratic Party became entrenched in Bourbon hands, and in the nation the Republicans were to rule supreme.

The mechanism which sustained the Bourbon rule deserves careful attention, however, as the disfranchisement of the Negro voter was,

in the terms developed above, a totalitarian act. The *total* tendency
is to handle difference through its elimination. While in antebellum
Louisiana the constitution had imposed limits on who should vote,
it was not completely restrictive since any citizen who met the
qualifications was granted suffrage. The Constitution of 1898 effectively closed suffrage for most of the Negro population, as the
Bourbons insured that only their kind of people should vote and
control the political destiny of the state.

That is not all, however, since the mechanism, which sustains the
total tendency of closing social relations to those who are different,
requires what may be called an obliterative ideology. The rest of the
population asserts a common identity which distinguishes this *All*,
(union) from the *Other* (difference) who is eliminated or placed
outside of and below the rest.

Twentieth-century totalitarianism has been labeled *sui generis*
because it is argued that the political system of a modern nation-state
can be captured only by a single mass party with official ideology,
through means of controlling the military and mass communications
and the perfection of terroristic police tactics. Yet, at least one leading
tendency can be said to run through totalitarianism wherever it is
found—the *elimination of difference*. It is possible to argue about what
constitutes a totalitarian political *system*, but there is no question
concerning the total *tendency*—it is a matter of the extent to which an
obliterative force is allowed to operate.

The total tendency is present in Southern society (as in all others,
of course). But the claim here is that the total tendency in the South
was peculiarly consequent upon *one* way of making accommodation
to the endemic communual-mass (planter-farmer) cleavage. This
historic tension, in a time of great stress, as in the Populist threat to
the Bourbon ascendancy, may lead to the assertion of the total
tendency—the elimination of all that is different from the accepted
identity.

To preserve this forced union of all whites, however, it too becomes
trapped. For, once the total solution is used, the only escape lies in the
willingness to handle *difference* some way. To preserve the union of
white supremacy, however, it was necessary only to "push the race

button," to holler "nigger," and a perennial source of political power was tapped. This is what happened in Louisiana as, from 1900 until the Dixiecrat revolt of 1948, the voters within the state did their part in maintaining the Democratic "Solid South." Across the South, a demagogue could appeal to the white masses in the name of white supremacy and gain political power—and provide little by way of improvement in social and economic conditions. But Table 11–3 shows that the total solution did not stick in Louisiana, and the realism of Huey Long encouraged a competitive politics which boded well for a break in Bourbon rule.

The heavy repression of the Bourbons was eased as Longism mobilized the farmer masses, and, although the margin of victory was close, for the first time in Louisiana political history, the lower classes captured political power. The economic realism of the Longs upset Bourbon power in 1928, and, while economic welfare was spread among the "have-nots," the race issue remained dormant. It was demonstrated above that Huey Long, where others (like the Progressive Parker) had failed before him, successfully won and sustained the support of the depressed lower classes of Louisiana and provided a vehicle whereby they might have a voice in government.

Huey Long has been regarded as an American fascist dictator. In the light of the analysis here, this interpretation is to a great extent unjustified. While his control of the state of Louisiana at one time was seemingly absolute, his power rested upon the assertion of difference (mass tendency). There was no racism, and the factional organization bore little resemblance to the European fascist groups except in tactics. On the other hand, as far as the ecological base goes, the analogy is pretty strong. The kind of rural area where Huey Long had his main support is quite similar to those areas of Germany where Adolph Hitler had his main support in 1929–32.[13]

Nilson has pointed out that both in France and Germany, in the plains of Caen studied by Siegfried, and in the *Geest* in the Province of Schleswig-Holstein studied by Heberle, traditional politics had been weak. The rural farmer class predominated both areas, and it

[13] Sten S. Nilson, *Histoire et Sciences Politiques* (Bergen, 1950), in particular pp. 43–48.

had little experience in political activity and tended to be susceptible to the appeals of demagogues and strong in support of new political movement. Both areas contained small agricultural villages where social control and pressure exercised by political leaders was quite effective, for social solidarity was strong. A whole village might vote *en bloc*.

In the European situation, then, conditions of political life are found to be similar to those of the uplands of Louisiana. There subsistence farming predominated and economic pressure was constant. Yet, in the Louisiana Hills a persistent tradition of protest had been found, manifest in the votes on Secession, Populism, Socialism, and Longism. Huey Long falls into the line of upland farmers' movements and southern demagogues, and a strong case can be made that the Long movement was a continuation of Populism.[14] Finally, while Hitler proceeded to obliterate all difference in Germany, in Louisiana Long's actions manifested something other than this aspect of total tendency.

It was ironic, perhaps, that in the elections of 1948 Earl Long's victory promised the continuation of Longism while the success of the States' Rights Party in the presidential election hailed a renewed attempt to use the total tendency to resist the social and economic changes advocated by the national Democratic Party. With support from representatives of the Longs, the Democratic Party carried Louisiana in 1952, and with the appealing candidacy of John F. Kennedy (at least in South Louisiana) they carried the state with a minimum majority of 50.4 percent in 1960. Yet, since 1948, as Louisiana voters anguished over the issue of desegregation, the Democratic Party average presidential support has been but 46 percent of the total votes cast.

---

[14] D. F. Saposs, "The Role of the Middle Class in Social Development: Fascism, Populism, Communism, Socialism," *Economic Essays in Honor of Wesley C. Mitchell* (New York, 1935), 104.

## II. *The Potentials of Change*

It has been argued elsewhere[15] that there is nothing inherent in the processes of industrialization and urbanization which foster liberal tendencies. Recent symposiums on change in the South have consisted of papers in which authors wait impatiently for the liberalization of the South and the increasing competitiveness of a two-party politics.[16] The implied causal relation may not in fact exist. As the Louisiana economy became increasingly industrial and the state's residents more urban, attention was given in the analysis within the chapters above to the impact of these factors on politics. It can be concluded that while such trends may help to explain increased variance in the vote which appeared with the North-South Louisiana cleavage of the 1960's, just as pertinent may be the impasse into which the accommodation of difference had led the electorate.

If such a position has merit, it lies in the assertion that social *change* must be explained in terms of socially relevant variables, related ultimately to the possible types of social order. If the Solid South was maintained by inhibiting the expression of difference, extreme difficulty would be found in accepting a national Democratic Party reorganized into the national majority party through an alignment of the support of a multiplicity of ethnic minorities. A party now committed to civil rights would evoke the strongest resistance and counteractions in those regions least affected by the national trends.

North Louisiana parishes, rural and urban alike, manifested the predictable conservative reaction. It had been the hard core of the old Democratic support in the state, it was the region with the greatest proportionate concentration of Negroes, and the one in which least change in race relations such as voter registration had taken place. It was likewise the region dominated by white Anglo-Saxon protestantism which found its self-interpretation of Democratic Party symbolism rudely perverted.

[15] Howard and Brent, "Social Change," 73.

[16] *Journal of Politics*. Silver Aniversary Issue, "The American South; 1950–1970," XXVI (1964) 1–240; Allan P. Sindler (ed.), *Change in the Contemporary South* (Durham, 1963).

At the same time, it could be concluded that South Louisiana was adjusting itself to new social and economic conditions, not by resistance, but by developing tendencies in the direction of a pluralistic group politics. The success of "Chep" Morrison as Mayor of New Orleans in building an alliance of upper white and Negro voters must be counted as the expression of plural alternative to the total tendency. In the past, there had been differences in North Louisiana as great as those in the southern parishes and, in fact, analysis has shown how Longism built upon these differences by successfully bridging the two areas of the state. But this electoral coalition was overriden in 1960 by the issues of race and religion, and the bulk of the North Louisiana vote went against the entire tendency of national politics as it was represented in the choices open to the electorate in both gubernatorial and presidential elections. The candidacies of Morrison and Kennedy produced ideal conditions for those intent upon making North Louisiana a solid electoral bloc opposed to the acceptance of difference.

Talk is heard about a "new" leadership within southern states, and there are numerous, if widely scattered, examples. It involves a willingness to use the potentials of change to lead the electorate away from the dialectic trap of white supremacy and a closed society, toward the expression of more open tendencies. It is a leadership willing to resist "pushing the race button" as a source of electoral power, a willingness to take on the solution of a variety of issues and problems. In this sense, Governor John J. McKeithen, while he gained his office partly by using the race issue to his advantage, began to display such tendencies. For, as discussion brought out above, Governor McKeithen in building and sustaining a consensus politics (Louisiana style) has taken alternatives which enhance the spread of plural tendencies in the toleration of difference.

Louisiana was part of what Dewey Grantham has called the "Democratic South,"[17] in which the natural electoral majority consisted of farmers and laborers whose perennial political preference had been the Democratic Party. This tendency was associated with a

[17] Dewey Grantham, *The Democratic South* (Athens, 1963).

populist liberalism in the rural areas, however, and even with the race issue aside, there is great difficulty in assimilating this kind of liberalism with the urban industrial liberalism characteristic of general American politics today. Only the Longs had managed to do so with some degree of success in Louisiana, and this proves a partial explanation for the relatively stronger ecological base of Long strength in comparison to that of the national Democrats in recent presidential elections. This is not to say that a more open politics will necessarily be liberal. There is, after all, a conservative position, and the Louisiana electorate may come to find it more desirable.

All potential factional divisions lay dormant following the overwhelming endorsement of Governor McKeithen's second term by the electorate. The unique position of the Governor was seen as November, 1968, approached, and he faced what promised to be a situation similar to the multi-party contest which had faced Governor Earl Long twenty years before, when, mostly by his insistence, the Truman-Barkley ticket was placed on the ballot. Then, the States' Rights Party won a plurality of the electorate's votes. Due to the action of the present governor, again all parties are guaranteed a place on the ballot but, now there is widespread agreement that the position taken by Governor McKeithen could significantly affect the outcome of an election.

History will record the eventual assertions of difference made as political hopefuls announce candidacy for office. What occurs in the gubernatorial elections of 1971–72 will depend greatly upon how the Governor has invested the great powers of his office. Conditions may be prepared for a more open political climate if such social problems as race relations, labor-management relations, and fiscal matters are dealt with actively. On this will rest future manifestation of political tendencies in Louisiana.

# Appendixes

*Table 1*
THE POLITICAL ARITHMETIC OF LOUISIANA, 1810–1964

| | Presidential | | | Gubernatorial | | | Population | |
|---|---|---|---|---|---|---|---|---|
| Year | Total | Demo. | % | Total | Demo. | % | Total | Voting Age Total |
| 1810 | | | | | | | 34,311(wh) | 9,520*Est |
| 1812 | Madison | | | Claiborne | | | | |
| 1816 | Monroe | | | Villeré | | | | |
| 1820 | Monroe | | | Robertson | | | 73,867(wh) | 20,700*Est |
| 1824 | Jackson/Adams (tie) | | | 6,242 Whig(Fr.) | | | | |
| 1828 | 8,600 | 4,605 | 53.5 | 7,367 Whig(Fr.) | | | | |
| 1830 | | | | | | | 89,231(wh) | 24,914*Est |
| 1831 | | | | 8,318 Whig(Fr.) | | | | |
| 1832 | 6,622 | 4,094 | 63.6 | | | | | |
| 1834 | | | | 10,211 | 4,149 | 40.7 | | |
| 1836 | 7,425 | 3,842 | 51.7 | | | | | |
| 1838 | | | | 13,748 | 6,486 | 47.2 | | |
| 1840 | 18,912 | 7,616 | 40.3 | | | | 158,457(wh) | 48,031*Est |
| 1842 | | | | 14,307 | 6,375 | 55.4 | | |
| 1844 | 26,865 | 13,782 | 51.3 | | | | | |
| 1846 | | | | 23,354 | 12,629 | 54.0 | | |
| 1848 | 33,866 | 15,379 | 45.4 | | | | | |
| 1850 | | | | 36,115 | 18,566 | 51.4 | 255,491(wh) | 77,528*Est |
| 1852 | 35,902 | 18,647 | 51.9 | 33,061 | 17,529 | 53.0 | | |
| 1856 | 42,873 | 22,164 | 51.7 | 42,707 | 22,952 | 53.7 | | |
| 1860 | 50,500 | 7,625 | 15.1 | 41,041 | 25,454 | 62.0 | 357,629(wh) | 104,166*Est |
| | So.Dem.- | 22,681 | 44.9 | | | | | |
| | Union- | 20,194 | 40.0 | | | | | |
| 1868 | 113,588 | 80,325 | 70.7 | 102,947 | 38,046 | 36.8 (contested) | | |
| 1870 | | | | (White & Negro) | | | 729,915 | 167,880*Est |
| 1872 | 128,692 | 57,029 | 44.3 | 128,139 | 55,249 | 43.0 (contested) | | |
| 1876 | 145,823 | 70,508 | 48.3 | 150,964 | 84,487 | 55.5 (contested) | | |
| 1879 | | | | 130,892 | 74,098 | 63.5 | | |
| 1880 | 103,457 | 65,066 | 62.9 | | | | 940,263 | 216,260*Est |

*Table I (cont.)*

| | Presidential | | | Gubernatorial | | | Population | |
|---|---|---|---|---|---|---|---|---|
| Year | Total | Demo. | % | Total | Demo. | % | Total | Voting Age Total |
| 1884 | 108,948 | 62,601 | 57.4 | 132,296 | 88,794 | 67.1 | | |
| 1888 | 115,713 | 85,012 | 69.2 | 186,739 | 136,746 | 72.4 | | |
| 1890 | | | | | | | 1,118,588 | 250,553 |
| 1892 | 114,054 | 87,922 | 77.1 | 178,035 | 79,388 | 44.3 | | |
| 1896 | 101,179 | 77,172 | 76.3 | 206,354 | 116,216 | 56.3 | | |
| 1900 | 67,902 | 53,668 | 79.0 | 76,870 | 60,206 | 78.3 | 1,381,625 | 325,943 |
| 1904 | 53,947 | 47,747 | 88.5 | 54,222 | 48,345 | 89.0 | | |
| 1908 | 75,502 | 63,948 | 84.7 | 106,905 | (Democratic Primary) | | | |
| 1910 | | | | | | | 1,656,386 | 414,919 |
| 1912 | 78,803 | 60,435 | 76.7 | 123,408 | » | | | |
| 1916 | 92,982 | 79,875 | 85.9 | 114,519 | » | | | |
| 1920 | 126,396 | 87,519 | 69.2 | 143,553 | » | | 1,798,509 | 924,184 |
| 1924 | 121,951 | 93,218 | 76.4 | 239,529 | » | | | |
| 1928 | 215,833 | 164,655 | 76.3 | 288,915 | » | | | |
| 1930 | | | | | | | 2,101,593 | 1,134,852 |
| 1932 | 268,804 | 249,418 | 92.8 | 379,949 | » | | | |
| 1936 | 329,778 | 292,894 | 88.8 | 540,370 | » | | | |
| 1940 | 372,305 | 319,751 | 85.9 | 553,723 | » | | 2,363,880 | 1,374,947 |
| 1944 | 349,383 | 281,564 | 80.6 | 479,354 | » | | | |
| 1948 | 416,336 | 136,344 | 32.7 | 656,499 | (2nd Primary) | | | |
| 1950 | | | | | | | 2,683,516 | 1,587,145 |
| 1952 | 651,952 | 345,027 | 52.9 | 785,045 | (2nd Primary) | | | |
| 1956 | 617,544 | 243,977 | 39.5 | 819,709 | (1st Primary) | | | |
| 1960 | 807,891 | 407,339 | 50.4 | 901,791 | (2nd Primary) | | 3,257,022 | 1,803,805 |
| 1964 | 896,293 | 387,068 | 43.2 | 944,066 | (2nd Primary) | | | |

*Table 1 (cont.)*

| Year | White Voting Age | Negro Voting Age | Registration Total | White | Negro | Per-cent Negro | Turnout Pres. | Gubn. | |
|------|------|------|------|------|------|------|------|------|------|
| 1812 | | | | | | | | | |
| 1816 | | | | | | | | | |
| 1820 | | | | | | | | | |
| 1824 | | | | | | | | | Est. of |
| 1828 | ................................................ | | | | | | 34.4 | 29.7 | White |
| 1830 | | | | | | | | | Male |
| 1831 | ....................................................... | | | | | | | 33.2 | Voting |
| 1832 | ................................................ | | | | | | 26.4 | | Age |
| 1834 | | | | | | | | | Voting |
| 1836 | | | | | | | | | |
| 1838 | ....................................................... | | | | | | | 29.2 | |
| 1840 | ................................................ | | | | | | 39.4 | | |
| 1842 | | | | | | | | | |
| 1844 | | | | | | | | | |
| 1848 | ................................................ | | | | | | 43.7 | | |
| 1850 | ........................................................... | | | | | | | 46.6 | |
| 1852 | ................................................ | | | | | | 46.3 | | |
| 1856 | | | | | | | | | |
| 1860 | ................................................ | | | | | | 48.4 | 39.4 | |
| 1868 | ............... | | 146,398 | ...................... | | | 77.5 | 70.0 | Per- |
| 1870 | | | | | | | | | cent of |
| 1872 | | | | | | | | | Registered |
| 1876 | | | | | | | | | Voters |
| 1879 | ............... | | 172,943 | 87,978 | 84,965 | 49.1 | — | 74.0 | Voting |
| 1880 | ............... | | 173,475 | 85,451 | 88,024 | 50.7 | 59.6 | — | |
| 1884 | ............... | | 218,906 | 108,644 | 110,262 | 50.7 | 49.8 | 60.4 | |
| 1888 | ............... | | 254,807 | 126,884 | 127,923 | 50.2 | 45.4 | 73.3 | |
| 1890 | 130,748 | 119,815 | | | | | | | |
| 1892 | ............... | | 267,000* | 140,000* | 127,000 | 47.6 | 42.7 | 66.6*Est. | |
| 1896 | ............... | | 280,018 | 153,169 | 126,849 | 45.3 | 36.1 | 73.7 | |

* U.S. Census, Louisiana State Reports.

*Table 1 (cont.)*

| | White Voting | Negro Voting | Registration | | | Per- cent | Turnout | |
|---|---|---|---|---|---|---|---|---|
| Year | Age | Age | Total | White | Negro | Negro | Pres. | Gubn. |
| 1900 | 177,878 | 148,065 | 130,725 | 125,437 | 5,320 | 4.1 | 51.9 | 55.9 |
| 1904 | ............... | ....... | 108,079 | 106,360 | 1,718 | 1.6 | 49.9 | 50.2 |
| 1908 | ............... | ....... | 154,142 | 152,142 | 1,743 | 1.1 | 49.0 | 69.3 |
| 1910 | 240,001 | 174,918 | | | | | | |
| 1912 | ............... | ....... | 154,828 | 153,044 | 1,684 | 1.1 | 50.9 | 79.7 |
| 1916 | ............... | ....... | 187,312 | 185,313 | 1,979 | 1.1 | 49.6 | 61.1 |
| 1920 | 564,017 | 360,167 | 260,815 | 257,282 | 3,533 | 1.4 | 48.5 | 55.0 |
| 1924 | ............... | ....... | 323,555 | 322,600 | 955 | 0.3 | 37.7 | 74.0 |
| 1928 | ............... | ....... | 379,270 | 377,246 | 2,054 | 0.5 | 56.9 | 76.2 |
| 1930 | 703,239 | 431,613 | 352,704 | 350,425 | 2,279 | 0.6 | | |
| 1932 | ............... | ....... | 559,233 | 557,674 | 1,559 | 0.3 | 48.1 | 67.9 |
| 1936 | ............... | ....... | 643,632 | 641,589 | 2,043 | 0.3 | 51.2 | 83.9 |
| 1940 | 899,960 | 474,987 | 702,545 | 701,659 | 886 | 0.1 | 53.0 | 78.8 |
| 1944 | ............... | ....... | 722,715 | 721,043 | 1,672 | 0.2 | 48.3 | 66.3 |
| 1948 | ............... | ....... | 924,705 | 896,417 | 28,177 | 3.1 | 45.0 | 70.9 |
| 1950 | 1,105,861 | 481,284 | 818,031 | 756,356 | 61,675 | 7.5 | | |
| 1952 | ............... | ....... | 1,056,720 | 945,038 | 107,844 | 10.2 | 61.7 | 74.2 |
| 1956 | ............... | ....... | 1,057,687 | 905,614 | 152,073 | 14.4 | 58.3 | 77.5 |
| 1960 | 1,289,216 | 514,589 | 1,152,398 | 992,586 | 159,812 | 13.9 | 70.1 | 78.2 |
| 1964 | ............... | ....... | 1,202,056 | 1,037,339 | 164,717 | 13.7 | 73.2 | 77.1 |

*Table 2*
DEMOCRATIC PERCENTAGE IN PRESIDENTIAL ELECTIONS:
1836–1964

| Year | U.S. | "South" | Louisiana | δ La./U.S. | δ La./South |
|------|------|---------|-----------|------------|-------------|
| 1836 | 50.8 | 49.4 | 51.7 | +0.9 | −2.3 |
| 1840 | 46.8 | 45.0 | 40.2 | −6.6 | −5.2 |
| 1844 | 49.5 | 50.8 | 51.3 | +1.8 | +0.5 |
| 1848 | 42.5 | 47.9 | 45.4 | +2.9 | −2.5 |
| 1852 | 50.7 | 53.4 | 51.9 | +1.2 | −1.5 |
| Ave. | 49.8 | 49.3 | 48.1 | −1.7 | −1.2 |
| 1856 | 45.3 | 56.0 | 51.6 | +6.3 | −4.4 |
| 1860 | 29.5 | 9.4 | 15.0 | −14.5 | +5.6 |
| Ave. | 37.4 | 32.7 | 33.3 | −4.1 | +0.6 |
| 1864 | 44.9 | 54.6 | — | | |
| 1868 | 47.3 | 55.5 | 70.7 | +26.3 | +15.2 |
| 1872 | 44.0 | 47.4 | 44.3 | +0.3 | −3.1 |
| 1876 | 50.9 | 59.5 | 48.3 | −2.6 | −11.2 |
| Ave. | 46.7 | 54.2 | 54.4 | +8.1 | +0.2 |
| 1880 | 47.9 | 51.7 | 62.8 | +14.9 | +5.7 |
| 1884 | 48.9 | 57.8 | 57.4 | +8.5 | −0.4 |
| 1888 | 48.6 | 42.2 | 73.4 | +24.8 | +31.2 |
| 1892 | 46.0 | 56.4 | 77.0 | +31.0 | +20.6 |
| Ave. | 47.8 | 53.4 | 69.0 | +21.2 | +15.6 |
| 1896 | 45.9 | 56.2 | 76.3 | +30.4 | +20.1 |
| 1900 | 45.5 | 58.1 | 79.0 | +33.9 | +20.9 |
| 1904 | 37.6 | 60.6 | 88.5 | +50.9 | +27.9 |
| 1908 | 43.1 | 57.8 | 84.7 | +41.6 | +26.9 |
| 1912 | 41.9 | 58.3 | 76.7 | +34.8 | +18.4 |
| 1916 | 49.3 | 62.7 | 85.9 | +34.6 | +23.2 |
| Ave. | 49.4 | 59.5 | 82.9 | +33.5 | +23.4 |

*Table 2 (cont.)*

| Year | U.S. | "South" | Louisiana | δ La./U.S. | δ La./South |
|------|------|---------|-----------|------------|-------------|
| 1920 | 34.1 | 53.6 | 69.2 | +35.1 | +15.6 |
| 1924 | 28.8 | 56.8 | 76.4 | +47.6 | +19.6 |
| 1928 | 40.8 | 46.7 | 76.3 | +35.5 | +29.6 |
| Ave. | 34.4 | 52.7 | 73.9 | +39.5 | +21.2 |
| 1932 | 57.4 | 70.9 | 92.8 | +35.4 | +21.9 |
| 1936 | 60.8 | 76.1 | 88.8 | +28.0 | +12.7 |
| 1940 | 54.7 | 73.4 | 85.9 | +31.2 | +12.5 |
| 1944 | 53.4 | 68.6 | 80.6 | +27.2 | +12.0 |
| Ave. | 58.5 | 72.2 | 84.5 | +26.0 | +12.3 |
| 1948 | 49.6 | 45.8 | 32.7 | −16.9 | −13.1 |
| 1952 | 44.4 | 52.0 | 52.9 | +8.5 | +0.9 |
| 1956 | 42.0 | 49.8 | 39.5 | −12.5 | −10.3 |
| 1960 | 49.7 | 49.7 | 50.4 | +0.7 | +0.7 |
| Ave. | 45.3 | 49.8 | 47.9 | +2.6 | −1.9 |
| 1964 | 61.1 | 49.5 | 43.2 | −17.9 | −6.3 |

## Table 3

### Parish Percentages for Winning Candidate in Selected Elections: Gubernatorial, 1865–1900*

| Parish | Wells 1865 | Warmoth 1868 | Kellogg 1872 | Nicholls 1876 | Wiltz 1879 | McEnery 1884 | Nicholls 1888 | Foster 1892 | Foster 1896 | Heard 1900 |
|---|---|---|---|---|---|---|---|---|---|---|
| Acadia | — | — | — | — | — | — | 91.8 | 72.4 | 34.7 | 66.1 |
| Ascension | 100.0 | 98.3 | 73.4 | 37.2 | 23.5 | 39.4 | 67.0 | 58.4 | 50.4 | 46.2 |
| Assumption | 93.4 | 75.1 | 59.9 | 50.1 | 43.9 | 36.4 | 46.8 | 27.1 | 28.7 | 72.1 |
| Avoyelles | 64.7 | 57.0 | 59.4 | 48.7 | 54.2 | 65.1 | 64.9 | 49.7 | 61.4 | 88.4 |
| Bienville | 55.2 | 55.4 | 32.9 | 80.9 | 100.0 | 99.8 | 98.1 | 56.5 | 61.7 | 82.8 |
| Bossier | 60.9 | 54.4 | 100.0 | 34.0 | 84.6 | 77.3 | 97.7 | 89.7 | 98.3 | 98.5 |
| Caddo | 32.7 | 57.0 | 66.4 | 39.5 | 81.8 | 79.1 | 93.6 | 70.9 | 92.0 | 98.0 |
| Calcasieu | 100.0 | 21.0 | 14.9 | 93.8 | 91.6 | 89.7 | 76.4 | 36.3 | 36.7 | 84.6 |
| Caldwell | 82.4 | 14.1 | 43.1 | 68.9 | 74.9 | 78.7 | 70.8 | 29.6 | 31.5 | 69.4 |
| Cameron | — | — | 24.1 | 82.5 | 81.0 | 84.7 | 99.5 | 64.5 | 56.2 | 45.0 |
| Carroll | 97.6 | 97.7 | 79.2 | 21.0 | Divided into East Carroll and West Carroll | | | | | |
| Catahoula | 73.0 | 44.8 | 56.4 | 54.4 | 62.4 | 94.2 | 52.8 | 20.0 | 29.4 | 76.2 |
| Claiborne | 56.6 | 46.3 | 40.7 | 78.8 | 79.5 | 78.4 | 75.7 | 63.0 | 44.6 | 83.6 |
| Concordia | 94.6 | 96.0 | 89.9 | 13.4 | 55.3 | 76.5 | 06.6 | 65.4 | 97.4 | 84.9 |
| De Soto | 58.8 | 38.1 | 56.4 | 59.5 | 99.1 | 99.7 | 96.1 | 45.9 | 76.6 | 94.3 |
| E. Baton Rouge | 92.2 | 67.0 | 72.8 | 58.4 | 54.7 | 40.6 | 43.2 | 33.1 | 23.2 | 89.6 |
| E. Carroll | — | — | — | — | 11.5 | 34.7 | 90.3 | 6.5 | 100.0 | 95.2 |
| E. Feliciana | 68.5 | 58.3 | 72.1 | 69.0 | 81.1 | 84.2 | 99.7 | 79.6 | 91.3 | 92.7 |
| Franklin | 82.0 | 03.3 | 33.4 | 50.9 | 99.8 | 99.8 | 99.5 | 52.7 | 62.4 | 77.1 |

* Source: *Louisiana Senate Journal*, 1865, 1872, 1892–1900; *Report of Secretary of State, Louisiana*, 1886–88. Report of Committee of Senate of United States, 2nd Session, 43rd Congress 1876–79, Vol. 4, Part 3, Table pp. 2634–35.

## Table 4
### NUMBER OF WHITES, SLAVES, AND PERCENT CHANGE:
### 1810–60

| YEAR | TOTAL NUMBER OF WHITES | TOTAL NUMBER OF SLAVES | PERCENT SLAVES | PERCENT INCREASE BY DECADE | |
|---|---|---|---|---|---|
| | | | | WHITES | SLAVES |
| 1810 | 34,311 | 34,660 | 49% | — | — |
| 1820 | 73,867 | 69,064 | 48% | 117% | 99% |
| 1830 | 89,231 | 109,588 | 55% | 21% | 57% |
| 1840 | 158,457 | 168,452 | 51% | 77% | 54% |
| 1850 | 255,491 | 244,806 | 49% | 61% | 45% |
| 1860 | 357,629 | 331,726 | 48% | 40% | 35% |

## Table 5
### PROPORTION OF STATE TOTAL WHITE AND SLAVE POPULATIONS
### BY VOTER TYPE AREAS IN PERCENTAGES

| | 1810 | | 1820 | | 1830 | | 1840 | | 1850 | | 1860 | |
|---|---|---|---|---|---|---|---|---|---|---|---|---|
| | W | S | W | S | W | S | W | S | W | S | W | S |
| North La. Hills | — | — | — | — | 2 | 1 | 5 | 4 | 7 | 4 | 7 | 7 |
| Central Pine Hills | 6 | 6 | 8 | 4 | 6 | 4 | 7 | 4 | 4 | 5 | 5 | 6 |
| Macon Ridge | — | — | — | — | — | — | — | — | 1 | 1 | 1 | 1 |
| North La. Planter | 11 | 10 | 7 | 9 | 7 | 10 | 7 | 18 | 9 | 24 | 10 | 31 |
| South La. Planter | 21 | 30 | 14 | 25 | 15 | 28 | 10 | 23 | 8 | 22 | 8 | 20 |
| Florida Parishes | 4 | 3 | 18 | 16 | 16 | 16 | 11 | 15 | 9 | 13 | 7 | 11 |
| South La. Bayou | 14 | 7 | 11 | 9 | 17 | 15 | 12 | 13 | 10 | 13 | 9 | 13 |
| Southwest La. | 20 | 14 | 15 | 14 | 11 | 7 | 8 | 6 | 7 | 6 | 6 | 5 |
| Jefferson | — | — | — | — | 2 | 4 | 3 | 3 | 7 | 2 | 3 | 2 |
| Orleans | 23 | 30 | 27 | 23 | 24 | 15 | 37 | 14 | 36 | 10 | 44 | 4 |

STATE = 100% ......................................................

### Table 6
#### PERCENTAGE INCREASE BY DECADE, WHITE AND SLAVE POPULATIONS

| | 1810 | | 1820 | | 1830 | | 1840 | | 1850 | | 1860 | |
|---|---|---|---|---|---|---|---|---|---|---|---|---|
| | W | S | W | S | W | S | W | S | W | S | W | S |
| North La. Hills | — | — | — | — | — | — | 100 | 967 | 422 | 473 | 54 | 20 |
| Central Pine Hills | — | — | 210 | 38 | 18 | 46 | 77 | 42 | −6 | 97 | 99 | 38 |
| Macon Ridge | — | — | — | — | — | — | — | — | — | — | 38 | 53 |
| North La. Planter | — | — | 35 | 55 | 14 | 81 | 90 | 177 | 110 | 92 | 14 | 73 |
| South La. Planter | — | — | 45 | 57 | 25 | 77 | 19 | 22 | 33 | 43 | 11 | 22 |
| Florida Parishes | — | — | — | — | 5 | 57 | 17 | 35 | 30 | 27 | 11 | 14 |
| South La. Bayou | — | — | 57 | 168 | 88 | 152 | 29 | 38 | 36 | 48 | 29 | 32 |
| Southwest La. | — | — | 62 | 101 | −9 | −24 | 31 | 48 | 39 | 48 | 20 | 140 |
| Jefferson | — | — | — | — | — | — | 205 | 2 | 271 | 20 | −56 | −10 |
| Orleans | — | — | 140 | 38 | 10 | 11 | 180 | 41 | 53 | −23 | 39 | −19 |
| STATE | — | — | 117 | 99 | 21 | 57 | 77 | 54 | 61 | 45 | 40 | 35 |

### Table 7
#### ANTEBELLUM GUBERNATORIAL AND PRESIDENTIAL VOTES BY VOTER TYPE AREAS

| UNIT | Gubernatorial Average Percent "French" 1824/28/31 | Presidential Average Percent Anti-Jackson 1828/32 | Gubernatorial Average Percent Democratic 1834–52 | 1856–60 | Presidential Average Percent Democratic 1836–52 | 1856 |
|---|---|---|---|---|---|---|
| North La. Hills | — | — | 59.4 | 66.2 | 59.1 | 60.4 |
| Central Pine Hills | — | — | 60.1 | 63.8 | 61.4 | 63.2 |
| Macon Ridge | — | — | 54.9 | 57.9 | 58.1 | 59.1 |
| North La. Planter | 35.4 | 30.0 | 53.5 | 57.5 | 48.4 | 52.6 |
| South La. Planter | 76.0 | 46.4 | 42.5 | 56.6 | 42.8 | 53.5 |
| Florida Parishes | 32.5 | 22.8 | 62.7 | 58.7 | 57.7 | 55.7 |
| South La. Bayou | 69.2 | 56.8 | 41.9 | 62.3 | 44.6 | 59.1 |
| Southwest La. | 70.9 | 40.1 | 58.5 | 77.7 | 55.0 | 73.6 |
| Jefferson | 86.5 | 73.5 | 40.9 | 45.4 | 42.3 | 11.5 |
| Orleans | 72.9 | 46.0 | 48.0 | 45.0 | 46.2 | 46.2 |
| STATE | 58.6 | 39.5 | 50.3 | 57.8 | 48.1 | 51.7 |

*Table 8*

PRESIDENTIAL VOTE, 1860, AND AVERAGE PERCENT TURNOUT (1831–60)
BY VOTER TYPE AREAS

| UNIT | Presidential 1860 Percent Vote for | | | Presidential Average Percent Turnout 1840/52/60 | Gubernatorial Average Percent Turnout 1831/52/60 |
|---|---|---|---|---|---|
| | Breckinridge | Douglas | Bell | | |
| North La. Hills | 55.5 | 6.2 | 36.3 | 76.5 | 67.3 |
| Central Pine Hills | 54.2 | 10.8 | 35.0 | 67.6 | 59.3 |
| Macon Ridge | 55.0 | 6.4 | 38.6 | 84.4 | 78.1 |
| North La. Planter | 53.5 | 7.1 | 39.4 | 72.7 | 69.6 |
| South La. Planter | 45.8 | 17.1 | 37.1 | 67.9 | 62.3 |
| Florida Parishes | 52.1 | 12.2 | 35.7 | 73.0 | 62.7 |
| South La. Bayou | 45.7 | 21.6 | 32.7 | 67.1 | 60.3 |
| Southwest La. | 64.0 | 8.0 | 35.2 | 53.8 | 51.8 |
| Jefferson | 12.5 | 25.6 | 61.9 | 36.5 | 26.7 |
| Orleans | 24.3 | 27.6 | 48.1 | 22.3 | 19.2 |
| STATE | 45.0 | 15.0 | 40.0 | 44.7 | 39.7 |

*Table 9*

ELECTION OF DELEGATES TO SECESSION CONVENTION, 1861,
BY VOTER TYPE AREAS

| UNIT | Election of Delegates to Secession Convention, 1861 | | | | |
|---|---|---|---|---|---|
| | Percent Secession | Percent of State Total | | Number of Parishes | |
| | | Secession | Cooperation | Secession | Cooperation |
| North La. Hills | 49.1 | 10.5 | 13.0 | 2 | 3 |
| Central Pine Hills | 35.7 | 5.3 | 11.2 | 0 | 4 |
| Macon Ridge | 59.6 | 1.1 | 1.0 | 1 | 0 |
| North La. Planter | 70.1 | 21.8 | 11.0 | 9 | 1 |
| South La. Planter | 44.0 | 8.6 | 13.1 | 4 | 4 |
| Florida Parishes | 47.5 | 6.3 | 8.3 | 3 | 4 |
| South La. Bayou | 62.2 | 16.4 | 11.5 | 4 | 3 |
| Southwest La. | 66.5 | 8.7 | 5.4 | 4 | 0 |
| Jefferson | 20.2 | 1.0 | 4.5 | 0 | 1 |
| Orleans | 52.5 | 20.3 | 21.0 | 1 | 0 |
| STATE | 54.1 | 100.0 | 100.0 | 28 | 20 |

*Table 10*

PERCENT SLAVES, RATIO WHITE MALES TO SLAVES, PERCENT WEALTH, 1860,
BY VOTER TYPE AREAS

| UNIT | Population 1860 Percent Slave | Ratio White Males 21 Years & Over To Slaves, 1860 | Percent Total Wealth 1860 | White Per Capita Wealth 1860 |
|---|---|---|---|---|
| North La. Hills | 41.8 | 1–3 | 4.46 | $1,048 |
| Central Pine Hills | 52.2 | 1–3 | 7.14 | 1,716 |
| Macon Ridge | 56.1 | 1–3 | 0.89 | 2,051 |
| North La. Planter | 72.9 | 1–10 | 26.11 | 6,118 |
| South La. Planter | 71.0 | 1–10 | 16.83 | 4,193 |
| Florida Parishes | 57.7 | 1–6 | 8.97 | 2,376 |
| South La. Bayou | 53.6 | 1–5 | 12.22 | 2,187 |
| Southwest La. | 43.5 | 1–3 | 5.18 | 1,189 |
| Jefferson | 33.0 | 1–2 | 1.91 | 1,777 |
| Orleans | 8.3 | 1–0.26 | 16.29 | 657 |
| STATE | 47.6 | 1–3 | 100.00% | $1,676 |

*Table 11*

RELATIONSHIP BETWEEN VOTE IN PRESIDENTIAL ELECTIONS IN 1860
AND SUBSEQUENT VOTE FOR SECESSION OR UNION IN SEVEN STATES
IN COUNTIES WITH DIFFERENT PROPORTIONS OF SLAVES

| | | Slaves | | | | | |
|---|---|---|---|---|---|---|---|
| Lipset | | High | | Medium | | Low | |
| | | Br. | Bell | Br. | Bell | Br. | Bell |
| VOTE ON SECESSION | | | | | | | |
| SECESSION | | 82% | 61% | 82% | 30% | 50% | 14% |
| UNION | | 18 | 39 | 18 | 70 | 50 | 86 |
| | (N) | (94) | (87) | (87) | (66) | (130) | (73) |
| Louisiana | | (65.0–100.0%) | | (50.0–64.9%) | | (0.0–49.9%) | |
| SECESSION | | 100% | 50% | 67% | 33% | 62% | 25% |
| UNION | | 0 | 50 | 33 | 67 | 38 | 75 |
| | (N) | (7) | (6) | (9) | (9) | (13) | (4) |

Louisiana Voter Types

SECESSION

| | | High Br. | High Bell | Medium Br. | Medium Bell | Low Br. | Low Bell |
|---|---|---|---|---|---|---|---|
| North La. Hills | (2) | — | — | — | — | 25% | — |
| Central Pine Hills | (–) | — | — | — | — | — | — |
| North La. Planter | (10) | 57% | 33% | 67% | 33% | — | — |
| South La. Planter | (4) | 29 | 67 | — | — | — | — |
| Florida Parishes | (3) | 14 | — | — | — | 25 | — |
| South La. Bayou | (4) | — | — | 33 | 67 | — | — |
| Southwest La. | (4) | — | — | — | — | 50 | — |
| Orleans | (1) | — | — | — | — | — | 100 |
| (N) | (28) | (7) | (3) | (6) | (3) | (8) | (1) |

UNION

| | | High Br. | High Bell | Medium Br. | Medium Bell | Low Br. | Low Bell |
|---|---|---|---|---|---|---|---|
| North La. Hills | (3) | — | — | — | — | 60 | — |
| Central Pine Hills | (4) | — | — | 67 | — | 20 | 33 |
| North La. Planter | (1) | — | — | — | 17 | — | — |
| South La. Planter | (4) | — | 67 | — | 33 | — | — |
| Florida Parishes | (4) | — | 33 | 33 | 17 | 20 | — |
| South La. Bayou | (3) | — | — | — | 33 | — | 33 |
| Southwest La. | (–) | — | — | — | — | — | — |
| Jefferson | (1) | — | — | — | — | — | 34 |
| (N) | (20) | — | (3) | (3) | (6) | (5) | (3) |

*Table 12*

LOUISIANA IN THE UNITED STATES CONGRESS

| Congress | 13th–24th | 25th–32nd | 33rd–36th | 37th–40th | 41st–44th | 45th–52nd |
|---|---|---|---|---|---|---|
| Years | 1813–36 | 1837–52 | 1853–60 | 1861–67 | 1869–76 | 1877–91 |
| **Senate** | | | | | | |
| Affiliation | | | | | | |
| Not Given | 43.7% | — | — | — | — | — |
| Democrat | 31.2 | 81.2% | 100.0% | 0.0% | 14.3% | 99.9% |
| Whig/Republican | 25.1 | 18.8 | 0.0 | 100.0 | 85.7 | 0.1 |
| **House** | | | | | | |
| Affiliation | | | | | | |
| Democrat | 35.5 | 57.9 | 92.3 | 20.0 | 34.5 | 99.9 |
| Whig/Republican | 64.5 | 42.1 | 7.7 | 80.0 | 64.5 | 0.1 |
| **Position of Incumbent Senator** | | | | | | |
| Lawyer | 90.6 | 87.5 | 100.0 | — | 14.3 | |
| Planter | 6.2 | 12.5 | — | — | 28.6 | |
| Military Officer | 3.2 | — | — | — | 42.8 | |
| Politician | — | — | — | — | 14.3 | |
| **Position of Incumbent Congressman** | | | | | | |
| Lawyer | 90.6 | 44.7 | 92.3 | — | 48.4 | |
| Planter | — | 23.7 | 7.7 | — | 29.0 | |
| Military Officer | 9.4 | 5.3 | — | — | 6.4 | |
| Medicine | — | 5.2 | — | — | — | |
| Politician | — | 13.2 | — | — | 3.3 | |
| Other | — | 7.9 | — | — | 12.6 | |

*Table 13*

Post-Bellum Louisiana Politics: An Ecological Panel
Subsequent Voting Behavior of Secession and Cooperation Parishes[†]

| Subsequent Voting Behavior | | Secession Parishes Total (28) | 100% | (One) Whig 1836–52 Union 1860 (6) | (Two) Whig 1836–52 So. Dem. 1860 (7) | (Three) Dem. 1836–52 So. Dem. 1860 (15) |
|---|---|---|---|---|---|---|
| Percent* | High | (11) | 39% | 66% | 29% | 33% |
| Slave | Medium | (8) | 32 | 17 | 42 | 27 |
| 1860 | Low | (9) | 29 | 17 | 29 | 40 |
| Percent | High | (14) | 50% | 66% | 42% | 47% |
| Negro | Medium | (5) | 21 | 17 | 14 | 20 |
| 1870–1900 | Low | (9) | 29 | 17 | 42 | 33 |
| % Negro | High | (12) | 46% | 66% | 29% | 40% |
| Registration | Medium | (7) | 25 | 17 | 42 | 20 |
| 1880–88 | Low | (9) | 29 | 17 | 29 | 40 |
| Ave. Gubn. | High | (4) | 16% | 0% | 0% | 27% |
| Dem. % | Medium | (8) | 32 | 17 | 29 | 33 |
| 1872–76 | Low | (15) | 52 | 83 | 71 | 40 |
| Ave. Gubn. | High | (10) | 36% | 33% | 29% | 53% |
| Dem. % | Medium | (8) | 32 | 33 | 42 | 20 |
| 1879–92 | Low | (8) | 32 | 33 | 29 | 27 |
| Ave. Pres. | High | (10) | 36% | 17% | 29% | 47% |
| Dem. % | Medium | (7) | 25 | 33 | 42 | 13 |
| 1868–76 | Low | (11) | 39 | 50 | 29 | 40 |
| Ave. Pres. | High | (21) | 75% | 83% | 71% | 74% |
| Dem. % | Medium | (4) | 16 | 0 | 29 | 13 |
| 1880–92 | Low | (3) | 9 | 17 | 29 | 13 |
| Gubn. Dem. | High | (15) | 52% | 50% | 71% | 46% |
| Percent | Medium | (7) | 25 | 33 | 14 | 27 |
| 1896 | Low | (6) | 23 | 17 | 14 | 27 |

* The percentage intervals are as follows:  High (65–100%)
Medium (50–64.9%)
Low (0–49.9%)

*Table 13 (cont.)*

| Subsequent Voting Behavior | | Cooperation Parishes Total (20) | 100% | (Four) Whig Union (8) | (Five) Dem. Union (5) | (Six) Whig So. Dem. (1) | (Seven) Dem. So. Dem (6) |
|---|---|---|---|---|---|---|---|
| Percent* | High | (3) | 15% | 25% | 20% | 0% | 0% |
| Slave | Medium | (9) | 45 | 37 | 60 | 0 | 50 |
| 1860 | Low | (8) | 40 | 37 | 20 | 100 | 50 |
| Percent | High | (4) | 20% | 37% | 20% | 0% | 0% |
| Negro | Medium | (9) | 45 | 37 | 60 | 0 | 50 |
| 1870–1900 | Low | (7) | 35 | 25 | 20 | 100 | 50 |
| % Negro | High | (7) | 35% | 50% | 60% | 0% | 0% |
| Registration | Medium | (4) | 20 | 25 | 20 | 0 | 17 |
| 1880–80 | Low | (9) | 45 | 25 | 20 | 100 | 83 |
| Ave. Gubn. | High | (4) | 20% | 0% | 20% | 100% | 33% |
| Dem. % | Medium | (4) | 20 | 25 | 0 | 0 | 33 |
| 1872–76 | Low | (12) | 60 | 75 | 80 | 0 | 33 |
| Ave. Gubn. | High | (7) | 35% | 0% | 60% | 100% | 50% |
| Dem. % | Medium | (5) | 25 | 25 | 0 | 0 | 50 |
| 1879–92 | Low | (8) | 40 | 75 | 40 | 0 | 0 |
| Ave. Pres. | High | (6) | 30% | 0% | 20% | 100% | 66% |
| Dem. % | Medium | (3) | 15 | 12 | 0 | 0 | 33 |
| 1868–76 | Low | (11) | 55 | 88 | 80 | 0 | 0 |
| Ave. Pres. | High | (12) | 60% | 25% | 60% | 100% | 100% |
| Dem. % | Medium | (5) | 25 | 37 | 40 | 0 | 0 |
| 1880–92 | Low | (3) | 15 | 37 | 0 | 0 | 0 |
| Gubn. Dem. | High | (4) | 20% | 25% | 40% | 0% | 0% |
| Percent | Medium | (5) | 25 | 50 | 20 | 0 | 0 |
| 1896 | Low | (11) | 55 | 25 | 40 | 100 | 100 |

* The percentage intervals are as follows:     High (65–100%)
Medium (50–64.9%)
Low (0–49.9%)

*Table 13 (cont.)*

| Subsequent Voting Behavior | | Secession Parishes Total | | (One) Whig 1836–52 Union 1860 (6) | (Two) Whig 1836–52 So. Dem. 1860 (7) | (Three) Dem. 1836–52 So. Dem. 1860 (15) |
|---|---|---|---|---|---|---|
| | | (28) | 100% | | | |
| Long* | High | (0) | 0% | 0% | 0% | 0% |
| Percent | Medium | (12) | 46 | 33 | 29 | 53 |
| 1928 | Low | (16) | 54 | 66 | 71 | 47 |
| Ave. Long | High | (0) | 0% | 0% | 0% | 0% |
| Percent | Medium | (11) | 38 | 17 | 57 | 40 |
| 1928–56 | Low | (17) | 61 | 83 | 42 | 60 |
| Ave. | High | (2) | 8% | 17% | 0% | 7% |
| Morrison % | Medium | (8) | 28 | 50 | 42 | 13 |
| 1960–64 | Low | (18) | 64 | 33 | 57 | 80 |
| Ave. Pres. | High | (27) | 96% | 83% | 100% | 100% |
| Dem. % | Medium | (1) | 4 | 17 | 0 | 0 |
| 1900–16 | Low | (0) | 0 | 0 | 0 | 0 |
| Ave. Pres. | High | (24) | 86% | 83% | 86% | 87% |
| Dem. % | Medium | (4) | 14 | 17 | 14 | 13 |
| 1920–28 | Low | (0) | 0 | 0 | 0 | 0 |
| Ave. Pres. | High | (27) | 96% | 100% | 100% | 93% |
| Dem. % | Medium | (1) | 4 | 0 | 0 | 7 |
| 1932–44 | Low | (0) | 0 | 0 | 0 | 0 |
| Percent | High | (0) | 0% | 0% | 0% | 0% |
| Dem. % | Medium | (3) | 10 | 0 | 0 | 10 |
| 1948 | Low | (25) | 90 | 100 | 100 | 80 |
| Ave. Pres. | High | (0) | 0% | 0% | 0% | 0% |
| Dem. % | Medium | (11) | 39 | 33 | 42 | 40 |
| 1952–60 | Low | (17) | 61 | 66 | 57 | 60 |
| Percent | High | (1) | 4% | 17% | 0% | 0% |
| Dem. % | Medium | (9) | 32 | 50 | 42 | 20 |
| 1964 | Low | (18) | 64 | 33 | 57 | 80 |

* The percentage intervals are as follows:  High (65–100%)
                                           Medium (50–64.9%)
                                           Low (0–49.9%)

*Table 13 (cont.)*

| Subsequent Voting Behavior | | Cooperation Parishes | | (Four) Whig Union | (Five) Dem. Union | (Six) Whig So. Dem. | (Seven) Dem. So. Dem. |
|---|---|---|---|---|---|---|---|
| | | Total (20) | 100% | (8) | (5) | (1) | (6) |
| Long* Percent 1928 | High | (4) | 20% | 12% | 20% | 0% | 33% |
| | Medium | (7) | 35 | 37 | 20 | 100 | 33 |
| | Low | (9) | 45 | 50 | 60 | 0 | 33 |
| Ave. Long Percent 1928–56 | High | (4) | 20% | 25% | 20% | 0% | 17% |
| | Medium | (9) | 45 | 63 | 0 | 100 | 50 |
| | Low | (7) | 35 | 12 | 80 | 0 | 33 |
| Ave. Morrison % 1960–64 | High | (2) | 10% | 25% | 0% | 0% | 0% |
| | Medium | (6) | 30 | 63 | 20 | 0 | 0 |
| | Low | (12) | 60 | 12 | 80 | 100 | 100 |
| Ave. Pres. Dem. % 1900–16 | High | (14) | 70% | 50% | 60% | 100% | 100% |
| | Medium | (6) | 30 | 50 | 40 | 0 | 0 |
| | Low | (0) | 0 | 0 | 0 | 0 | 0 |
| Ave. Pres. Dem. % 1920–28 | High | (15) | 75% | 50% | 80% | 100% | 100% |
| | Medium | (3) | 15 | 37 | 0 | 0 | 0 |
| | Low | (2) | 10 | 12 | 20 | 0 | 0 |
| Ave. Pres. Dem. % 1932–44 | High | (19) | 95% | 100% | 100% | 0% | 100% |
| | Medium | (1) | 5 | 0 | 0 | 100 | 0 |
| | Low | (0) | 0 | 0 | 0 | 0 | 0 |
| Percent Dem. % 1948 | High | (0) | 0% | 0% | 0% | 0% | 0% |
| | Medium | (0) | 0 | 0 | 0 | 0 | 0 |
| | Low | (20) | 100 | 100 | 100 | 100 | 100 |
| Ave. Pres. Dem. % 1952–60 | High | (1) | 5% | 12% | 0% | 0% | 0% |
| | Medium | (6) | 30 | 50 | 20 | 0 | 17 |
| | Low | (13) | 65 | 37 | 80 | 100 | 83 |
| Percent Dem. % 1964 | High | (3) | 15% | 37% | 0% | 0% | 0% |
| | Medium | (4) | 20 | 37 | 20 | 0 | 0 |
| | Low | (13) | 65 | 12 | 80 | 100 | 100 |

\* The percentage intervals are as follows:    High (65–100%)
Medium (50–64.9%)
Low (0–49.9%)

*Table 13 (cont.)*

† A List of the Categories of Secession and Cooperation Parishes:

| Secession | (one) | (two) | (three) |
|---|---|---|---|
| | Madison | Avoyelles | Bienville |
| | Morehouse | Caddo | Bossier |
| | Orleans | Concordia | Calcasieu |
| | St. Charles | St. Bernard | Carroll |
| | St. Martin | St. Landry | De Soto |
| | St. Mary | Tensas | Franklin |
| | | Vermilion | Iberville |
| | | | Jackson |
| | | | Lafayette |
| | | | Livingston |
| | | | Plaquemines |
| | | | Pt. Coupee |
| | | | Rapides |
| | | | Washington |
| | | | W. Feliciana |

| Cooperation | | | |
|---|---|---|---|
| (four) | (five) | (six) | (seven) |
| Assumption | Ascension | Union | Caldwell |
| LaFourche | E. Baton Rouge | | Catahoula |
| Jefferson | E. Feliciana | | Claiborne |
| St. James | Ouachita | | Natchitoches |
| St. John | Winn | | Sabine |
| St. Tammany | | | St. Helena |
| Terrebonne | | | |
| W. Baton Rouge | | | |

*Table 14*

PRESIDENTIAL VOTE CAST, 1860, AND VOTER REGISTRATION, 1867
BY VOTER TYPE AREA

| UNIT | Percent of State Vote Cast Pres. 1860 | Percent Slaves 1860 | Percent of State Registration of Voters, 1867 Total | White | Negro |
|------|------|------|------|------|------|
| North La. Hills | 12 | 7 | 6 | 10 | 5 |
| Central Pine Hills | 8 | 6 | 5 | 5 | 4 |
| Macon Ridge | 1 | 1 | 1 | 1 | 1 |
| North La. Planter | 17 | 31 | 20 | 7 | 27 |
| | 38% | 45% | 32% | 23% | 37% |
| South La. Planter | 10 | 20 | 14 | 12 | 15 |
| Florida Parishes | 9 | 11 | 9 | 8 | 10 |
| South La. Bayou | 12 | 13 | 12 | 13 | 11 |
| Southwest La. | 6 | 5 | 6 | 8 | 5 |
| | 37% | 49% | 41% | 41% | 41% |
| Jefferson | 3 | 2 | 4 | 3 | 4 |
| Orleans | 22 | 4 | 23 | 33 | 18 |
| | 25% | 6% | 27% | 36% | 22% |
| STATE | 100% | 100% | 100% | 100% | 100% |

*Table 15*

AVERAGE PROPORTION NEGRO, 1870–1900, PERCENT OF STATE REGISTRATION, 1888, AND PERCENT OF STATE DEMOCRATIC VOTE, 1888

| UNIT | Average Proportion Negro | | Percent of State Registration 1888 | | | Percent State Democratic Vote 1888 |
|---|---|---|---|---|---|---|
| | Population 1870–1900 | Registration 1880–88 | Total | White | Negro | |
| North La. Hills | 45.2 | 39.3 | 8.2 | 9.6 | 7.1 | 10 |
| Central Pine Hills | 36.1 | 38.0 | 4.9 | 5.6 | 4.3 | 6 |
| Macon Ridge | 60.0 | 54.8 | 2.1 | 1.2 | 0.7 | 2 |
| North La. Planter | 77.5 | 72.6 | 17.2 | 10.4 | 26.0 | 26 |
| South La. Planter | 77.5 | 72.3 | 14.0 | 8.1 | 20.1 | 9 |
| Florida Parishes | 49.7 | 47.6 | 8.6 | 8.0 | 9.5 | 7 |
| South La. Bayou | 48.9 | 52.6 | 13.7 | 13.0 | 15.0 | 10 |
| Southwest La. | 29.9 | 27.8 | 9.6 | 12.8 | 10.2 | 8 |
| Jefferson | 44.9 | 65.0 | 2.3 | 0.9 | 0.8 | 2 |
| Orleans | 26.7 | 25.1 | 19.5 | 30.1 | 9.4 | 20 |
| STATE | 49.1 | 50.8 | 100.0% | 100.0% | 100.0% | 100% |

*Table 16*

PROPORTION OF VOTER UNITS TO STATE TOTAL QUALIFIED VOTERS: 1860, 1888, 1908

| VOTER TYPE | Percent of State Total White Males 21 Years & 1860 | Percent of State Registration Voters 1888 | | | Percent of State Registration Voters 1908 | | |
|---|---|---|---|---|---|---|---|
| | | Total | White | Negro | Total | White | Negro |
| North La. Hills | 6.4 | 8.2 | 9.6 | 7.1 | 9.7 | 9.3 | |
| Central Pine Hills | 5.6 | 4.9 | 5.6 | 4.3 | 8.3 | 7.0 | |
| Macon Ridge | 0.4 | 2.1 | 1.2 | 0.7 | 0.5 | 3.4 | |
| North La. Planter | 9.4 | 17.2 | 10.4 | 26.0 | 9.9 | 9.9 | |
| South La. Planter | 6.1 | 14.0 | 8.1 | 20.1 | 7.7 | 8.0 | |
| Florida Parishes | 6.2 | 8.6 | 8.0 | 9.5 | 8.7 | 8.6 | |
| South La. Bayou | 8.0 | 13.7 | 13.0 | 15.0 | 11.4 | 11.2 | |
| Southwest La. | 5.3 | 9.6 | 12.8 | 10.2 | 13.9 | 13.8 | |
| Jefferson | 2.6 | 2.3 | 0.9 | 0.8 | 2.0 | 2.1 | |
| Orleans | 50.0 | 19.5 | 30.1 | 9.4 | 28.0 | 27.7 | |

*Table 17*

DEMOCRATIC GUBERNATORIAL AND PRESIDENTIAL VOTES, 1868–96

| UNIT | Presidential Average Percent Democratic | | Gubernatorial Average Percent Democratic | | Percent Democratic 1896 | |
|---|---|---|---|---|---|---|
| | 1868–76 | 1880–92 | 1872–76 | 1879–92 | Pres. | Gub. |
| North La. Hills | 83.5 | 91.1 | 60.6 | 80.3 | 94.9 | 51.6 |
| Central Pine Hills | 69.6 | 77.6 | 56.7 | 66.5 | 93.0 | 33.3 |
| Macon Ridge | 84.9 | 97.2 | 67.7 | 89.4 | 91.9 | 60.5 |
| North La. Planter | 40.8 | 84.7 | 30.2 | 75.2 | 87.4 | 88.5 |
| South La. Planter | 34.4 | 44.5 | 35.0 | 36.9 | 38.8 | 56.6 |
| Florida Parishes | 55.5 | 76.2 | 57.8 | 61.9 | 84.0 | 56.4 |
| South La. Bayou | 44.6 | 59.2 | 43.9 | 47.3 | 71.1 | 54.2 |
| Southwest La. | 80.0 | 72.1 | 71.6 | 68.2 | 82.8 | 53.1 |
| Jefferson | 47.9 | 43.1 | 34.8 | 36.7 | 79.3 | 78.6 |
| Orleans | 71.3 | 70.3 | 55.2 | 63.9 | 65.6 | 54.8 |
| STATE | 54.4 | 66.4 | 47.8 | 61.9 | 76.3 | 56.2 |

Table 18
REGISTRATION AND THE VOTE
1896–1900

| | Registration and the Vote | | | | | | Gubn. 1900 Vote as Percent 1896 Vote | 1896–1900 Ratio of Negro To White Percent Change in Registration |
|---|---|---|---|---|---|---|---|---|
| | 1896 | | | 1900 | | | | |
| UNIT | White | Negro | Gubn. Turnout | White | Negro | Gubn. Turnout | | |
| North La. Hills | 61.0 | 39.0 | 68.7 | 95.0 | 5.0 | 55.7 | 48.7 | 39.8 |
| Central Pine Hills | 70.1 | 29.9 | 65.2 | 97.5 | 2.5 | 55.8 | 58.7 | 51.5 |
| Macon Ridge | 36.4 | 63.6 | 84.9 | 87.1 | 12.9 | 54.7 | 21.4 | 31.1 |
| North La. Planter | 34.3 | 65.7 | 59.6 | 95.4 | 4.6 | 47.7 | 21.1 | 80.2 |
| South La. Planter | 32.3 | 67.7 | 65.6 | 89.4 | 10.6 | 89.4 | 30.8 | 60.9 |
| Florida Parishes | 59.8 | 40.2 | 54.9 | 94.0 | 6.0 | 54.0 | 25.9 | 25.5 |
| South La. Bayou | 54.0 | 46.0 | 62.9 | 97.3 | 2.7 | 73.5 | 42.8 | 51.9 |
| Southwest La. | 73.3 | 26.7 | 74.0 | 98.7 | 1.3 | 57.0 | 48.0 | 31.8 |
| Jefferson | 45.0 | 55.0 | (227.0) | 85.6 | 14.4 | 87.9 | 39.3 | 71.5 |
| Orleans | 76.4 | 23.6 | 76.4 | 96.3 | 3.7 | 56.9 | 45.5 | 8.0 |
| STATE | 54.7 | 45.3 | 73.7 | 95.9 | 4.1 | 55.9 | 37.2 | 19.4 |

## Table I

### Parish Percentage for Winning Party in Selected Elections: Gubernatorial, 1824–60, and Presidential, 1828 and 1832*

| Parish | Am. 1824 | Creole 1828 | Presidential Jackson 1828 | Jackson 1832 | Creole 1831 | Creole 1834 | Whig 1838 | Dem. 1842 | Dem. 1846 | Dem. 1850 | Dem. 1852 | Dem. 1856 | So. Dem. 1860 |
|---|---|---|---|---|---|---|---|---|---|---|---|---|---|
| Ascension | 71.7 | 80.3 | 50.0 | 87.4 | 12.5 | 82.4 | 31.0 | 48.6 | 54.2 | 50.0 | 53.8 | 63.8 | 63.8 |
| Assumption | 43.9 | 53.7 | 50.0 | 15.4 | 41.6 | 94.1 | 35.3 | 62.7 | 52.5 | 43.8 | 57.2 | 76.0 | 85.0 |
| Avoyelles | 51.1 | N | 24.5 | 58.3 | 42.4 | 66.2 | 71.6 | 51.6 | 60.5 | 59.7 | 46.9 | 59.6 | 62.7 |
| Bienville | — | — | — | — | — | — | — | — | — | 72.4 | 67.0 | 71.9 | 85.3 |
| Bossier | — | — | — | — | — | — | — | — | — | 67.6 | N | 55.2 | 73.8 |
| Caddo | — | — | — | — | — | — | 69.5 | D | 77.2 | 73.5 | 75.3 | 93.1 | 93.7 |
| Calcasieu | — | — | — | — | — | — | — | D | — | 54.8 | 45.3 | 48.8 | 51.9 |
| Caldwell | — | — | — | — | — | — | 23.1 | 64.0 | 76.5 | 67.1 | 67.1 | 76.9 | 71.0 |
| Carroll | — | — | — | — | — | — | 42.6 | D | 52.3 | 54.6 | N | 59.0 | 74.1 |
| Catahoula | 87.8 | 18.8 | 79.4 | 75.1 | 7.4 | 29.3 | 77.5 | D | 60.4 | 59.3 | 52.0 | 48.4 | 61.7 |
| Claiborne | — | — | — | — | — | — | — | 31.4 | 74.0 | 66.9 | 53.7 | 55.6 | 63.2 |
| Concordia | 54.1 | 44.8 | 62.5 | 67.1 | 28.5 | 54.6 | 96.5 | — | 48.0 | 40.6 | 29.8 | 27.5 | 58.4 |
| De Soto | — | — | — | — | — | — | — | — | 74.1 | 62.4 | 51.0 | 58.0 | 68.2 |
| E. Baton Rouge | 85.7 | 9.5 | 62.3 | 56.9 | 40.8 | 47.0 | 56.0 | 53.5 | 66.2 | 55.0 | 50.9 | 47.3 | 60.4 |
| E. Feliciana | 92.4 | 7.3 | 84.6 | 92.3 | 5.2 | 12.5 | N | 56.7 | 57.0 | 54.8 | 53.7 | 53.5 | 64.3 |
| Franklin | — | — | — | — | — | — | — | D | 53.1 | 61.3 | 60.3 | 57.3 | 58.5 |
| Iberville | 48.6 | 71.3 | 74.2 | 61.9 | 49.0 | 70.2 | 44.5 | D | 48.2 | 46.0 | 60.0 | 62.1 | 80.7 |
| Jackson | — | — | — | — | — | — | — | — | 54.6 | 66.2 | 54.7 | 61.9 | 72.0 |
| Jefferson | — | 82.0 | 27.6 | 25.5 | 83.4 | 74.8 | 64.4 | 33.6 | 47.4 | 53.0 | 48.8 | 40.1 | 50.7 |
| Lafayette | 24.6 | 28.0 | 56.8 | 63.0 | 52.5 | 63.1 | 25.0 | 65.0 | 68.3 | 60.3 | 71.9 | 74.3 | 98.2 |
| Lafourche | 36.0 | 86.0 | N | N | 73.8 | 96.8 | 24.6 | 17.8 | 21.4 | 17.6 | 17.3 | 66.3 | 68.2 |
| Livingston | — | — | — | — | — | 17.8 | 27.8 | 77.7 | 61.7 | 61.1 | 67.2 | 61.1 | 81.2 |
| Madison | — | — | — | — | — | — | 51.0 | 47.0 | 47.6 | 49.3 | 48.9 | 41.7 | 60.6 |
| Morehouse | — | — | — | — | — | — | — | — | 34.5 | 40.3 | 42.0 | N | 58.1 |

* Source: *Louisiana Senate Journal*, 1824–1860; Norton, "Origins of the Whig Party in Louisiana" (Master's thesis, Louisiana State University, 1933); *Whig Almanac*, 1844.

Table I (cont.)

| Parish | Am. 1824 | Creole 1828 | Presidential Jackson 1828 | Presidential Jackson 1832 | Creole 1831 | Creole 1834 | Whig 1838 | Dem. 1842 | Dem. 1846 | Dem. 1850 | Dem. 1852 | Dem. 1856 | So. Dem. 1860 |
|---|---|---|---|---|---|---|---|---|---|---|---|---|---|
| Natchitoches | 30.2 | 43.0 | 63.5 | 75.6 | 49.4 | 45.8 | N | D | 57.3 | 60.7 | 55.6 | 54.3 | 60.2 |
| Orleans | 23.3 | 56.0 | 52.9 | 59.1 | 47.3 | 63.8 | 49.9 | 44.3 | 50.0 | 51.1 | 56.4 | 49.1 | 40.5 |
| Ouachita | 65.7 | 25.2 | 60.7 | 75.3 | 20.8 | 44.0 | 41.7 | D | 62.4 | 57.5 | 52.6 | 58.1 | 61.7 |
| Plaquemines | 5.7 | 25.3 | 29.0 | 94.4 | 90.4 | 12.5 | 29.1 | 66.8 | 72.1 | 66.8 | 78.3 | 50.4 | 88.8 |
| Pointe Coupee | 43.4 | 65.4 | 57.7 | 84.9 | 5.2 | N | 21.0 | 72.2 | 59.2 | 59.1 | 62.8 | 59.8 | 89.7 |
| Rapides | N | 36.0 | 74.6 | 65.9 | 31.7 | 38.6 | 57.6 | 53.9 | 64.1 | 64.2 | 65.9 | 48.8 | 59.3 |
| Sabine | — | — | — | — | — | — | — | — | 60.8 | 52.6 | 54.0 | 62.9 | 74.4 |
| St. Bernard | N | 57.6 | 39.9 | 100.0 | 40.1 | 88.8 | 48.8 | 47.2 | 51.2 | 48.0 | 56.4 | 52.6 | 71.4 |
| St. Charles | N | 85.8 | 40.6 | 93.5 | 52.1 | 58.5 | 35.0 | W | 32.9 | 27.8 | 20.9 | 49.5 | 56.3 |
| St. Helena | 90.7 | 0.3 | 84.7 | 92.5 | 27.4 | N | 43.4 | 68.6 | 60.0 | 61.7 | 52.4 | 50.1 | 56.0 |
| St. James | 6.0 | 89.0 | 28.2 | 62.2 | 72.2 | 72.0 | 75.6 | W | 47.0 | 33.0 | 39.3 | 33.8 | 52.6 |
| St. John | 1.3 | 89.0 | 28.0 | 47.0 | 70.3 | 90.0 | 58.6 | W | 41.1 | 40.0 | 46.4 | 47.0 | 68.0 |
| St. Landry | 28.6 | 82.0 | 19.9 | N | 62.4 | 61.6 | 70.7 | 44.3 | 63.0 | 34.2 | 38.4 | 58.0 | 66.9 |
| St. Martin | 10.4 | 52.0 | 19.6 | 22.7 | 32.8 | 89.0 | 60.5 | 74.7 | 39.3 | 28.9 | 40.7 | 61.1 | 57.7 |
| St. Mary | 41.5 | 57.6 | 39.5 | 31.8 | 70.6 | 70.0 | 59.4 | 32.4 | N | 50.0 | 35.5 | 42.2 | 69.8 |
| St. Tammany | 80.8 | 23.7 | 78.0 | 74.8 | 69.0 | 15.0 | 51.3 | 62.4 | 57.5 | 51.5 | 41.4 | 27.7 | 52.0 |
| Tensas | — | — | — | — | — | — | — | — | 51.9 | 50.5 | 47.7 | 53.5 | 75.2 |
| Terrebonne | 84.7 | 9.8 | 43.7 | 18.8 | 72.0 | 88.0 | 82.5 | 12.5 | 31.0 | 37.2 | 43.1 | 49.3 | 43.5 |
| Union | — | — | — | — | — | — | — | D | 45.0 | 59.3 | 51.7 | 55.1 | 60.0 |
| Vermilion | — | — | — | — | — | — | — | — | 42.9 | 50.8 | 56.8 | 62.6 | 95.4 |
| Washington | 85.6 | 0.3 | 80.4 | 83.2 | 30.8 | 8.9 | 65.6 | 83.6 | 73.6 | 76.0 | 61.7 | 61.2 | 81.1 |
| W. Baton Rouge | 48.6 | 4.3 | 53.0 | 17.6 | 48.9 | 88.0 | 68.6 | 40.7 | 40.0 | 39.4 | 36.2 | 38.4 | 54.3 |
| W. Feliciana | — | 25.6 | 69.6 | 68.3 | 22.6 | 12.0 | 47.5 | 60.4 | 69.0 | 57.9 | 60.7 | 50.7 | 69.0 |
| Winn | — | — | — | — | — | — | — | — | — | — | 63.8 | 63.5 | 74.7 |
| STATE AVERAGE | 42.4 | 44.1 | 53.0 | 68.1 | 43.6 | 59.3 | 52.8 | 55.4 | 54.0 | 51.4 | 53.0 | 53.7 | 62.0 |

— Not yet a Parish   N No returns   W Whig Majority   D Democratic

## Table 2

VOTING PERCENTAGES, DEMOCRATIC PARTY PRESIDENTIAL
ELECTIONS 1836–60 BY PARISHES*

| Parish | Dem. 1836 | Dem. 1840 | Dem. 1844 | Dem. 1848 | Dem. 1852 | Dem. 1856 | Dem. 1860 | So. Dem. 1860 | Const. Union 1860 |
|---|---|---|---|---|---|---|---|---|---|
| Ascension | 76.1 | 50.0 | 52.5 | 45.0 | 54.9 | 63.4 | 45.7 | 18.5 | 35.8 |
| Assumption | 45.1 | 54.0 | 49.5 | 37.8 | 52.0 | 81.0 | 46.7 | 30.4 | 22.9 |
| Avoyelles | 18.2 | 47.4 | 65.8 | 54.5 | 56.3 | 64.4 | 6.6 | 71.6 | 21.8 |
| Bienville | .... | .... | .... | 62.4 | 64.5 | 70.4 | 12.1 | 61.5 | 26.4 |
| Bossier | .... | .... | 63.5 | .... | 57.9 | 48.6 | 6.9 | 61.3 | 31.8 |
| Caddo | .... | .... | 42.5 | 51.6 | 48.9 | 48.1 | 31.0 | 52.5 | 44.5 |
| Calcasieu | .... | .... | 75.3 | 81.5 | 86.7 | 92.2 | .... | 94.3 | 5.7 |
| Caldwell | .... | .... | 73.8 | 62.3 | 74.5 | 75.1 | 10.0 | 63.5 | 26.5 |
| Carroll | 53.8 | 54.3 | 53.8 | 46.7 | 54.4 | 60.5 | 5.9 | 53.7 | 40.4 |
| Catahoula | 56.3 | 47.1 | 55.6 | 54.7 | 52.5 | 52.1 | 1.8 | 59.5 | 38.7 |
| Claiborne | 77.0 | .... | 65.6 | 59.4 | 60.5 | 55.7 | 9.3 | 50.3 | 40.4 |
| Concordia | 35.0 | 29.6 | 33.6 | 33.8 | 41.5 | 46.5 | 1.5 | 52.7 | 45.8 |
| De Soto | .... | .... | 74.2 | 59.3 | 54.4 | 63.3 | 0.2 | 63.4 | 36.4 |
| E. Baton Rouge | 55.7 | 48.7 | 55.1 | 50.4 | 50.1 | 52.3 | 11.4 | 41.0 | 47.6 |
| E. Feliciana | 66.4 | 54.4 | 56.0 | 53.0 | 56.4 | 57.3 | 16.7 | 48.0 | 35.3 |
| Franklin | .... | .... | 54.1 | 56.6 | 63.6 | 59.1 | 6.4 | 54.9 | 38.7 |
| Iberville | 60.2 | 47.1 | 48.1 | 40.7 | 57.2 | 66.1 | 11.7 | 61.8 | 26.5 |
| Jackson | .... | .... | .... | 60.3 | 66.2 | 58.1 | 11.2 | 54.2 | 34.6 |
| Jefferson | 40.0 | 25.4 | 48.1 | 47.9 | 50.4 | 11.5 | 25.6 | 12.5 | 61.9 |
| Lafayette | 81.3 | .... | 67.4 | 67.1 | 70.3 | 78.0 | 0.2 | 86.7 | 13.1 |
| Lafourche | 24.9 | 75.6 | 22.5 | 17.9 | 16.6 | 71.5 | 48.6 | 20.4 | 31.0 |
| Livingston | 50.0 | 62.0 | 69.6 | 62.8 | 67.9 | 62.9 | 14.8 | 53.8 | 31.4 |
| Madison | .... | 43.0 | 49.0 | 40.4 | 46.2 | 46.8 | 17.7 | 33.1 | 49.2 |
| Morehouse | .... | .... | 22.5 | 36.2 | 41.1 | 48.6 | 6.1 | 49.2 | 44.7 |

* Source: W. Dean Burnham, *Presidential Ballots, 1836–1892* (Johns Hopkins, 1955).

*Table 2 (cont.)*

| Parish | Dem. 1836 | Dem. 1840 | Dem. 1844 | Dem. 1848 | Dem. 1852 | Dem. 1856 | Dem. 1860 | So. Dem. 1860 | Const. Union 1860 |
|---|---|---|---|---|---|---|---|---|---|
| Natchitoches | 36.0 | 47.8 | 59.0 | 56.3 | 58.5 | 58.3 | 7.6 | 54.1 | 38.3 |
| Orleans | 49.6 | 39.5 | 46.3 | 45.2 | 50.6 | 30.3 | 27.6 | 24.3 | 48.1 |
| Ouachita | 56.6 | 34.8 | 66.0 | 51.2 | 55.8 | 60.0 | 18.5 | 39.0 | 42.5 |
| Plaquemines | 83.0 | 86.2 | 96.4 | 65.2 | 71.1 | 54.7 | 28.3 | 59.6 | 12.1 |
| Pointe Coupee | 56.0 | 48.6 | 50.1 | 56.2 | 60.0 | 66.2 | 8.0 | 70.3 | 21.7 |
| Rapides | 40.7 | 44.6 | 58.3 | 58.6 | 60.8 | 56.6 | 5.6 | 59.1 | 35.3 |
| Sabine | .... | .... | 60.0 | 52.4 | 51.4 | 64.8 | 6.5 | 60.7 | 32.8 |
| St. Bernard | 71.4 | 34.5 | 31.2 | 38.5 | 48.0 | 49.8 | 13.9 | 66.2 | 19.9 |
| St. Charles | 97.0 | 32.3 | 30.4 | 20.6 | 27.8 | 60.8 | 9.8 | 48.4 | 41.8 |
| St. Helena | 81.5 | 58.0 | 59.0 | 50.4 | 54.1 | 46.8 | 2.8 | 51.6 | 45.6 |
| St. James | 32.8 | 8.9 | 56.6 | 21.3 | 33.0 | 31.1 | 19.3 | 28.6 | 52.1 |
| St. John | 100.0 | 25.3 | 44.3 | 35.9 | 44.2 | 52.5 | 22.2 | 32.9 | 44.9 |
| St. Landry | 30.5 | 34.2 | 34.0 | 33.3 | 45.1 | 57.7 | 1.1 | 51.5 | 47.4 |
| St. Martin | 24.8 | 18.2 | 38.7 | 34.5 | 38.3 | 43.9 | 4.1 | 48.1 | 47.8 |
| St. Mary | 30.7 | 22.0 | 28.7 | 26.1 | 38.4 | 45.4 | 9.3 | 49.0 | 41.7 |
| St. Tammany | 76.4 | 28.2 | 54.1 | 39.9 | 45.0 | 42.8 | 24.5 | 30.4 | 45.1 |
| Tensas | .... | .... | 40.7 | 38.5 | 47.1 | 56.6 | 0.7 | 65.0 | 34.3 |
| Terrebonne | 38.3 | 6.0 | 38.2 | 26.8 | 33.0 | 49.0 | 8.7 | 45.7 | 45.6 |
| Union | .... | 50.6 | 50.8 | 43.6 | 51.7 | 53.3 | 1.7 | 55.8 | 42.5 |
| Vermilion | .... | .... | 37.1 | 10.8 | 48.1 | 66.8 | 0.3 | 60.0 | 39.7 |
| Washington | 83.2 | 47.2 | 64.4 | 54.6 | 67.4 | 68.2 | 1.0 | 76.8 | 22.2 |
| W. Baton Rouge | 25.9 | 31.5 | 33.2 | 29.9 | 34.9 | 42.4 | 6.9 | 37.5 | 55.6 |
| W. Feliciana | 60.9 | 53.1 | 55.9 | 52.9 | 61.4 | 59.7 | 6.8 | 56.3 | 36.9 |
| Winn | .... | .... | .... | .... | 70.8 | 66.6 | 28.3 | 41.5 | 30.2 |
| STATE AVERAGE | 51.7 | 40.3 | 51.3 | 45.4 | 51.9 | 51.7 | 15.1 | 44.9 | 40.0 |

.... Not yet a Parish

Table 3

AGE CATEGORIES BY VOTER TYPES*

| | Census 1830 Years | | | | Census 1860 Years | | | | Census 1930 Years | | | | Census 1960 Years | | | |
|---|---|---|---|---|---|---|---|---|---|---|---|---|---|---|---|---|
| | 0–14 | 15–19 | 20–59 | 60 & over | 0–14 | 15–19 | 20–59 | 60 & over | 0–14 | 15–19 | 20–59 | 60 & over | 0–14 | 15–19 | 20–59 | 60 & over |
| North La. Hills | 50.4 | 10.2 | 37.4 | 2.0 | 48.5 | 11.0 | 38.2 | 2.3 | 37.7 | 11.4 | 45.4 | 5.5 | 32.0 | 9.6 | 43.8 | 14.6 |
| Central Pine Hills | 46.8 | 10.8 | 40.7 | 1.7 | 46.6 | 10.5 | 40.0 | 2.9 | 37.1 | 10.9 | 45.8 | 6.2 | 32.3 | 9.5 | 43.3 | 14.9 |
| Macon Ridge | — | — | — | — | 44.1 | 9.7 | 44.3 | 1.9 | 38.1 | 11.1 | 46.1 | 4.7 | 37.6 | 9.5 | 40.2 | 12.7 |
| North La. Planter | 43.3 | 9.9 | 44.7 | 2.1 | 52.5 | 10.0 | 45.4 | 2.1 | 33.5 | 10.3 | 50.0 | 6.2 | 38.1 | 8.2 | 42.5 | 11.2 |
| Caddo | | | | | | | | | 29.6 | 9.6 | 55.5 | 5.3 | 34.0 | 6.9 | 47.5 | 11.6 |
| Ouachita | | | | | | | | | 30.3 | 9.7 | 55.2 | 4.8 | 35.0 | 7.9 | 46.3 | 10.8 |
| Rapides | | | | | | | | | — | — | — | — | 34.1 | 7.9 | 46.7 | 11.3 |
| South La. Planter | 45.0 | 9.0 | 43.4 | 2.6 | 41.6 | 10.1 | 45.2 | 3.1 | 36.0 | 10.1 | 47.1 | 6.8 | 39.3 | 8.4 | 42.0 | 10.3 |
| Florida Parishes | 45.8 | 10.7 | 41.4 | 2.1 | 42.8 | 10.5 | 43.4 | 3.3 | 33.9 | 10.7 | 48.9 | 6.5 | 31.7 | 8.4 | 51.5 | 11.4 |
| E.B.R. | | | | | | | | | — | — | — | — | 35.3 | 8.5 | 48.5 | 7.7 |
| South La. Bayou | 48.3 | 8.8 | 40.3 | 2.6 | 45.2 | 10.9 | 41.4 | 2.5 | 38.9 | 11.2 | 57.0 | 6.9 | 38.8 | 8.2 | 44.3 | 8.7 |
| Southwest La. | 48.4 | 11.4 | 38.2 | 2.0 | 47.5 | 16.2 | 38.7 | 2.6 | 23.8 | 11.5 | 59.9 | 4.8 | 36.7 | 8.7 | 44.0 | 10.6 |
| Calcasieu | | | | | | | | | | | | | 37.2 | 7.5 | 48.5 | 6.8 |
| Lafayette | | | | | | | | | | | | | 36.6 | 8.3 | 47.6 | 7.5 |
| Jefferson | 37.7 | 7.5 | 51.5 | 3.3 | 43.0 | 9.0 | 45.9 | 2.1 | 34.8 | 9.8 | 50.2 | 5.2 | 38.0 | 6.5 | 49.1 | 6.4 |
| Orleans | 33.9 | 9.4 | 53.6 | 3.1 | 34.4 | 8.9 | 54.6 | 2.1 | 25.9 | 8.8 | 58.0 | 7.3 | 30.5 | 7.1 | 50.5 | 12.8 |
| STATE | 42.1 | 10.1 | 45.3 | 2.5 | 39.5 | 9.7 | 48.5 | 2.3 | 33.6 | 10.3 | 50.3 | 5.8 | 35.2 | 8.0 | 46.1 | 10.7 |

* 1830 and 1860 white only. U.S. Census.

Table 3 (cont.)

| Parish | Wells 1865 | Warmoth 1868 | Kellogg 1872 | Nicholls 1876 | Wiltz 1879 | McEnery 1884 | Nicholls 1888 | Foster 1892 | Foster 1896 | Heard 1900 |
|---|---|---|---|---|---|---|---|---|---|---|
| Grant | — | — | 82.5 | 26.1 | 76.8 | 44.4 | 59.1 | 29.4 | 23.5 | 72.7 |
| Iberia | — | — | 61.0 | 35.7 | 37.7 | 63.8 | 76.5 | 38.2 | 44.8 | 57.9 |
| Iberville | 91.2 | 66.9 | 76.4 | 96.5 | 21.8 | 35.3 | 40.8 | 38.3 | 92.4 | 70.5 |
| Jackson | 53.0 | 60.5 | 54.8 | 21.2 | 100.0 | 100.0 | 99.2 | 55.9 | 31.2 | 56.7 |
| Jefferson | 91.2 | 62.9 | 64.1 | 33.7 | N | 23.3 | 40.0 | 46.7 | 78.5 | 92.5 |
| Lafayette | 57.7 | 86.0 | 35.2 | 63.6 | 63.5 | 56.0 | 58.0 | 63.4 | 69.7 | 62.9 |
| Lafourche | 88.8 | 73.8 | 51.4 | 50.1 | 55.6 | 55.4 | 63.5 | 25.3 | 48.4 | 57.5 |
| Lincoln | — | — | — | 76.9 | 100.0 | 99.2 | 100.0 | 81.7 | 40.5 | 59.3 |
| Livingston | 17.0 | 30.5 | 21.5 | 86.5 | 87.1 | 28.6 | 79.9 | 47.2 | 43.1 | 83.1 |
| Madison | 100.0 | 94.6 | 85.2 | 11.8 | 96.8 | 51.8 | 100.0 | 91.4 | 100.0 | 87.3 |
| Morehouse | 69.3 | 53.1 | 66.9 | 64.7 | 85.2 | 97.8 | 99.1 | 75.4 | 72.1 | 95.0 |
| Natchitoches | 86.7 | 78.8 | 100.0 | 46.9 | 72.4 | 80.4 | 92.2 | 37.6 | 46.4 | 87.4 |
| Orleans | 83.8 | 50.1 | 40.6 | 51.0 | 70.3 | 83.7 | 71.4 | 30.3 | 54.8 | 83.3 |
| Ouachita | 92.0 | 80.3 | 70.3 | 69.8 | 99.4 | 99.9 | 99.9 | 66.1 | 73.3 | 70.6 |
| Plaquemines | 79.6 | 85.9 | 82.4 | 29.5 | 33.6 | 27.5 | 36.6 | 37.8 | 53.6 | 87.1 |
| Pointe Coupee | 98.9 | 68.7 | 57.1 | 35.8 | 60.0 | 61.1 | 57.0 | 19.0 | 52.8 | 95.6 |
| Rapides | 38.7 | 68.3 | 64.6 | 48.8 | 68.3 | 59.6 | 91.2 | 60.3 | 75.6 | 94.8 |
| Red River | — | — | 71.6 | 33.1 | 89.7 | 50.9 | 95.5 | 52.2 | 65.3 | 95.9 |
| Richland | — | — | 25.2 | 78.6 | 98.1 | 99.9 | 95.3 | 70.4 | 49.6 | 90.2 |
| Sabine | 72.1 | 43.1 | 7.2 | 97.6 | 99.9 | 100.0 | 99.8 | 52.9 | 47.4 | 83.9 |
| St. Bernard | 95.6 | 65.5 | 64.3 | 48.4 | 65.5 | 50.8 | 69.5 | 11.4 | 74.0 | 96.9 |
| St. Charles | 94.8 | 93.1 | 71.2 | 20.1 | 9.3 | 0.4 | 11.1 | 5.5 | 56.1 | 97.3 |
| St. Helena | 11.8 | 45.2 | 55.3 | 55.8 | 56.8 | 49.4 | 69.5 | 53.6 | 41.7 | 89.6 |
| St. James | 99.9 | 93.4 | 73.8 | 33.1 | 35.6 | 27.6 | 29.0 | 26.1 | 50.1 | 37.4 |

## Table 3 (cont.)

| Parish | Wells 1865 | Warmoth 1868 | Kellogg 1872 | Nicholls 1878 | Wiltz 1879 | McEnery 1884 | Nicholls 1888 | Foster 1892 | Foster 1896 | Heard 1900 |
|---|---|---|---|---|---|---|---|---|---|---|
| St. John | 100.0 | 73.8 | 68.4 | 37.0 | 49.8 | 21.7 | 32.7 | 14.5 | 66.9 | 85.0 |
| St. Landry | 95.3 | 79.5 | 44.6 | 62.5 | 59.9 | 59.2 | 54.3 | 43.6 | 92.8 | 75.7 |
| St. Martin | 90.3 | 53.6 | 51.7 | 50.7 | 44.3 | 54.3 | 40.5 | 72.6 | 85.5 | 96.7 |
| St. Mary | 97.7 | 71.3 | 69.2 | 37.7 | 30.5 | 11.8 | 63.6 | 77.1 | 24.0 | 63.2 |
| St. Tammany | 61.5 | 49.5 | 50.2 | 63.9 | 59.4 | 45.1 | 59.7 | 37.0 | 50.2 | 77.1 |
| Tangipahoa | — | — | 55.6 | 62.6 | 58.6 | 54.6 | 66.5 | 43.5 | 50.5 | 82.4 |
| Tensas | 95.8 | 90.5 | 93.1 | 13.2 | 84.8 | 99.9 | 97.6 | 11.1 | 100.0 | 99.9 |
| Terrebonne | 93.9 | 36.2 | 53.1 | 41.6 | 34.2 | 36.9 | 45.3 | 29.7 | 36.8 | 63.8 |
| Union | 70.2 | 41.4 | 51.5 | 94.5 | 95.3 | 75.9 | 96.3 | 78.4 | 47.8 | 75.5 |
| Vermilion | 95.7 | 77.3 | 47.1 | 76.9 | 76.1 | 74.8 | 73.1 | 58.8 | 28.5 | 76.9 |
| Vernon | — | — | 5.3 | 99.9 | 100.0 | 100.0 | 100.0 | 20.5 | 40.6 | 63.1 |
| Washington | 7.8 | 28.3 | 26.2 | 76.0 | 76.6 | 50.7 | 73.7 | 53.5 | 48.4 | 88.4 |
| Webster | — | — | 58.8 | 51.0 | 50.6 | 41.1 | 82.2 | 84.2 | 74.5 | 89.9 |
| W. Baton Rouge | 99.9 | 55.0 | 100.0 | 32.8 | 37.5 | 66.0 | 79.0 | 23.9 | 60.4 | 90.1 |
| W. Carroll | — | — | — | — | 89.9 | 99.1 | 83.8 | 60.8 | 79.6 | 90.1 |
| W. Feliciana | — | 76.4 | 82.7 | 90.6 | 90.1 | 87.7 | 84.3 | 44.7 | 99.9 | 96.2 |
| Winn | 77.8 | 45.2 | 15.9 | 87.6 | 99.8 | 98.5 | 93.5 | 10.4 | 28.6 | 57.2 |
| STATE AVERAGE | 80.2 | 63.0 | 56.8 | 52.4 | 63.5 | 67.1 | 72.4 | 44.5 | 56.2 | 78.3 |

— Not yet a Parish.  N No returns.

*Table 4*

VOTING PERCENTAGES, DEMOCRATIC PARTY PRESIDENTIAL
ELECTIONS, 1868–96 BY PARISHES*

| Parish | 1868 | 1872 | 1876 | 1880 | 1884 | 1888 | 1892 | 1896 |
|---|---|---|---|---|---|---|---|---|
| Acadia | .... | .... | .... | .... | .... | 99.3 | 69.3 | 81.5 |
| Ascension | 42.8 | 16.6 | 36.6 | 20.0 | 28.7 | 68.8 | 90.1 | 49.0 |
| Assumption | 49.8 | 40.6 | 49.9 | 35.3 | 38.8 | 68.1 | 63.5 | 23.7 |
| Avoyelles | 72.1 | 40.5 | 49.4 | 50.4 | 51.6 | 71.3 | 92.8 | 88.0 |
| Bienville | 99.9 | 67.1 | 80.8 | 100.0 | 89.2 | 99.9 | 78.5 | 96.0 |
| Bossier | 99.9 | 100.0 | 27.1 | 92.0 | 91.9 | 92.6 | 97.9 | 97.3 |
| Caddo | 99.9 | 33.6 | 38.1 | 99.7 | 85.1 | 95.3 | 95.5 | 83.9 |
| Calcasieu | 98.9 | 89.3 | 93.7 | 88.8 | 80.9 | 83.9 | 68.9 | 74.2 |
| Caldwell | 94.7 | 56.8 | 69.5 | 79.1 | 81.3 | 97.5 | 74.1 | 95.5 |
| Cameron | .... | 81.5 | 82.5 | 74.3 | 78.5 | 94.4 | 98.9 | 85.4 |
| Catahoula | 84.3 | 43.6 | 51.2 | 79.6 | 81.1 | 69.1 | 71.6 | 91.3 |
| Claiborne | 99.9 | 59.0 | 76.3 | 89.4 | 80.6 | 99.0 | 57.5 | 95.9 |
| Concordia | 11.4 | 90.4 | 10.9 | 64.4 | 16.2 | 84.2 | 99.1 | 92.6 |
| De Soto | 100.0 | 43.6 | 46.1 | 100.0 | 98.6 | 99.8 | 85.4 | 91.5 |
| E. Baton Rouge | 52.0 | 27.2 | 35.2 | 52.1 | 49.2 | 40.9 | 62.6 | 68.4 |
| E. Carroll | 36.2 | 20.8 | 19.6(†) | 14.4 | 13.4 | 84.2 | 97.3 | 52.9 |
| E. Feliciana | 68.7 | 27.9 | .... | 86.8 | 80.4 | 98.1 | 95.3 | 98.5 |
| Franklin | 100.0 | 67.3 | 87.6 | 100.0 | 96.1 | 95.6 | 97.2 | 94.9 |
| Grant | .... | 18.1 | .... | 79.1 | 71.1 | 86.0 | 28.7 | 85.1 |
| Iberia | .... | 37.4 | 39.1 | 35.0 | 52.9 | 99.4 | 93.2 | 70.0 |
| Iberville | 25.2 | 23.7 | 29.3 | 19.1 | 20.5 | 35.0 | 70.9 | 36.7 |
| Jackson | 100.0 | 42.2 | 95.2 | 100.0 | 100.0 | 100.0 | 60.0 | 97.2 |
| Jefferson | 76.8 | 36.2 | 30.7 | 30.9 | 21.3 | 35.9 | 84.4 | 79.3 |
| Lafayette | 100.0 | 64.7 | 49.2 | 57.4 | 57.7 | 97.7 | 99.4 | 81.8 |
| Lafourche | 52.6 | 48.6 | 47.5 | 76.6 | 50.8 | 76.1 | 93.6 | 73.9 |
| Lincoln | .... | .... | 76.4 | 39.6 | 99.6 | 100.0 | 46.2 | 95.0 |
| Livingston | 81.8 | 79.1 | 76.4 | 78.9 | 74.2 | 76.5 | 57.6 | 90.2 |
| Madison | 10.1 | 15.1 | 11.3 | 67.0 | 30.9 | 93.8 | 99.5 | 92.2 |

* Source: W. Dean Burnham, *Presidential Ballots, 1836–1892* (Johns Hopkins, 1955);
 Edgar E. Robinson, *The Presidential Vote, 1896–1932* (Stanford, 1934).
(†) Carroll Parish until 1876. Afterwards, Carroll divided into East and West.

*Table 4 (cont.)*

| Parish | 1868 | 1872 | 1876 | 1880 | 1884 | 1888 | 1892 | 1896 |
|---|---|---|---|---|---|---|---|---|
| Morehouse | 99.7 | 38.3 | 48.0 | 95.0 | 86.0 | 99.7 | 93.6 | 94.0 |
| Natchitoches | 41.8 | 100.0 | 40.4 | 75.7 | 78.4 | 82.5 | 68.8 | 98.1 |
| Orleans | 95.4 | 62.3 | 61.5 | 71.2 | 71.3 | 65.4 | 73.5 | 65.6 |
| Ouachita | 50.9 | 30.3 | 31.9 | 99.2 | 95.7 | 99.8 | 91.0 | 94.5 |
| Plaquemines | 17.0 | 17.5 | 28.9 | 42.8 | 31.6 | 33.9 | 44.9 | 73.2 |
| Pointe Coupee | 36.6 | 42.9 | 35.3 | 54.0 | 43.3 | 52.6 | 73.4 | 64.1 |
| Rapides | 42.7 | 35.3 | 48.0 | 75.1 | 66.5 | 89.4 | 88.1 | 93.5 |
| Red River | .... | 28.4 | 33.1 | 87.4 | 85.4 | 95.3 | 74.3 | 96.4 |
| Richland | .... | 74.8 | 61.8 | 97.2 | 80.9 | 100.0 | 97.9 | 90.9 |
| Sabine | 99.8 | 92.7 | 97.5 | 100.0 | 100.0 | 100.0 | 99.2 | 97.2 |
| St. Bernard | 99.9 | 36.9 | 32.7 | 53.3 | 41.5 | 61.6 | 63.2 | 89.5 |
| St. Charles | 16.5 | 10.6 | 15.7 | 94.9 | 77.8 | 77.6 | 32.9 | 30.0 |
| St. Helena | 88.9 | 53.0 | 55.1 | 60.1 | 60.2 | 83.6 | 82.9 | 88.6 |
| St. James | 26.4 | 26.4 | 33.0 | 27.9 | 20.3 | 22.9 | 29.1 | 12.6 |
| St. John | 67.0 | 31.6 | 36.6 | 26.6 | 23.8 | 26.7 | 31.0 | 24.3 |
| St. Landry | 100.0 | 55.4 | 60.2 | 62.4 | 52.8 | 74.0 | 54.7 | 87.1 |
| St. Martin | 98.1 | 47.5 | 48.2 | 40.0 | 37.1 | 99.6 | 97.4 | 89.0 |
| St. Mary | 61.4 | 28.3 | 37.7 | 20.7 | 24.6 | 55.5 | 82.2 | 49.2 |
| St. Tammany | 60.0 | 49.8 | 54.1 | 54.7 | 56.1 | 56.0 | 67.7 | 60.9 |
| Tangipahoa | .... | 45.0 | 60.2 | 67.8 | 68.8 | 69.8 | 85.7 | 76.9 |
| Tensas | 27.3 | 6.7 | 12.6 | 77.7 | 74.8 | 83.1 | 91.7 | 82.1 |
| Terrebonne | 45.7 | 46.9 | 41.4 | 37.2 | 40.7 | 56.2 | 67.6 | 62.1 |
| Union | 99.9 | 48.5 | 94.1 | 95.7 | 86.8 | 100.0 | 87.1 | 93.4 |
| Vermilion | 100.0 | 74.2 | 76.6 | 76.3 | 71.9 | 85.9 | 66.1 | 77.3 |
| Vernon | .... | 95.9 | 72.5 | 100.0 | 100.0 | 100.0 | 59.0 | 94.6 |
| Washington | 100.0 | 73.1 | 75.7 | 88.7 | 83.3 | 84.1 | 76.6 | 95.1 |
| Webster | .... | 41.1 | 40.2 | 82.1 | 52.3 | 96.9 | 83.2 | 88.4 |
| W. Baton Rouge | 42.5 | 24.2 | 32.6 | 47.7 | 70.0 | 57.2 | 86.7 | 43.7 |
| W. Carroll | 36.2 | 20.8 | 19.6 | 85.5 | 63.8 | 100.0 | 98.3 | 99.9 |
| W. Feliciana | 36.3 | 17.6 | 27.6 | 89.7 | 80.4 | 97.5 | 100.0 | 93.6 |
| Winn | 94.3 | 83.4 | 87.8 | 100.0 | 85.5 | 97.2 | 21.4 | 93.4 |
| STATE AVERAGE | 70.7 | 44.3 | 48.3 | 62.9 | 57.4 | 69.2 | 77.1 | 76.3 |

## Table 5
### PARISH PERCENTAGES, SELECTED ELECTIONS, GUBERNATORIAL, 1904–24*

GUBERNATORIAL VOTE

Winner in Primary

| Parish | Dem. 1904 | 1908 | 1912 Aswell | 1912 Hall | 1912 Michel | 1916 | 1920 | 1924 Bouan. | 1924 Fuqua | 1924 Long | 1924 Runoff Fuqua |
|---|---|---|---|---|---|---|---|---|---|---|---|
| Acadia | 89.7 | 43.4 | 28.5 | 43.7 | 27.8 | 48.5 | 65.6 | 55.3 | 35.0 | 9.7 | 42.0 |
| Allen | — | — | — | — | — | 60.5 | 67.4 | 31.4 | 36.3 | 32.3 | 61.5 |
| Ascension | 59.0 | 54.9 | 16.1 | 56.5 | 27.4 | 79.2 | 56.2 | 54.2 | 17.5 | 28.3 | 37.1 |
| Assumption | 62.9 | 61.5 | 6.3 | 63.4 | 30.3 | 87.3 | 72.4 | 77.9 | 3.7 | 18.4 | 22.7 |
| Avoyelles | 98.9 | 61.3 | 24.3 | 49.9 | 25.8 | 77.9 | 58.8 | 59.7 | 17.1 | 23.3 | 34.0 |
| Beauregard | — | — | — | — | — | 64.7 | 69.0 | 8.5 | 36.1 | 55.4 | 69.5 |
| Bienville | 94.1 | 54.7 | 52.7 | 39.3 | 8.0 | 41.7 | 56.2 | 3.3 | 24.5 | 72.2 | 84.1 |
| Bossier | 99.7 | 41.9 | 37.3 | 54.5 | 8.2 | 52.8 | 44.9 | 8.5 | 36.3 | 55.2 | 85.6 |
| Caddo | 98.7 | 47.2 | 33.5 | 25.8 | 40.7 | 58.8 | 50.1 | 19.5 | 40.1 | 40.4 | 68.4 |
| Calcasieu | 91.6 | 54.2 | 29.6 | 52.5 | 17.9 | 63.1 | 54.1 | 37.2 | 41.3 | 21.5 | 58.5 |
| Caldwell | 95.3 | 39.5 | 37.9 | 51.7 | 10.4 | 65.4 | 75.9 | 6.7 | 25.7 | 67.6 | 65.7 |
| Cameron | 94.5 | 52.6 | 11.5 | 80.1 | 8.4 | 71.5 | 45.3 | 75.0 | 11.3 | 13.7 | 28.0 |
| Catahoula | 86.7 | 51.0 | 47.6 | 31.5 | 20.9 | 59.7 | 75.3 | 9.2 | 43.8 | 47.0 | 71.5 |
| Claiborne | 97.8 | 29.5 | 31.1 | 60.9 | 8.0 | 67.7 | 35.0 | 4.6 | 40.1 | 55.3 | 93.0 |
| Concordia | 100.0 | 57.8 | 32.1 | 46.9 | 21.0 | 81.0 | 65.6 | 17.5 | 49.9 | 32.6 | 80.5 |
| De Soto | 99.6 | 61.6 | 23.0 | 53.1 | 23.9 | 56.2 | 52.9 | 10.2 | 50.5 | 39.3 | 85.0 |
| E. Baton Rouge | 97.2 | 55.5 | 7.2 | 51.0 | 41.8 | 68.1 | 57.7 | 30.0 | 55.6 | 14.4 | 74.8 |
| E. Carroll | 98.7 | 44.1 | 23.8 | 52.4 | 23.8 | 88.3 | 28.8 | 13.2 | 58.8 | 28.0 | 83.6 |
| E. Feliciana | 97.3 | 52.4 | 14.3 | 60.3 | 25.4 | 69.7 | 72.2 | 9.4 | 47.5 | 43.1 | 82.5 |
| Evangeline | — | — | 15.7 | 48.2 | 36.1 | 61.5 | 68.1 | 75.7 | 10.8 | 13.5 | 29.4 |
| Franklin | 99.3 | 54.1 | 53.1 | 30.3 | 16.6 | 72.1 | 39.7 | 17.6 | 43.7 | 38.7 | 90.0 |

* Source: *Report of Secretary of State; Compilation of Primary Election Returns*, State of Louisiana.

*Table 5 (cont.)*

GUBERNATORIAL VOTE

Winner in Primary

| Parish | Dem. 1904 | 1908 | 1912 Aswell | 1912 Hall | 1912 Michel | 1916 | 1920 | 1924 Bouan. | 1924 Fuqua | 1924 Long | 1924 Runoff Fuqua |
|---|---|---|---|---|---|---|---|---|---|---|---|
| Grant | 90.5 | 48.1 | 46.2 | 38.8 | 15.0 | 70.8 | 37.5 | 10.7 | 21.5 | 67.8 | 71.5 |
| Iberia | 81.1 | 50.6 | 20.5 | 53.3 | 26.2 | 75.0 | 72.0 | 73.3 | 16.8 | 9.9 | 26.3 |
| Iberville | 72.8 | 57.6 | 1.5 | 44.7 | 53.8 | 62.4 | 63.6 | 65.4 | 9.8 | 24.8 | 28.0 |
| Jackson | 98.7 | 38.3 | 59.2 | 35.2 | 5.6 | 74.6 | 46.2 | 9.7 | 14.9 | 75.4 | 75.1 |
| Jefferson | 96.2 | 72.7 | 0.8 | 23.9 | 75.3 | 72.0 | 58.3 | 35.3 | 24.2 | 40.5 | 52.5 |
| Jefferson Davis | — | — | — | — | — | 63.7 | 62.7 | 55.3 | 38.0 | 6.7 | 48.0 |
| Lafayette | 95.4 | 56.3 | 10.9 | 54.8 | 34.3 | 66.9 | 66.3 | 70.1 | 18.8 | 11.1 | 27.0 |
| Lafourche | 82.5 | 55.4 | 20.4 | 64.7 | 14.9 | 86.0 | 56.2 | 67.7 | 8.4 | 23.9 | 21.2 |
| LaSalle | — | — | 40.3 | 33.1 | 26.6 | 53.6 | 59.2 | 5.0 | 27.7 | 67.3 | 76.5 |
| Lincoln | 95.0 | 46.4 | 59.1 | 34.9 | 6.0 | 75.3 | 51.8 | 3.6 | 33.3 | 63.1 | 90.0 |
| Livingston | 98.9 | 43.9 | 12.0 | 70.2 | 17.8 | 61.9 | 66.9 | 14.9 | 25.6 | 59.5 | 69.7 |
| Madison | 100.0 | 70.0 | 20.8 | 35.1 | 44.1 | 87.6 | 28.2 | 4.7 | 86.2 | 9.1 | 96.0 |
| Morehouse | 98.8 | 41.3 | 17.9 | 76.4 | 5.7 | 65.1 | 38.0 | 23.8 | 55.6 | 20.6 | 77.7 |
| Natchitoches | 86.0 | 60.5 | 51.2 | 26.2 | 22.6 | 68.7 | 51.5 | 31.7 | 21.4 | 46.8 | 59.3 |
| Orleans | 90.1 | 65.1 | 6.6 | 35.4 | 58.0 | 88.7 | 45.1 | 33.9 | 48.3 | 17.8 | 60.7 |
| Ouachita | 95.9 | 62.3 | 19.4 | 52.6 | 28.0 | 62.2 | 15.6 | 24.4 | 34.1 | 41.5 | 65.0 |
| Plaquemines | 97.1 | 4.7 | 0.5 | 46.8 | 52.7 | 93.1 | 37.4 | 50.8 | 46.1 | 3.1 | 46,7 |
| Pointe Coupee | 99.8 | 45.3 | 5.9 | 65.5 | 28.6 | 75.0 | 83.7 | 84.4 | 11.4 | 4.2 | 16.0 |
| Rapides | 94.3 | 53.3 | 29.1 | 33.5 | 37.4 | 63.7 | 54.5 | 24.1 | 25.1 | 50.8 | 71.6 |
| Red River | 98.4 | 35.0 | 53.0 | 33.4 | 13.6 | 61.2 | 34.3 | 3.2 | 20.4 | 76.4 | 82.0 |
| Richland | 98.4 | 46.6 | 52.1 | 33.5 | 14.4 | 74.2 | 31.3 | 8.4 | 34.0 | 57.6 | 80.0 |
| Sabine | 98.2 | 60.0 | 47.0 | 37.2 | 15.8 | 54.8 | 60.6 | 24.0 | 14.1 | 61.9 | 62.8 |
| St. Bernard | 96.5 | 94.4 | 0.0 | 29.4 | 70.6 | 94.0 | 52.2 | 62.2 | 32.1 | 5.7 | 30.8 |
| St. Charles | 93.2 | 46.7 | 2.8 | 55.5 | 41.7 | 74.8 | 68.1 | 56.2 | 48.4 | 25.4 | 27.5 |

Table 5 (cont.)

GUBERNATORIAL VOTE

Winner in Primary

| Parish | Dem. 1904 | 1908 | 1912 | | | 1916 | 1920 | Bouan. | 1924 | | 1924 Runoff Fuqua |
|---|---|---|---|---|---|---|---|---|---|---|---|
| | | | Aswell | Hall | Michel | | | | Fuqua | Long | |
| St. Helena | 91.2 | 66.3 | 16.9 | 50.3 | 32.8 | 50.2 | 58.9 | 7.5 | 21.3 | 71.2 | 55.0 |
| St. James | 61.6 | 59.0 | 6.6 | 57.5 | 35.9 | 76.2 | 84.9 | 76.7 | 8.4 | 14.9 | 18.8 |
| St. John | 93.1 | 67.8 | 2.9 | 27.5 | 69.6 | 52.8 | 56.5 | 67.6 | 7.0 | 25.4 | 38.3 |
| St. Landry | 92.8 | 57.2 | 11.4 | 46.5 | 42.1 | 57.4 | 68.0 | 65.3 | 22.3 | 12.4 | 36.0 |
| St. Martin | 94.9 | 52.2 | 7.6 | 52.2 | 40.2 | 86.6 | 60.5 | 79.3 | 12.0 | 8.7 | 25.8 |
| St. Mary | 77.7 | 63.0 | 14.9 | 40.8 | 44.3 | 76.4 | 76.0 | 62.4 | 25.5 | 12.1 | 34.6 |
| St. Tammany | 97.6 | 55.7 | 17.3 | 50.9 | 31.8 | 68.6 | 65.6 | 28.8 | 24.8 | 46.1 | 62.3 |
| Tangipahoa | 91.3 | 44.0 | 38.2 | 38.3 | 23.5 | 60.3 | 65.1 | 22.4 | 35.2 | 42.4 | 63.5 |
| Tensas | 96.4 | 69.9 | 15.5 | 35.4 | 49.1 | 89.5 | 49.2 | 18.6 | 77.2 | 4.2 | 87.5 |
| Terrebonne | 71.1 | 48.8 | 8.2 | 53.3 | 38.5 | 74.3 | 58.2 | 62.5 | 14.7 | 22.8 | 35.0 |
| Union | 99.0 | 60.2 | 40.8 | 42.8 | 16.4 | 89.5 | 45.2 | 9.1 | 23.2 | 67.7 | 79.0 |
| Vermilion | 88.8 | 41.7 | 11.4 | 68.5 | 20.1 | 70.1 | 59.7 | 46.4 | 11.3 | 42.3 | 46.4 |
| Vernon | 92.3 | 63.0 | 39.2 | 43.3 | 17.5 | 72.3 | 56.8 | 13.5 | 15.1 | 71.4 | 68.5 |
| Washington | 87.1 | 40.7 | 46.9 | 39.7 | 13.4 | 58.3 | 67.0 | 5.7 | 27.2 | 67.1 | 86.4 |
| Webster | 96.4 | 46.7 | 42.7 | 46.6 | 10.7 | 63.9 | 58.1 | 3.3 | 37.8 | 58.9 | 85.6 |
| W. Baton Rouge | 94.2 | 51.5 | 2.3 | 71.0 | 26.7 | 65.1 | 63.1 | 75.1 | 14.5 | 10.4 | 21.3 |
| W. Feliciana | 98.0 | 49.3 | 6.2 | 52.4 | 40.4 | 70.3 | 73.2 | 24.5 | 40.0 | 35.5 | 69.0 |
| Winn | 76.2 | 39.8 | 50.4 | 34.4 | 15.2 | 73.3 | 63.6 | 4.7 | 25.2 | 70.1 | 64.2 |
| W. Carroll | 97.4 | 67.5 | 47.8 | 40.6 | 11.6 | 73.3 | 65.1 | 2.4 | 29.6 | 68.0 | 79.0 |
| STATE AVERAGE | 89.2 | 56.3 | 19.3 | 43.3 | 37.4 | 73.7 | 54.2 | 35.1 | 34.0 | 30.9 | 59.0 |

— Not yet a Parish.

*Table 6*
VOTING PERCENTAGES, DEMOCRATIC PARTY PRESIDENTIAL
ELECTIONS, 1900–28, BY PARISHES*

| Parish | 1900 | 1904 | 1908 | 1912 | 1916 | 1920 | 1924 | 1928 |
|---|---|---|---|---|---|---|---|---|
| Acadia | 70.0 | 77.1 | 74.1 | 74.9 | 83.8 | 48.1 | 68.2 | 77.2 |
| Allen | .... | .... | .... | .... | 89.5 | 80.6 | 71.2 | 64.3 |
| Ascension | 56.4 | 74.1 | 82.6 | 65.9 | 76.1 | 55.6 | 71.0 | 76.3 |
| Assumption | 53.5 | 78.7 | 72.0 | 56.9 | 45.1 | 21.8 | 33.7 | 75.5 |
| Avoyelles | 85.1 | 95.3 | 94.9 | 84.2 | 95.7 | 66.3 | 76.3 | 87.4 |
| Beauregard | .... | .... | .... | .... | 94.1 | 85.0 | 83.5 | 76.4 |
| Bienville | 93.2 | 93.8 | 82.4 | 81.9 | 97.1 | 84.7 | 92.0 | 78.0 |
| Bossier | 99.1 | 93.9 | 96.5 | 87.8 | 98.7 | 94.3 | 94.0 | 84.1 |
| Caddo | 96.0 | 96.9 | 91.2 | 88.4 | 95.2 | 91.4 | 81.0 | 65.4 |
| Calcasieu | 70.9 | 69.5 | 69.3 | 65.9 | 91.1 | 83.7 | 68.8 | 63.9 |
| Caldwell | 80.6 | 91.7 | 80.0 | 72.7 | 94.5 | 80.8 | 85.2 | 73.6 |
| Cameron | 72.0 | 90.8 | 97.5 | 90.0 | 94.2 | 93.0 | 94.6 | 90.5 |
| Catahoula | 78.5 | 79.3 | 76.5 | 73.9 | 95.6 | 74.5 | 73.6 | 67.6 |
| Claiborne | 96.3 | 97.5 | 93.3 | 92.3 | 98.7 | 96.2 | 95.9 | 86.2 |
| Concordia | 95.5 | 95.0 | 95.4 | 91.1 | 95.3 | 96.9 | 87.4 | 81.6 |
| De Soto | 98.2 | 97.6 | 93.7 | 88.7 | 97.2 | 95.6 | 90.7 | 73.6 |
| E. Baton Rouge | 84.9 | 95.3 | 91.3 | 85.4 | 90.0 | 84.1 | 81.9 | 60.4 |
| E. Carroll | 95.6 | 99.1 | 96.5 | 86.1 | 98.6 | 96.9 | 79.6 | 77.0 |
| E. Feliciana | 96.5 | 97.7 | 97.7 | 96.1 | 95.7 | 94.6 | 95.3 | 79.5 |
| Evangeline | .... | .... | .... | 83.6 | 89.9 | 48.0 | 78.8 | 86.2 |
| Franklin | 92.3 | 98.3 | 94.4 | 77.0 | 98.5 | 83.8 | 82.8 | 69.9 |
| Grant | 69.1 | 74.5 | 74.0 | 62.4 | 91.4 | 86.1 | 78.1 | 67.0 |
| Iberia | 60.6 | 76.3 | 68.3 | 51.4 | 44.9 | 25.6 | 52.1 | 86.1 |
| Iberville | 64.5 | 87.7 | 91.9 | 65.8 | 72.0 | 45.3 | 58.7 | 85.4 |
| Jackson | 80.2 | 91.0 | 78.9 | 73.2 | 97.1 | 88.1 | 88.6 | 100.0 |
| Jefferson | 95.6 | 97.1 | 97.4 | 82.3 | 94.2 | 86.6 | 84.9 | 87.8 |
| Jefferson Davis | .... | .... | .... | .... | 73.9 | 44.9 | 52.4 | 60.3 |
| Lafayette | 67.3 | 88.9 | 74.3 | 63.3 | 66.0 | 44.1 | 64.8 | 84.4 |
| Lafourche | 59.8 | 84.5 | 78.1 | 57.3 | 32.5 | 24.4 | 52.6 | 89.1 |
| LaSalle | .... | .... | .... | 65.8 | 95.6 | 83.9 | 81.7 | 66.2 |
| Lincoln | 89.4 | 94.7 | 89.0 | 84.4 | 95.1 | 84.4 | 86.5 | 60.8 |
| Livingston | 96.4 | 88.2 | 90.1 | 80.2 | 90.5 | 75.6 | 85.7 | 51.8 |
| Madison | 96.8 | 100.0 | 96.3 | 95.5 | 99.5 | 98.8 | 95.5 | 67.8 |
| Morehouse | 98.3 | 96.2 | 92.1 | 89.1 | 98.8 | 94.2 | 80.5 | 71.2 |
| Natchitoches | 88.2 | 83.4 | 81.0 | 75.4 | 93.9 | 88.7 | 85.0 | 80.0 |

* Source: Edgar E. Robinson, *The Presidential Vote, 1896–1932* (Stanford, 1934).

*Table 6 (cont.)*

| Parish | 1900 | 1904 | 1908 | 1912 | 1916 | 1920 | 1924 | 1928 |
|---|---|---|---|---|---|---|---|---|
| Orleans | 80.0 | 91.0 | 87.8 | 79.7 | 91.0 | 64.7 | 82.8 | 79.5 |
| Ouachita | 93.5 | 94.3 | 90.5 | 83.7 | 96.8 | 90.0 | 76.3 | 66.5 |
| Plaquemines | 83.1 | 93.1 | 74.5 | 82.5 | 90.2 | 72.3 | 76.3 | 91.5 |
| Pointe Coupee | 96.4 | 98.0 | 96.6 | 66.8 | 85.3 | 94.0 | 71.7 | 92.9 |
| Rapides | 81.6 | 87.6 | 86.7 | 79.8 | 93.2 | 86.1 | 67.9 | 64.2 |
| Red River | 98.7 | 94.6 | 83.2 | 76.8 | 99.3 | 80.4 | 94.5 | 73.8 |
| Richland | 95.9 | 97.6 | 98.1 | 89.9 | 98.9 | 93.0 | 85.4 | 81.7 |
| Sabine | 91.3 | 87.8 | 87.5 | 79.8 | 97.0 | 91.8 | 84.4 | 65.8 |
| St. Bernard | 89.6 | 92.6 | 95.2 | 88.6 | 92.8 | 86.5 | 97.6 | 96.8 |
| St. Charles | 90.2 | 96.3 | 90.7 | 74.6 | 90.0 | 66.5 | 78.7 | 91.2 |
| St. Helena | . . . . | 88.3 | 88.9 | 88.8 | 95.5 | 91.0 | 91.1 | 80.8 |
| St. James | 48.6 | 72.7 | 73.2 | 53.9 | 71.5 | 39.1 | 68.9 | 92.1 |
| St. John | 78.6 | 91.9 | 89.1 | 62.4 | 70.1 | 48.9 | 63.4 | 89.2 |
| Zt. Landry | 85.0 | 92.9 | 84.6 | 76.9 | 36.9 | 51.9 | 79.1 | 82.5 |
| St. Martin | 82.6 | 96.4 | 91.9 | 64.2 | 69,4 | 43.2 | 72.8 | 88.7 |
| St. Mary | 57.4 | 79.2 | 71.7 | 61.3 | 45.9 | 40.6 | 50.2 | 74.4 |
| St. Tammany | 76.4 | 83.3 | 80.6 | 82.1 | 87.7 | 77.8 | 78.3 | 66.7 |
| Tangipahoa | 80.4 | 79.4 | 80.6 | 80.0 | 88.6 | 77.3 | 77.2 | 66.7 |
| Tensas | 97.7 | 97.1 | 97.7 | 91.7 | 96.7 | 94.2 | 94.2 | 78.5 |
| Terrebonne | 60.1 | 82.5 | 62.6 | 55.1 | 46.4 | 40.1 | 53.7 | 86.0 |
| Union | 87.7 | 96.9 | 89.2 | 88.1 | 97.2 | 92.6 | 99.2 | 72.0 |
| Vermilion | 62.7 | 86.6 | 72.6 | 58.9 | 55.3 | 27.9 | 59.0 | 85.1 |
| Vernon | 66.7 | 61.3 | 54.2 | 59.0 | . . . . | 84.8 | 90.6 | 81.4 |
| Washington | 89.3 | 90.8 | 91.5 | 82.8 | 93.2 | 86.9 | 87.7 | 56.9 |
| Webster | 98.5 | 97.1 | 85.7 | 83.9 | 97.8 | 90.0 | 94.7 | 80.1 |
| W. Baton Rouge | 82.9 | 97.9 | 95.6 | 83.2 | 87.8 | 66.8 | 67.5 | 88.6 |
| W. Carroll | 98.8 | 89.8 | 76.8 | 63.5 | 91.2 | 76.9 | 83.4 | 75.9 |
| W. Feliciana | 94.4 | 96.1 | 94.1 | 89.5 | 95.2 | 91.3 | 95.9 | 82.4 |
| Winn | 55.6 | 63.1 | 59.5 | 58.4 | 85.3 | 76.8 | 86.9 | 68.5 |
| STATE AVERAGE | 79.0 | 88.5 | 84.7 | 76.7 | 85.9 | 69.2 | 76.4 | 76.3 |

. . . . Not yet a Parish.

*Table 7*

VOTING PERCENTAGES, DEMOCRATIC PARTY PRESIDENTIAL
ELECTIONS, 1932–48, BY PARISHES*

| Parish | Dem. 1932 | Dem. 1936 | Dem. 1940 | Dem. 1944 | Dem. 1948 | Rep. 1948 | States' Rights 1948 |
|---|---|---|---|---|---|---|---|
| Acadia | 91.1 | 91.1 | 87.5 | 81.3 | 35.7 | 11.7 | 52.6 |
| Allen | 93.9 | 87.2 | 90.3 | 86.8 | 62.0 | 7.5 | 30.5 |
| Ascension | 86.6 | 87.0 | 86.4 | 86.3 | 37.7 | 14.5 | 47.8 |
| Assumption | 79.9 | 39.1 | 70.9 | 76.9 | 19.7 | 25.6 | 54.7 |
| Avoyelles | 96.0 | 90.7 | 96.4 | 92.5 | 19.1 | 4.0 | 76.9 |
| Beauregard | 94.1 | 79.9 | 83.5 | 74.6 | 47.6 | 12.9 | 39.5 |
| Bienville | 98.5 | 92.4 | 88.8 | 71.9 | 14.1 | 6.4 | 79.5 |
| Bossier | 97.5 | 91.0 | 91.2 | 79.6 | 29.6 | 8.7 | 61.7 |
| Caddo | 89.7 | 87.7 | 84.5 | 68.6 | 27.1 | 21.6 | 51.3 |
| Calcasieu | 89.7 | 85.6 | 83.0 | 80.8 | 56.9 | 15.6 | 27.5 |
| Caldwell | 94.0 | 85.4 | 84.0 | 69.3 | 44.5 | 8.6 | 46.9 |
| Cameron | 98.9 | 98.5 | 96.1 | 92.3 | 66.1 | 7.7 | 26.2 |
| Catahoula | 97.9 | 93.3 | 91.9 | 80.6 | 30.9 | 5.2 | 63.9 |
| Claiborne | 97.8 | 94.5 | 94.2 | 79.7 | 16.4 | 9.5 | 74.1 |
| Concordia | 98.0 | 95.1 | 90.8 | 82.9 | 21.0 | 6.3 | 72.7 |
| De Soto | 96.4 | 96.2 | 93.2 | 77.5 | 22.2 | 9.7 | 68.1 |
| E. Baton Rouge | 85.5 | 90.3 | 88.3 | 83.0 | 39.9 | 21.4 | 38.7 |
| E. Carroll | 96.9 | 89.5 | 79.2 | 72.2 | 29.3 | 10.5 | 60.2 |
| E. Feliciana | 94.8 | 91.2 | 86.6 | 79.8 | 21.6 | 10.3 | 68.1 |
| Evangeline | 98.4 | 91.3 | 94.2 | 91.7 | 19.9 | 3.6 | 76.5 |
| Franklin | 97.3 | 92.5 | 91.5 | 80.6 | 47.8 | 3.8 | 48.4 |
| Grant | 96.0 | 98.3 | 91.6 | 77.7 | 39.4 | 9.6 | 51.0 |
| Iberia | 75.1 | 67.8 | 70.6 | 76.2 | 16.5 | 47.3 | 36.2 |
| Iberville | 75.3 | 88.1 | 83.5 | 84.0 | 55.3 | 16.5 | 28.2 |
| Jackson | 98.1 | 91.4 | 90.7 | 81.5 | 31.1 | 7.4 | 61.5 |
| Jefferson | 93.9 | 92.7 | 89.5 | 85.2 | 28.8 | 16.2 | 55.0 |
| Jefferson Davis | 81.7 | 80.9 | 70.6 | 66.8 | 47.2 | 21.8 | 31.0 |
| Lafayette | 93.2 | 93.7 | 77.4 | 86.6 | 23.5 | 27.2 | 49.3 |
| Lafourche | 87.8 | 57.4 | 76.8 | 85.1 | 26.8 | 21.1 | 52.1 |
| LaSalle | 93.6 | 86.8 | 88.4 | 79.2 | 26.0 | 9.7 | 64.3 |
| Lincoln | 92.1 | 91.4 | 86.9 | 62.3 | 19.5 | 11.0 | 69.5 |
| Livingston | 95.0 | 83.0 | 92.2 | 87.8 | 53.0 | 7.8 | 39.4 |
| Madison | 89.1 | 93.9 | 84.8 | 69.3 | 14.4 | 9.3 | 76.3 |

* Source: Richard M. Scammon, *America Votes*, Washington, D.C., Governmental
   Affairs Institute, 1964.

*Table 7 (cont.)*

| Parish | Dem. 1932 | Dem. 1936 | Dem. 1940 | Dem. 1944 | Dem. 1948 | Rep. 1948 | States' Rights 1948 |
|---|---|---|---|---|---|---|---|
| Morehouse | 96.0 | 93.5 | 91.6 | 79.5 | 41.8 | 8.6 | 49.6 |
| Natchitoches | 95.2 | 87.4 | 84.8 | 69.6 | 31.6 | 14.3 | 54.1 |
| Orleans | 93.9 | 91.3 | 85.6 | 81.7 | 33.8 | 23.8 | 42.4 |
| Ouachita | 92.9 | 87.3 | 84.9 | 70.7 | 39.0 | 16.0 | 45.0 |
| Plaquemines | 98.1 | 95.9 | 90.7 | 84.0 | 2.8 | 3.2 | 94.0 |
| Pointe Coupee | 94.0 | 92.4 | 88.4 | 84.1 | 20.3 | 10.0 | 69.7 |
| Rapides | 91.8 | 86.4 | 91.3 | 84.2 | 36.2 | 13.1 | 50.7 |
| Red River | 98.3 | 92.6 | 59.1 | 70.4 | 21.5 | 5.4 | 73.1 |
| Richland | 97.4 | 93.5 | 88.6 | 81.0 | 37.9 | 4.7 | 57.4 |
| Sabine | 96.2 | 85.4 | 83.7 | 66.3 | 34.1 | 11.4 | 54.5 |
| St. Bernard | 94.1 | 98.9 | 94.0 | 96.2 | 3.7 | 4.4 | 91.9 |
| St. Charles | 94.1 | 94.0 | 91.0 | 91.8 | 37.9 | 11.9 | 50.2 |
| St. Helena | 97.4 | 92.2 | 92.6 | 86.3 | 39.4 | 5.0 | 55.6 |
| St. James | 87.7 | 85.9 | 74.3 | 84.0 | 40.6 | 21.4 | 38.0 |
| St. John | 79.6 | 86.9 | 80.7 | 87.2 | 42.5 | 20.2 | 37.3 |
| St. Landry | 92.7 | 92.7 | 91.9 | 84.9 | 15.2 | 10.7 | 74.1 |
| St. Martin | 93.0 | 96.3 | 84.4 | 94.0 | 8.0 | 18.0 | 74.0 |
| St. Mary | 81.4 | 80.0 | 83.3 | 87.0 | 26.2 | 73.5 | 0.3 |
| St. Tammany | 94.6 | 85.4 | 87.0 | 83.1 | 23.1 | 15.7 | 61.2 |
| Tangipahoa | 90.6 | 77.1 | 82.1 | 73.8 | 29.5 | 17.4 | 53.1 |
| Tensas | 95.5 | 92.2 | 91.0 | 79.9 | 22.9 | 6.9 | 70.2 |
| Terrebonne | 90.8 | 78.3 | 84.3 | 86.5 | 29.1 | 24.2 | 46.7 |
| Union | 97.5 | 86.7 | 88.5 | 68.7 | 25.4 | 9.1 | 65.5 |
| Vermilion | 91.6 | 89.0 | 65.5 | 87.4 | 28.8 | 19.4 | 51.8 |
| Vernon | 96.6 | 75.2 | 91.7 | 75.1 | 42.3 | 6.5 | 51.2 |
| Washington | 93.4 | 94.2 | 95.1 | 92.2 | 41.9 | 4.8 | 53.3 |
| Webster | 97.6 | 90.1 | 91.8 | 80.3 | 36.5 | 8.6 | 54.9 |
| W. Baton Rouge | 86.1 | 91.5 | 89.4 | 92.3 | 47.7 | 12.1 | 40.2 |
| W. Carroll | 97.9 | 86.1 | 83.8 | 70.5 | 40.1 | 6.6 | 53.3 |
| W. Feliciana | 91.9 | 88.1 | 83.3 | 70.5 | 17.4 | 17.5 | 65.1 |
| Winn | 96.7 | 90.4 | 87.0 | 61.4 | 32.1 | 11.4 | 56.5 |
| STATE AVERAGE | 92.8 | 88.8 | 85.9 | 80.6 | 32.7 | 17.5 | 49.8 |

*Table 8*
VOTING PERCANTAGES, DEMOCRATIC PARTY PRESIDENTIAL
ELECTIONS, 1952–64 BY PARISHES*

| Parish | Dem. 1952 | Dem. 1956 | Dem. 1960 | Rep. 1960 | States' Rights 1960 | Dem. 1964 |
|---|---|---|---|---|---|---|
| Acadia | 58.5 | 58.2 | 75.8 | 17.3 | 6.9 | 58.5 |
| Allen | 72.0 | 46.7 | 59.8 | 27.0 | 13.2 | 58.3 |
| Ascension | 66.8 | 57.5 | 74.8 | 13.3 | 11.9 | 60.4 |
| Assumption | 57.6 | 41.4 | 71.7 | 18.2 | 10.1 | 59.1 |
| Avoyelles | 64.0 | 49.6 | 76.0 | 12.7 | 11.3 | 51.1 |
| Beauregard | 53.8 | 44.2 | 48.7 | 40.8 | 10.5 | 47.7 |
| Bienville | 48.9 | 46.3 | 17.6 | 34.7 | 47.7 | 18.6 |
| Bossier | 42.7 | 30.8 | 25.2 | 39.3 | 35.5 | 16.5 |
| Caddo | 34.3 | 27.7 | 24.8 | 54.3 | 20.9 | 19.4 |
| Calcasieu | 58.8 | 45.8 | 64.4 | 27.2 | 8.4 | 57.7 |
| Caldwell | 54.7 | 28.0 | 34.0 | 35.1 | 30.9 | 19.4 |
| Cameron | 59.5 | 58.4 | 83.1 | 13.8 | 3.1 | 64.4 |
| Catahoula | 60.2 | 39.2 | 26.2 | 45.5 | 28.3 | 19.0 |
| Claiborne | 35.4 | 20.8 | 12.7 | 34.7 | 52.6 | 11.0 |
| Concordia | 53.0 | 33.0 | 23.1 | 30.3 | 46.6 | 16.7 |
| De Soto | 42.2 | 32.0 | 26.7 | 36.1 | 37.2 | 24.1 |
| E. Baton Rouge | 54.0 | 40.3 | 46.6 | 31.5 | 21.9 | 41.4 |
| E. Carroll | 54.8 | 40.5 | 23.9 | 29.4 | 46.7 | 15.0 |
| E. Feliciana | 53.8 | 53.6 | 24.6 | 16.2 | 59.2 | 20.4 |
| Evangeline | 58.2 | 58.7 | 80.6 | 11.3 | 8.1 | 16.8 |
| Franklin | 63.7 | 39.1 | 30.0 | 33.1 | 36.9 | 12.2 |
| Grant | 64.7 | 43.6 | 31.4 | 32.3 | 36.3 | 30.6 |
| Iberia | 41.6 | 33.4 | 59.7 | 23.0 | 17.3 | 49.8 |
| Iberville | 67.2 | 51.4 | 72.2 | 15.9 | 11.9 | 56.4 |
| Jackson | 63.6 | 32.0 | 34.1 | 43.9 | 22.0 | 25.6 |
| Jefferson | 53.1 | 39.0 | 51.3 | 27.5 | 21.2 | 46.1 |
| Jefferson Davis | 51.0 | 35.4 | 67.8 | 25.8 | 6.4 | 57.5 |
| Lafayette | 49.9 | 39.9 | 62.3 | 26.7 | 11.0 | 53.9 |
| Lafourche | 59.1 | 36.4 | 76.3 | 18.2 | 5.5 | 66.1 |
| LaSalle | 54.2 | 31.1 | 21.9 | 55.3 | 22.8 | 16.7 |
| Lincoln | 39.5 | 22.4 | 20.6 | 54.1 | 25.3 | 22.9 |
| Livingston | 71.4 | 58.8 | 43.5 | 14.4 | 42.1 | 38.9 |
| Madison | 35.7 | 16.3 | 12.4 | 33.3 | 54.3 | 16.8 |

* Source: Richard M. Scammon, *America Votes*, Washington, D.C., Governmental
Affairs Institute, 1964.

*Table 8 (cont.)*

| Parish | Dem. 1952 | Dem. 1956 | Dem. 1960 | Rep. 1960 | States' Rights 1960 | Dem. 1964 |
|---|---|---|---|---|---|---|
| Morehouse | 53.9 | 29.2 | 22.7 | 53.4 | 23.9 | 12.5 |
| Natchitoches | 55.5 | 35.1 | 39.4 | 36.3 | 24.3 | 35.0 |
| Orleans | 51.3 | 39.5 | 49.6 | 26.8 | 23.6 | 50.3 |
| Ouachita | 52.3 | 28.8 | 27.0 | 54.6 | 18.4 | 16.6 |
| Plaquemines | 7.0 | 14.5 | 21.1 | 13.8 | 65.1 | 13.6 |
| Pointe Coupee | 54.1 | 52.1 | 71.8 | 16.4 | 11.8 | 49.1 |
| Rapides | 58.2 | 35.2 | 40.6 | 34.3 | 25.1 | 35.5 |
| Red River | 70.2 | 44.9 | 19.7 | 21.2 | 59.1 | 13.0 |
| Richland | 60.3 | 30.8 | 25.7 | 35.6 | 38.7 | 14.2 |
| Sabine | 61.7 | 43.5 | 41.0 | 41.1 | 17.9 | 33.3 |
| St. Bernard | 48.3 | 45.5 | 42.6 | 13.1 | 44.3 | 43.4 |
| St. Charles | 71.2 | 40.6 | 71.3 | 20.9 | 7.8 | 65.2 |
| St. Helena | 60.4 | 59.0 | 37.5 | 16.4 | 46.1 | 34.9 |
| St. James | 61.5 | 48.7 | 82.1 | 11.7 | 6.2 | 74.2 |
| St. John | 76.5 | 47.1 | 80.1 | 10.3 | 9.6 | 70.0 |
| St. Landry | 47.3 | 44.5 | 72.2 | 15.2 | 12.6 | 52.0 |
| St. Martin | 56.4 | 54.7 | 78.0 | 12.1 | 9.9 | 62.6 |
| St. Mary | 49.0 | 35.9 | 61.6 | 27.6 | 10.8 | 57.0 |
| St. Tammany | 55.4 | 44.2 | 46.8 | 25.8 | 27.4 | 45.9 |
| Tangipahoa | 53.1 | 43.2 | 46.3 | 22.9 | 30.8 | 42.2 |
| Tensas | 49.5 | 31.6 | 20.4 | 42.2 | 37.4 | 10.4 |
| Terrebonne | 52.5 | 32.0 | 68.1 | 23.7 | 8.2 | 56.0 |
| Union | 52.0 | 25.7 | 25.4 | 49.6 | 25.0 | 20.3 |
| Vermilion | 57.6 | 52.5 | 77.1 | 14.9 | 8.0 | 64.9 |
| Vernon | 64.3 | 45.3 | 51.1 | 32.3 | 16.6 | 49.1 |
| Washington | 75.3 | 57.9 | 49.0 | 16.2 | 34.8 | 39.3 |
| Webster | 56.9 | 34.9 | 16.6 | 40.9 | 42.5 | 17.7 |
| W. Baton Rouge | 64.5 | 52.2 | 73.7 | 12.4 | 13.9 | 50.8 |
| W. Carroll | 59.3 | 33.4 | 32.4 | 30.6 | 37.0 | 11.6 |
| W. Feliciana | 35.7 | 37.8 | 30.4 | 22.0 | 47.6 | 19.9 |
| Winn | 53.5 | 35.0 | 27.1 | 44.9 | 28.0 | 21.5 |
| STATE AVERAGE | 52.9 | 39.5 | 50.4 | 28.6 | 21.0 | 43.2 |

## Table 9

PERCENTAGE FOR LONG CANDIDATES, 1928–56; MORRISON, 1960–64; AND LYONS, 1964, BY PARISHES* (†)

| Parish | Long Candidates | | | | | | | | Morrison | | Lyons |
| | 1928 | 1932 | 1936 | 1940 | 1944 | 1948 | 1952 | 1956 | 1960 | 1964 | 1964 |
|---|---|---|---|---|---|---|---|---|---|---|---|
| Acadia | 55.9 | 37.0 | 69.0 | 44.1 | 53.0 | 66.0 | 44.0 | 59.1 | 57.3 | 48.0 | 29.2 |
| Allen | 66.1 | 52.0 | 69.0 | 57.4 | 56.0 | 69.0 | 46.0 | 67.6 | 40.2 | 37.9 | 24.1 |
| Ascension | 53.7 | 36.0 | 51.0 | 46.5 | 42.0 | 64.0 | 53.0 | 66.1 | 57.1 | 59.4 | 23.2 |
| Assumption | 66.8 | 48.0 | 71.0 | 47.6 | 33.0 | 74.0 | 47.0 | 64.8 | 63.7 | 64.2 | 19.8 |
| Avoyelles | 48.2 | 43.0 | 63.0 | 52.7 | 45.0 | 74.0 | 48.0 | 60.4 | 52.0 | 52.4 | 27.8 |
| Beauregard | 69.2 | 58.0 | 75.0 | 51.1 | 49.0 | 68.0 | 49.0 | 67.5 | 29.7 | 29.1 | 27.8 |
| Bienville | 59.8 | 51.0 | 68.0 | 48.2 | 45.0 | 71.0 | 51.0 | 65.0 | 11.1 | 18.3 | 36.8 |
| Bossier | 53.5 | 51.0 | 65.0 | 47.5 | 39.0 | 73.0 | 34.0 | 54.4 | 18.8 | 18.1 | 52.9 |
| Caddo | 38.9 | 37.0 | 54.0 | 33.2 | 25.0 | 54.0 | 25.0 | 38.8 | 28.8 | 30.7 | 71.4 |
| Calcasieu | 57.3 | 56.0 | 71.0 | 44.1 | 47.0 | 65.0 | 41.0 | 54.3 | 43.4 | 49.7 | 44.0 |
| Caldwell | 60.0 | 63.0 | 70.0 | 46.5 | 50.0 | 75.0 | 49.0 | 66.8 | 14.3 | 8.5 | 7.2 |
| Cameron | 73.6 | 63.0 | 68.0 | 55.7 | 54.0 | 66.0 | 33.0 | 51.8 | 45.8 | 47.7 | 18.7 |
| Catahoula | 39.8 | 52.0 | 73.0 | 57.5 | 56.0 | 80.0 | 46.0 | 68.7 | 16.7 | 10.7 | 14.5 |
| Claiborne | 56.8 | 49.0 | 63.0 | 46.4 | 43.0 | 63.0 | 34.0 | 42.6 | 9.9 | 12.5 | 53.1 |
| Concordia | 41.6 | 63.0 | 66.0 | 52.0 | 42.0 | 74.0 | 42.0 | 60.9 | 16.8 | 20.1 | 31.9 |
| De Soto | 47.9 | 45.0 | 52.0 | 40.9 | 34.0 | 64.0 | 39.0 | 56.3 | 11.9 | 22.8 | 51.5 |
| E. Baton Rouge | 23.4 | 45.0 | 51.0 | 34.2 | 33.0 | 47.0 | 36.0 | 39.1 | 45.4 | 54.5 | 47.6 |
| E. Carroll | 32.8 | 68.0 | 65.0 | 50.3 | 42.0 | 71.0 | 38.0 | 60.2 | 10.6 | 22.5 | 45.0 |
| E. Feliciana | 37.7 | 54.0 | 46.0 | 38.9 | 35.0 | 51.0 | 30.0 | 66.2 | 17.4 | 18.4 | 20.6 |

* Source: *Compilation of Primary Election Returns*, State of Louisiana.

(†) All elections are second primary except Lyons (general election) and 1928, 1932, 1936, 1956 (first primary).

Table 9 (cont.)

Long Candidates

| Parish | 1928 | 1932 | 1936 | 1940 | 1944 | 1948 | 1952 | 1956 | Morrison 1960 | 1964 | Lyons 1964 |
|---|---|---|---|---|---|---|---|---|---|---|---|
| Evangeline | 73.0 | 41.0 | 74.0 | 44.1 | 48.0 | 75.0 | 41.0 | 70.6 | 59.4 | 54.3 | 16.0 |
| Franklin | 51.2 | 65.0 | 74.0 | 55.5 | 49.0 | 77.0 | 42.0 | 57.5 | 12.6 | 8.7 | 19.9 |
| Grant | 66.9 | 43.0 | 63.0 | 49.9 | 52.0 | 70.0 | 51.0 | 65.0 | 21.8 | 19.0 | 22.0 |
| Iberia | 55.1 | 51.0 | 71.0 | 46.4 | 48.0 | 67.0 | 30.0 | 53.2 | 62.6 | 58.5 | 40.4 |
| Iberville | 52.2 | 54.0 | 55.0 | 42.2 | 46.0 | 63.0 | 51.0 | 64.7 | 55.4 | 57.3 | 27.7 |
| Jackson | 62.7 | 56.0 | 70.0 | 51.2 | 33.0 | 78.0 | 59.0 | 69.8 | 16.8 | 23.0 | 29.9 |
| Jefferson | 36.1 | 79.0 | 89.0 | 43.3 | 30.0 | 71.0 | 22.0 | 42.4 | 54.6 | 60.6 | 42.7 |
| Jefferson Davis | 55.1 | 55.0 | 59.0 | 39.7 | 40.0 | 56.0 | 37.0 | 49.5 | 55.3 | 50.3 | 45.4 |
| Lafayette | 57.9 | 40.0 | 55.0 | 34.5 | 47.0 | 57.0 | 33.0 | 43.8 | 76.9 | 62.2 | 44.9 |
| Lafourche | 63.3 | 62.0 | 74.0 | 46.2 | 40.0 | 67.0 | 36.0 | 50.1 | 59.3 | 64.8 | 29.7 |
| LaSalle | 60.5 | 52.0 | 61.0 | 59.3 | 51.0 | 70.0 | 46.0 | 64.7 | 12.9 | 10.2 | 19.7 |
| Lincoln | 46.8 | 49.0 | 59.0 | 46.5 | 41.0 | 66.0 | 37.0 | 46.0 | 11.8 | 30.2 | 52.2 |
| Livingston | 63.3 | 51.0 | 62.0 | 48.9 | 58.0 | 74.0 | 42.0 | 61.1 | 20.5 | 23.7 | 13.5 |
| Madison | 18.2 | 69.0 | 59.0 | 39.7 | 33.0 | 66.0 | 29.0 | 55.8 | 12.6 | 22.9 | 34.3 |
| Morehouse | 43.3 | 57.0 | 68.0 | 43.6 | 30.0 | 66.0 | 38.0 | 48.0 | 15.4 | 15.1 | 42.9 |
| Natchitoches | 64.0 | 45.0 | 64.0 | 52.4 | 53.0 | 71.0 | 53.0 | 62.9 | 43.4 | 34.6 | 41.6 |
| Orleans | 22.7 | 71.0 | 72.0 | 55.4 | 54.0 | 63.0 | 36.0 | 39.7 | 59.2 | 66.9 | 43.6 |
| Ouachita | 38.8 | 57.0 | 67.0 | 37.6 | 36.0 | 69.0 | 35.0 | 48.7 | 25.6 | 22.9 | 39.7 |
| Plaquemines | 44.9 | 77.0 | 98.0 | 67.6 | 74.0 | 91.0 | 3.6 | 18.9 | 38.4 | 19.6 | 7.2 |
| Pointe Coupee | 40.1 | 56.0 | 62.0 | 41.9 | 46.0 | 61.0 | 43.0 | 60.0 | 59.3 | 62.0 | 28.8 |
| Rapides | 46.8 | 51.0 | 55.0 | 42.4 | 42.0 | 63.0 | 43.0 | 51.6 | 35.1 | 36.5 | 36.5 |
| Red River | 68.7 | 59.0 | 75.0 | 61.4 | 59.0 | 77.0 | 64.0 | 77.4 | 10.5 | 8.9 | 35.4 |
| Richland | 47.6 | 64.0 | 71.0 | 57.7 | 52.0 | 77.0 | 43.0 | 56.3 | 15.7 | 14.5 | 31.2 |

Table 9 (cont.)

Long Candidates

| Parish | 1928 | 1932 | 1936 | 1940 | 1944 | 1948 | 1952 | 1956 | 1960 | Morrison 1964 | Lyons 1964 |
|---|---|---|---|---|---|---|---|---|---|---|---|
| Sabine | 67.1 | 51.0 | 69.0 | 61.7 | 58.0 | 79.0 | 59.0 | 75.1 | 27.0 | 23.7 | 30.1 |
| St. Bernard | 61.6 | 100.0 | 98.0 | 80.8 | 32.0 | 93.0 | 70.0 | 57.3 | 43.5 | 46.1 | 25.1 |
| St. Charles | 42.7 | 46.0 | 73.0 | 44.0 | 36.0 | 66.0 | 46.0 | 59.4 | 65.3 | 70.5 | 31.6 |
| St. Helena | 69.2 | 53.0 | 58.0 | 48.0 | 46.0 | 68.0 | 41.0 | 71.7 | 37.7 | 28.5 | 14.6 |
| St. James | 34.2 | 68.0 | 80.0 | 50.1 | 46.0 | 71.0 | 49.0 | 72.0 | 74.6 | 74.0 | 20.7 |
| St. John | 46.1 | 60.0 | 77.0 | 48.2 | 27.0 | 76.0 | 64.0 | 68.7 | 71.5 | 70.0 | 21.9 |
| St. Landry | 41.9 | 34.0 | 58.0 | 43.4 | 49.0 | 65.0 | 33.0 | 65.4 | 59.6 | 53.7 | 32.5 |
| St. Martin | 56.4 | 44.0 | 62.0 | 44.1 | 56.0 | 61.0 | 45.0 | 58.2 | 66.8 | 61.4 | 23.1 |
| St. Mary | 53.3 | 60.0 | 54.0 | 35.2 | 33.0 | 64.0 | 27.0 | 51.2 | 55.0 | 57.4 | 43.7 |
| St. Tammany | 49.9 | 70.0 | 71.0 | 47.0 | 67.0 | 65.0 | 38.0 | 60.6 | 42.0 | 44.9 | 33.3 |
| Tangipahoa | 52.3 | 49.0 | 66.0 | 47.0 | 52.0 | 68.0 | 38.0 | 58.1 | 39.8 | 39.2 | 28.5 |
| Tensas | 15.8 | 69.0 | 66.0 | 46.5 | 33.0 | 62.0 | 31.0 | 43.0 | 9.6 | 14.7 | 35.9 |
| Terrebonne | 58.0 | 52.0 | 72.0 | 37.8 | 47.0 | 78.0 | 24.0 | 51.6 | 57.3 | 64.4 | 43.8 |
| Union | 54.3 | 57.9 | 67.0 | 53.4 | 50.0 | 76.0 | 47.0 | 51.5 | 15.4 | 17.8 | 30.7 |
| Vermilion | 60.4 | 37.0 | 59.0 | 47.2 | 49.0 | 66.0 | 44.0 | 54.0 | 65.5 | 48.8 | 23.4 |
| Vernon | 73.5 | 52.0 | 71.0 | 65.8 | 64.0 | 82.0 | 49.0 | 72.9 | 28.3 | 21.4 | 19.9 |
| Washington | 46.4 | 60.0 | 72.0 | 56.4 | 49.0 | 70.0 | 44.0 | 64.6 | 22.8 | 28.1 | 18.3 |
| Webster | 56.7 | 54.0 | 68.0 | 38.6 | 43.0 | 75.0 | 42.0 | 62.0 | 9.6 | 12.8 | 47.1 |
| W. Baton Rouge | 50.2 | 43.0 | 47.0 | 43.3 | 45.0 | 59.0 | 41.0 | 59.4 | 54.2 | 57.6 | 32.7 |
| W. Feliciana | 38.2 | 46.0 | 49.0 | 47.4 | 35.0 | 38.0 | 29.0 | 43.6 | 27.5 | 27.7 | 34.1 |
| Winn | 69.6 | 57.0 | 63.0 | 55.6 | 45.0 | 77.0 | 54.0 | 71.1 | 19.8 | 22.0 | 28.2 |
| West Carroll | 65.9 | 68.0 | 71.0 | 53.6 | 55.0 | 78.0 | 45.0 | 62.2 | 10.6 | 9.0 | 26.9 |
| STATE AVERAGE | 43.9 | 57.0 | 67.0 | 48.2 | 46.0 | 66.0 | 39.0 | 51.4 | 45.9 | 47.8 | 39.0 |

# Name Index

# Source Index

# Subject Index

Acadians, 7, 9–10, 44, 66. *See also* French, Louisiana

Aggregate data, xv, xix, xx. *See also* Political ecology

Agrarian myth, xvii

Agrarian protest: growth of, 160–61, 172–75; and state convention system, 176; mentioned, 187, 246–47, 409

Agriculture: systems of, xvii; arpent field type of, 9; on cutover land, 11–12; planter economy of 30–32; crop lien and sharecropping systems of, 151; and tenancy, 161–67; and crises of 1920's, pp. 219–20. *See also* Farm; Farmer; Plantation; Planter

Alabama, 14, 87, 307, 360, 392

Alexandria, 324, 380

AFL–CIO, 349

American Party (Know-Nothings): and Whigs, 53; rise and decline of, 76–86 *passim*

American society: as developed from European *fragments*, 400; plural and mass sectors of, 404. *See also Fragments*; Mass tendency

Amite, 271

Amite River, 3

Anglo-Saxons: in Florida Parishes, 10; in North Louisiana, 12

Archives, datum, xx

Arkansas, 4, 360

Atchafalaya River, 3, 4, 10

"Atlanta Solution," 343

Avoyelles Parish: and Acadians, 7; in Bayou voter type area, 9

Bastrop, 217

Bastrop Hills, 4

Baton Rouge: ecology of, 285–86; voting behavior in, pp. 268–88; 1948 precinct votes compared in, 313–14; continued Democratic disaffection in, 325–26; mentioned, 3, 67, 274, 290, 323, 324–325, 343, 348, 352, 367, 389, 930

Black Codes: effects on Congress of, 122; Radical Republican's use of, 122–23

Blufflands, 10

Bogalusa, 393–94

Bogalusa Voters League, 394

Bourbons: and New South, 153; and reaction to Reconstruction, 153; and as Redeemers, 153; financial retrenchment of, 154; and repression of Negro vote, 154; and rigged state convention delegate apportionment, 170–71; economic and political power of, 171; and white supremacy, 172; and political discipline, 187; and their "reconstruction," 188; and capture of Democrat Party, 193; and New Orleans allies, 193–94; and local politics, 209; organization of, 212; ruling elite of, 218–19; ascendancy at polls by, 222; voter turnout depressed by, 232–34, 297 and Huey Long 248; sustaining mechanism of, 409–10

Caen: plains of, 411

Catholicism, 245

Central Pine Hills, 11–14, 42–43

Chicago, 317–20

Choctaws. *See* Old Regulars

Cleavage: geographic and social, 28–29. *See also* Political Cleavage

Clinton, 67

Colfax Riots, 142

Colonial experience, 18–20

Committee for a Better Louisiana (CABL), 395

Comparative method, ix

Compromise of 1850: and squatter sovereignty, 77; Millard Fillmore sponsor of, 82

Confederates: discredited, 113; postwar behavior of, 119; proscription against, 120; legal status of, 121–24 *passim*

Congress of Racial Equality (CORE), 394, 395

Congressional delegation: and issues of nativity, 30; composition of, 67–68, 146–49

Conservatism: and state electorate, 415

Conservative government: not inhibited from using power for law and order, 217

Conservatives: in two-pronged rebellion, 315

Constitution, 19

Constitution: of 1812, pp. 20–21, 47; of 1845, pp. 47–48, 69; of 1852, pp. 69–71, 98; of 1864, pp. 117–19; of 1868, pp. 125–27; of 1879, pp. 149, 153, 188;